Yuto Tsukuda

Even when storyboard after storyboard gets scrapped and I feel like crumbling, the moment the characters move and act on their own I feel as though I've been saved. It gives me the momentum I need to keep going.

Shun Saeki

I made salt-grilled horse mackerel! Food always seems to taste better when you make it yourself. Once again I see just how fun and amazing cooking can be, even when all I did was clean the fish, sprinkle on some salt and pop it on the grill.

About the authors

Yuto Tsukuda won the 34th Jump Juniketsu Newcomers' Manga Award for his one-shot story *Kiba ni Naru*. He made his *Weekly Shonen Jump* debut in 2010 with the series *Shonen Shikku*. His follow-up series, *Food Wars!: Shokugeki no Soma*, is his first English-language release.

Shun Saeki made his *Jump NEXT!* debut in 2011 with the one-shot story *Kimi to Watashi no Renai Soudan*. *Food Wars!: Shokugeki no Soma* is his first *Shonen Jump* series.

Food Wars!
SHOKUGEKI NO SOMA

Volume 32
Shonen Jump Manga Edition
Story by Yuto Tsukuda, Art by Shun Saeki
Contributor Yuki Morisaki

Translation: Adrienne Beck
Touch-Up Art & Lettering: James Gaubatz, Mara Coman
Design: Alice Lewis
Editor: Jennifer LeBlanc

Printed in the U.S.A.

Published by VIZ Media, LLC
P.O. Box 77010
San Francisco, CA 94107

10 9 8 7 6 5 4 3 2 1
First printing, October 2019

ratings.viz.com RATED T+ OLDER TEEN

PARENTAL ADVISORY
FOOD WARS! is rated T+ for Older Teen and is recommended for ages 16 and up. This volume contains sexual situations/humor.

VIZ MEDIA
viz.com

SHONEN JUMP
shonenjump.com

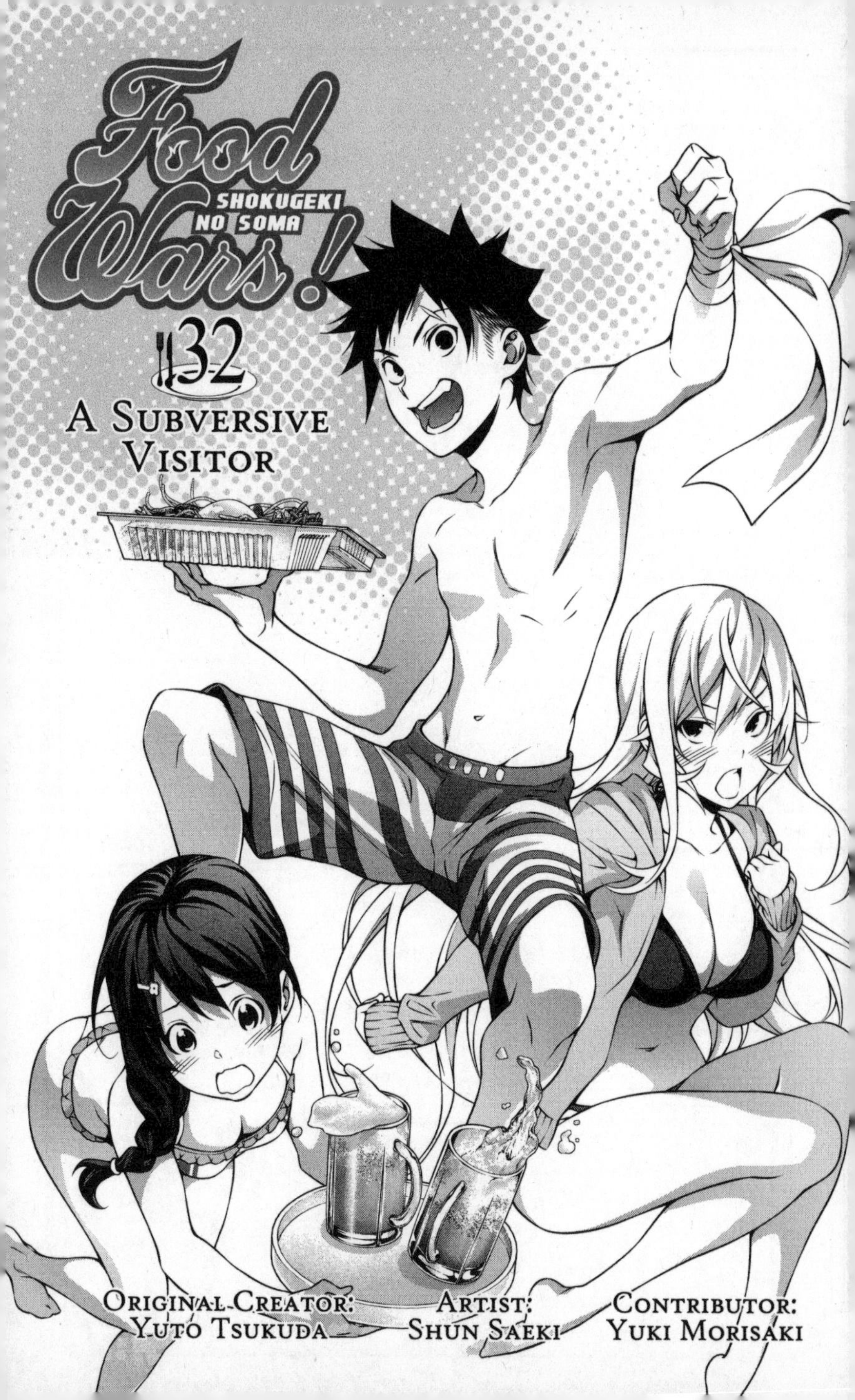
Food Wars!
SHOKUGEKI NO SOMA
32
A Subversive Visitor
Original Creator: Yuto Tsukuda
Artist: Shun Saeki
Contributor: Yuki Morisaki

CHARACTERS

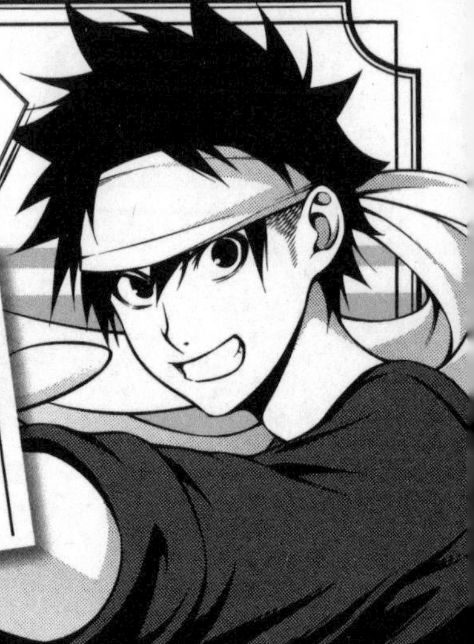

SOMA YUKIHIRA Second Year High School

The current first seat on Totsuki's Council of Ten. Unbound by traditional notions and with a natural inquisitiveness and passion for cooking, his fresh take on cuisine leads him to create dishes no one has ever thought of before. Resides in Polaris Dormitory.

Shokugeki no SOMA

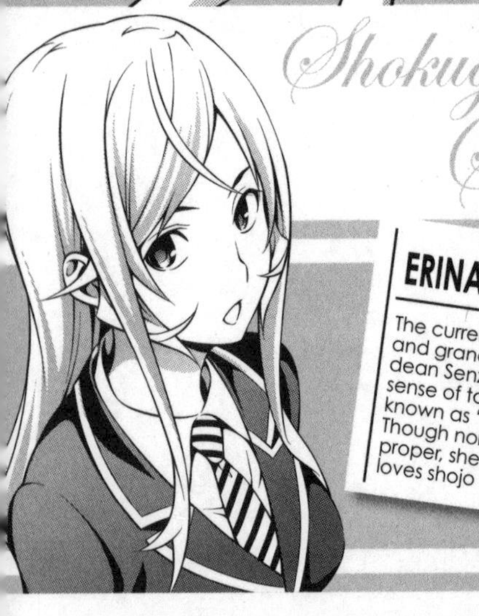

ERINA NAKIRI Second Year High School

The current dean of Totsuki Institute and granddaughter of former dean Senzaemon Nakiri. Her sense of taste is so refined it's known as "the Divine Tongue." Though normally strict and proper, she has a girly side and loves shojo manga.

STORY

Soma grew up helping to cook at his family's restaurant, Yukihira. But one day his father enrolls him in Japan's premier culinary school, Totsuki Institute. Having met other students as skilled as he is and with similar goals, Soma has grown a little as a chef.

Soma and the others enjoy the spring of their first term cooking and learning, having advanced to their second years while earning seats on the Council of Ten. But one day, newly appointed Dean Erina sends Soma and Megumi to a hot springs resort town to investigate a strange incident. There the two discover a secret invasion by underworld chefs called cuisiniers noir, who are using shokugeki to take over Japanese restaurants. Behind this invasion is a mysterious man known only as "Saiba"!

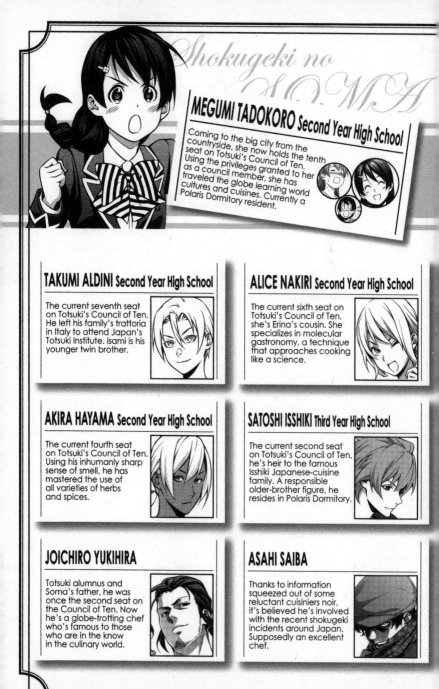

Shokugeki no SOMA

MEGUMI TADOKORO Second Year High School

Coming to the big city from the countryside, she now holds the tenth seat on Totsuki's Council of Ten. Using the privileges granted to her as a council member, she has traveled the globe learning world cultures and cuisines. Currently a Polaris Dormitory resident.

TAKUMI ALDINI Second Year High School

The current seventh seat on Totsuki's Council of Ten. He left his family's trattoria in Italy to attend Japan's Totsuki Institute. Isami is his younger twin brother.

ALICE NAKIRI Second Year High School

The current sixth seat on Totsuki's Council of Ten, she's Erina's cousin. She specializes in molecular gastronomy, a technique that approaches cooking like a science.

AKIRA HAYAMA Second Year High School

The current fourth seat on Totsuki's Council of Ten. Using his inhumanly sharp sense of smell, he has mastered the use of all varieties of herbs and spices.

SATOSHI ISSHIKI Third Year High School

The current second seat on Totsuki's Council of Ten, he's heir to the famous Isshiki Japanese-cuisine family. A responsible older-brother figure, he resides in Polaris Dormitory.

JOICHIRO YUKIHIRA

Totsuki alumnus and Soma's father, he was once the second seat on the Council of Ten. Now he's a globe-trotting chef who's famous to those who are in the know in the culinary world.

ASAHI SAIBA

Thanks to information squeezed out of some reluctant cuisiniers noir, it's believed he's involved with the recent shokugeki incidents around Japan. Supposedly an excellent chef.

Food Wars! SHOKUGEKI NO SOMA

32

Table of Contents

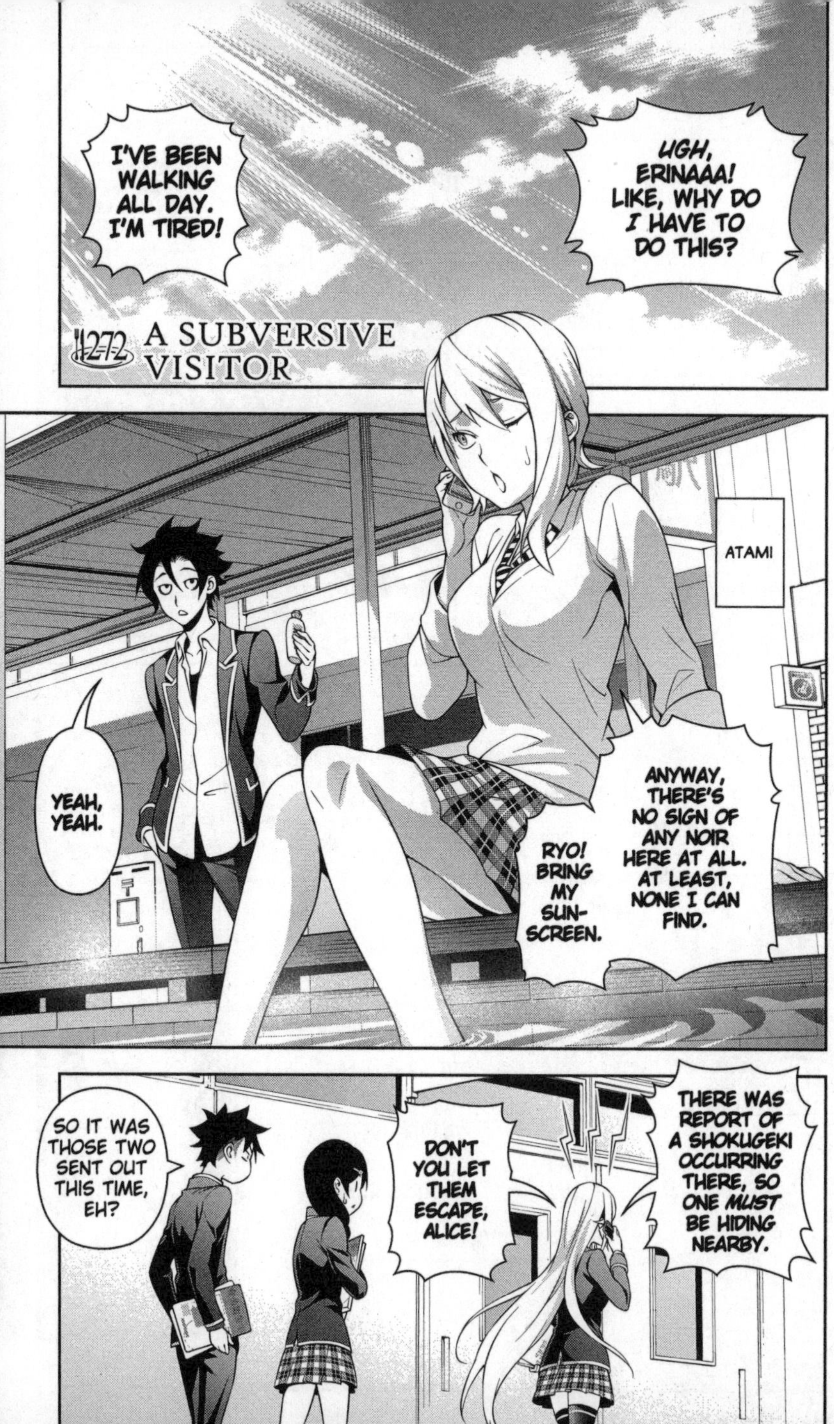
UGH, ERINAAA! LIKE, WHY DO I HAVE TO DO THIS?
I'VE BEEN WALKING ALL DAY. I'M TIRED!
272 A SUBVERSIVE VISITOR
ATAMI
ANYWAY, THERE'S NO SIGN OF ANY NOIR HERE AT ALL. AT LEAST, NONE I CAN FIND.
RYO! BRING MY SUN-SCREEN.
YEAH, YEAH.
THERE WAS REPORT OF A SHOKUGEKI OCCURRING THERE, SO ONE MUST BE HIDING NEARBY.
DON'T YOU LET THEM ESCAPE, ALICE!
SO IT WAS THOSE TWO SENT OUT THIS TIME, EH?

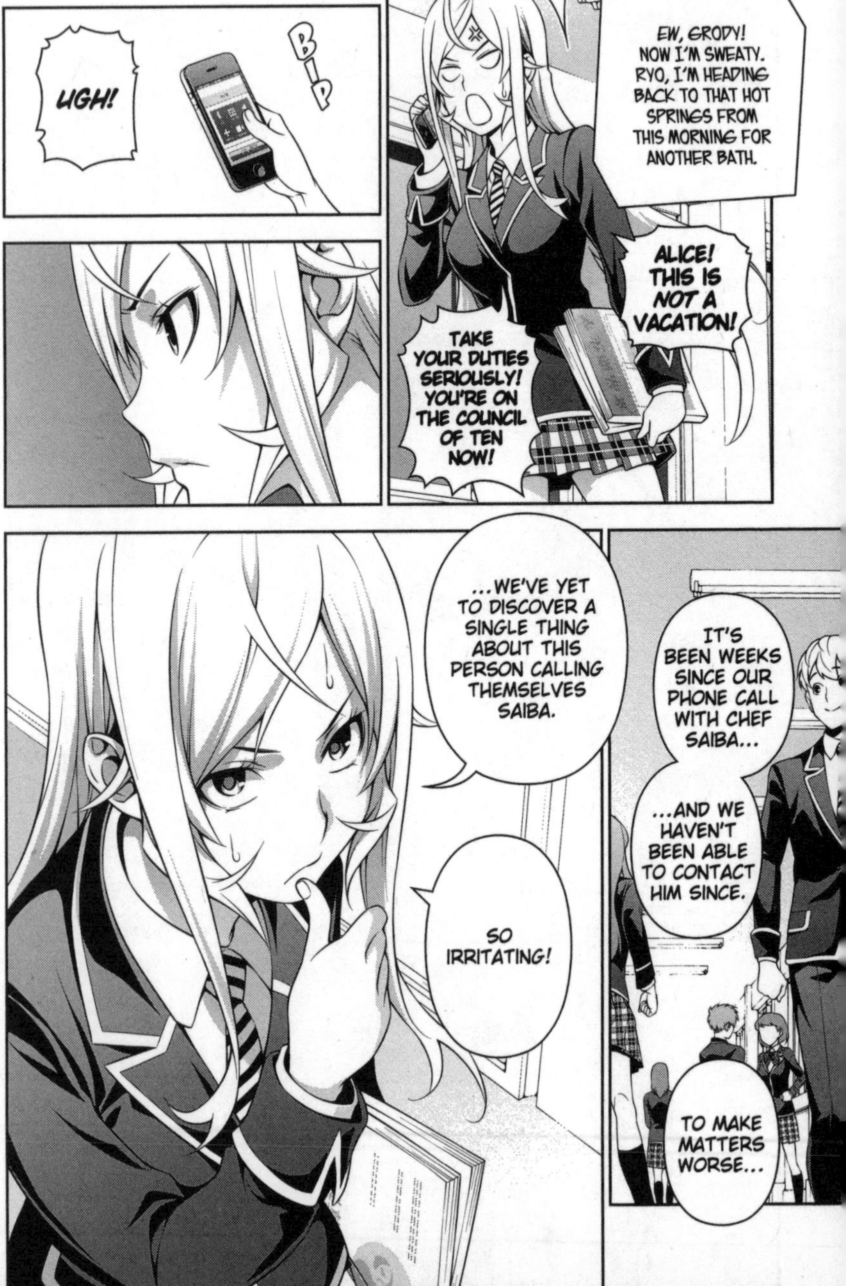
EW, GRODY! NOW I'M SWEATY. RYO, I'M HEADING BACK TO THAT HOT SPRINGS FROM THIS MORNING FOR ANOTHER BATH.
ALICE! THIS IS *NOT* A VACATION!
TAKE YOUR DUTIES SERIOUSLY! YOU'RE ON THE COUNCIL OF TEN NOW!
BIP
UGH!
IT'S BEEN WEEKS SINCE OUR PHONE CALL WITH CHEF SAIBA...
...AND WE HAVEN'T BEEN ABLE TO CONTACT HIM SINCE.
TO MAKE MATTERS WORSE...
...WE'VE YET TO DISCOVER A SINGLE THING ABOUT THIS PERSON CALLING THEMSELVES SAIBA.
SO IRRITATING!

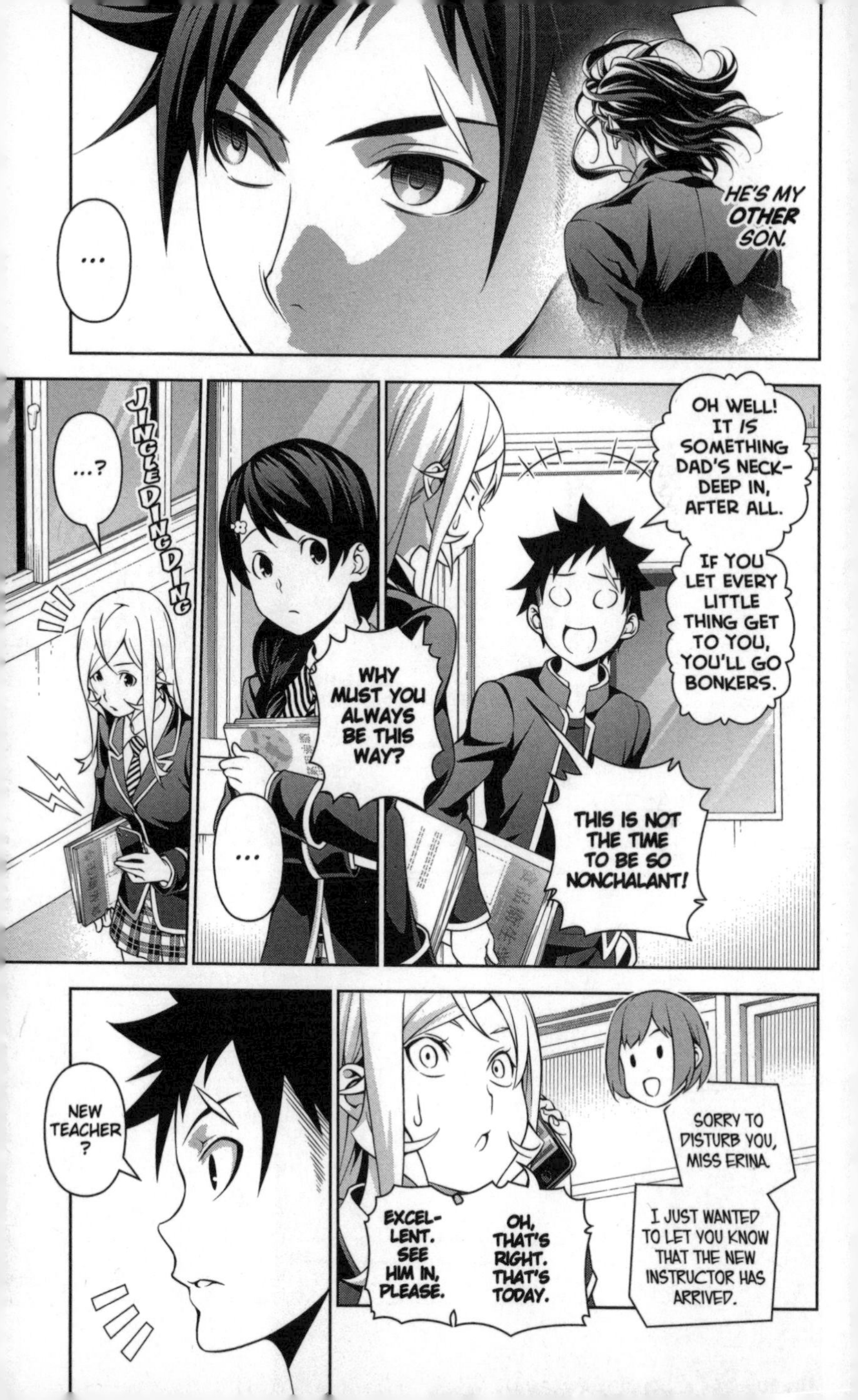
HE'S MY OTHER SON.
...
OH WELL! IT IS SOMETHING DAD'S NECK-DEEP IN, AFTER ALL.
IF YOU LET EVERY LITTLE THING GET TO YOU, YOU'LL GO BONKERS.
THIS IS NOT THE TIME TO BE SO NONCHALANT!
WHY MUST YOU ALWAYS BE THIS WAY?
...
JINGLEDINGDING
...?
SORRY TO DISTURB YOU, MISS ERINA.
I JUST WANTED TO LET YOU KNOW THAT THE NEW INSTRUCTOR HAS ARRIVED.
OH, THAT'S RIGHT. THAT'S TODAY.
EXCEL-LENT. SEE HIM IN, PLEASE.
NEW TEACHER?

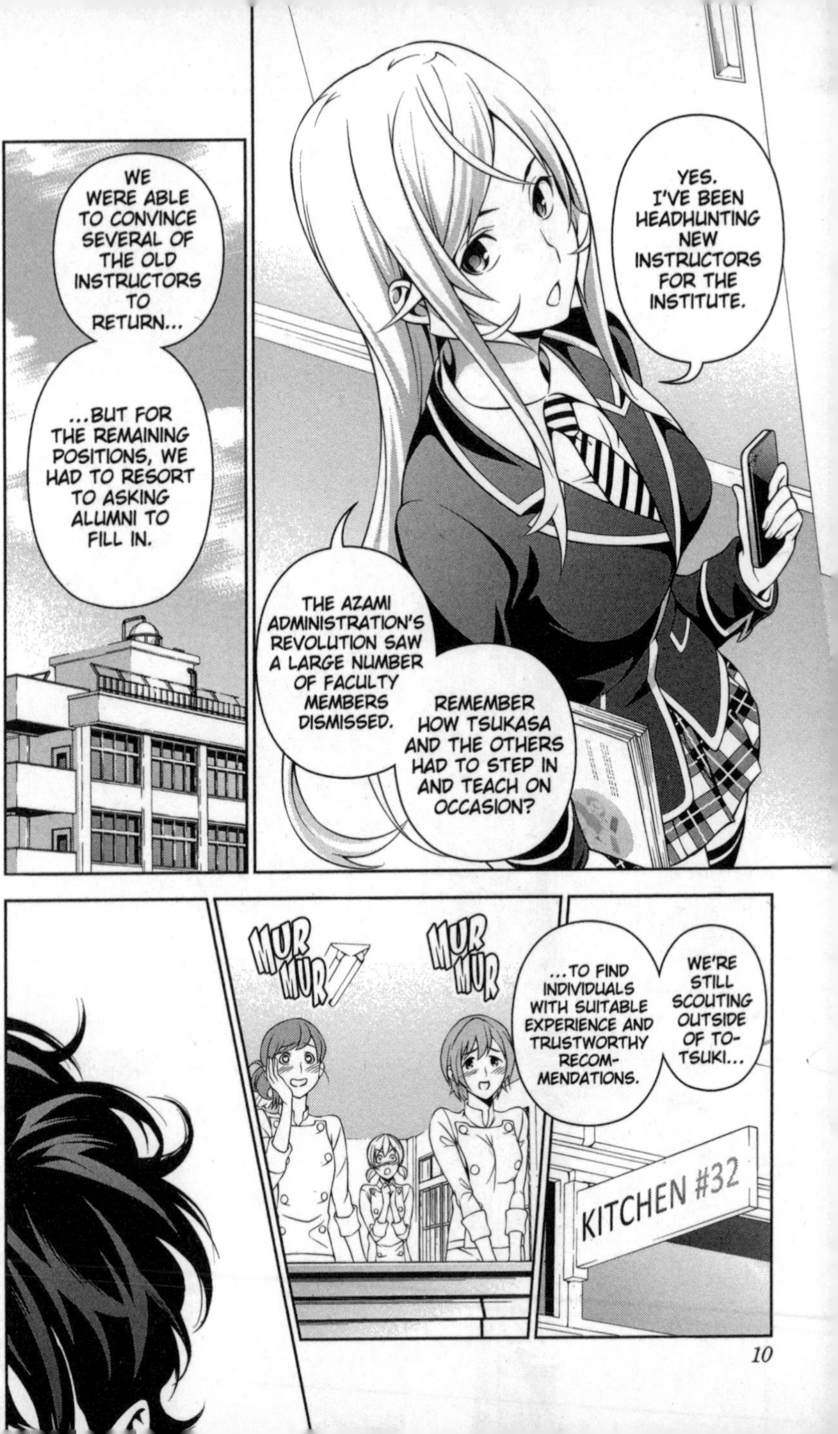
YES. I'VE BEEN HEADHUNTING NEW INSTRUCTORS FOR THE INSTITUTE.
THE AZAMI ADMINISTRATION'S REVOLUTION SAW A LARGE NUMBER OF FACULTY MEMBERS DISMISSED.
REMEMBER HOW TSUKASA AND THE OTHERS HAD TO STEP IN AND TEACH ON OCCASION?
WE WERE ABLE TO CONVINCE SEVERAL OF THE OLD INSTRUCTORS TO RETURN...
...BUT FOR THE REMAINING POSITIONS, WE HAD TO RESORT TO ASKING ALUMNI TO FILL IN.
WE'RE STILL SCOUTING OUTSIDE OF TO-TSUKI...
...TO FIND INDIVIDUALS WITH SUITABLE EXPERIENCE AND TRUSTWORTHY RECOM-MENDATIONS.
KITCHEN #32
MUR MUR
MUR MUR

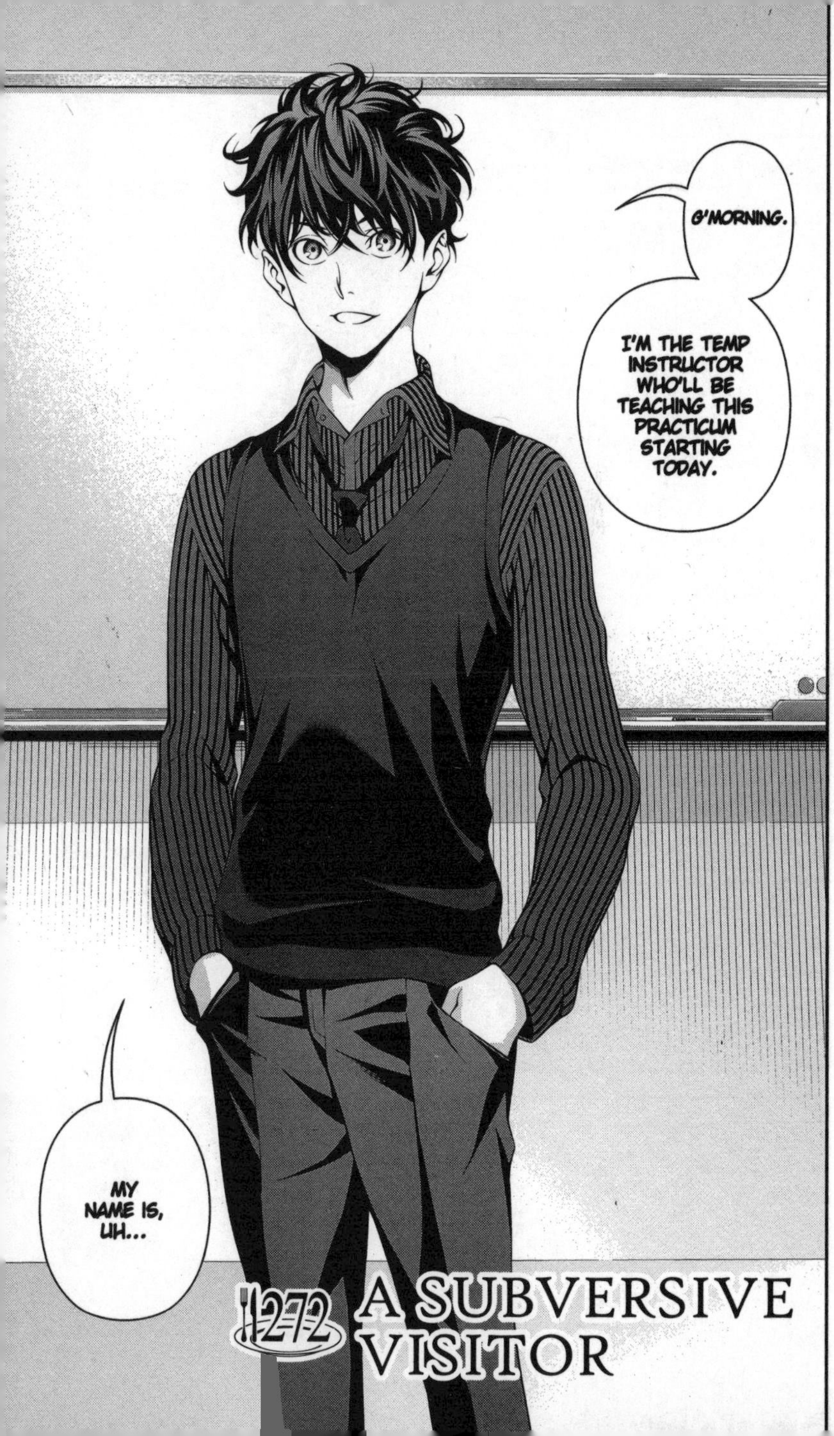
G'MORNING.
I'M THE TEMP INSTRUCTOR WHO'LL BE TEACHING THIS PRACTICUM STARTING TODAY.
MY NAME IS, UH...
272 A SUBVERSIVE VISITOR

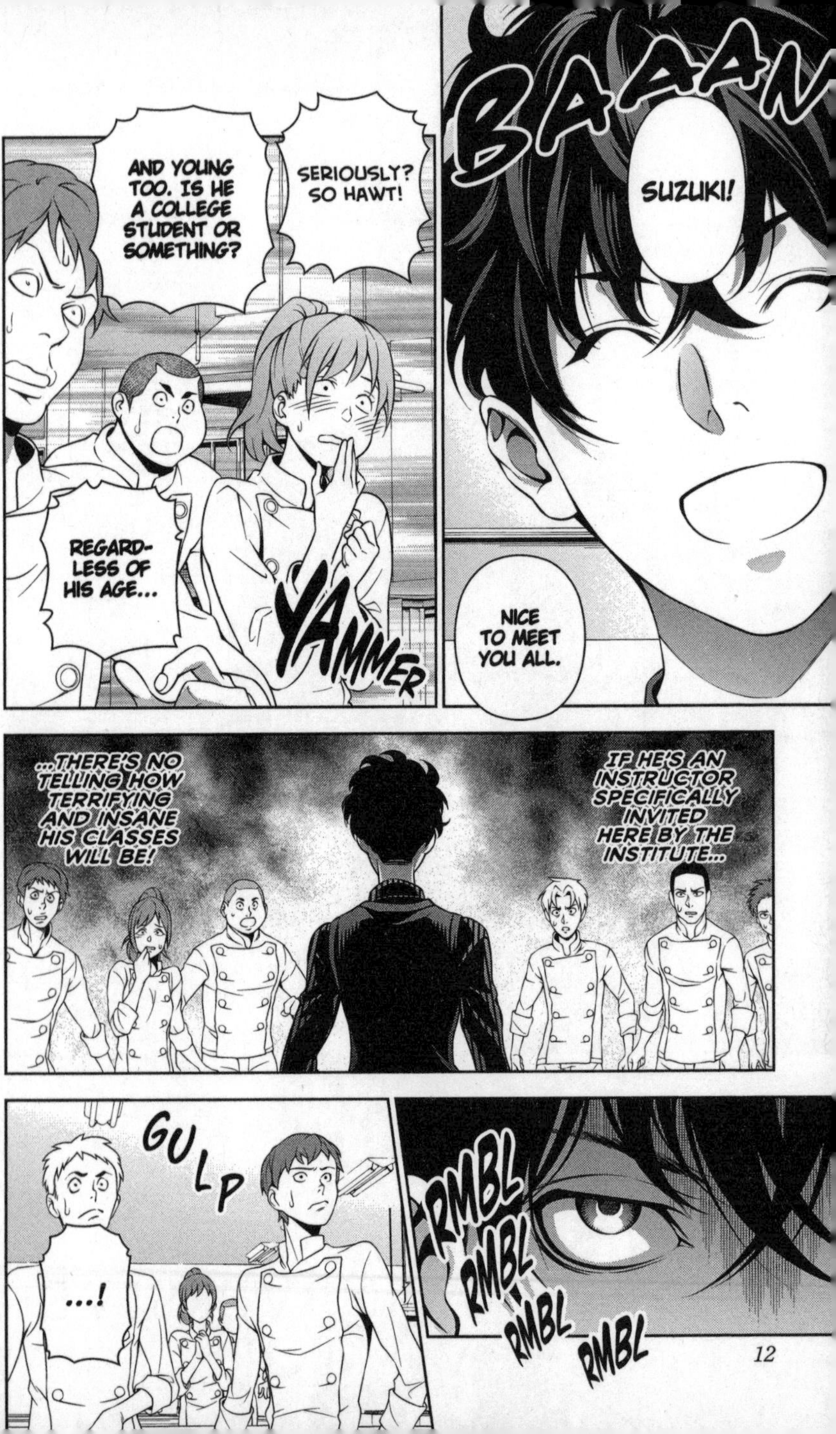
BAAAN
SUZUKI!
NICE TO MEET YOU ALL.
SERIOUSLY? SO HAWT!
AND YOUNG TOO. IS HE A COLLEGE STUDENT OR SOMETHING?
REGARD-LESS OF HIS AGE...
YAMMER
IF HE'S AN INSTRUCTOR SPECIFICALLY INVITED HERE BY THE INSTITUTE...
...THERE'S NO TELLING HOW TERRIFYING AND INSANE HIS CLASSES WILL BE!
RMBL RMBL RMBL RMBL RMBL
GULP
...!

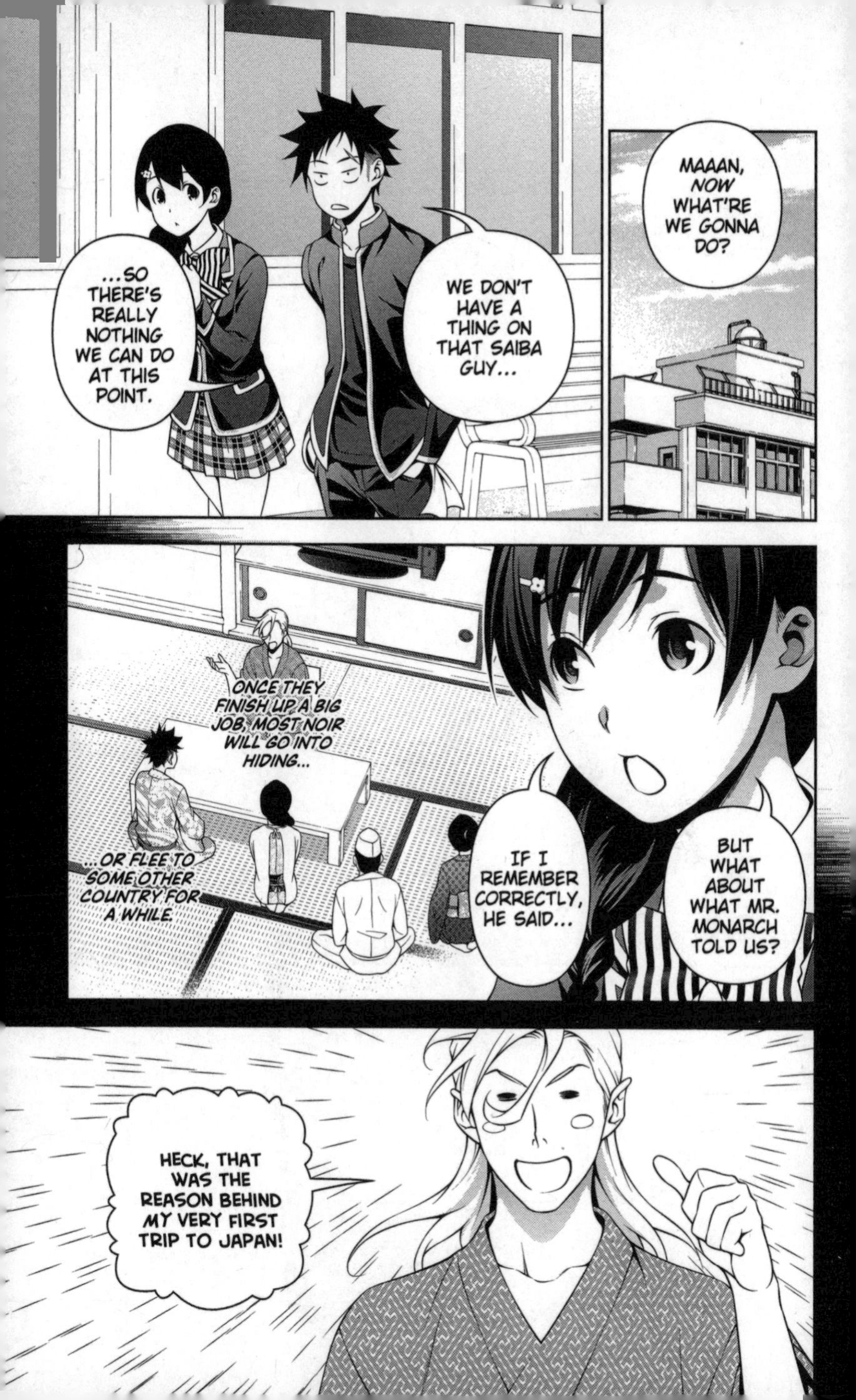
MAAAN, NOW WHAT'RE WE GONNA DO?
WE DON'T HAVE A THING ON THAT SAIBA GUY...
...SO THERE'S REALLY NOTHING WE CAN DO AT THIS POINT.
BUT WHAT ABOUT WHAT MR. MONARCH TOLD US?
IF I REMEMBER CORRECTLY, HE SAID...
ONCE THEY FINISH UP A BIG JOB, MOST NOIR WILL GO INTO HIDING...
...OR FLEE TO SOME OTHER COUNTRY FOR A WHILE.
HECK, THAT WAS THE REASON BEHIND MY VERY FIRST TRIP TO JAPAN!

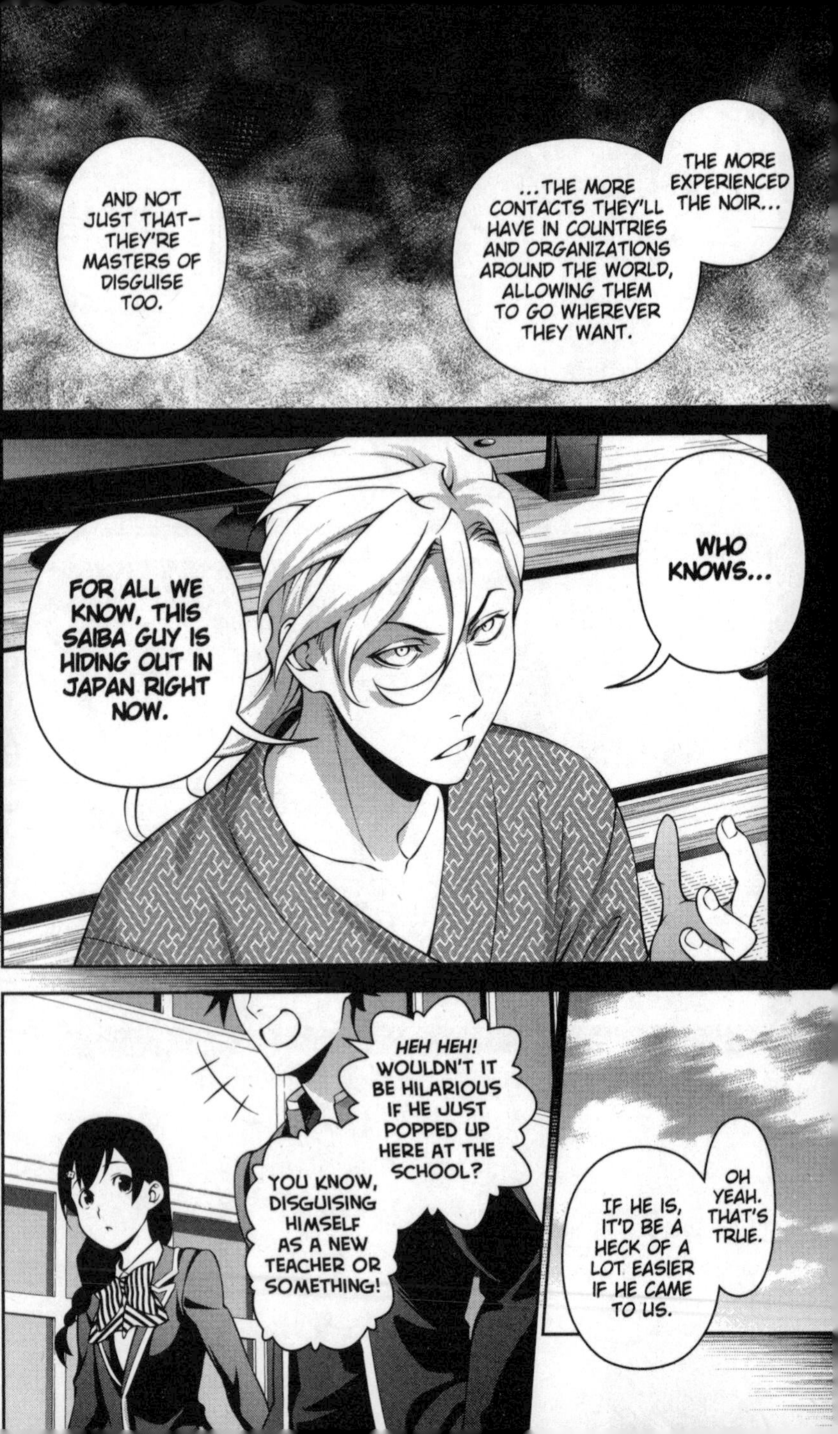
THE MORE EXPERIENCED THE NOIR...
...THE MORE CONTACTS THEY'LL HAVE IN COUNTRIES AND ORGANIZATIONS AROUND THE WORLD, ALLOWING THEM TO GO WHEREVER THEY WANT.
AND NOT JUST THAT- THEY'RE MASTERS OF DISGUISE TOO.
WHO KNOWS...
FOR ALL WE KNOW, THIS SAIBA GUY IS HIDING OUT IN JAPAN RIGHT NOW.
OH YEAH. THAT'S TRUE.
IF HE IS, IT'D BE A HECK OF A LOT EASIER IF HE CAME TO US.
HEH HEH! WOULDN'T IT BE HILARIOUS IF HE JUST POPPED UP HERE AT THE SCHOOL?
YOU KNOW, DISGUISING HIMSELF AS A NEW TEACHER OR SOMETHING!

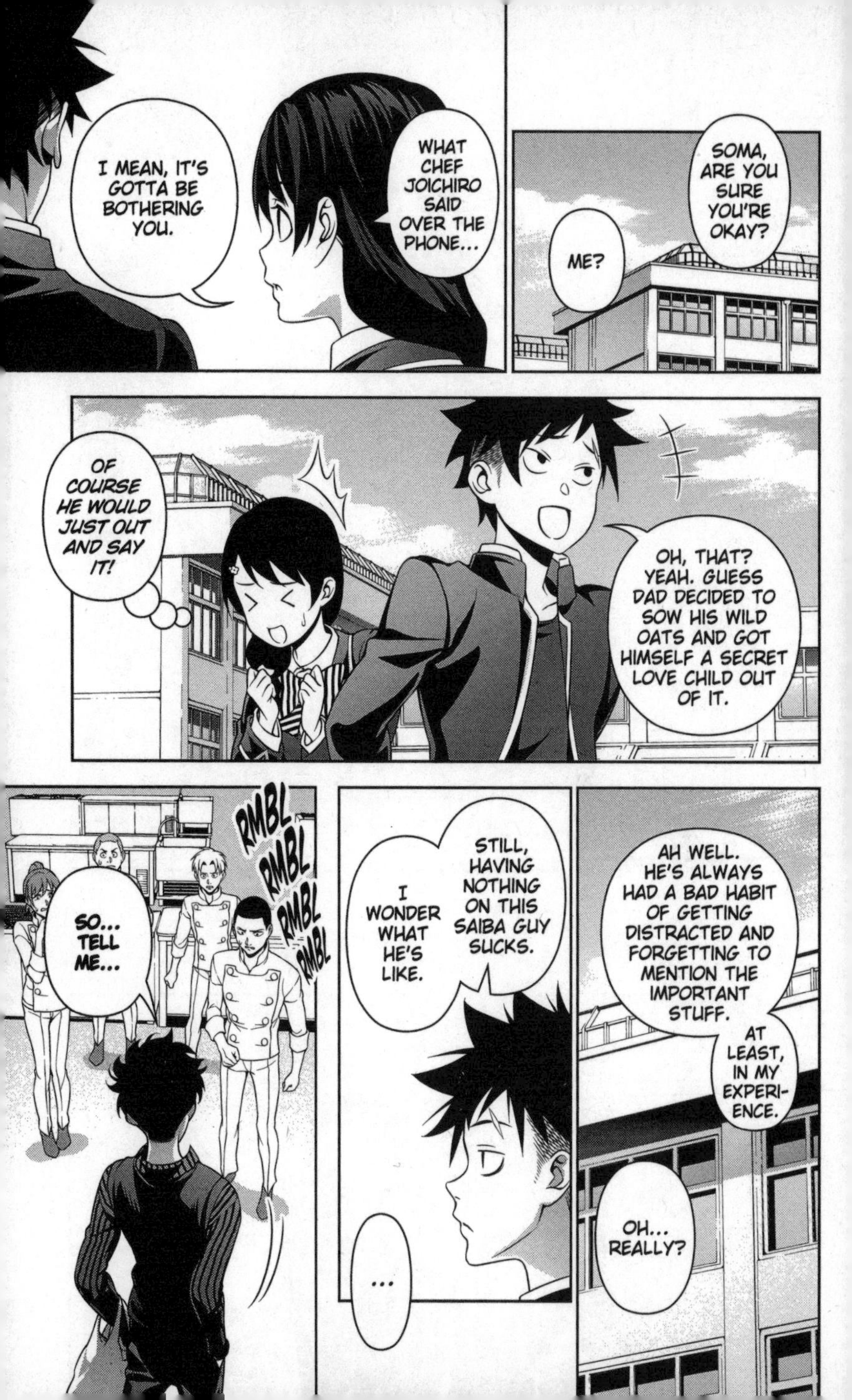
SOMA, ARE YOU SURE YOU'RE OKAY?
ME?
WHAT CHEF JOICHIRO SAID OVER THE PHONE...
I MEAN, IT'S GOTTA BE BOTHERING YOU.
OH, THAT? YEAH. GUESS DAD DECIDED TO SOW HIS WILD OATS AND GOT HIMSELF A SECRET LOVE CHILD OUT OF IT.
OF COURSE HE WOULD JUST OUT AND SAY IT!
AH WELL. HE'S ALWAYS HAD A BAD HABIT OF GETTING DISTRACTED AND FORGETTING TO MENTION THE IMPORTANT STUFF.
AT LEAST, IN MY EXPERIENCE.
OH... REALLY?
STILL, HAVING NOTHING ON THIS SAIBA GUY SUCKS.
I WONDER WHAT HE'S LIKE.
...
RMBL RMBL RMBL RMBL RMBL
SO... TELL ME...

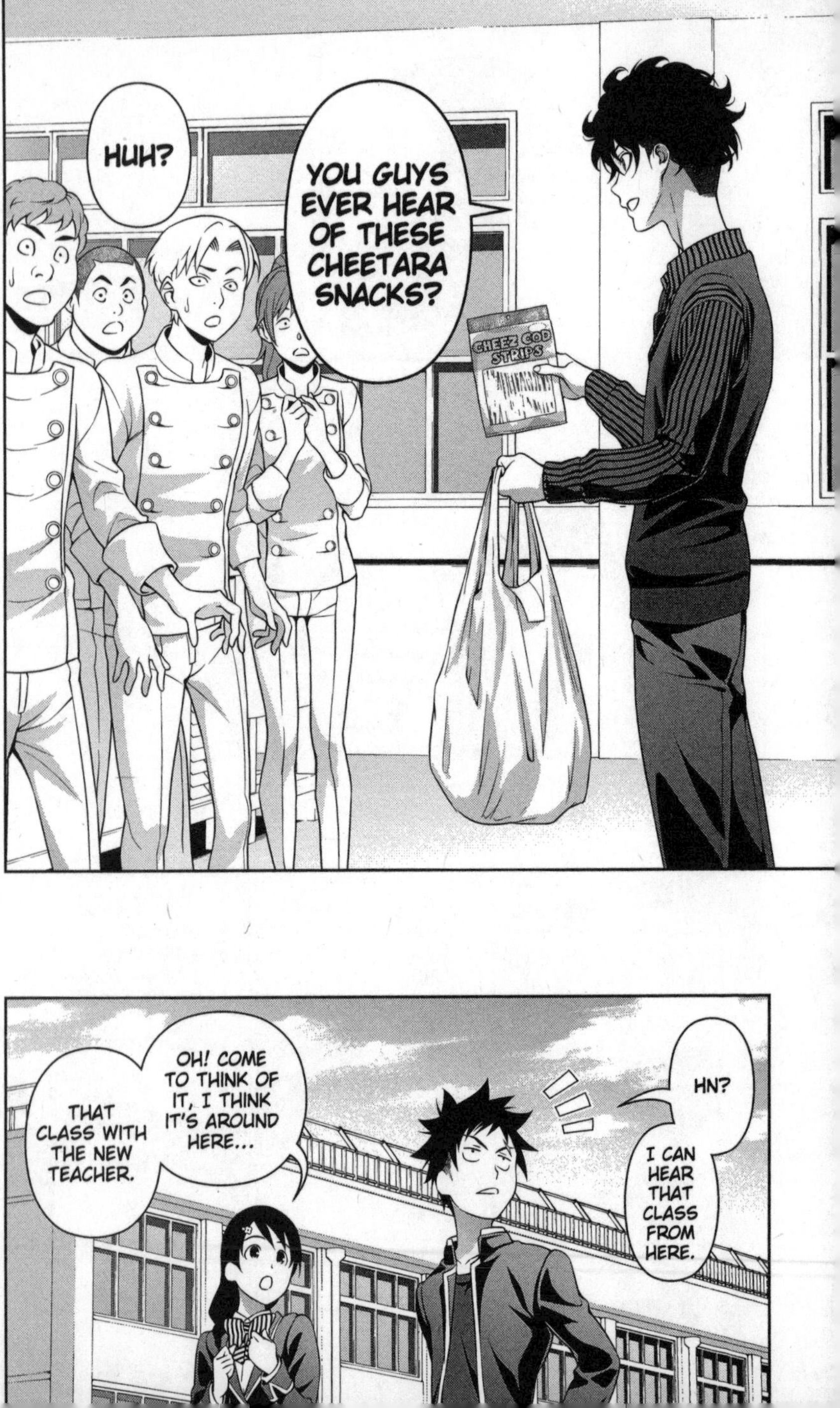
YOU GUYS EVER HEAR OF THESE CHEETARA SNACKS?
CHEEZ COD STRIPS
HUH?
HN?
I CAN HEAR THAT CLASS FROM HERE.
OH! COME TO THINK OF IT, I THINK IT'S AROUND HERE...
THAT CLASS WITH THE NEW TEACHER.

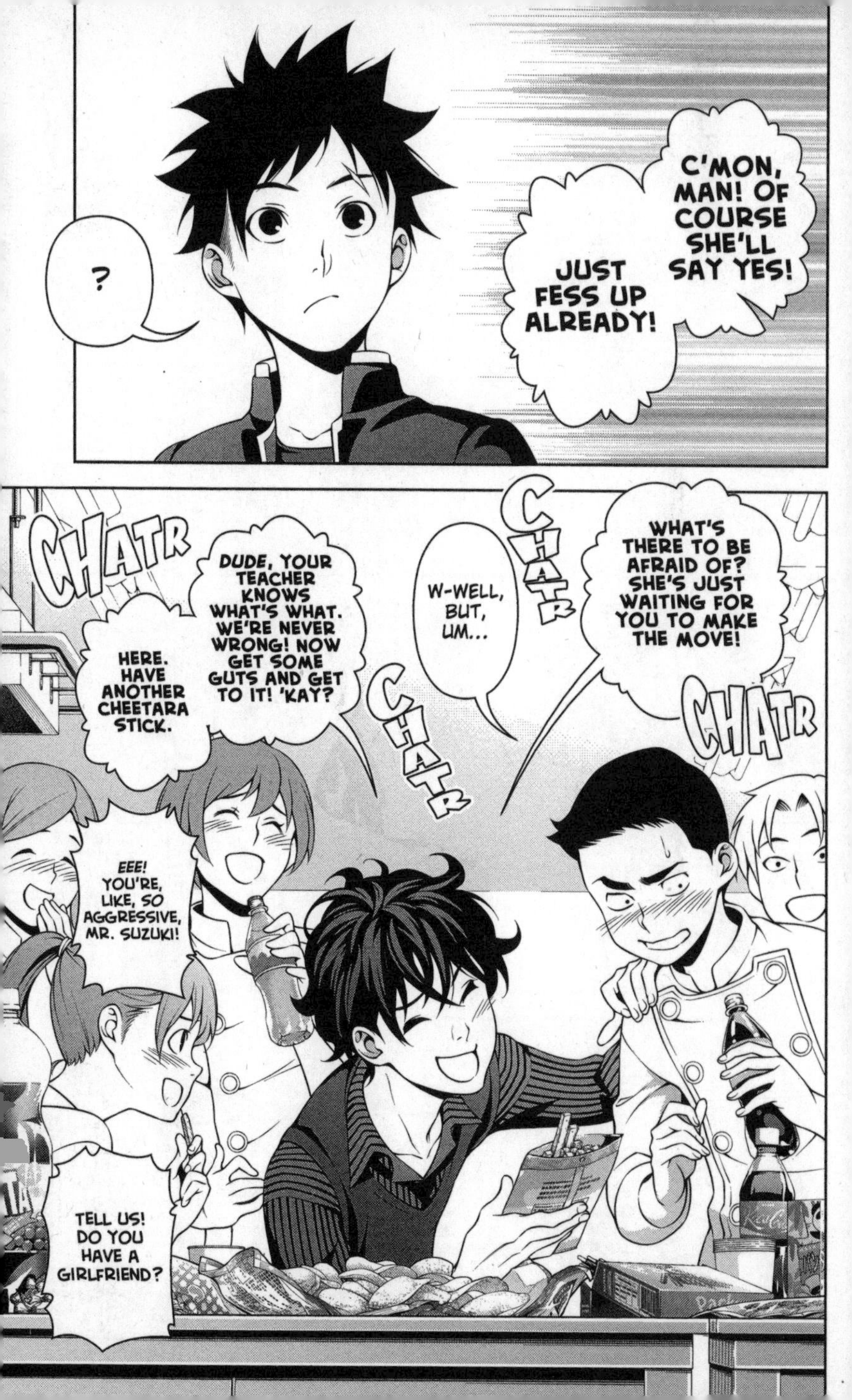
C'MON, MAN! OF COURSE SHE'LL SAY YES!
JUST FESS UP ALREADY!
?
CHATR
WHAT'S THERE TO BE AFRAID OF? SHE'S JUST WAITING FOR YOU TO MAKE THE MOVE!
CHATR
W-WELL, BUT, UM...
CHATR
DUDE, YOUR TEACHER KNOWS WHAT'S WHAT. WE'RE NEVER WRONG! NOW GET SOME GUTS AND GET TO IT! 'KAY?
CHATR
HERE. HAVE ANOTHER CHEETARA STICK.
EEE! YOU'RE, LIKE, SO AGGRESSIVE, MR. SUZUKI!
TELL US! DO YOU HAVE A GIRLFRIEND?

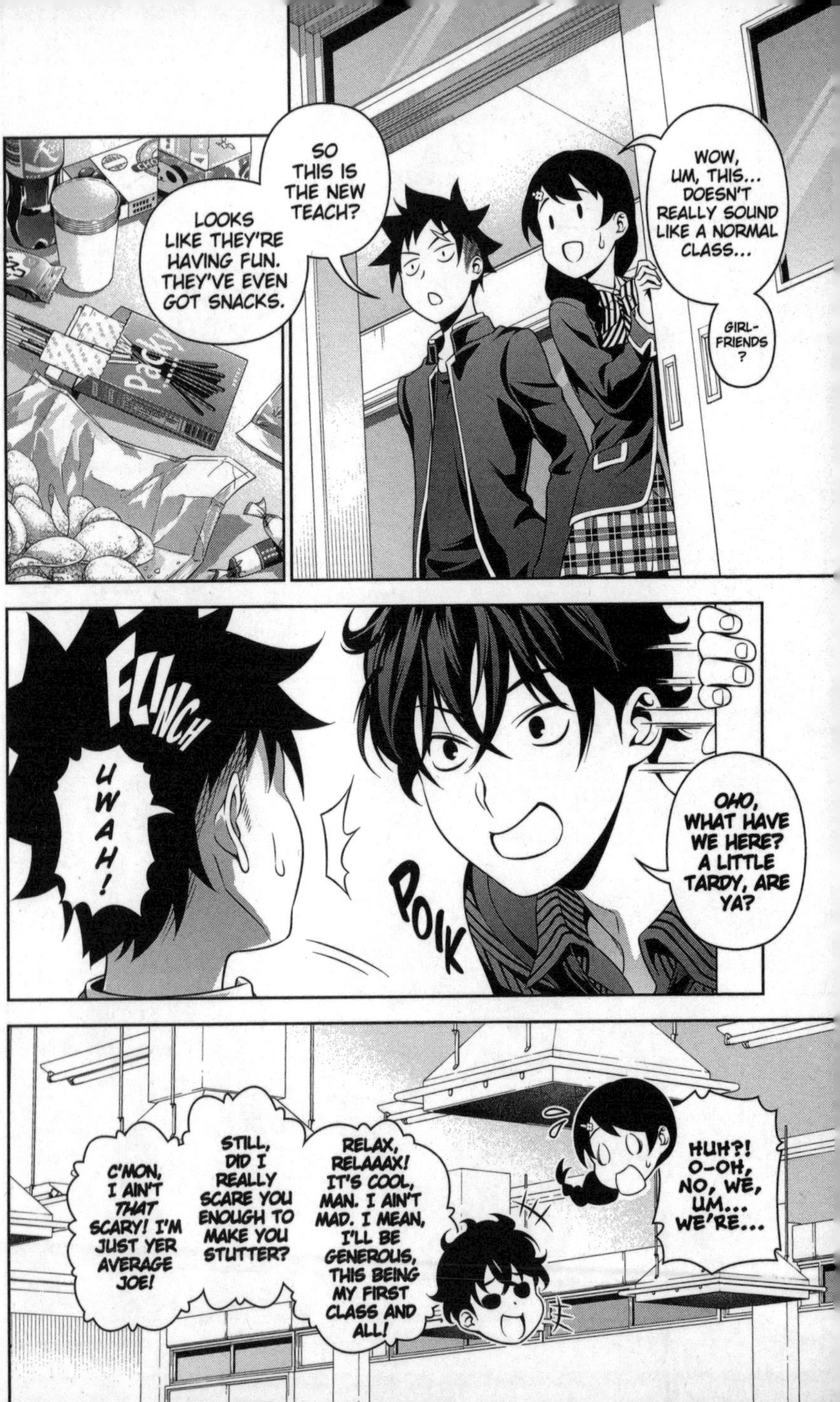
WOW, UM, THIS... DOESN'T REALLY SOUND LIKE A NORMAL CLASS...
SO THIS IS THE NEW TEACH?
GIRL-FRIENDS?
LOOKS LIKE THEY'RE HAVING FUN. THEY'VE EVEN GOT SNACKS.
OHO, WHAT HAVE WE HERE? A LITTLE TARDY, ARE YA?
POIK
FLINCH
UWAH!
HUH?! O-OH, NO, WE, UM... WE'RE...
RELAX, RELAAAX! IT'S COOL, MAN. I AIN'T MAD. I MEAN, I'LL BE GENEROUS, THIS BEING MY FIRST CLASS AND ALL!
STILL, DID I REALLY SCARE YOU ENOUGH TO MAKE YOU STUTTER?
C'MON, I AIN'T *THAT* SCARY! I'M JUST YER AVERAGE JOE!

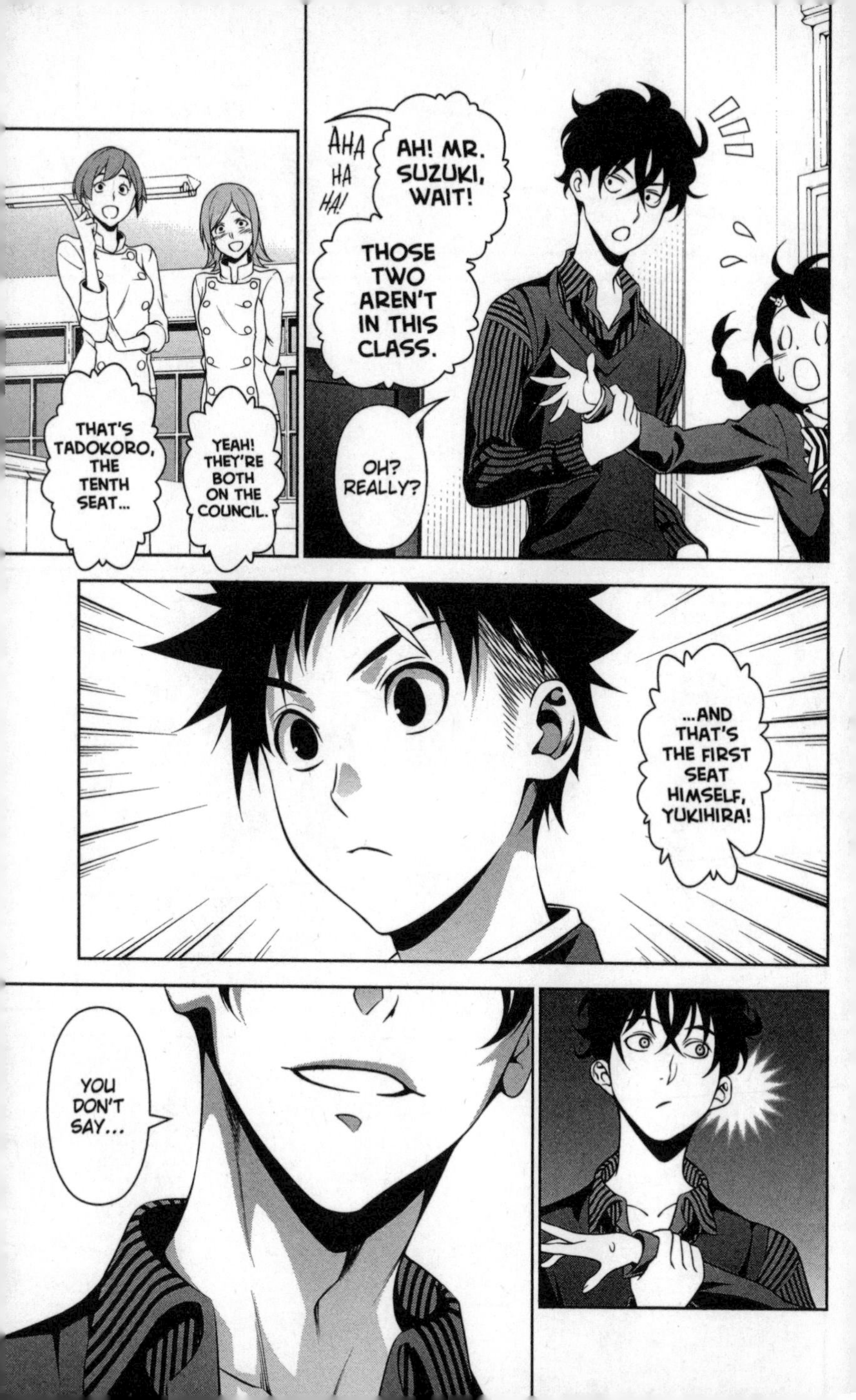
AHA HA HA!
AH! MR. SUZUKI, WAIT!
THOSE TWO AREN'T IN THIS CLASS.
OH? REALLY?
THAT'S TADOKORO, THE TENTH SEAT...
YEAH! THEY'RE BOTH ON THE COUNCIL.
...AND THAT'S THE FIRST SEAT HIMSELF, YUKIHIRA!
YOU DON'T SAY...

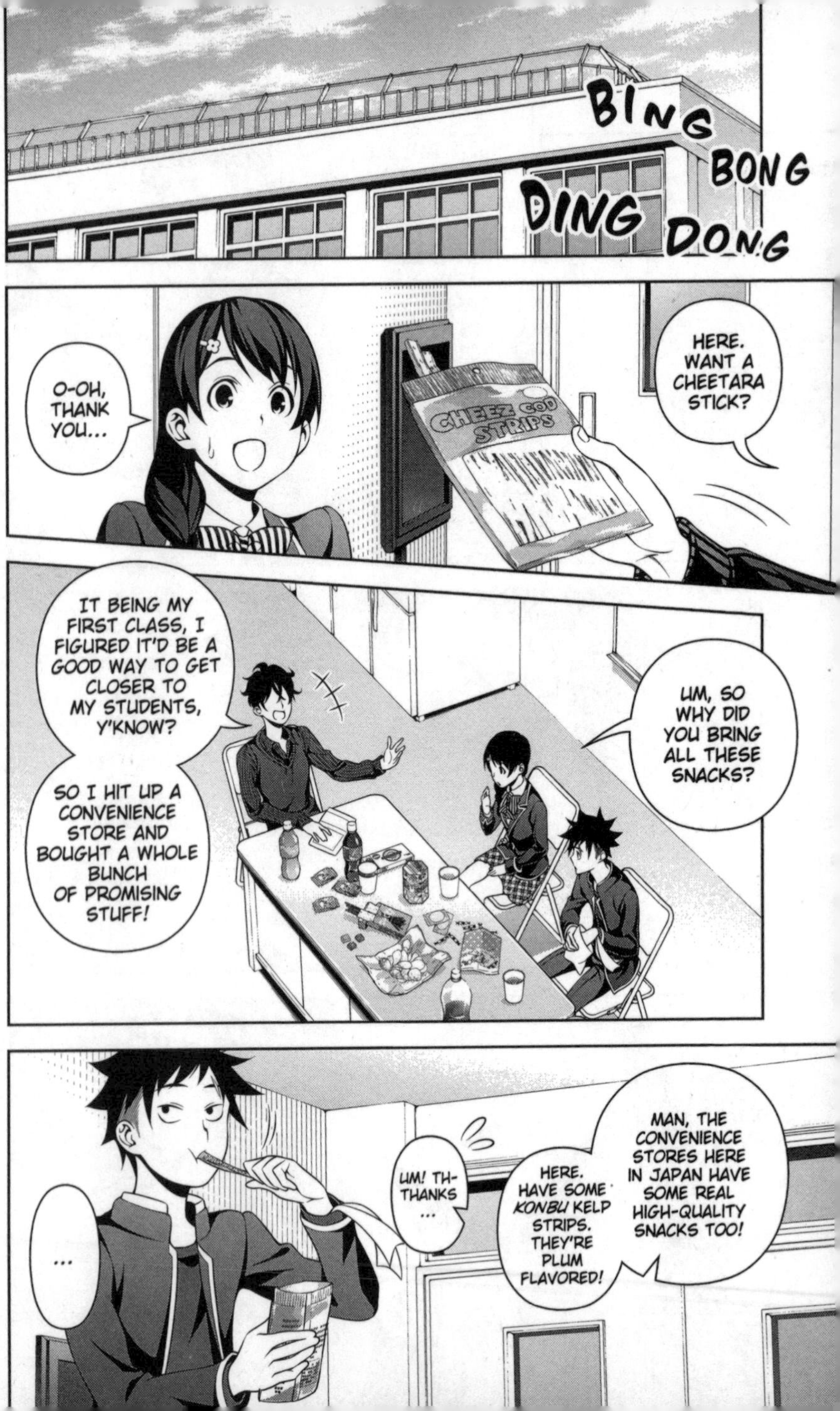
BING BONG
DING DONG
HERE. WANT A CHEETARA STICK?
CHEEZ COD STRIPS
O-OH, THANK YOU...
UM, SO WHY DID YOU BRING ALL THESE SNACKS?
IT BEING MY FIRST CLASS, I FIGURED IT'D BE A GOOD WAY TO GET CLOSER TO MY STUDENTS, Y'KNOW?
SO I HIT UP A CONVENIENCE STORE AND BOUGHT A WHOLE BUNCH OF PROMISING STUFF!
MAN, THE CONVENIENCE STORES HERE IN JAPAN HAVE SOME REAL HIGH-QUALITY SNACKS TOO!
HERE. HAVE SOME *KONBU* KELP STRIPS. THEY'RE PLUM FLAVORED!
UM! TH-THANKS ...
...

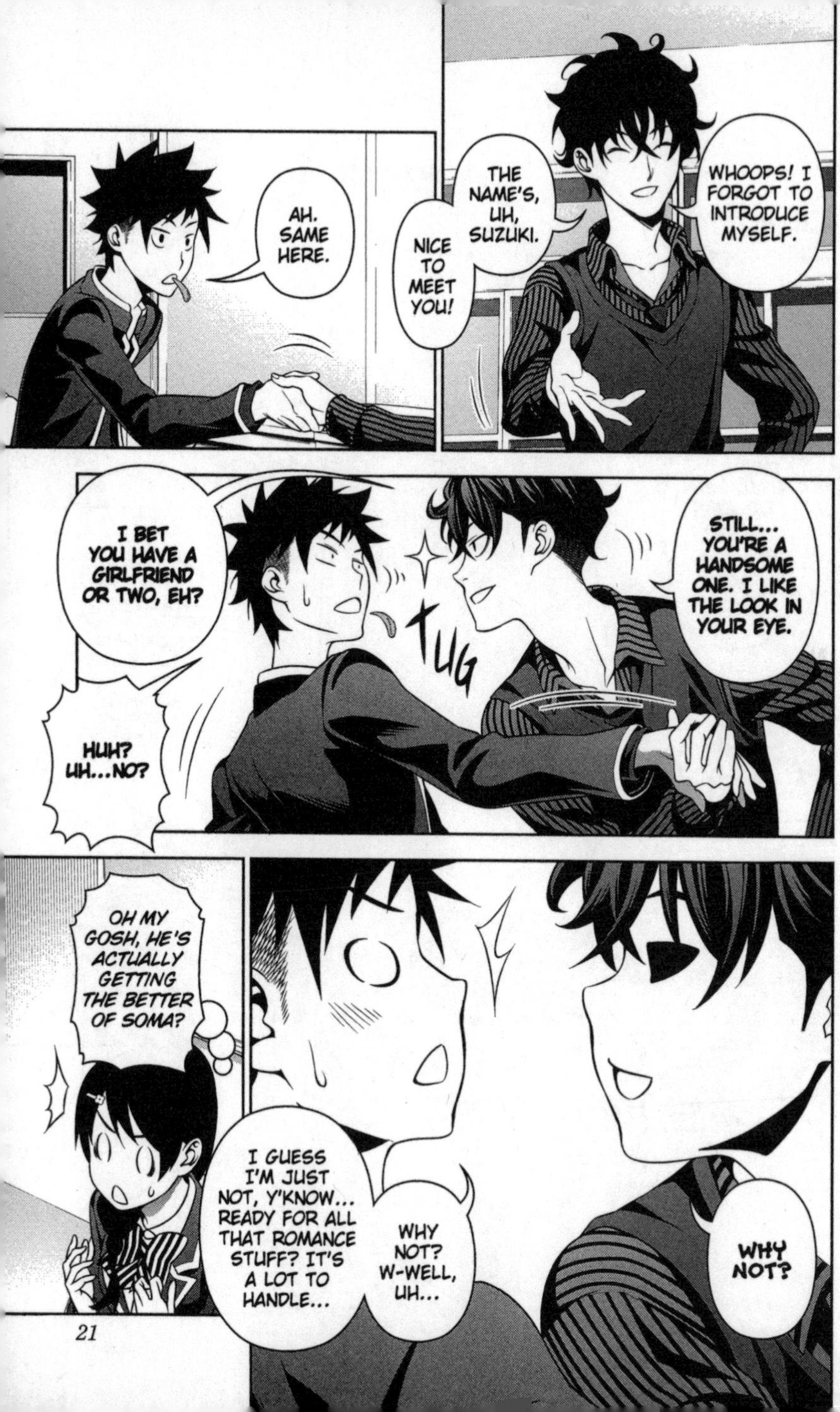
WHOOPS! I FORGOT TO INTRODUCE MYSELF.
THE NAME'S, UH, SUZUKI.
NICE TO MEET YOU!
AH. SAME HERE.
STILL... YOU'RE A HANDSOME ONE. I LIKE THE LOOK IN YOUR EYE.
TUG
I BET YOU HAVE A GIRLFRIEND OR TWO, EH?
HUH? UH...NO?
WHY NOT?
WHY NOT? W-WELL, UH...
I GUESS I'M JUST NOT, Y'KNOW... READY FOR ALL THAT ROMANCE STUFF? IT'S A LOT TO HANDLE...
OH MY GOSH, HE'S ACTUALLY GETTING THE BETTER OF SOMA?

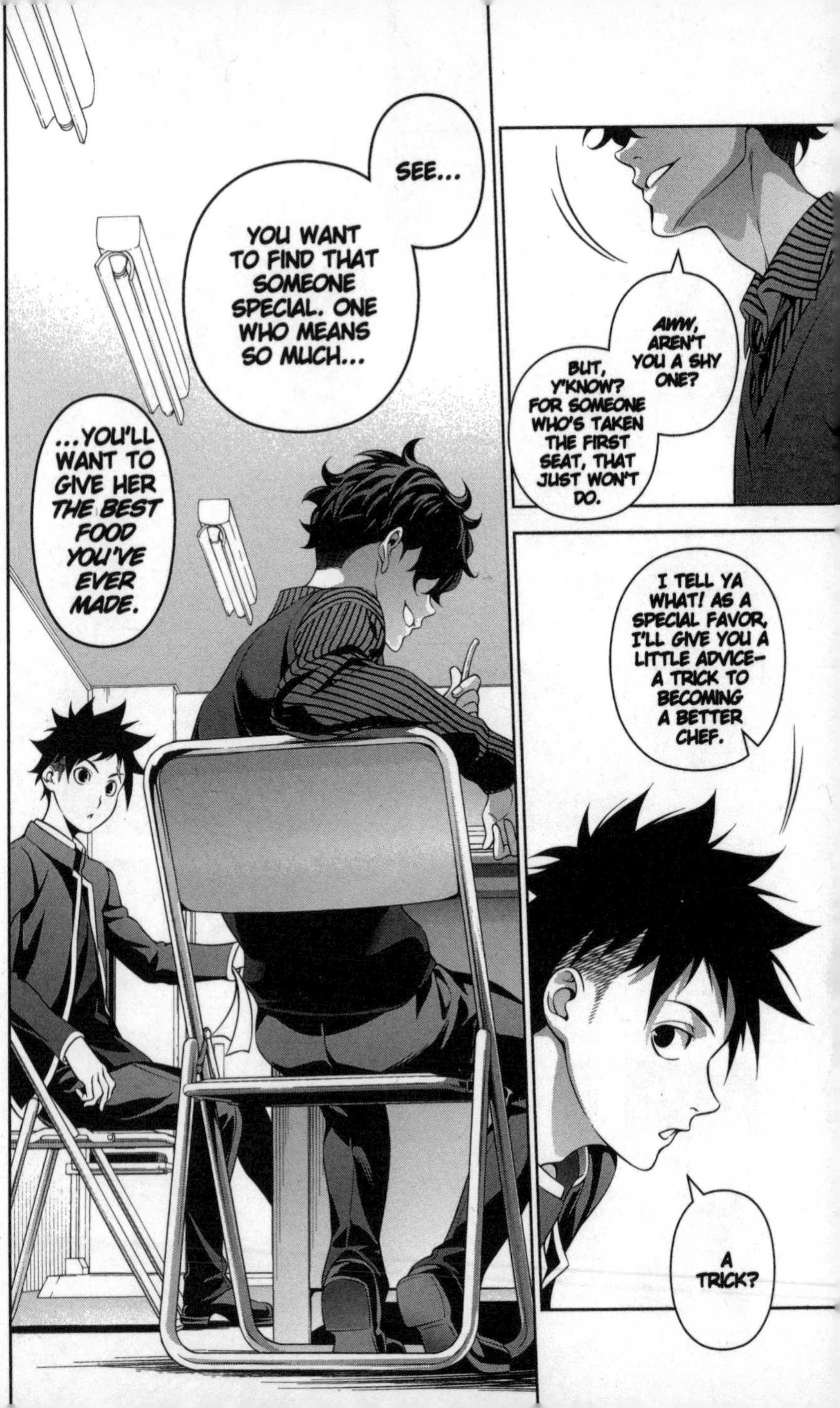
AWW, AREN'T YOU A SHY ONE?
BUT, Y'KNOW? FOR SOMEONE WHO'S TAKEN THE FIRST SEAT, THAT JUST WON'T DO.
I TELL YA WHAT! AS A SPECIAL FAVOR, I'LL GIVE YOU A LITTLE ADVICE— A TRICK TO BECOMING A BETTER CHEF.
A TRICK?
SEE...
YOU WANT TO FIND THAT SOMEONE SPECIAL. ONE WHO MEANS SO MUCH...
...YOU'LL WANT TO GIVE HER *THE BEST FOOD YOU'VE EVER MADE.*

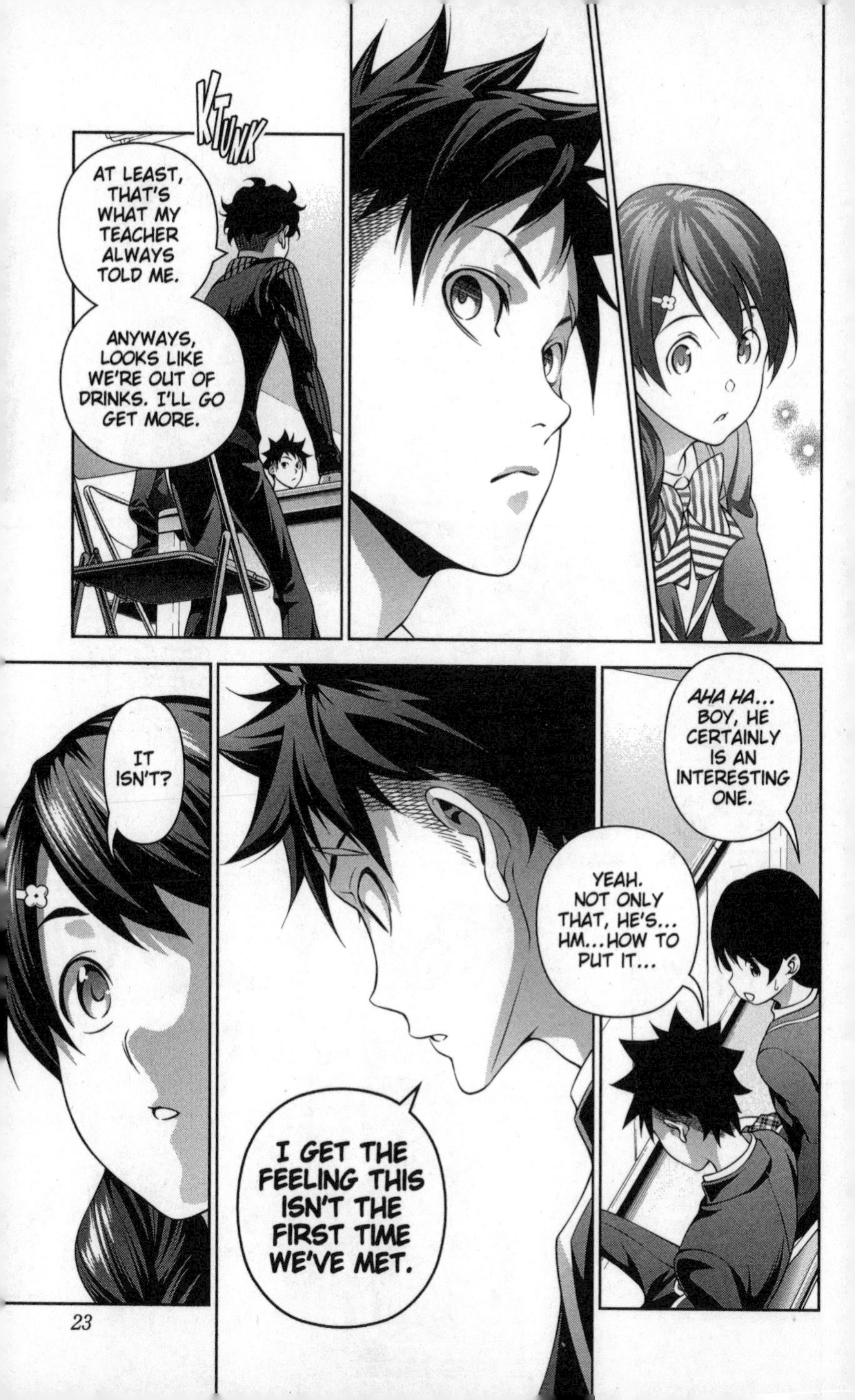
KTUNK
AT LEAST, THAT'S WHAT MY TEACHER ALWAYS TOLD ME.
ANYWAYS, LOOKS LIKE WE'RE OUT OF DRINKS. I'LL GO GET MORE.
AHA HA... BOY, HE CERTAINLY IS AN INTERESTING ONE.
YEAH. NOT ONLY THAT, HE'S... HM...HOW TO PUT IT...
I GET THE FEELING THIS ISN'T THE FIRST TIME WE'VE MET.
IT ISN'T?

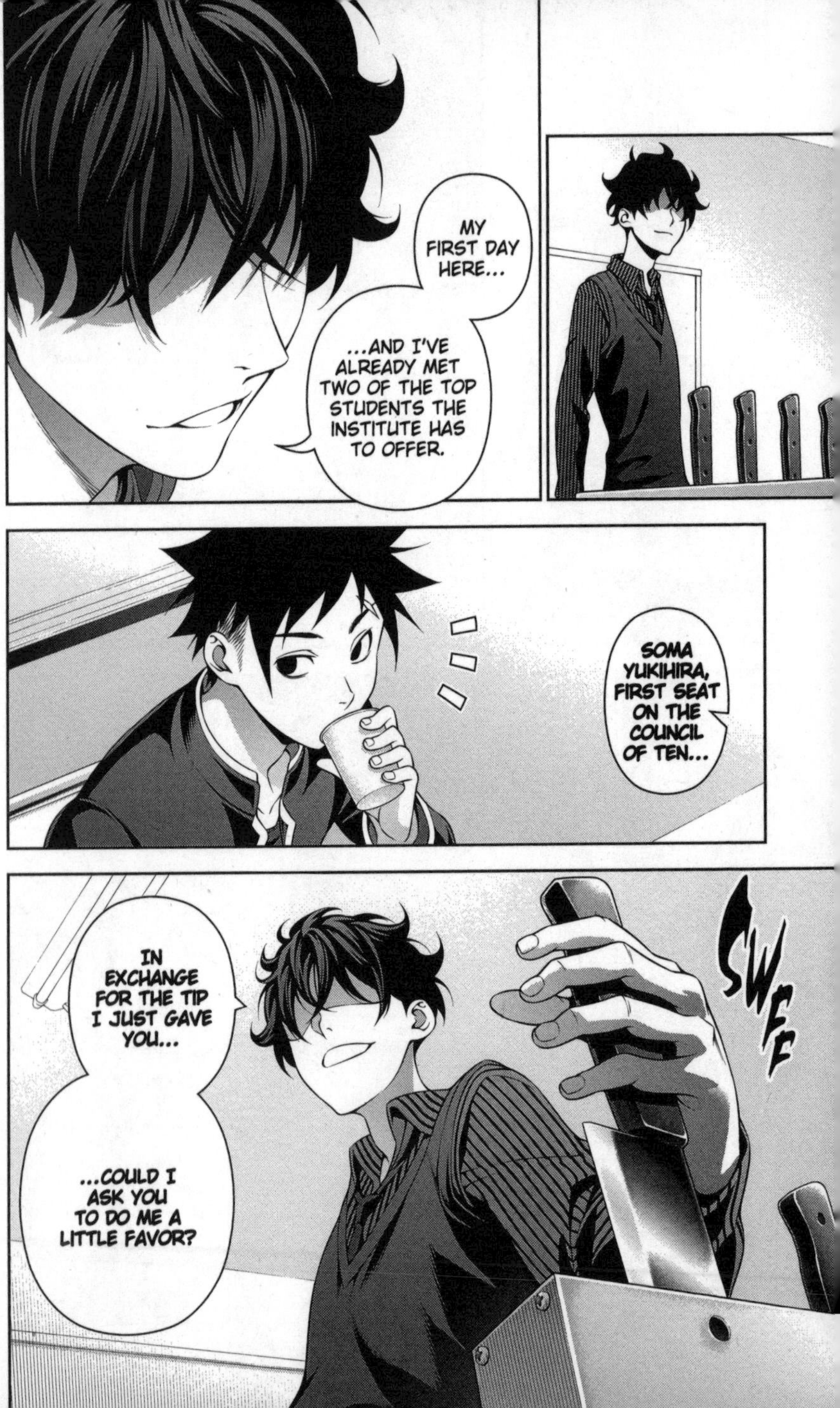
MY FIRST DAY HERE...
...AND I'VE ALREADY MET TWO OF THE TOP STUDENTS THE INSTITUTE HAS TO OFFER.
SOMA YUKIHIRA, FIRST SEAT ON THE COUNCIL OF TEN...
SWFF
IN EXCHANGE FOR THE TIP I JUST GAVE YOU...
...COULD I ASK YOU TO DO ME A LITTLE FAVOR?

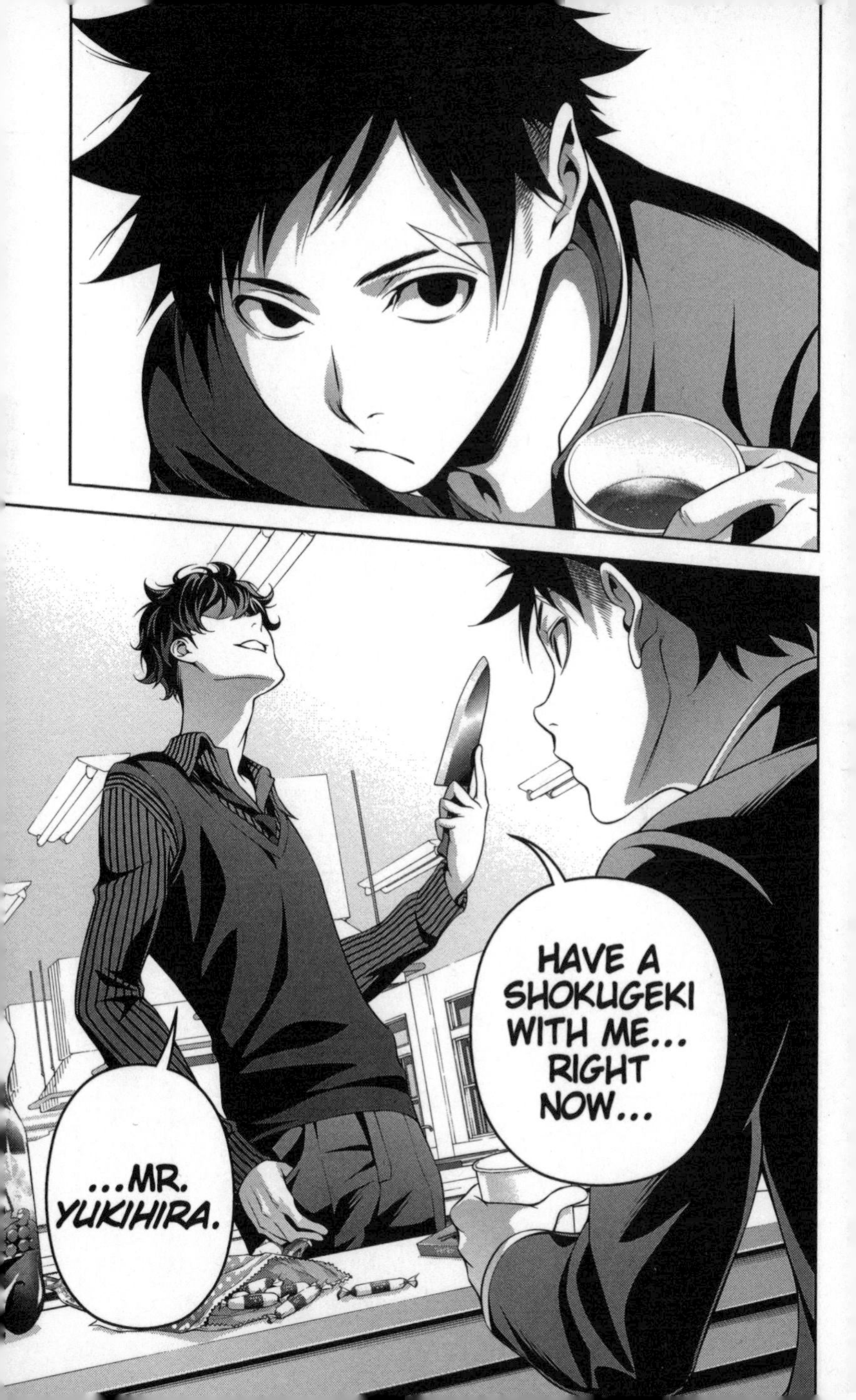
HAVE A SHOKUGEKI WITH ME... RIGHT NOW...
...MR. YUKIHIRA.

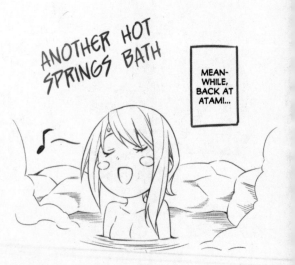

MEAN-WHILE, BACK AT ATAMI...
ANOTHER HOT SPRINGS BATH

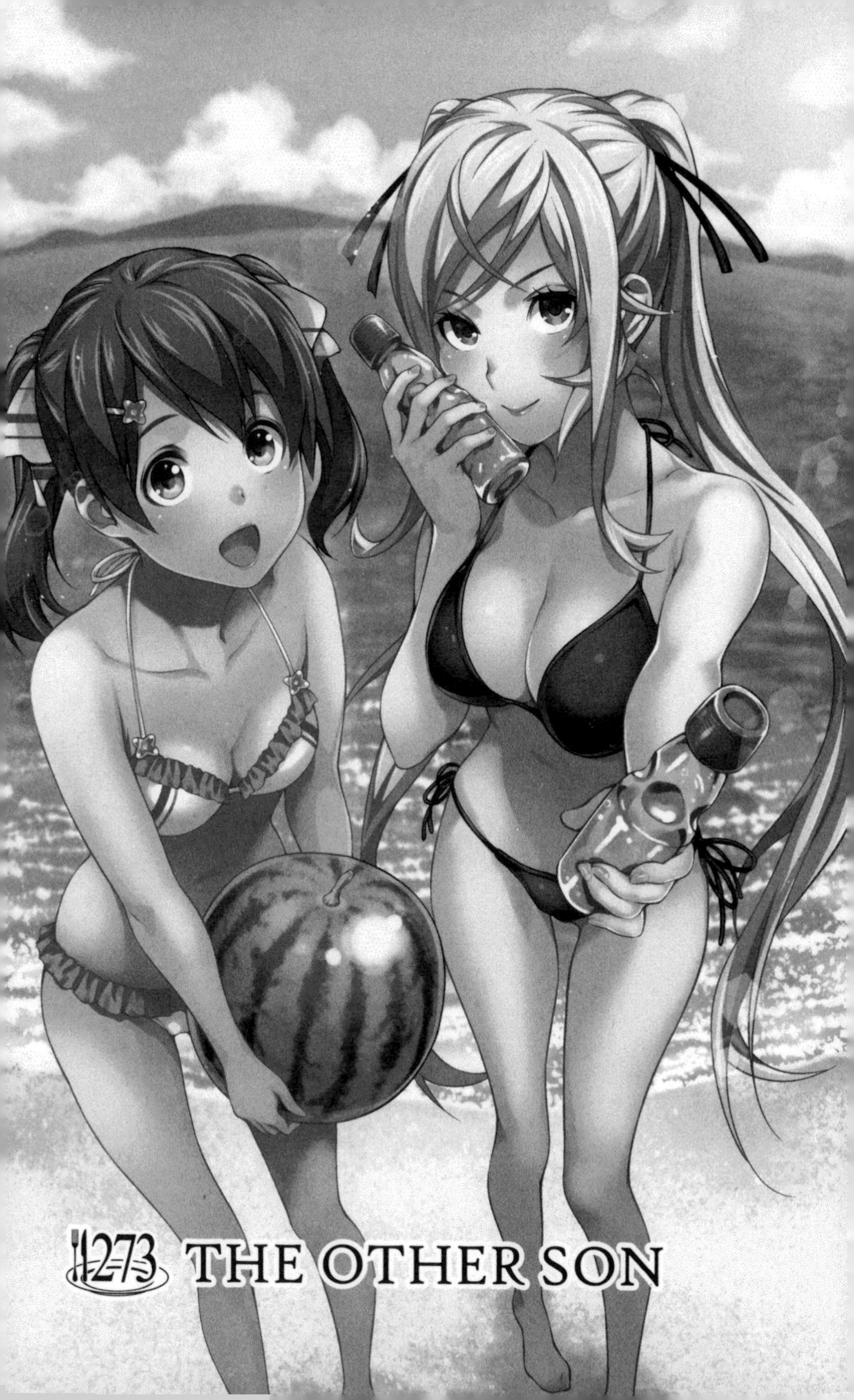

273 THE OTHER SON

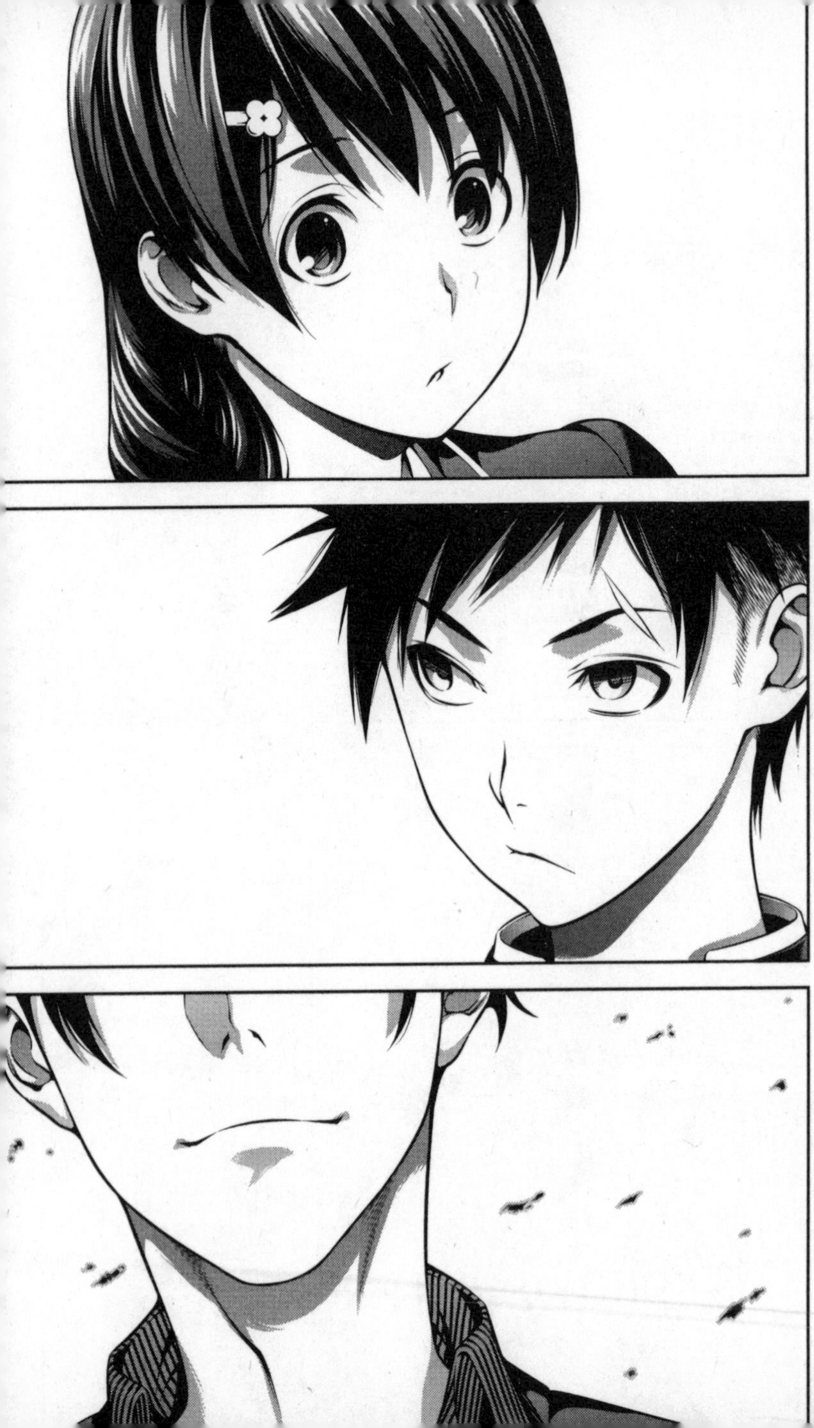

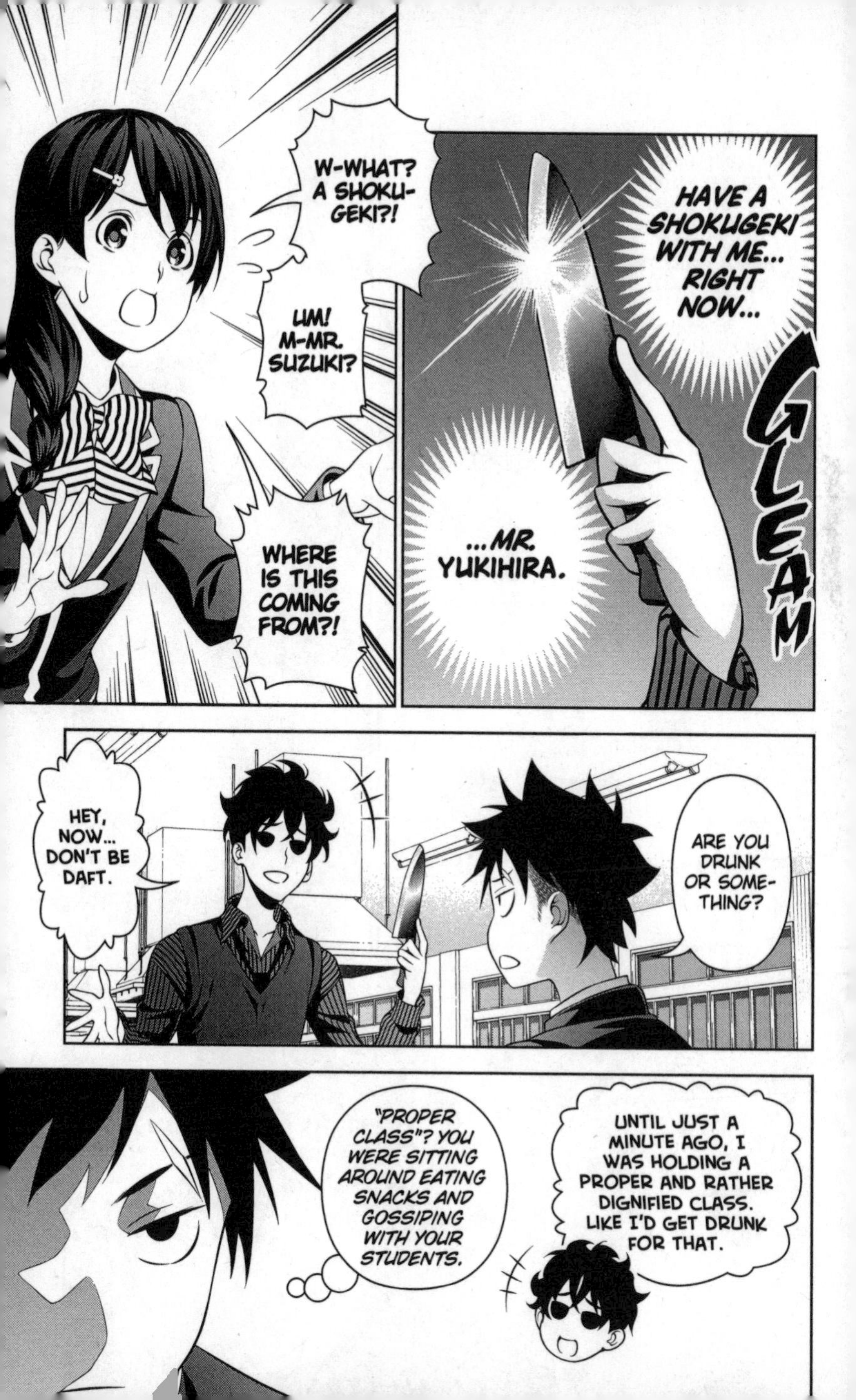
HAVE A SHOKUGEKI WITH ME... RIGHT NOW...
...MR. YUKIHIRA.
GLEAM
W-WHAT? A SHOKU-GEKI?!
UM! M-MR. SUZUKI?
WHERE IS THIS COMING FROM?!
ARE YOU DRUNK OR SOME-THING?
HEY, NOW... DON'T BE DAFT.
UNTIL JUST A MINUTE AGO, I WAS HOLDING A PROPER AND RATHER DIGNIFIED CLASS. LIKE I'D GET DRUNK FOR THAT.
"PROPER CLASS"? YOU WERE SITTING AROUND EATING SNACKS AND GOSSIPING WITH YOUR STUDENTS.

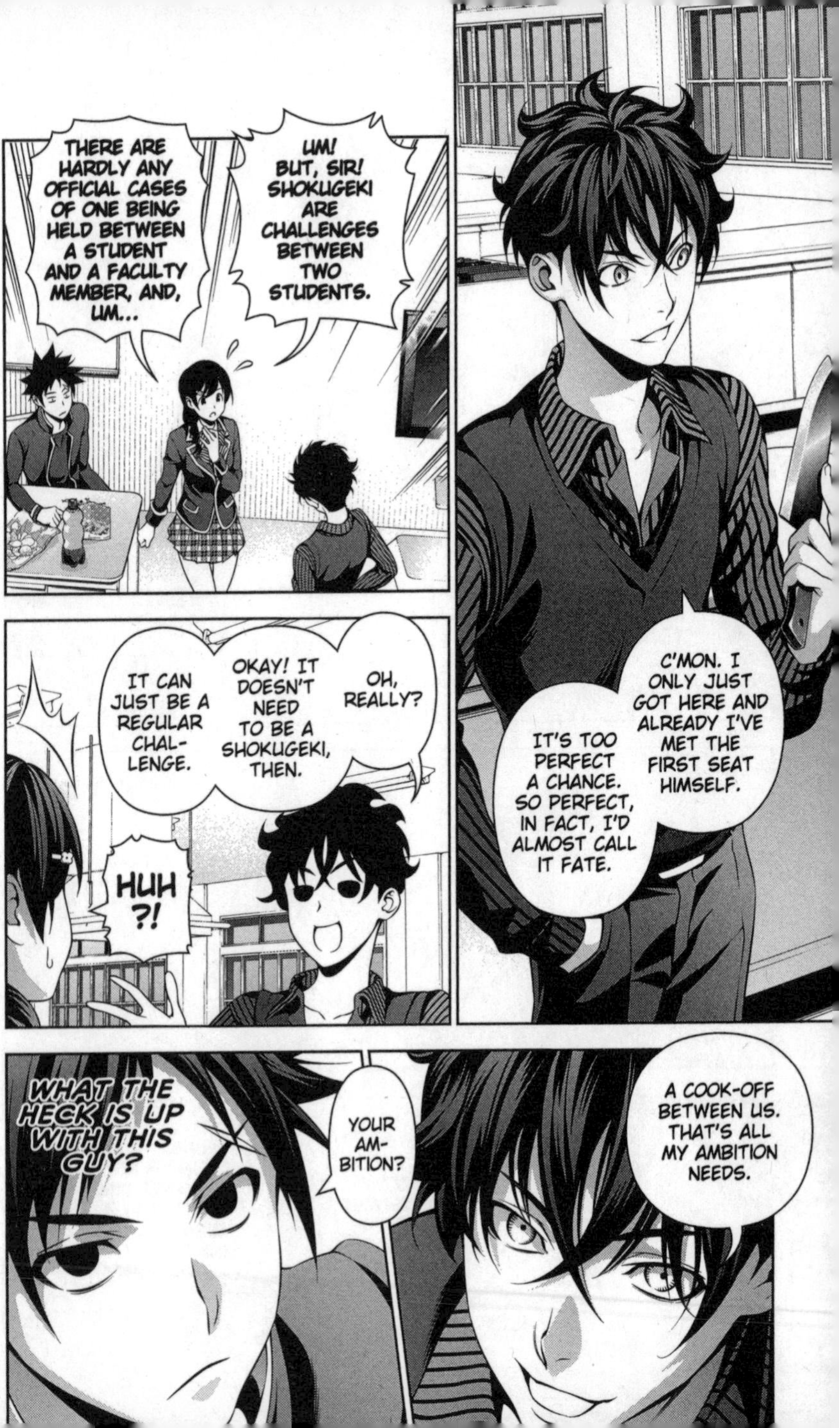
C'MON. I ONLY JUST GOT HERE AND ALREADY I'VE MET THE FIRST SEAT HIMSELF.
IT'S TOO PERFECT A CHANCE. SO PERFECT, IN FACT, I'D ALMOST CALL IT FATE.
UM! BUT, SIR! SHOKUGEKI ARE CHALLENGES BETWEEN TWO STUDENTS.
THERE ARE HARDLY ANY OFFICIAL CASES OF ONE BEING HELD BETWEEN A STUDENT AND A FACULTY MEMBER, AND, UM...
OH, REALLY?
OKAY! IT DOESN'T NEED TO BE A SHOKUGEKI, THEN.
IT CAN JUST BE A REGULAR CHAL-LENGE.
HUH?!
A COOK-OFF BETWEEN US. THAT'S ALL MY AMBITION NEEDS.
YOUR AM-BITION?
WHAT THE HECK IS UP WITH THIS GUY?

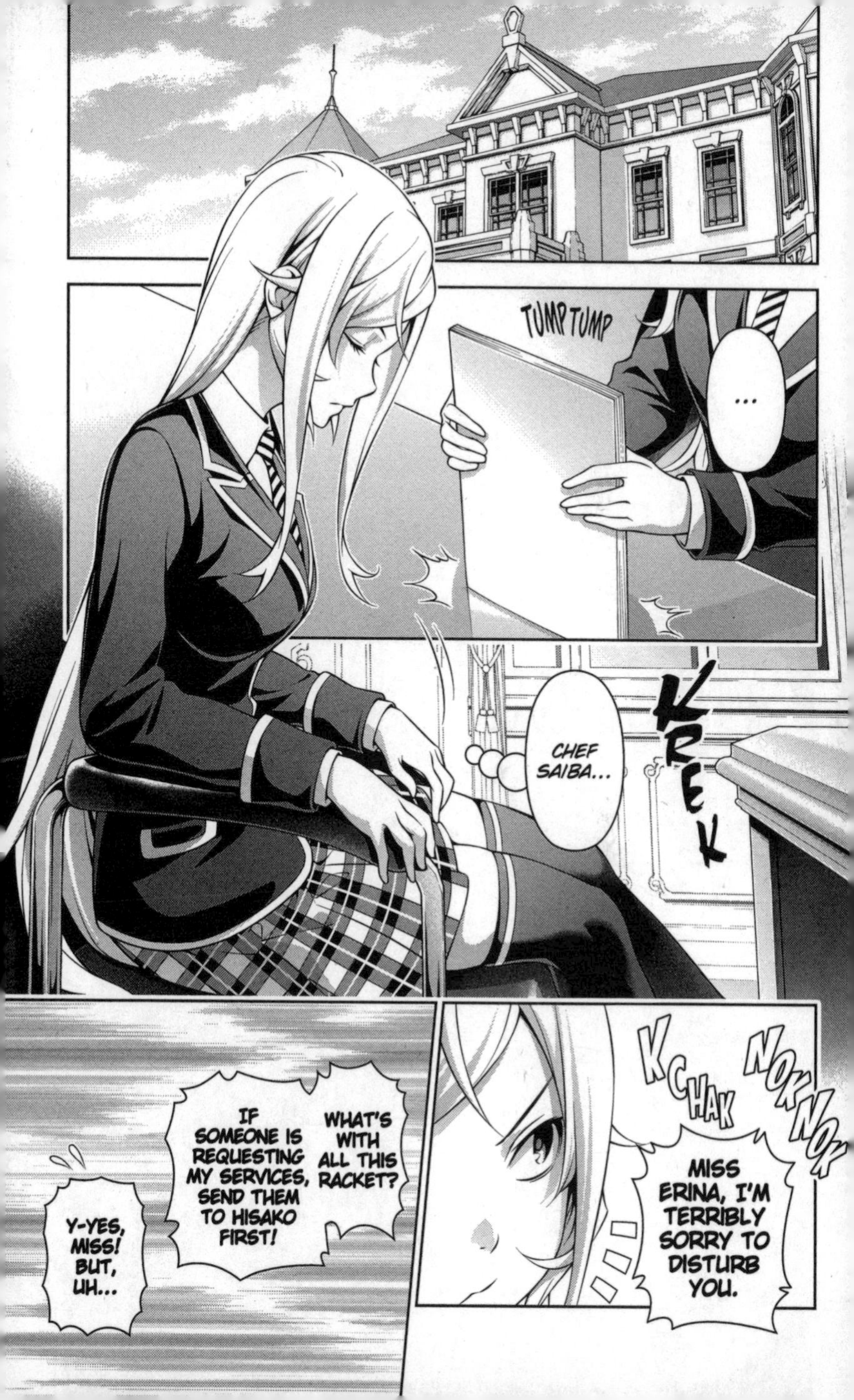

TUMP TUMP
...
KREK
CHEF SAIBA...
NOK NOK
KCHAK
MISS ERINA, I'M TERRIBLY SORRY TO DISTURB YOU.
WHAT'S WITH ALL THIS RACKET?
IF SOMEONE IS REQUESTING MY SERVICES, SEND THEM TO HISAKO FIRST!
Y-YES, MISS! BUT, UH...

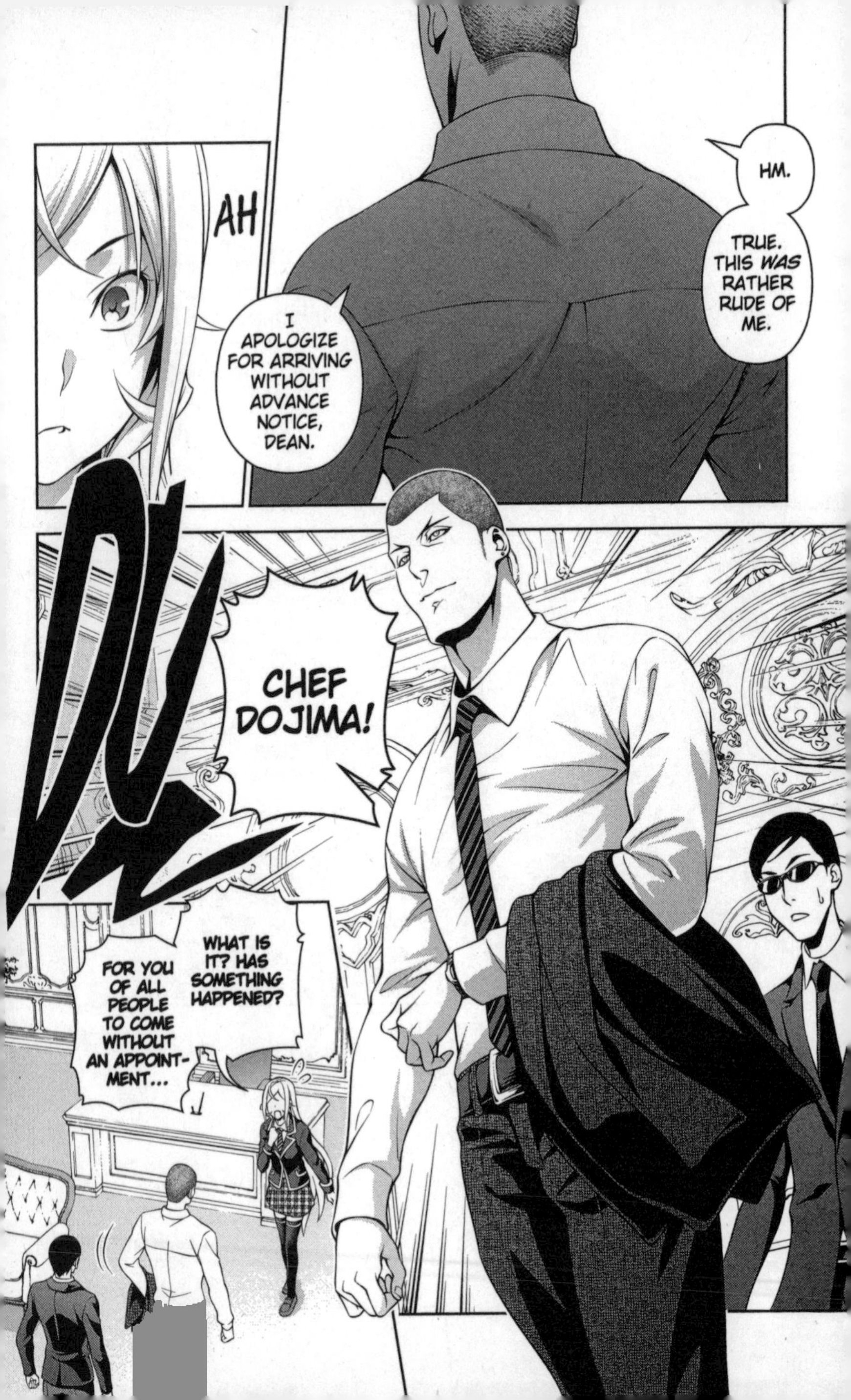
HM.
TRUE. THIS *WAS* RATHER RUDE OF ME.
I APOLOGIZE FOR ARRIVING WITHOUT ADVANCE NOTICE, DEAN.
AH
CHEF DOJIMA!
WHAT IS IT? HAS SOMETHING HAPPENED?
FOR YOU OF ALL PEOPLE TO COME WITHOUT AN APPOINT-MENT...

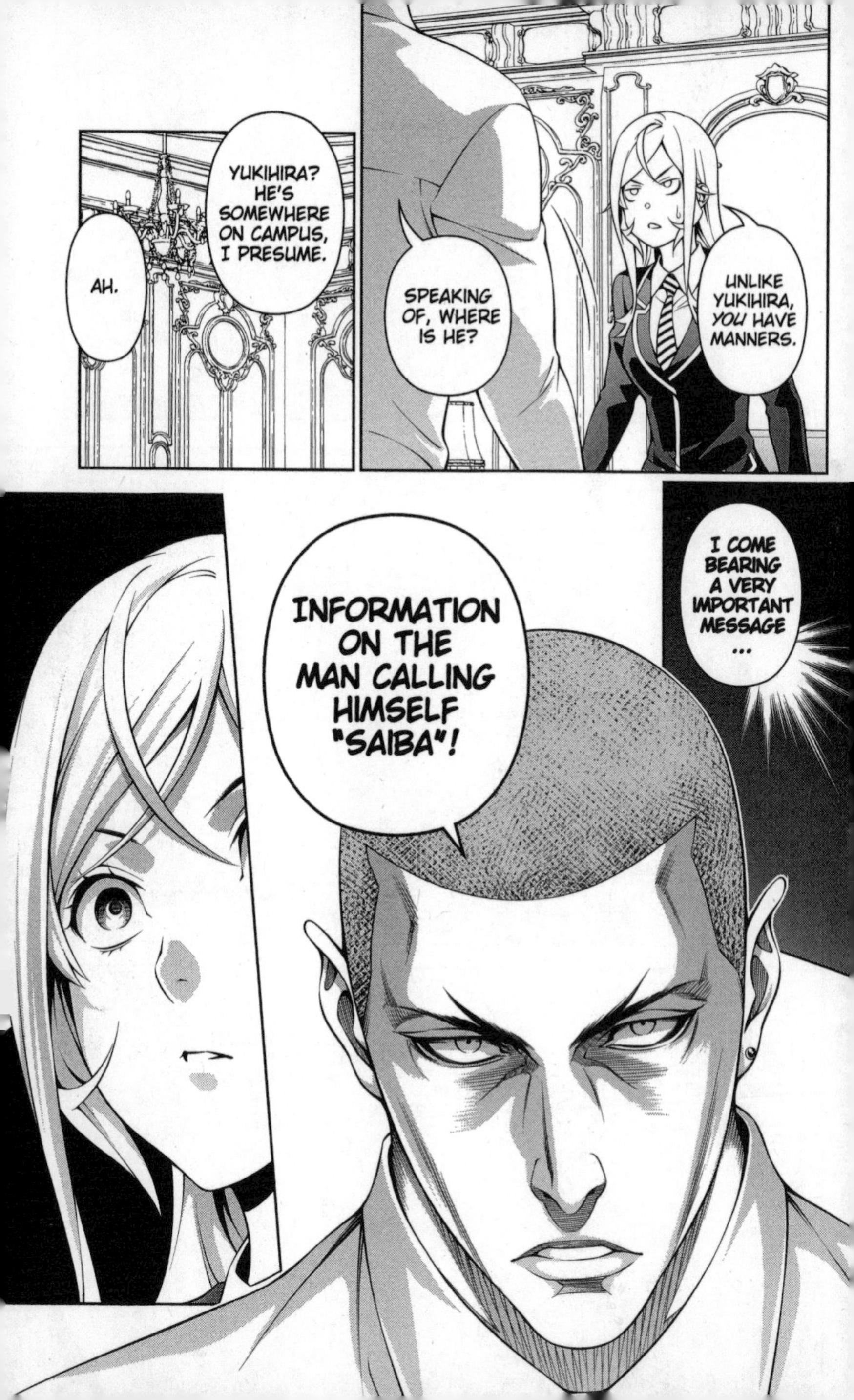
UNLIKE YUKIHIRA, *YOU* HAVE MANNERS.
SPEAKING OF, WHERE IS HE?
YUKIHIRA? HE'S SOMEWHERE ON CAMPUS, I PRESUME.
AH.
I COME BEARING A VERY IMPORTANT MESSAGE...
INFORMATION ON THE MAN CALLING HIMSELF "SAIBA"!

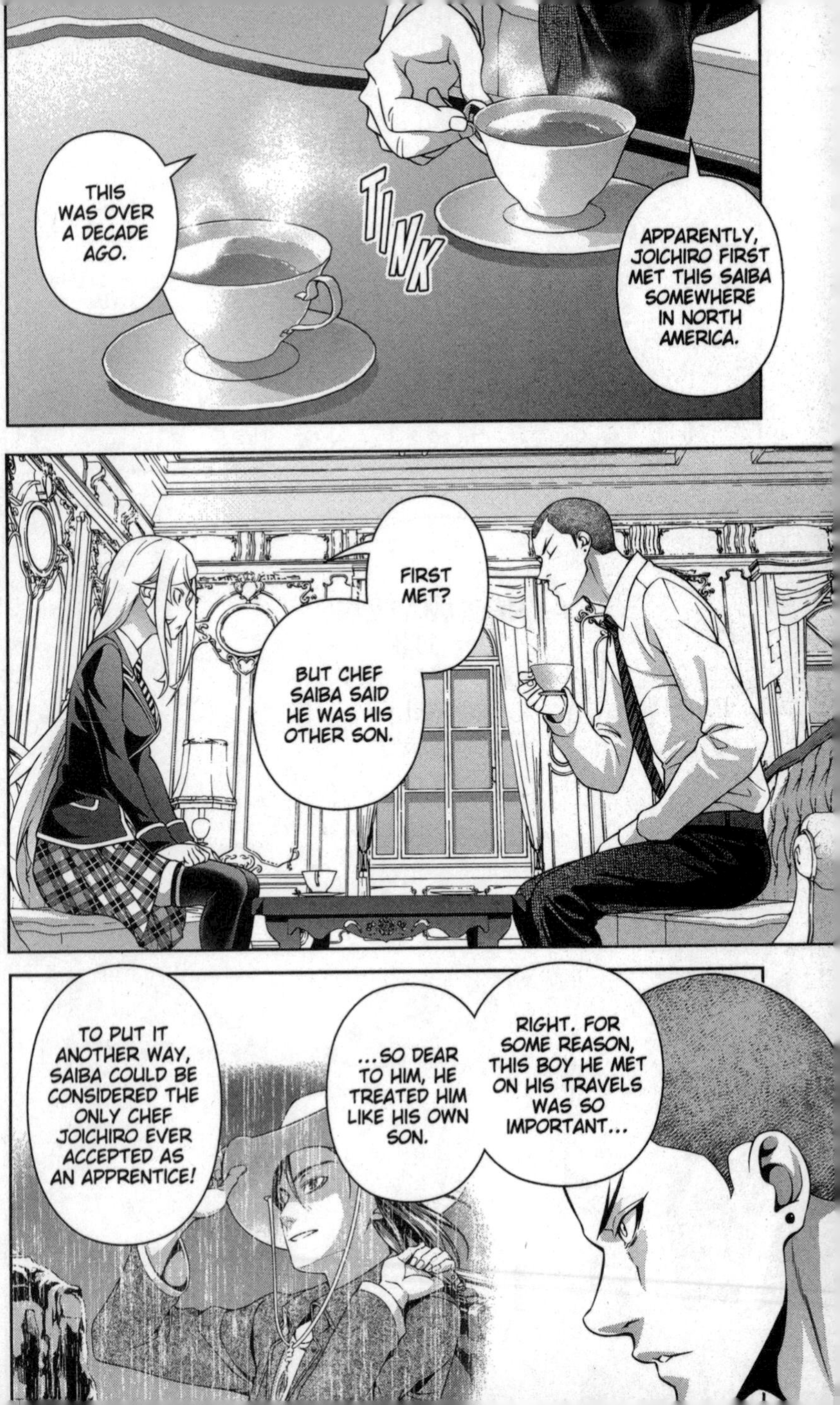
APPARENTLY, JOICHIRO FIRST MET THIS SAIBA SOMEWHERE IN NORTH AMERICA.
TINK
THIS WAS OVER A DECADE AGO.
FIRST MET?
BUT CHEF SAIBA SAID HE WAS HIS OTHER SON.
RIGHT. FOR SOME REASON, THIS BOY HE MET ON HIS TRAVELS WAS SO IMPORTANT...
...SO DEAR TO HIM, HE TREATED HIM LIKE HIS OWN SON.
TO PUT IT ANOTHER WAY, SAIBA COULD BE CONSIDERED THE ONLY CHEF JOICHIRO EVER ACCEPTED AS AN APPRENTICE!

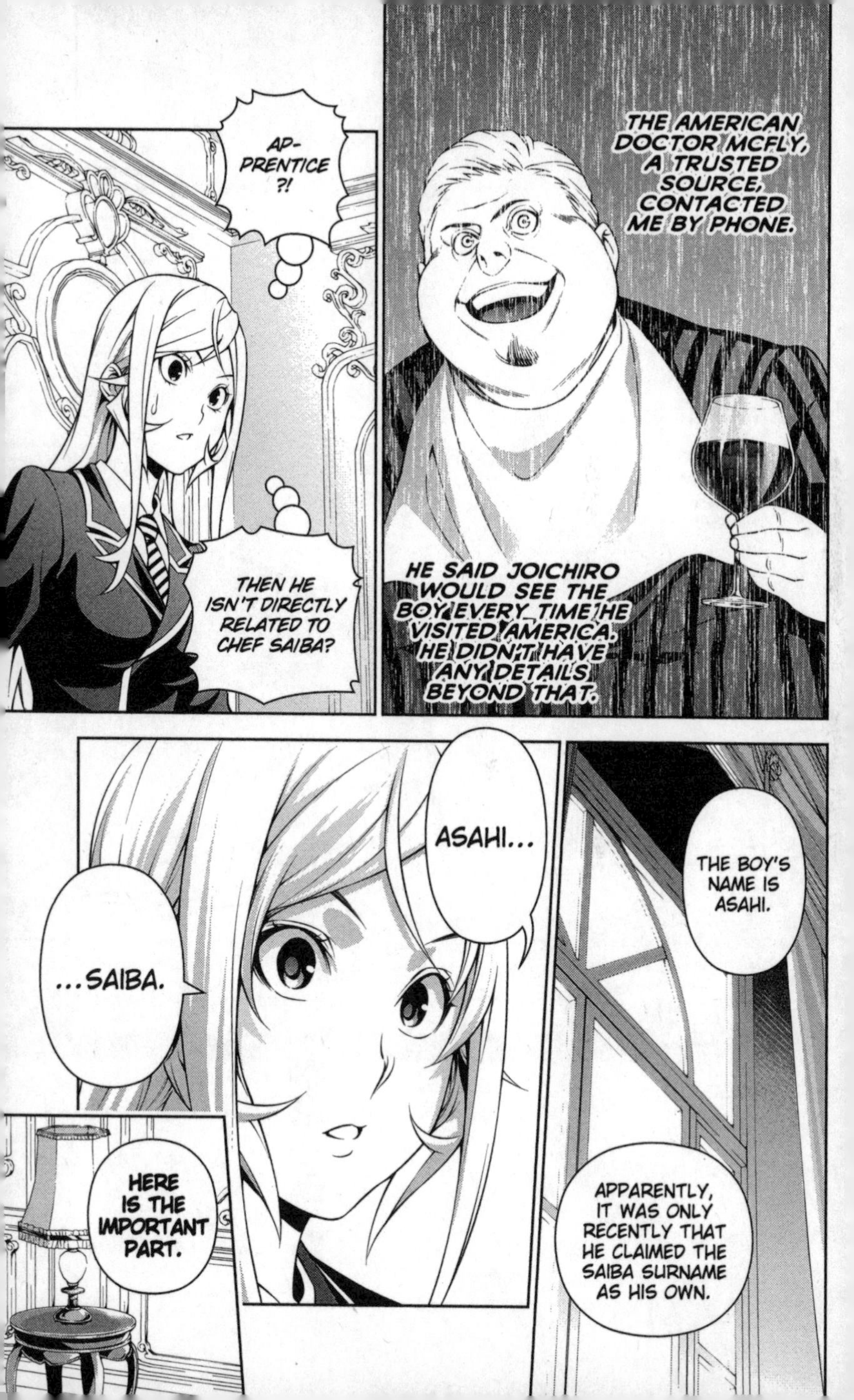
THE AMERICAN DOCTOR MCFLY, A TRUSTED SOURCE, CONTACTED ME BY PHONE.
HE SAID JOICHIRO WOULD SEE THE BOY EVERY TIME HE VISITED AMERICA. HE DIDN'T HAVE ANY DETAILS BEYOND THAT.
AP-PRENTICE?!
THEN HE ISN'T DIRECTLY RELATED TO CHEF SAIBA?
THE BOY'S NAME IS ASAHI.
APPARENTLY, IT WAS ONLY RECENTLY THAT HE CLAIMED THE SAIBA SURNAME AS HIS OWN.
ASAHI...
...SAIBA.
HERE IS THE IMPORTANT PART.

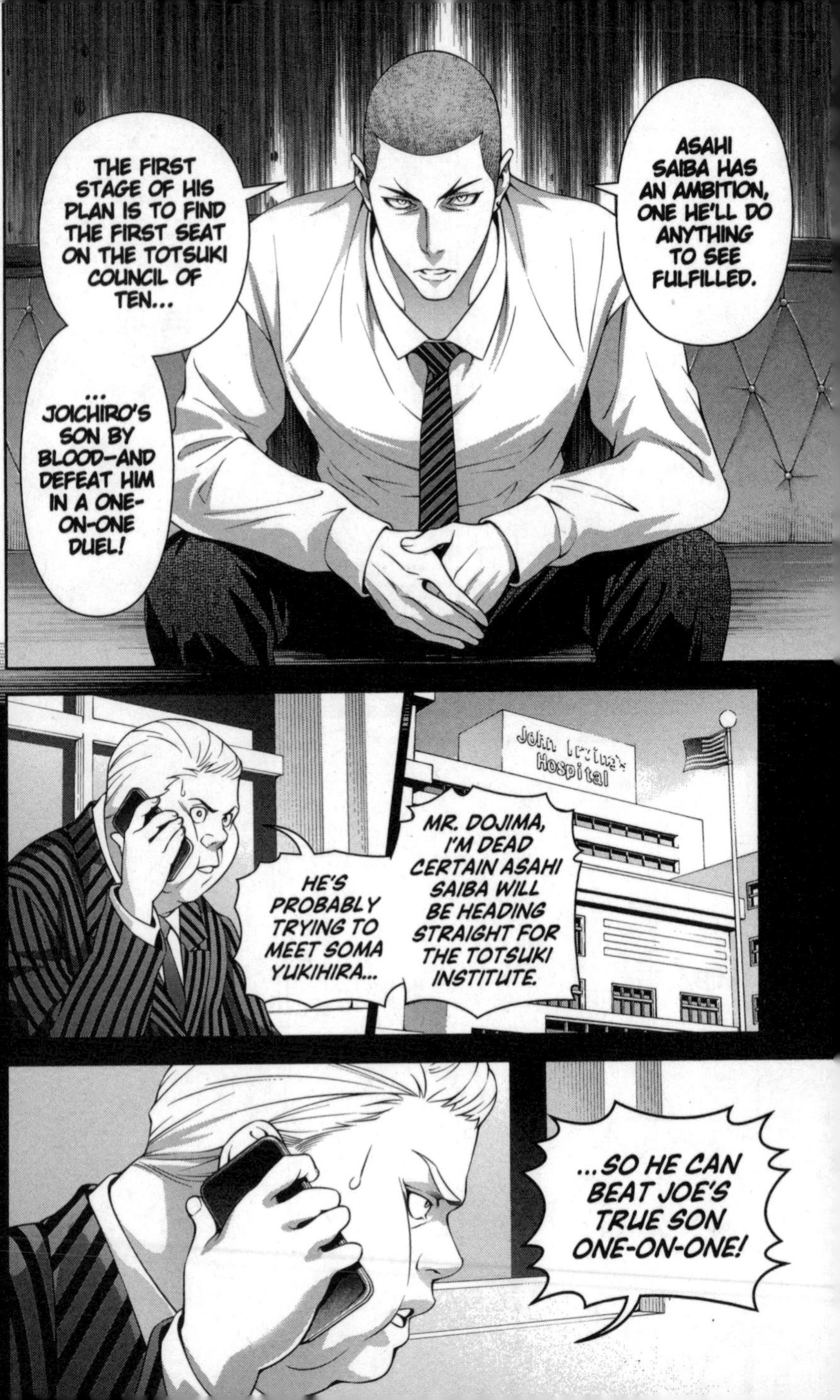
ASAHI SAIBA HAS AN AMBITION, ONE HE'LL DO ANYTHING TO SEE FULFILLED.
THE FIRST STAGE OF HIS PLAN IS TO FIND THE FIRST SEAT ON THE TOTSUKI COUNCIL OF TEN...
...JOICHIRO'S SON BY BLOOD—AND DEFEAT HIM IN A ONE-ON-ONE DUEL!
Hospital
MR. DOJIMA, I'M DEAD CERTAIN ASAHI SAIBA WILL BE HEADING STRAIGHT FOR THE TOTSUKI INSTITUTE.
HE'S PROBABLY TRYING TO MEET SOMA YUKIHIRA...
...SO HE CAN BEAT JOE'S TRUE SON ONE-ON-ONE!

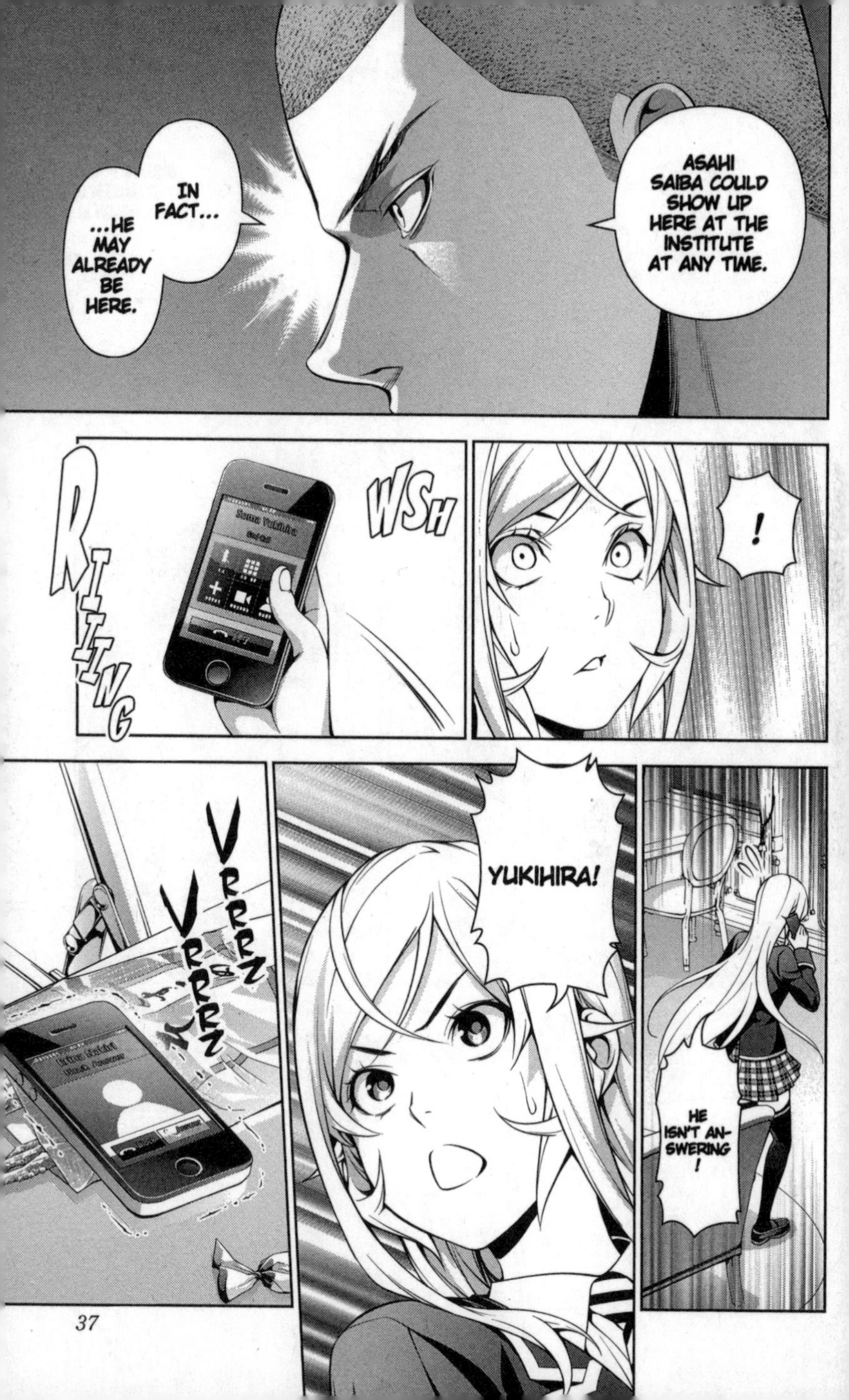
ASAHI SAIBA COULD SHOW UP HERE AT THE INSTITUTE AT ANY TIME.
IN FACT...
...HE MAY ALREADY BE HERE.
!
WSH
RIIIING
HE ISN'T AN-SWERING!
YUKIHIRA!
VRRRZ
VRRRZ

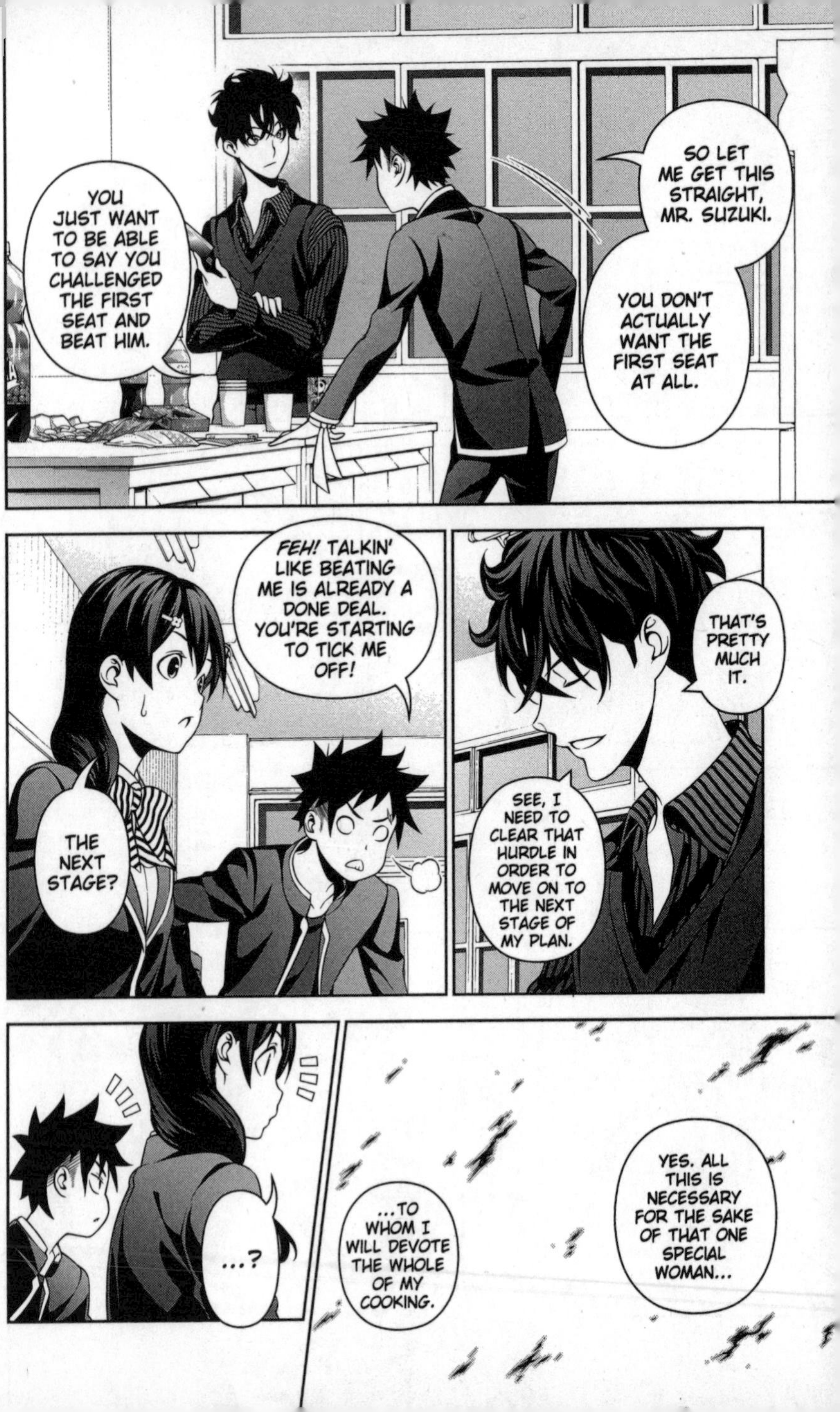
SO LET ME GET THIS STRAIGHT, MR. SUZUKI.
YOU DON'T ACTUALLY WANT THE FIRST SEAT AT ALL.
YOU JUST WANT TO BE ABLE TO SAY YOU CHALLENGED THE FIRST SEAT AND BEAT HIM.
THAT'S PRETTY MUCH IT.
SEE, I NEED TO CLEAR THAT HURDLE IN ORDER TO MOVE ON TO THE NEXT STAGE OF MY PLAN.
FEH! TALKIN' LIKE BEATING ME IS ALREADY A DONE DEAL. YOU'RE STARTING TO TICK ME OFF!
THE NEXT STAGE?
YES. ALL THIS IS NECESSARY FOR THE SAKE OF THAT ONE SPECIAL WOMAN...
...TO WHOM I WILL DEVOTE THE WHOLE OF MY COOKING.
...?

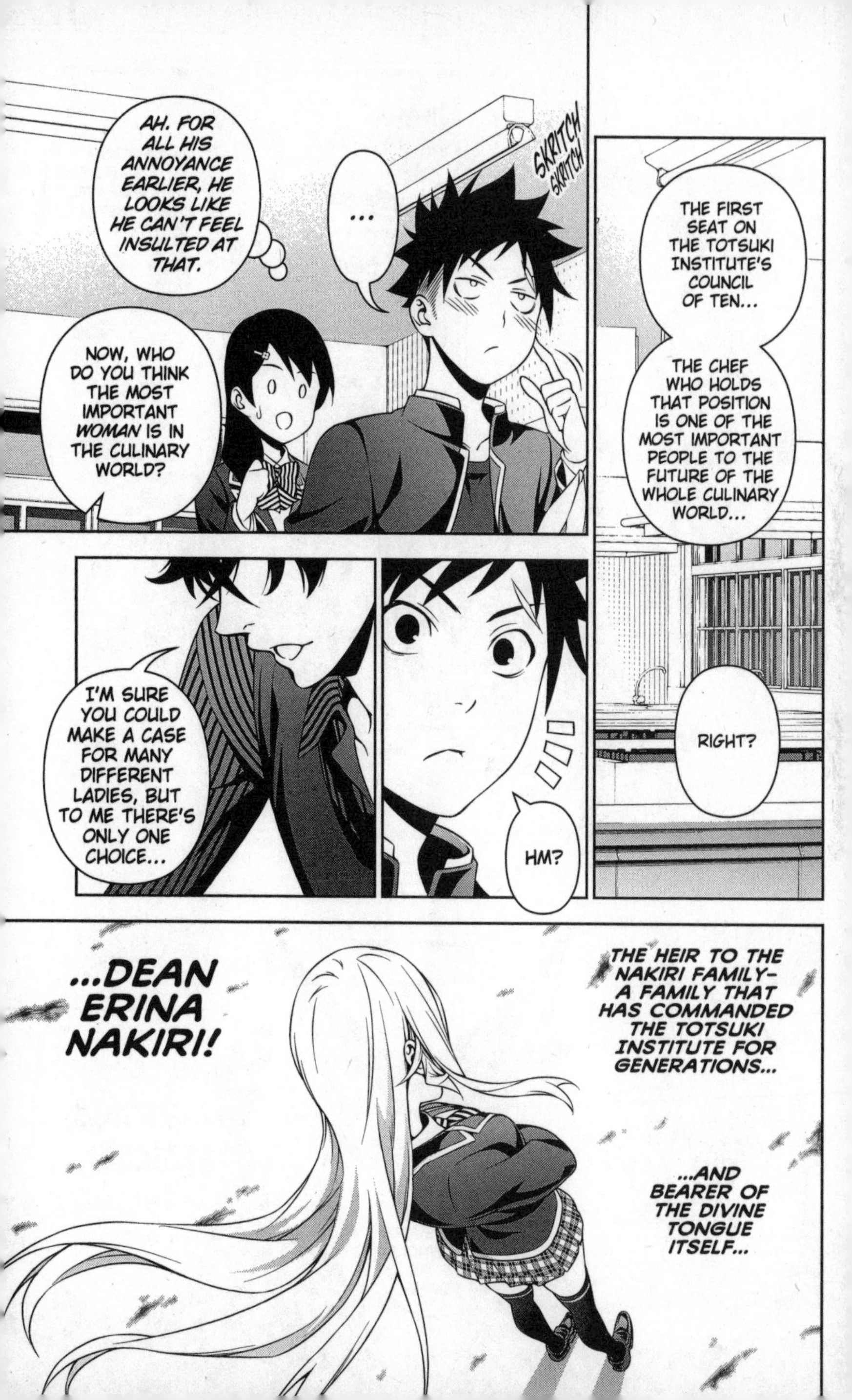
THE FIRST SEAT ON THE TOTSUKI INSTITUTE'S COUNCIL OF TEN...
THE CHEF WHO HOLDS THAT POSITION IS ONE OF THE MOST IMPORTANT PEOPLE TO THE FUTURE OF THE WHOLE CULINARY WORLD...
RIGHT?
SKRITCH SKRITCH
...
AH. FOR ALL HIS ANNOYANCE EARLIER, HE LOOKS LIKE HE CAN'T FEEL INSULTED AT THAT.
NOW, WHO DO YOU THINK THE MOST IMPORTANT *WOMAN* IS IN THE CULINARY WORLD?
HM?
I'M SURE YOU COULD MAKE A CASE FOR MANY DIFFERENT LADIES, BUT TO ME THERE'S ONLY ONE CHOICE...
THE HEIR TO THE NAKIRI FAMILY– A FAMILY THAT HAS COMMANDED THE TOTSUKI INSTITUTE FOR GENERATIONS...
...AND BEARER OF THE DIVINE TONGUE ITSELF...
...DEAN ERINA NAKIRI!

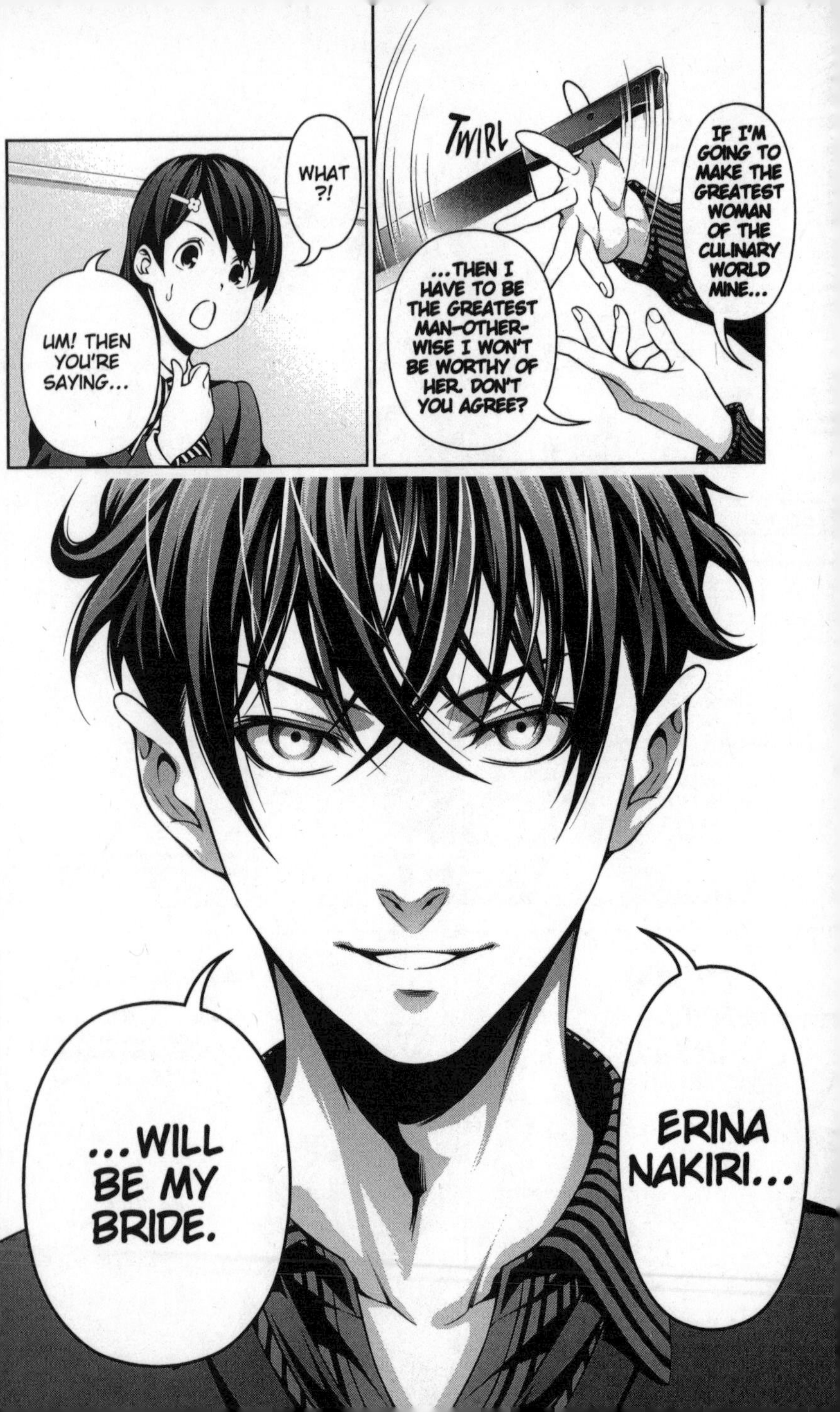
TWIRL
IF I'M GOING TO MAKE THE GREATEST WOMAN OF THE CULINARY WORLD MINE...
...THEN I HAVE TO BE THE GREATEST MAN—OTHER-WISE I WON'T BE WORTHY OF HER. DON'T YOU AGREE?
WHAT?!
UM! THEN YOU'RE SAYING...
ERINA NAKIRI...
...WILL BE MY BRIDE.

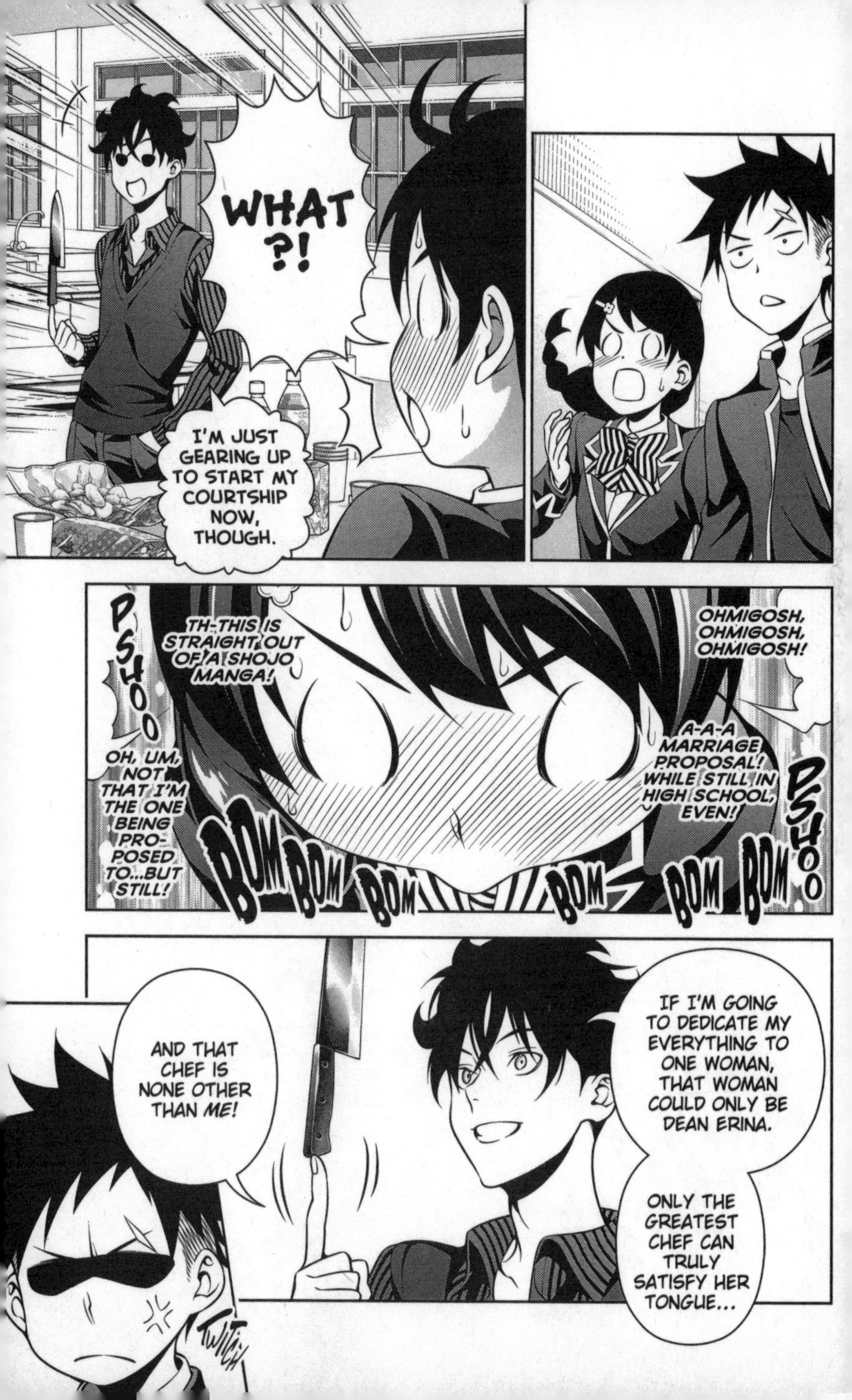
WHAT ?!
I'M JUST GEARING UP TO START MY COURTSHIP NOW, THOUGH.
OHMIGOSH, OHMIGOSH, OHMIGOSH!
A-A-A MARRIAGE PROPOSAL! WHILE STILL IN HIGH SCHOOL, EVEN!
PSHOO
TH-THIS IS STRAIGHT OUT OF A SHOJO MANGA!
PSHOO
OH, UM, NOT THAT I'M THE ONE BEING PRO-POSED TO...BUT STILL!
BOM BOM BOM BOM BOM BOM
IF I'M GOING TO DEDICATE MY EVERYTHING TO ONE WOMAN, THAT WOMAN COULD ONLY BE DEAN ERINA.
ONLY THE GREATEST CHEF CAN TRULY SATISFY HER TONGUE...
AND THAT CHEF IS NONE OTHER THAN *ME*!
TWITCH

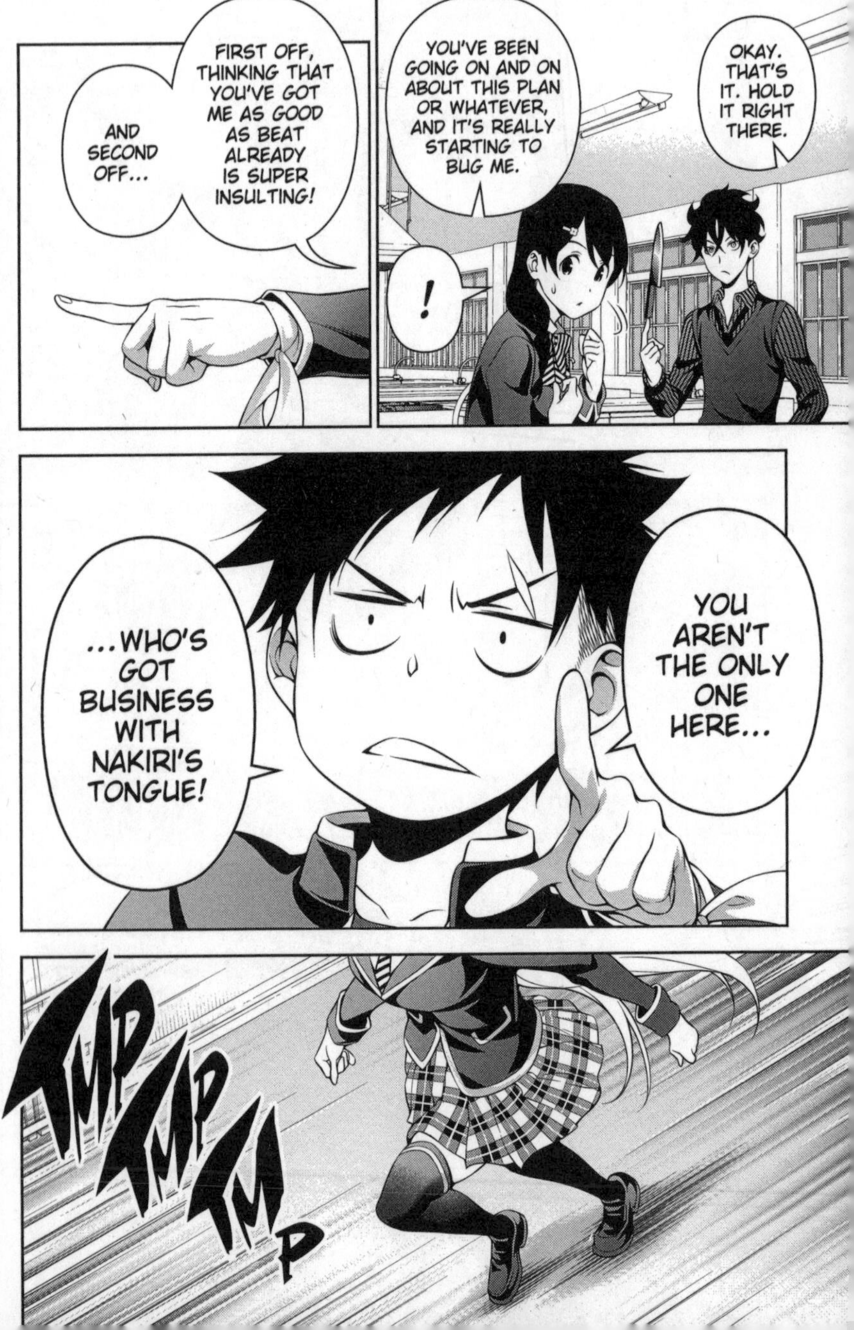
OKAY. THAT'S IT. HOLD IT RIGHT THERE.
YOU'VE BEEN GOING ON AND ON ABOUT THIS PLAN OR WHATEVER, AND IT'S REALLY STARTING TO BUG ME.
!
FIRST OFF, THINKING THAT YOU'VE GOT ME AS GOOD AS BEAT ALREADY IS SUPER INSULTING!
AND SECOND OFF...
YOU AREN'T THE ONLY ONE HERE...
...WHO'S GOT BUSINESS WITH NAKIRI'S TONGUE!
TMP TMP TMP

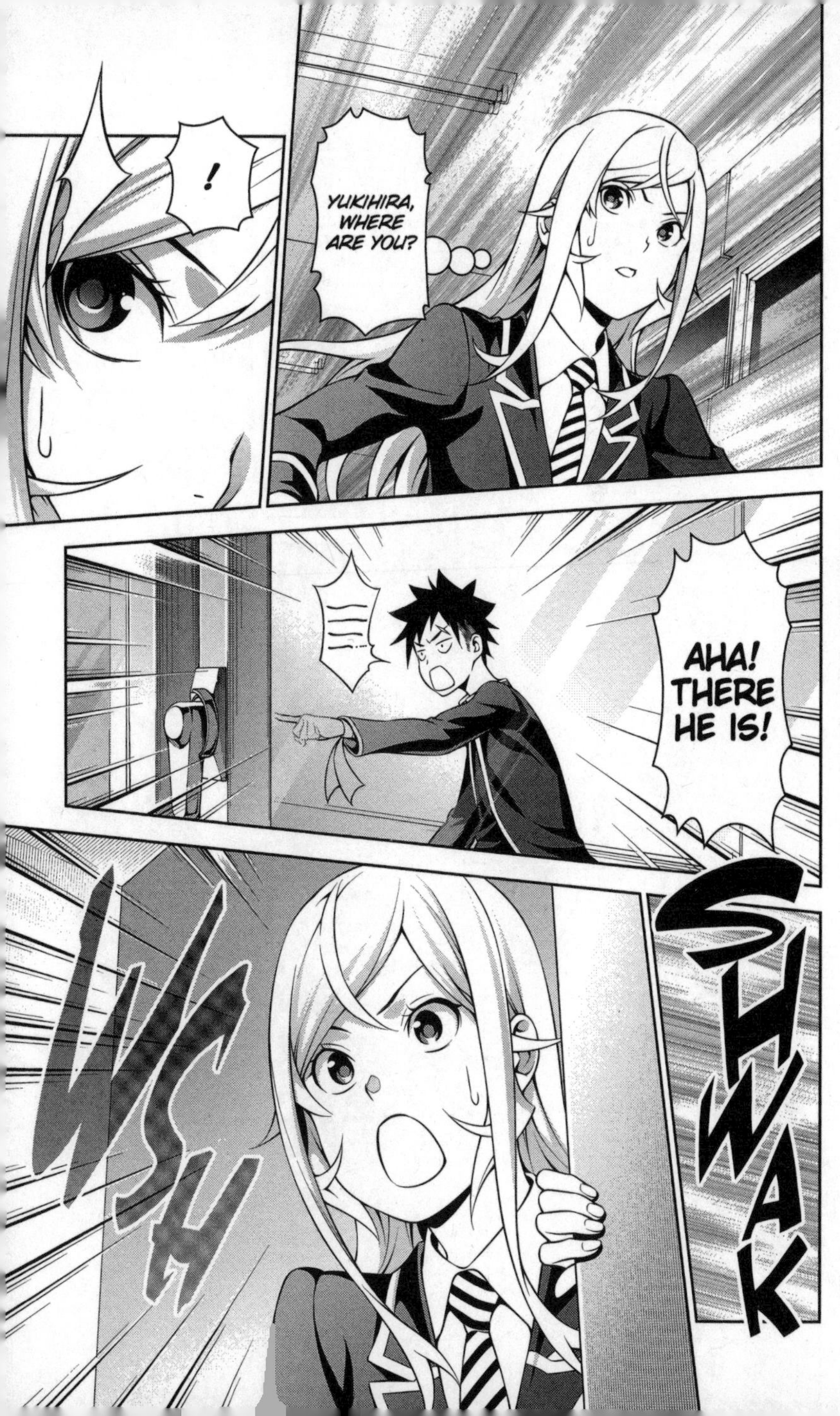
YUKIHIRA, WHERE ARE YOU?
!
AHA! THERE HE IS!
SHWAK
WHSH

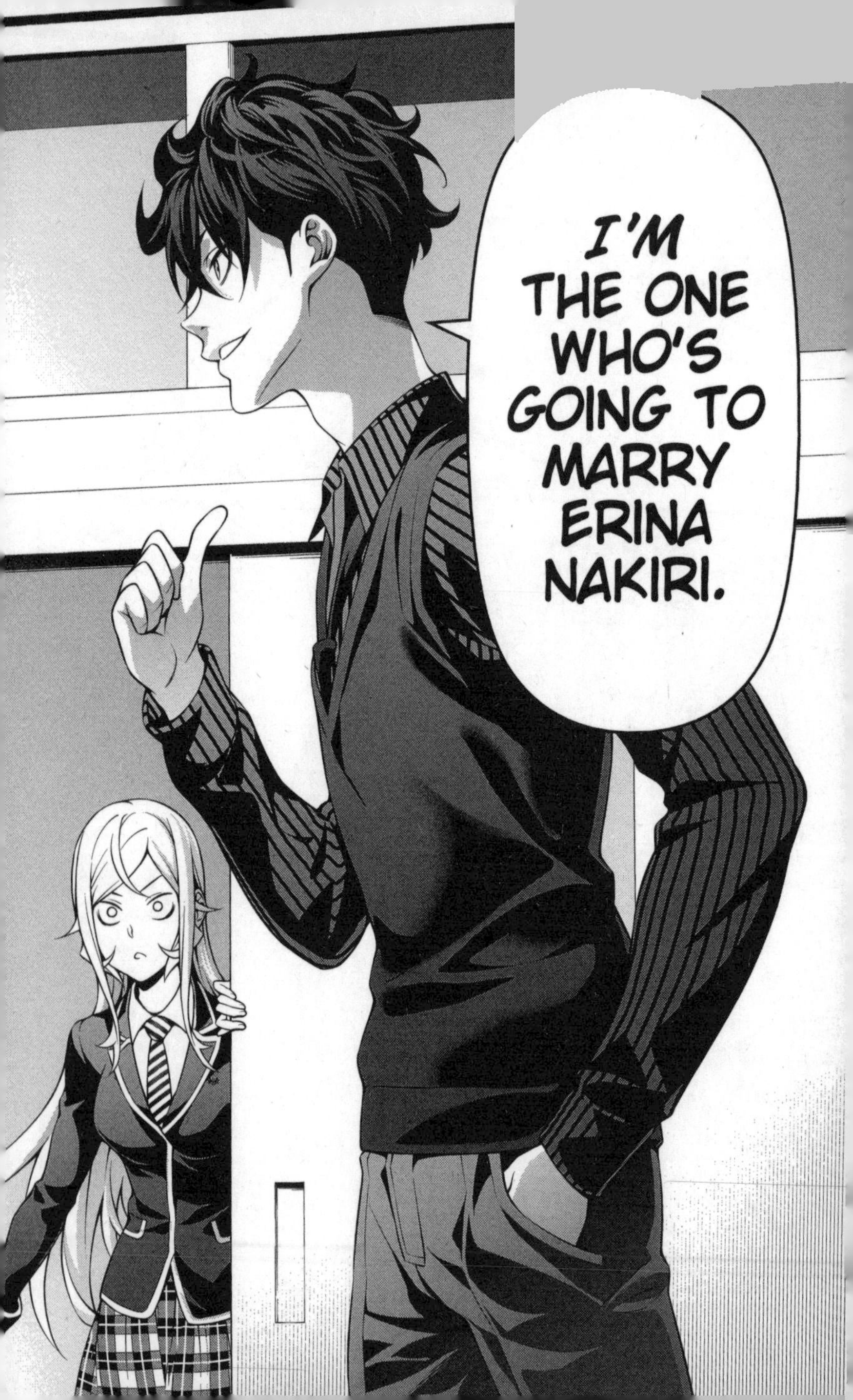
I'M THE ONE WHO'S GOING TO MARRY ERINA NAKIRI.

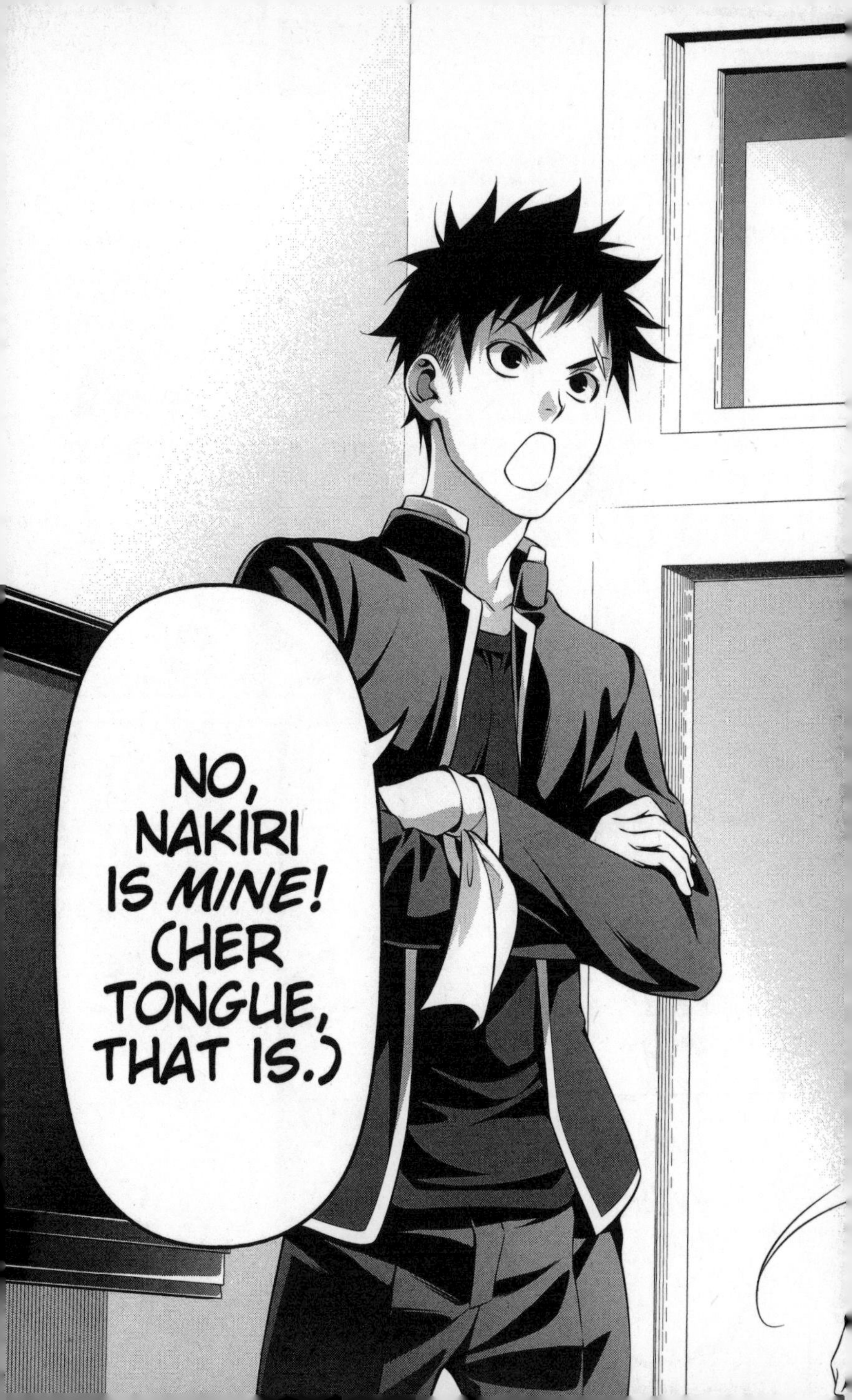
NO, NAKIRI IS *MINE*! (HER TONGUE, THAT IS.)

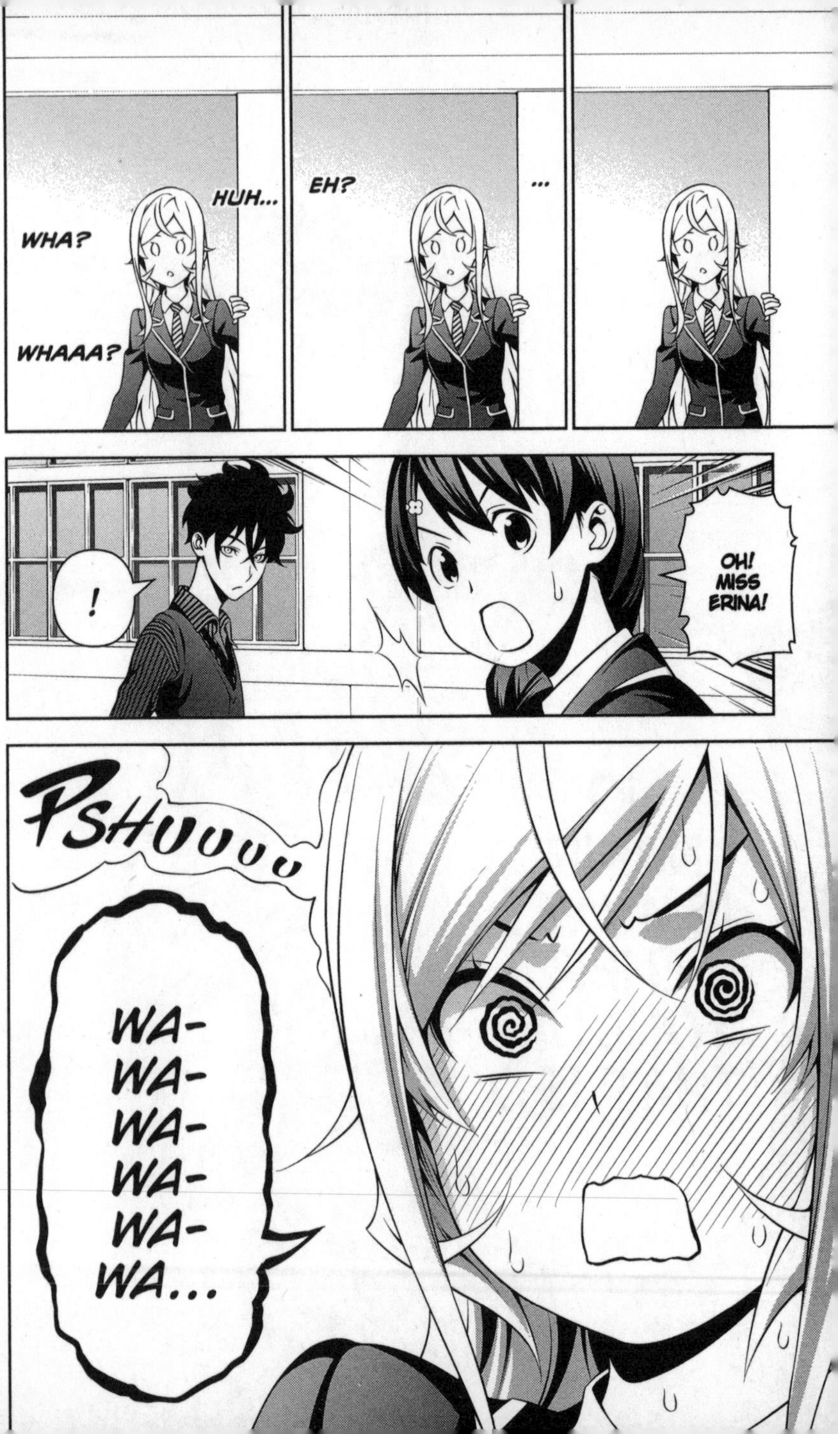
...
EH?
HUH...
WHA?
WHAAA?
OH! MISS ERINA!
!
PSHUUUUU
WA-WA-WA-WA-WA-WA...

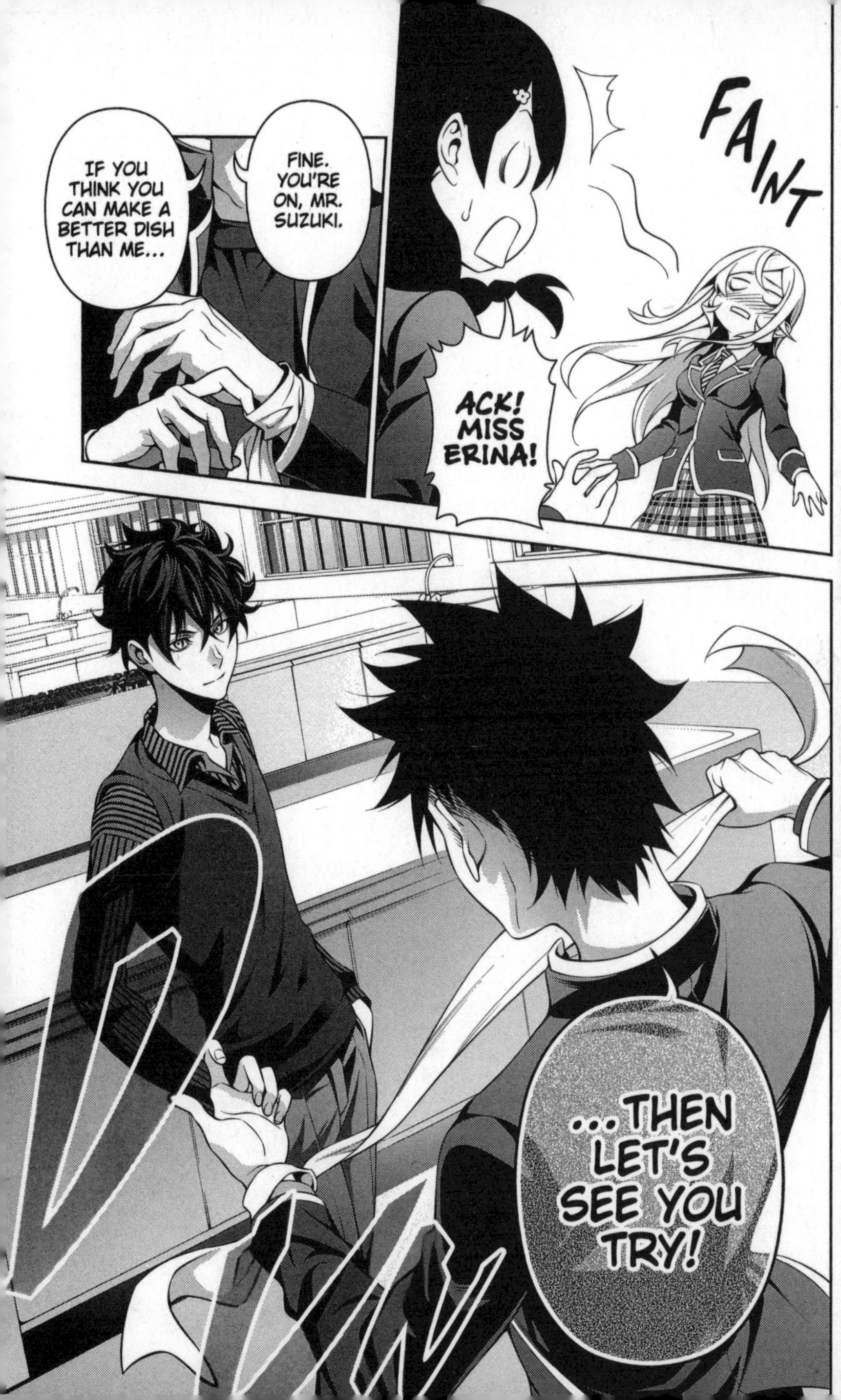
FAINT
ACK! MISS ERINA!
FINE. YOU'RE ON, MR. SUZUKI.
IF YOU THINK YOU CAN MAKE A BETTER DISH THAN ME...
...THEN LET'S SEE YOU TRY!

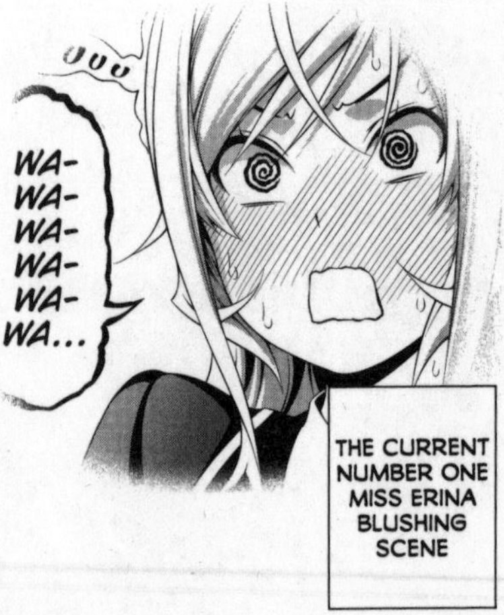
WA-
WA-
WA-
WA-
WA-
WA...
THE CURRENT NUMBER ONE MISS ERINA BLUSHING SCENE

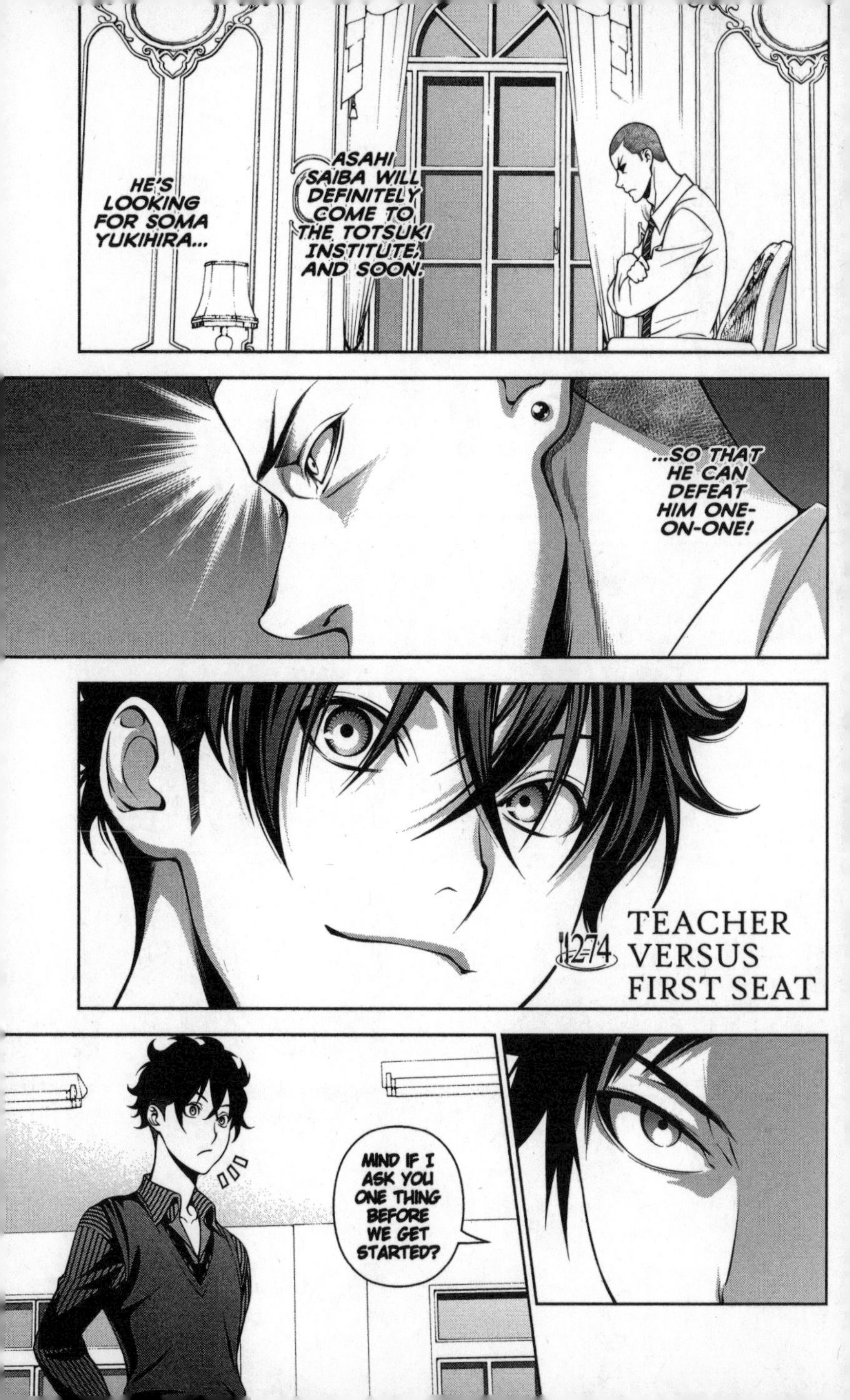
ASAHI SAIBA WILL DEFINITELY COME TO THE TOTSUKI INSTITUTE, AND SOON.
HE'S LOOKING FOR SOMA YUKIHIRA...
...SO THAT HE CAN DEFEAT HIM ONE-ON-ONE!
274
TEACHER VERSUS FIRST SEAT
MIND IF I ASK YOU ONE THING BEFORE WE GET STARTED?

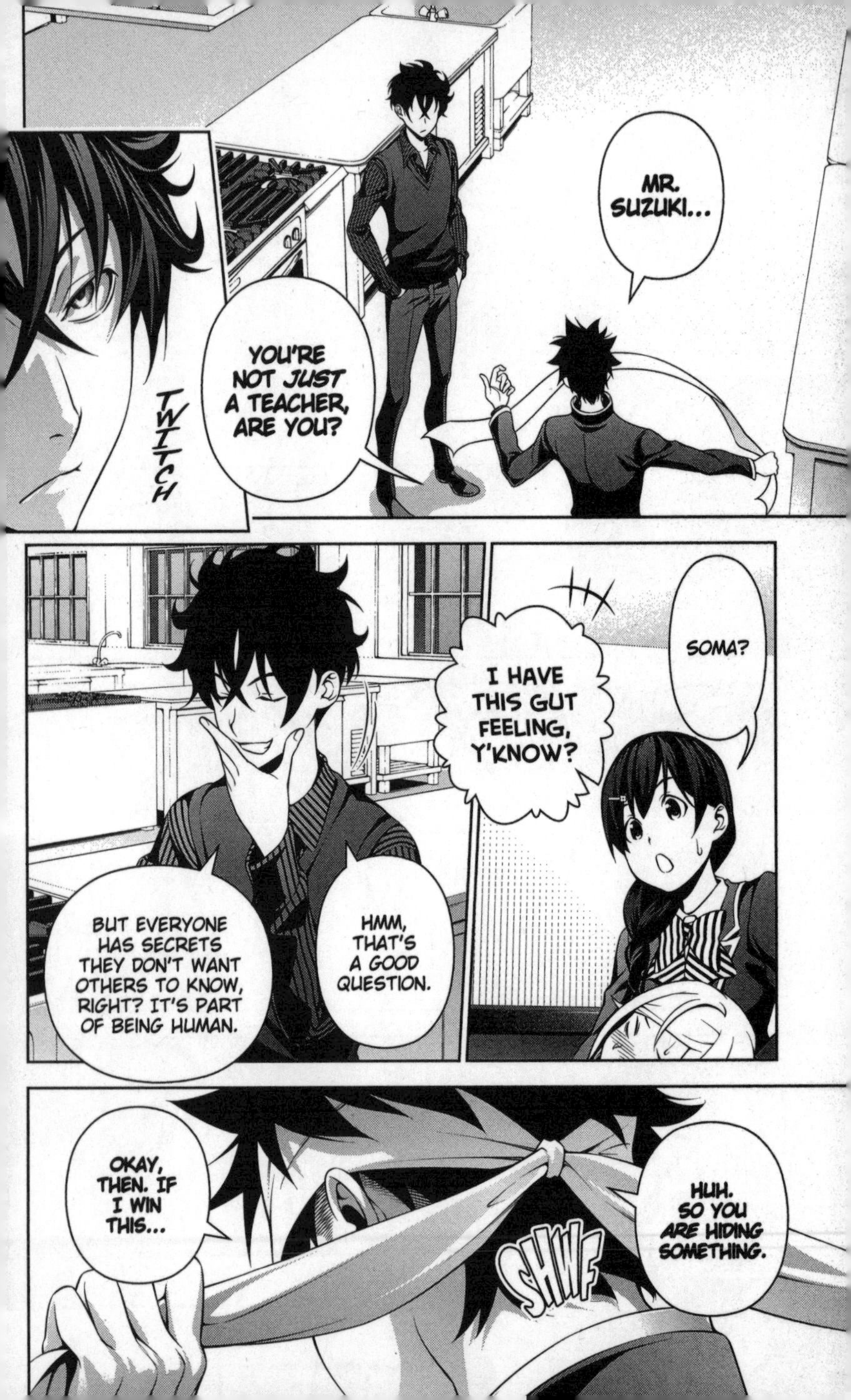
MR. SUZUKI...
YOU'RE NOT *JUST* A TEACHER, ARE YOU?
TWITCH
SOMA?
I HAVE THIS GUT FEELING, Y'KNOW?
HMM, THAT'S A GOOD QUESTION.
BUT EVERYONE HAS SECRETS THEY DON'T WANT OTHERS TO KNOW, RIGHT? IT'S PART OF BEING HUMAN.
HUH. SO YOU *ARE* HIDING SOMETHING.
SHWF
OKAY, THEN. IF I WIN THIS...

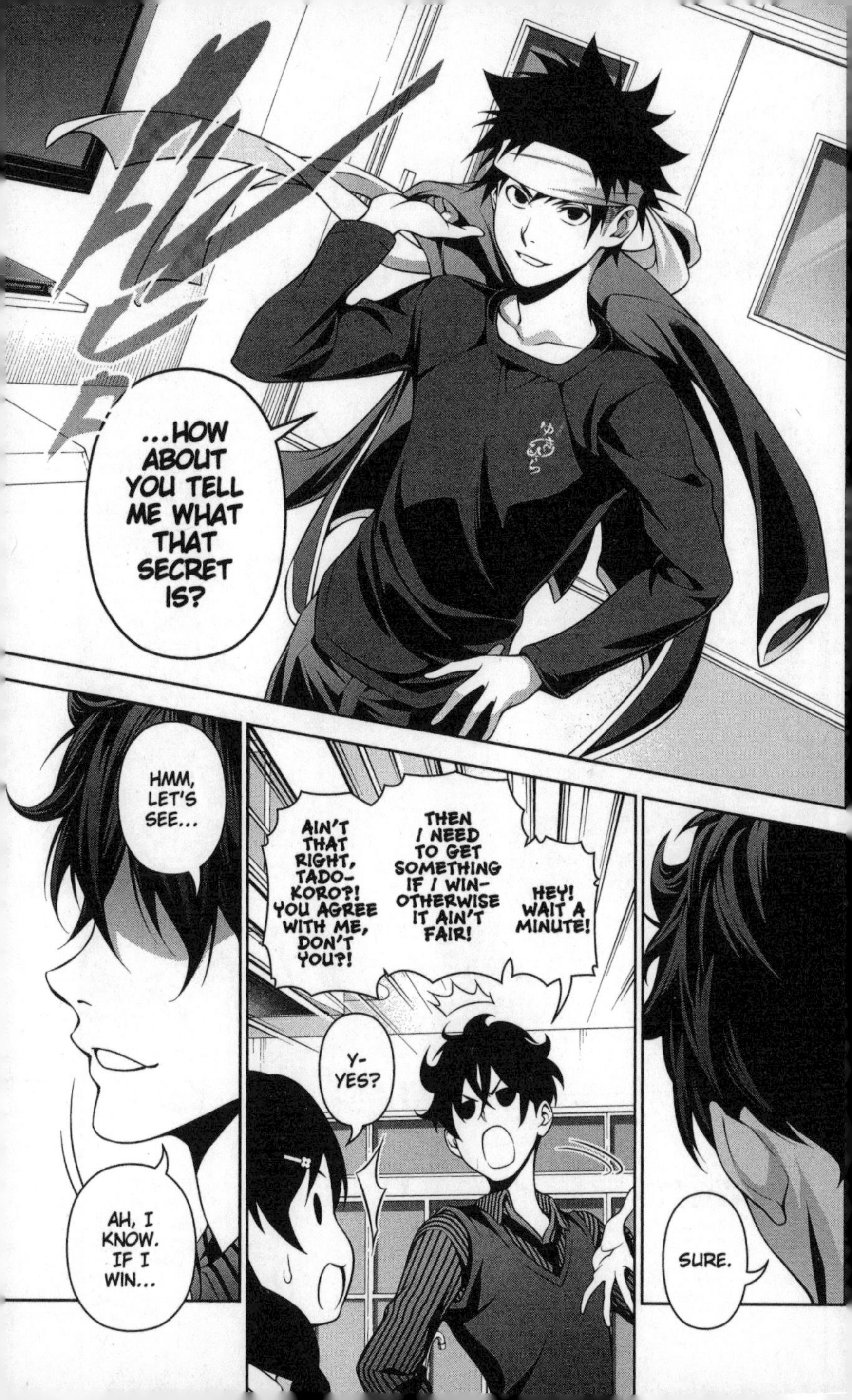
...HOW ABOUT YOU TELL ME WHAT THAT SECRET IS?
SURE.
HEY! WAIT A MINUTE!
THEN I NEED TO GET SOMETHING IF I WIN-OTHERWISE IT AIN'T FAIR!
AIN'T THAT RIGHT, TADOKORO?! YOU AGREE WITH ME, DON'T YOU?!
Y-YES?
HMM, LET'S SEE...
AH, I KNOW. IF I WIN...

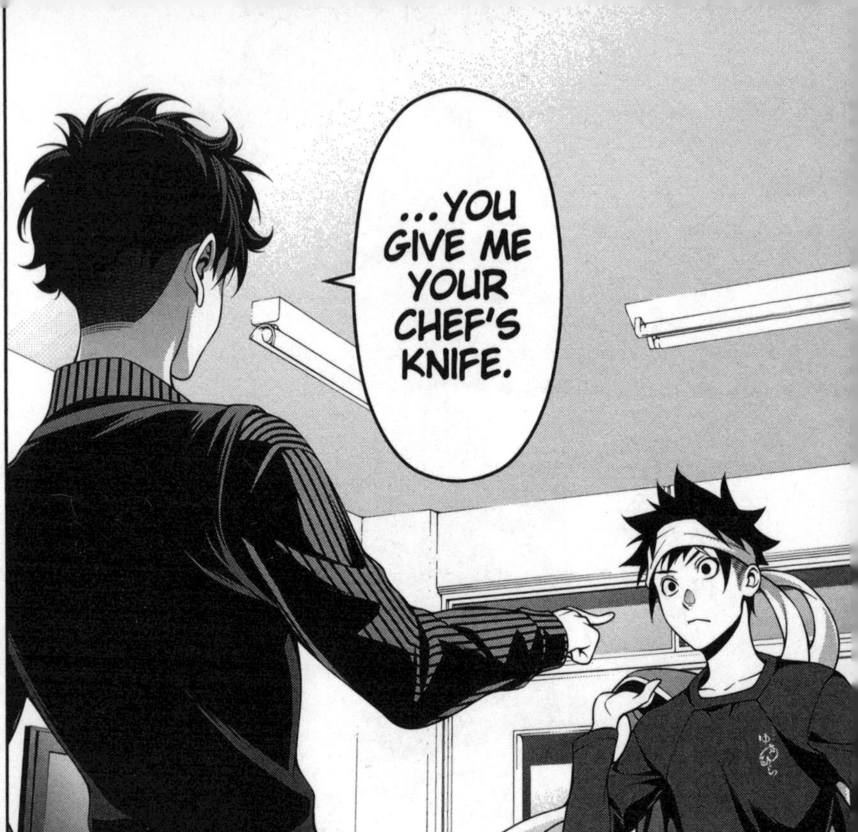
...YOU GIVE ME YOUR CHEF'S KNIFE.
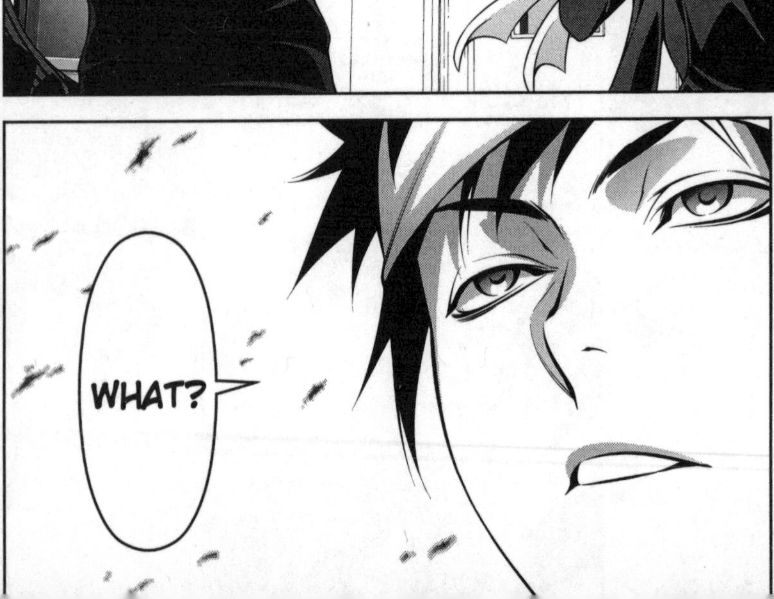
WHAT?

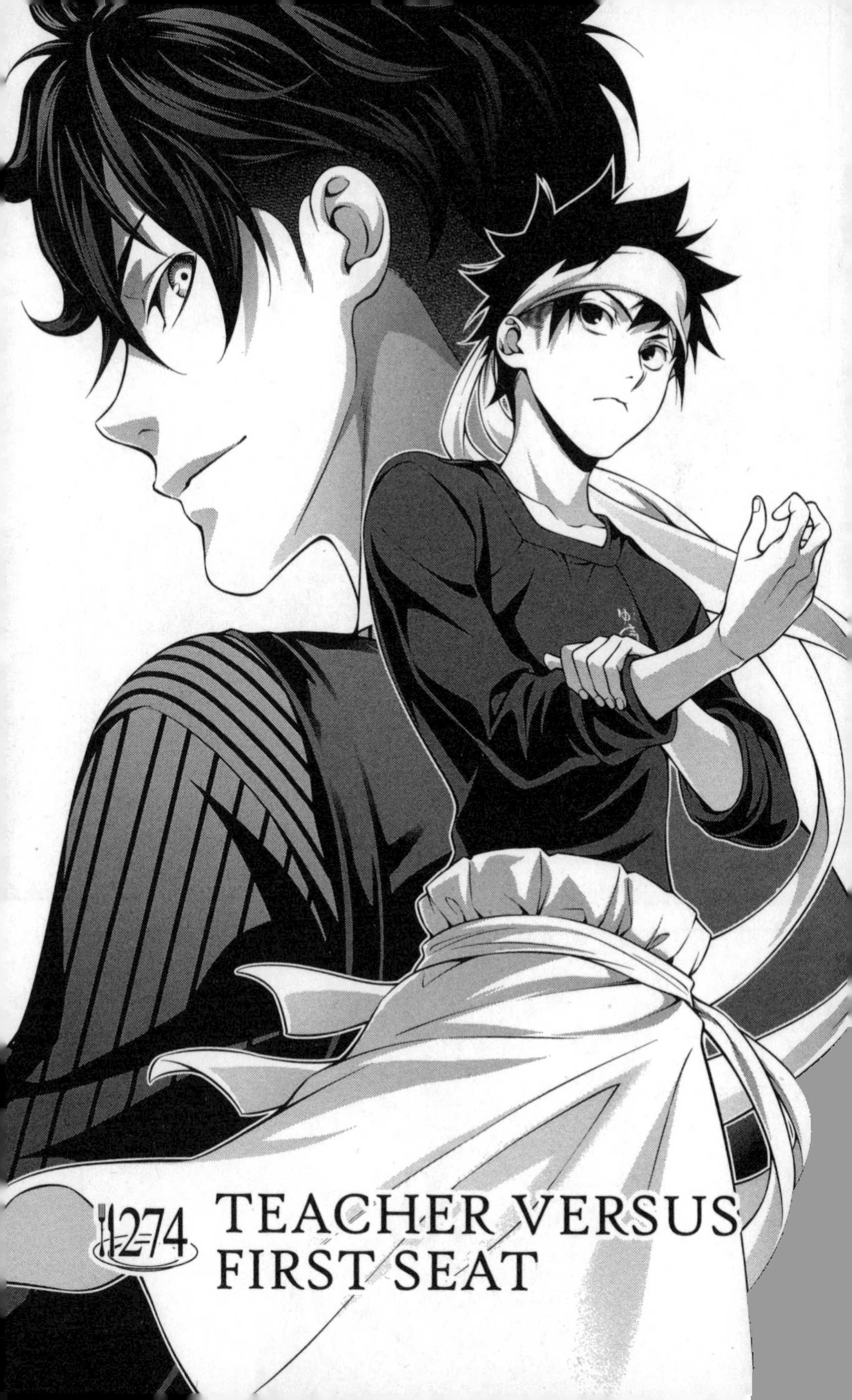
274 TEACHER VERSUS FIRST SEAT

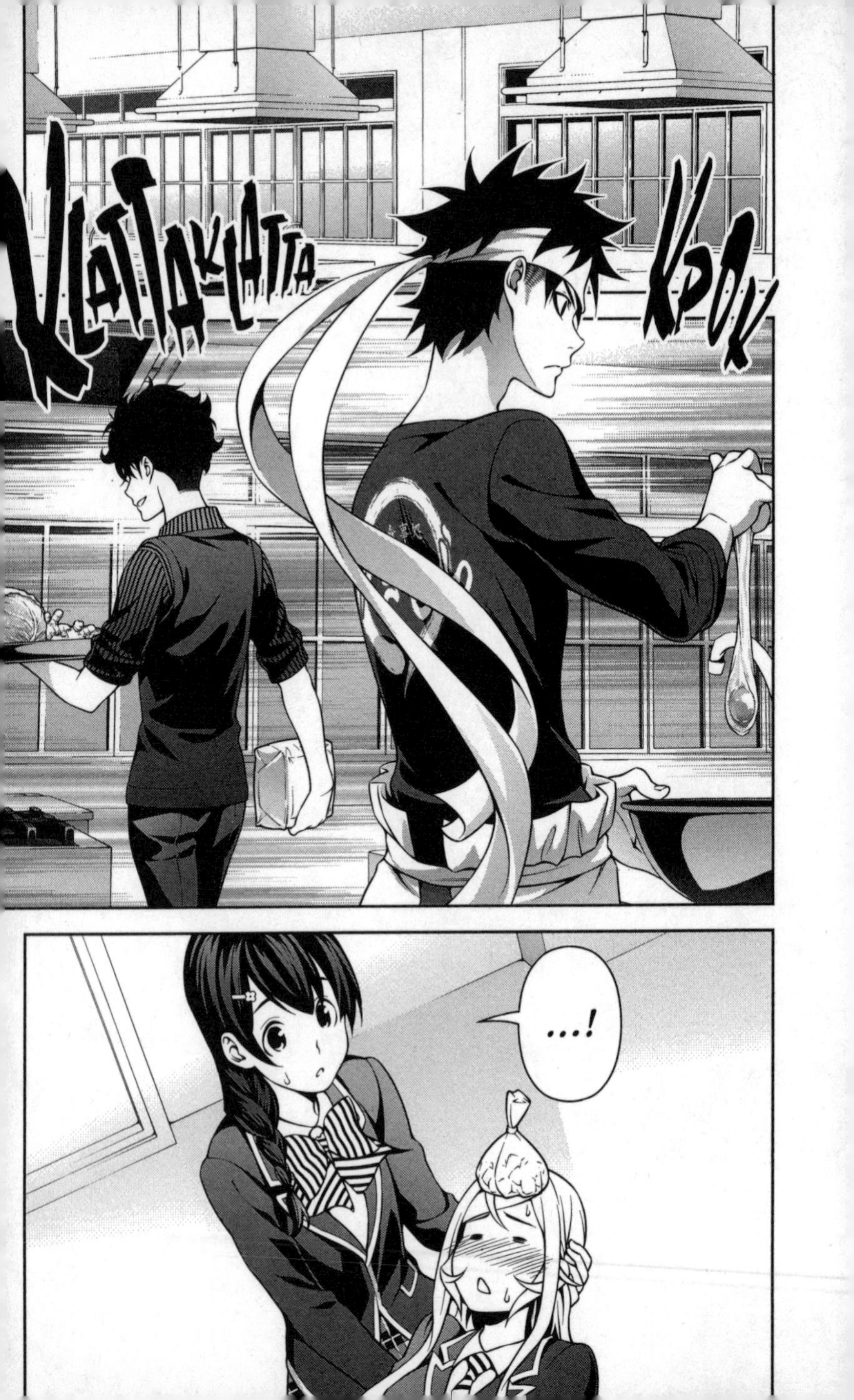
KPOK
KLATTAKLATTA
...!

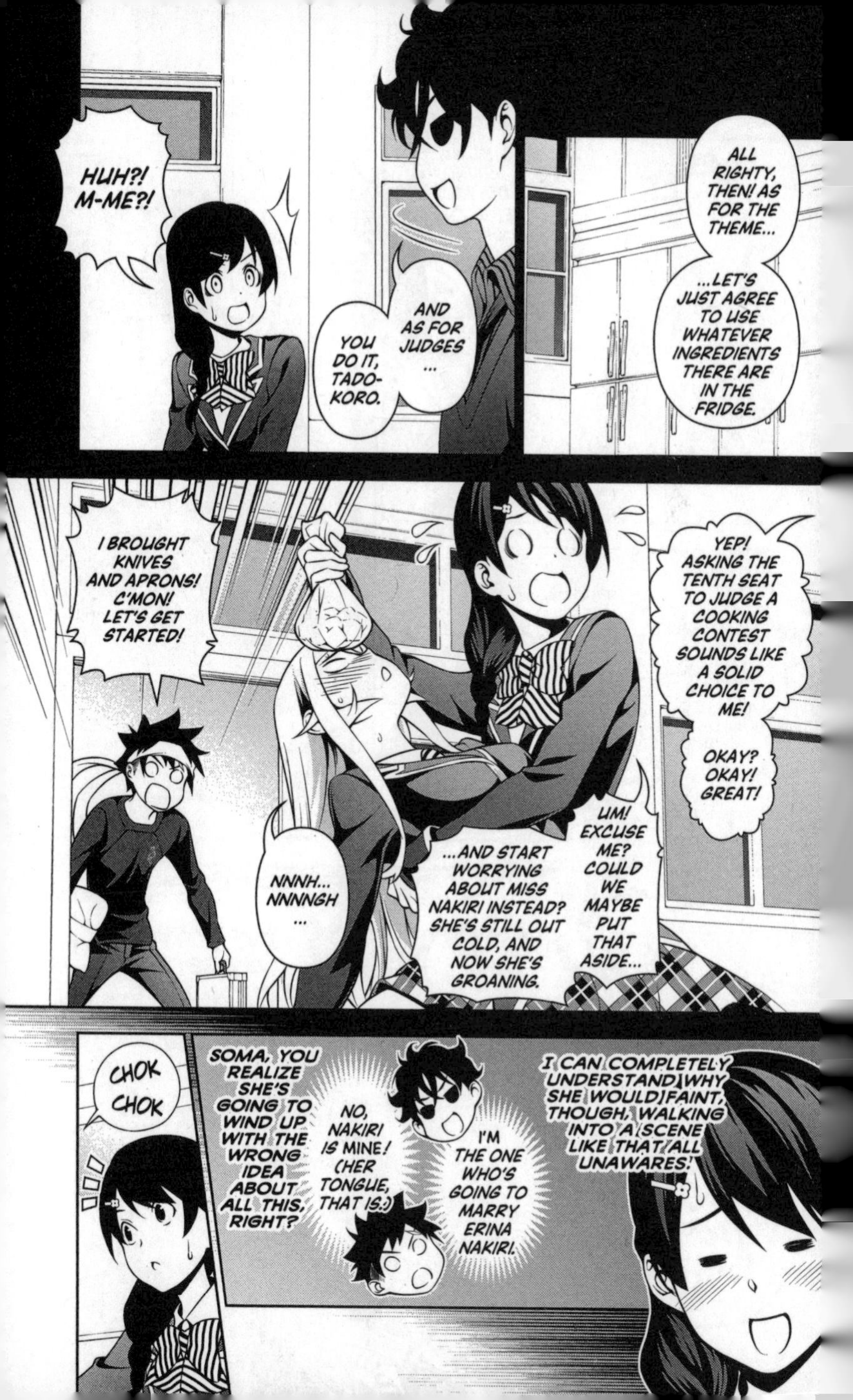

ALL RIGHTY, THEN! AS FOR THE THEME...
...LET'S JUST AGREE TO USE WHATEVER INGREDIENTS THERE ARE IN THE FRIDGE.
AND AS FOR JUDGES...
YOU DO IT, TADOKORO.
HUH?! M-ME?!
YEP! ASKING THE TENTH SEAT TO JUDGE A COOKING CONTEST SOUNDS LIKE A SOLID CHOICE TO ME!
OKAY? OKAY! GREAT!
UM! EXCUSE ME? COULD WE MAYBE PUT THAT ASIDE...
...AND START WORRYING ABOUT MISS NAKIRI INSTEAD? SHE'S STILL OUT COLD, AND NOW SHE'S GROANING.
NNNH... NNNNGH...
I BROUGHT KNIVES AND APRONS! C'MON! LET'S GET STARTED!
I CAN COMPLETELY UNDERSTAND WHY SHE WOULD FAINT, THOUGH, WALKING INTO A SCENE LIKE THAT ALL UNAWARES!
I'M THE ONE WHO'S GOING TO MARRY ERINA NAKIRI.
NO, NAKIRI IS MINE! (HER TONGUE, THAT IS.)
SOMA, YOU REALIZE SHE'S GOING TO WIND UP WITH THE WRONG IDEA ABOUT ALL THIS, RIGHT?
CHOK CHOK

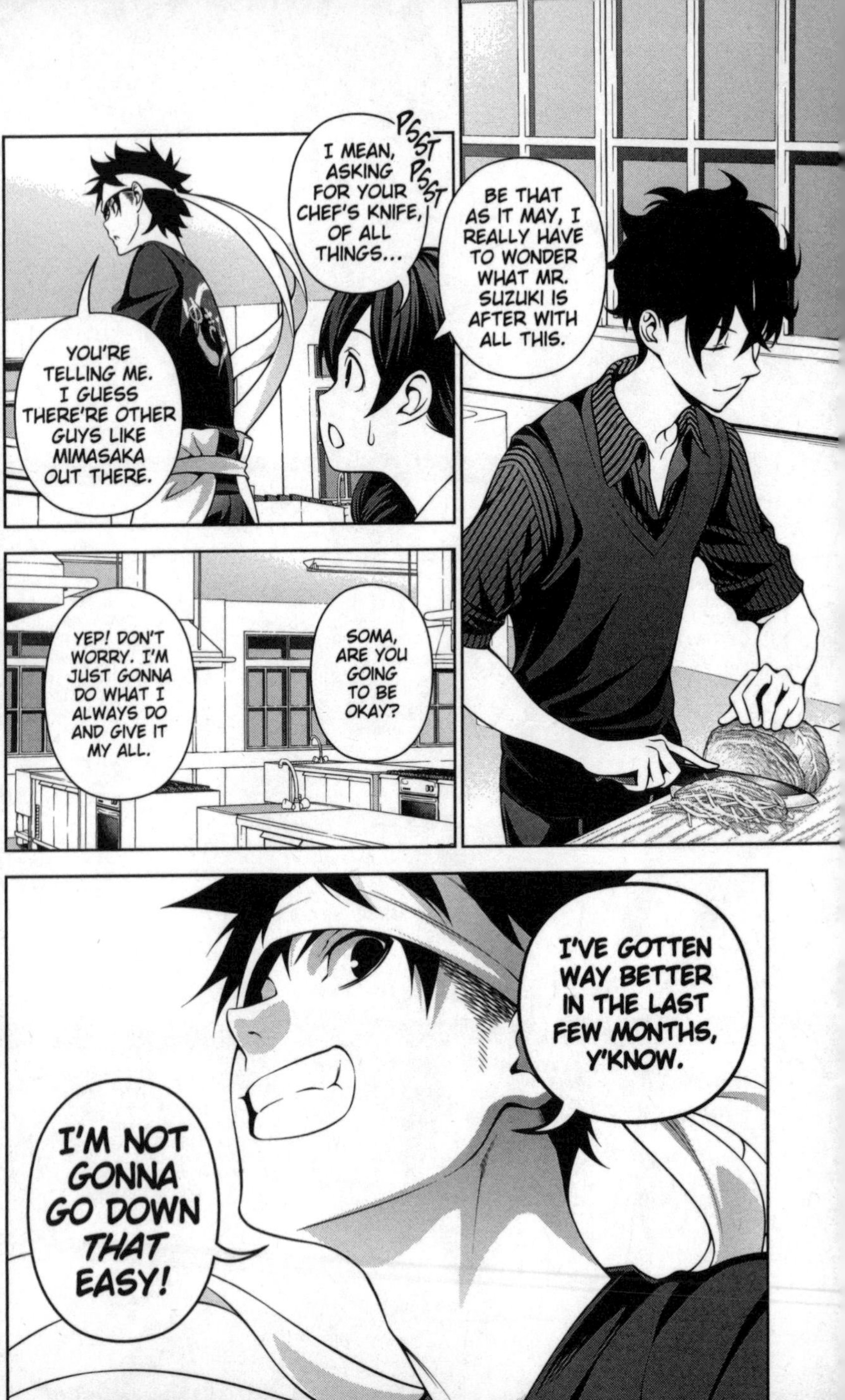
BE THAT AS IT MAY, I REALLY HAVE TO WONDER WHAT MR. SUZUKI IS AFTER WITH ALL THIS.
I MEAN, ASKING FOR YOUR CHEF'S KNIFE, OF ALL THINGS...
PSST PSST
YOU'RE TELLING ME. I GUESS THERE'RE OTHER GUYS LIKE MIMASAKA OUT THERE.
SOMA, ARE YOU GOING TO BE OKAY?
YEP! DON'T WORRY. I'M JUST GONNA DO WHAT I ALWAYS DO AND GIVE IT MY ALL.
I'VE GOTTEN WAY BETTER IN THE LAST FEW MONTHS, Y'KNOW.
I'M NOT GONNA GO DOWN *THAT* EASY!

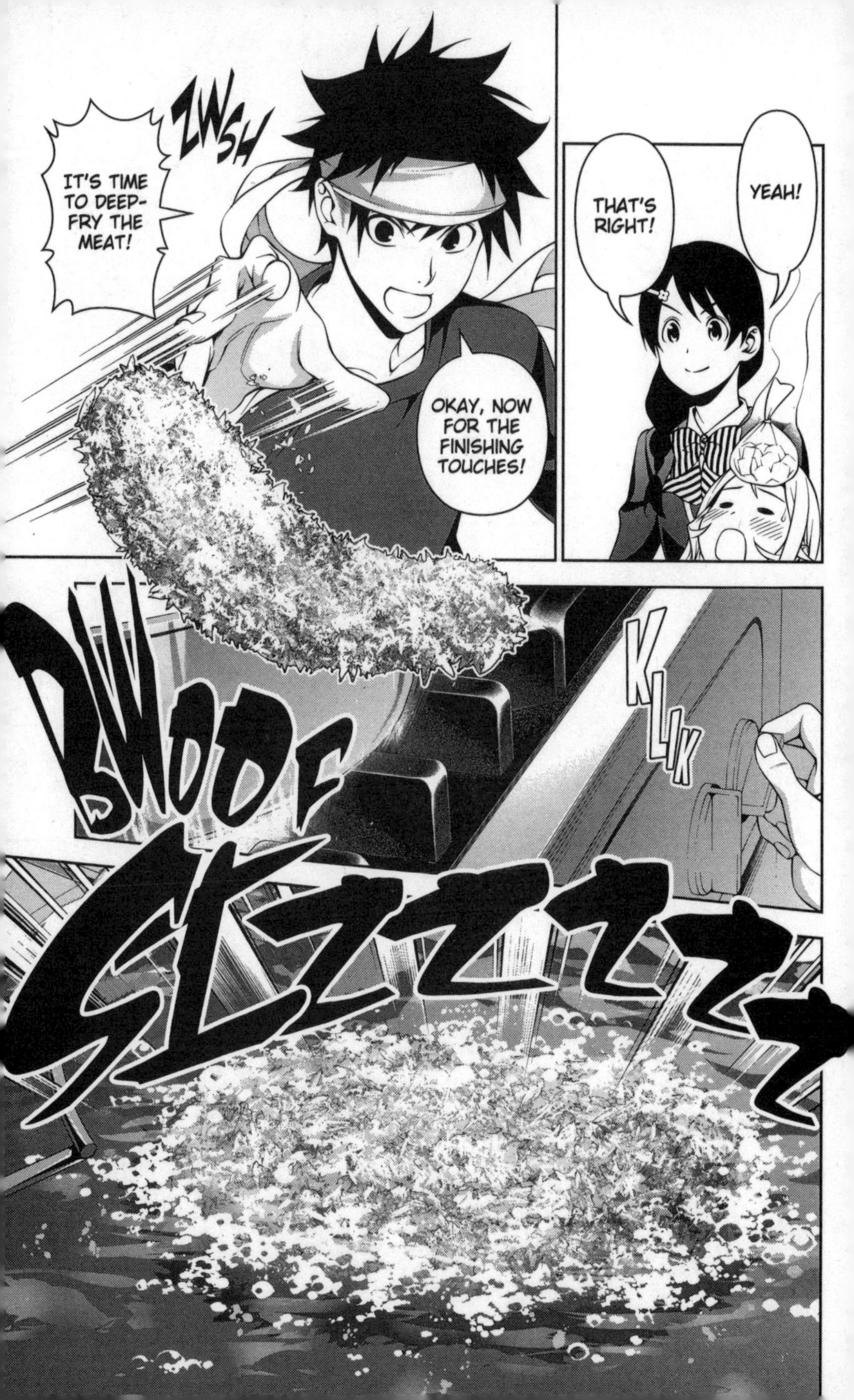
YEAH!
THAT'S RIGHT!
IT'S TIME TO DEEP-FRY THE MEAT!
ZWSH
OKAY, NOW FOR THE FINISHING TOUCHES!
KLIK
BWOOF
SIZZZZZ

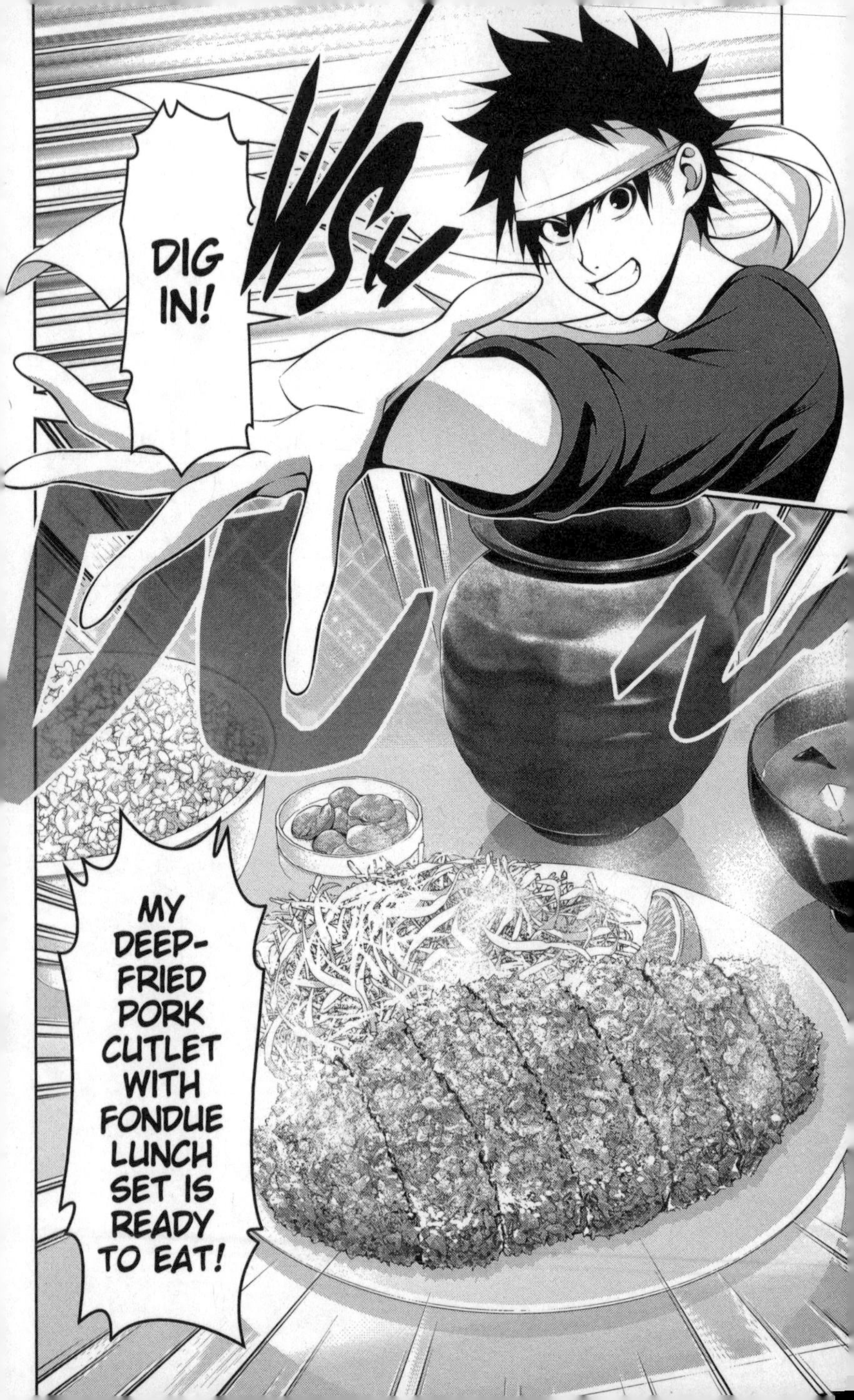
WSH
DIG IN!
MY DEEP-FRIED PORK CUTLET WITH FONDUE LUNCH SET IS READY TO EAT!

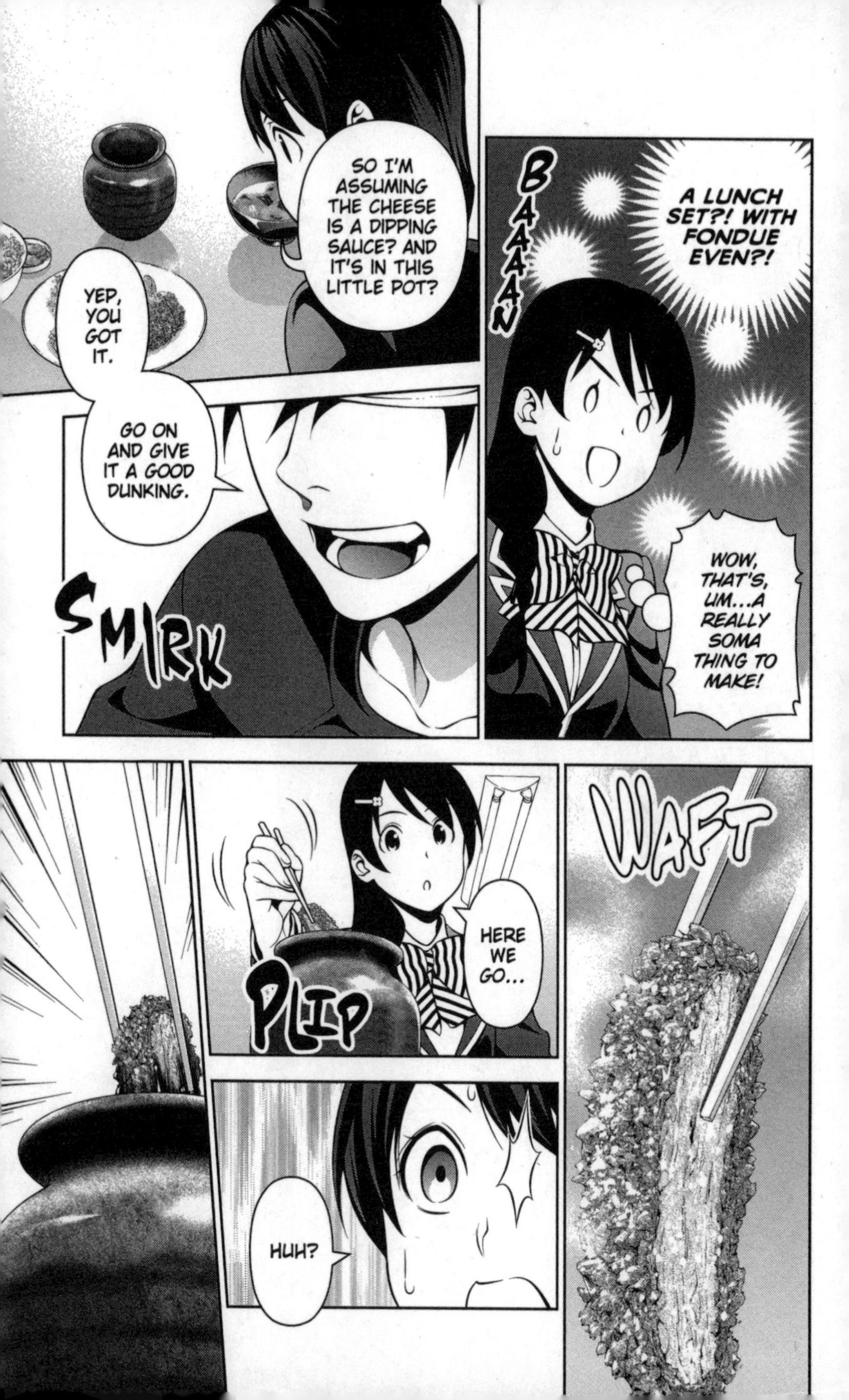
BAAAAN
A LUNCH SET?! WITH FONDUE EVEN?!
WOW, THAT'S, UM...A REALLY SOMA THING TO MAKE!
SO I'M ASSUMING THE CHEESE IS A DIPPING SAUCE? AND IT'S IN THIS LITTLE POT?
YEP, YOU GOT IT.
GO ON AND GIVE IT A GOOD DUNKING.
SMIRK
WAFT
HERE WE GO...
PLIP
HUH?

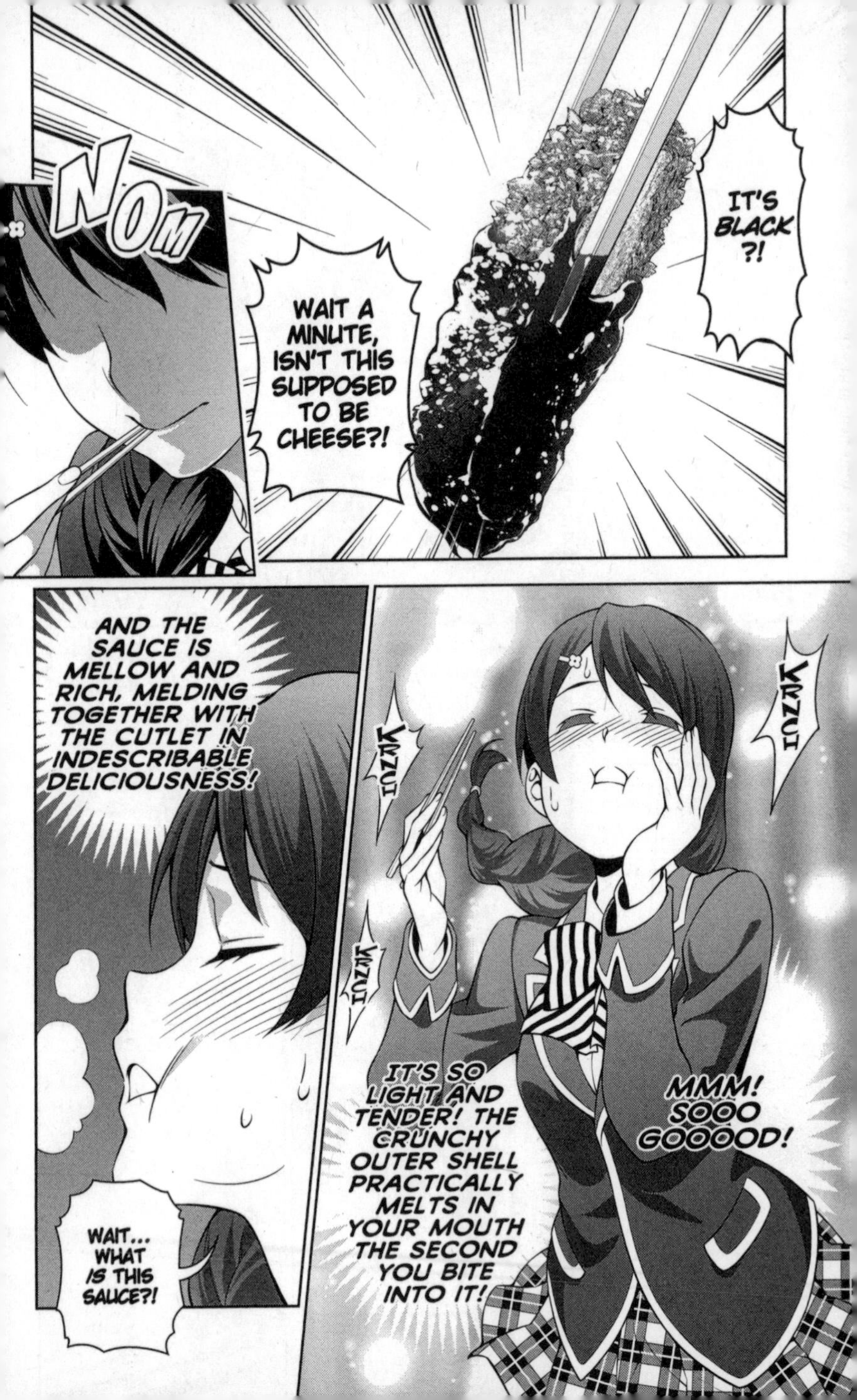

IT'S BLACK?!
WAIT A MINUTE, ISN'T THIS SUPPOSED TO BE CHEESE?!
NOM
KRNCH
MMM! SOOO GOOOOD!
IT'S SO LIGHT AND TENDER! THE CRUNCHY OUTER SHELL PRACTICALLY MELTS IN YOUR MOUTH THE SECOND YOU BITE INTO IT!
KRNCH
KRNCH
AND THE SAUCE IS MELLOW AND RICH, MELDING TOGETHER WITH THE CUTLET IN INDESCRIBABLE DELICIOUSNESS!
WAIT... WHAT IS THIS SAUCE?!

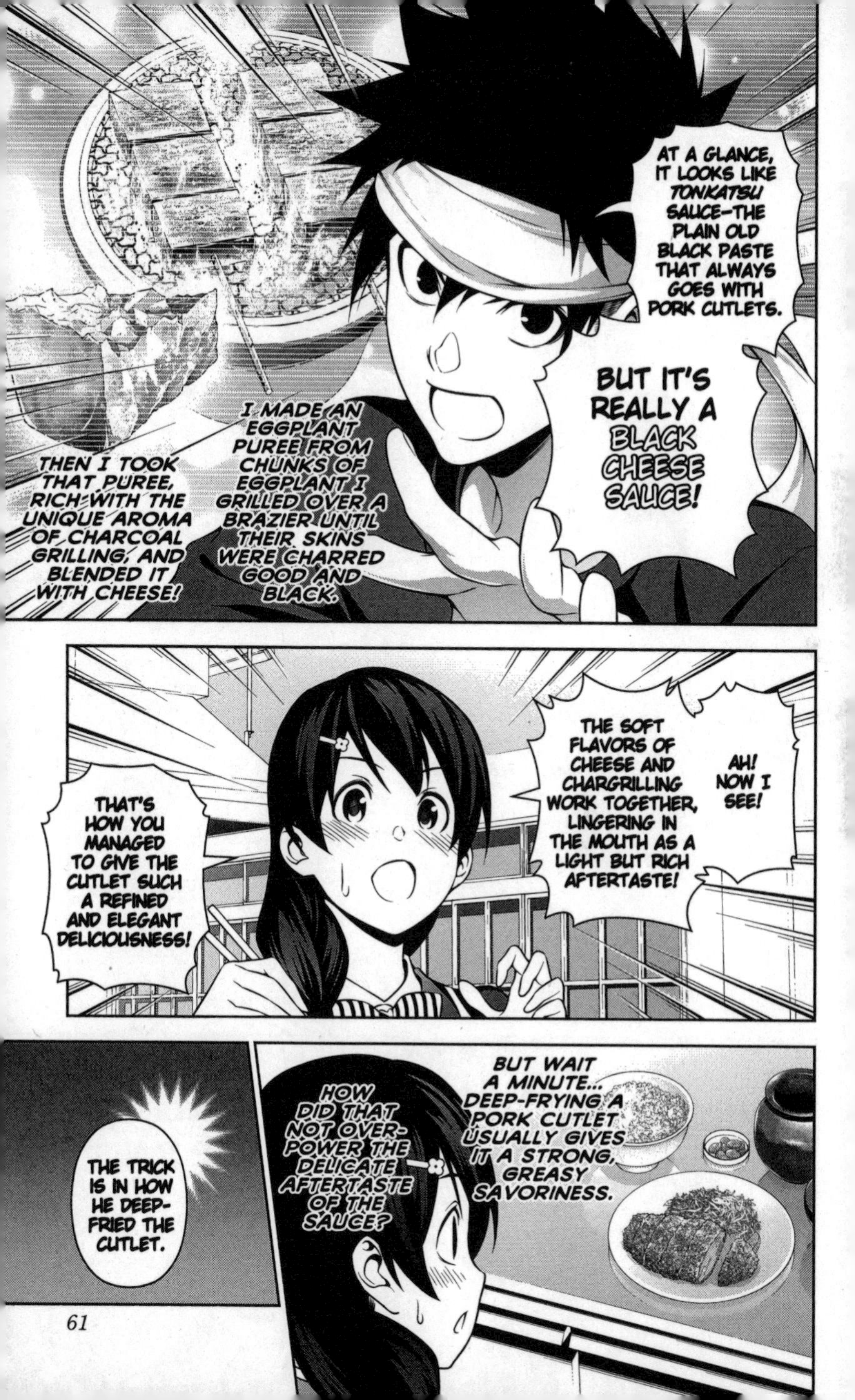
AT A GLANCE, IT LOOKS LIKE TONKATSU SAUCE—THE PLAIN OLD BLACK PASTE THAT ALWAYS GOES WITH PORK CUTLETS.
BUT IT'S REALLY A BLACK CHEESE SAUCE!
I MADE AN EGGPLANT PUREE FROM CHUNKS OF EGGPLANT I GRILLED OVER A BRAZIER UNTIL THEIR SKINS WERE CHARRED GOOD AND BLACK.
THEN I TOOK THAT PUREE, RICH WITH THE UNIQUE AROMA OF CHARCOAL GRILLING, AND BLENDED IT WITH CHEESE!
AH! NOW I SEE!
THE SOFT FLAVORS OF CHEESE AND CHARGRILLING WORK TOGETHER, LINGERING IN THE MOUTH AS A LIGHT BUT RICH AFTERTASTE!
THAT'S HOW YOU MANAGED TO GIVE THE CUTLET SUCH A REFINED AND ELEGANT DELICIOUSNESS!
BUT WAIT A MINUTE... DEEP-FRYING A PORK CUTLET USUALLY GIVES IT A STRONG, GREASY SAVORINESS.
HOW DID THAT NOT OVER-POWER THE DELICATE AFTERTASTE OF THE SAUCE?
THE TRICK IS IN HOW HE DEEP-FRIED THE CUTLET.

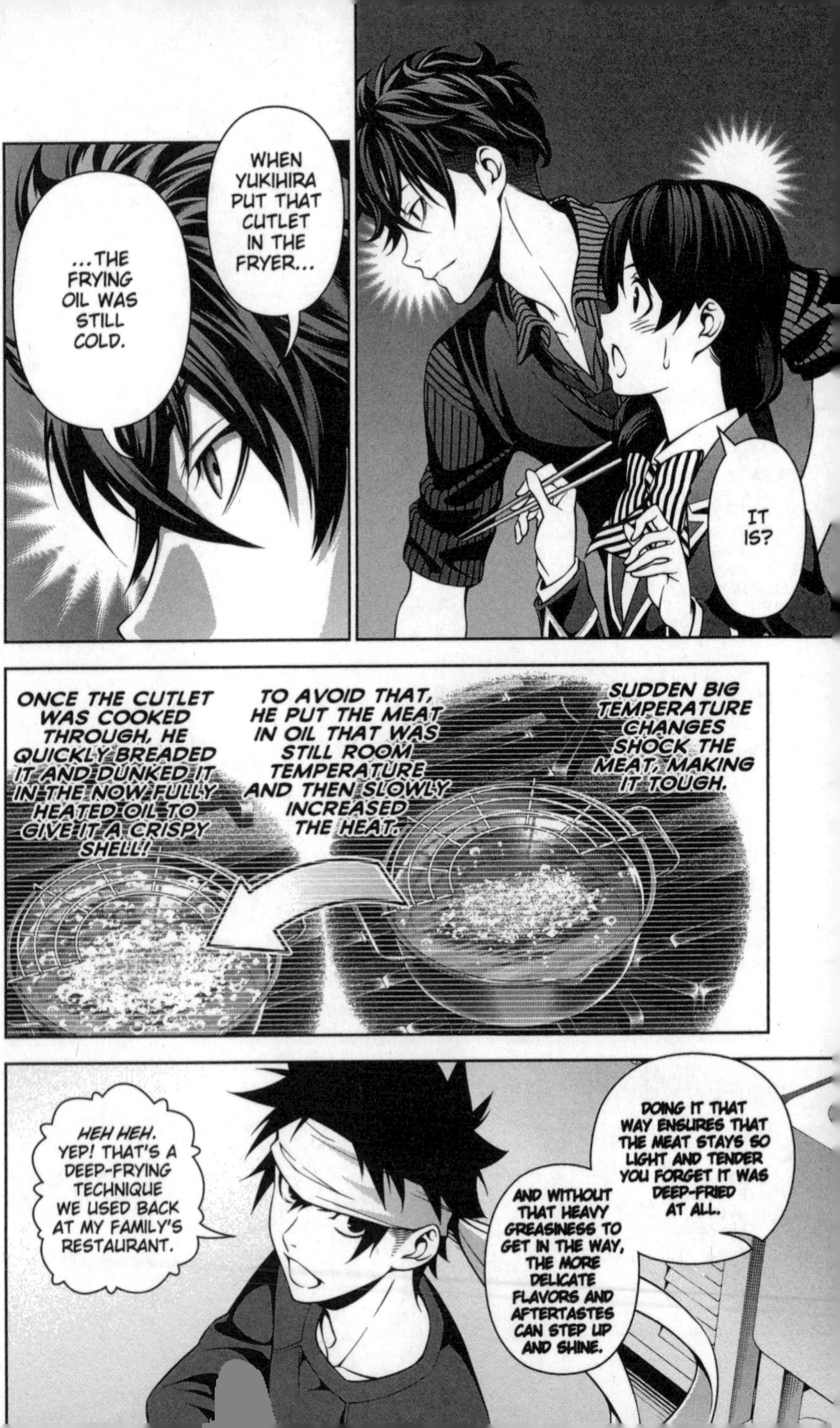
IT IS?
WHEN YUKIHIRA PUT THAT CUTLET IN THE FRYER...
...THE FRYING OIL WAS STILL COLD.
SUDDEN BIG TEMPERATURE CHANGES SHOCK THE MEAT, MAKING IT TOUGH.
TO AVOID THAT, HE PUT THE MEAT IN OIL THAT WAS STILL ROOM TEMPERATURE AND THEN SLOWLY INCREASED THE HEAT.
ONCE THE CUTLET WAS COOKED THROUGH, HE QUICKLY BREADED IT AND DUNKED IT IN THE NOW-FULLY HEATED OIL TO GIVE IT A CRISPY SHELL!
DOING IT THAT WAY ENSURES THAT THE MEAT STAYS SO LIGHT AND TENDER YOU FORGET IT WAS DEEP-FRIED AT ALL.
AND WITHOUT THAT HEAVY GREASINESS TO GET IN THE WAY, THE MORE DELICATE FLAVORS AND AFTERTASTES CAN STEP UP AND SHINE.
HEH HEH. YEP! THAT'S A DEEP-FRYING TECHNIQUE WE USED BACK AT MY FAMILY'S RESTAURANT.

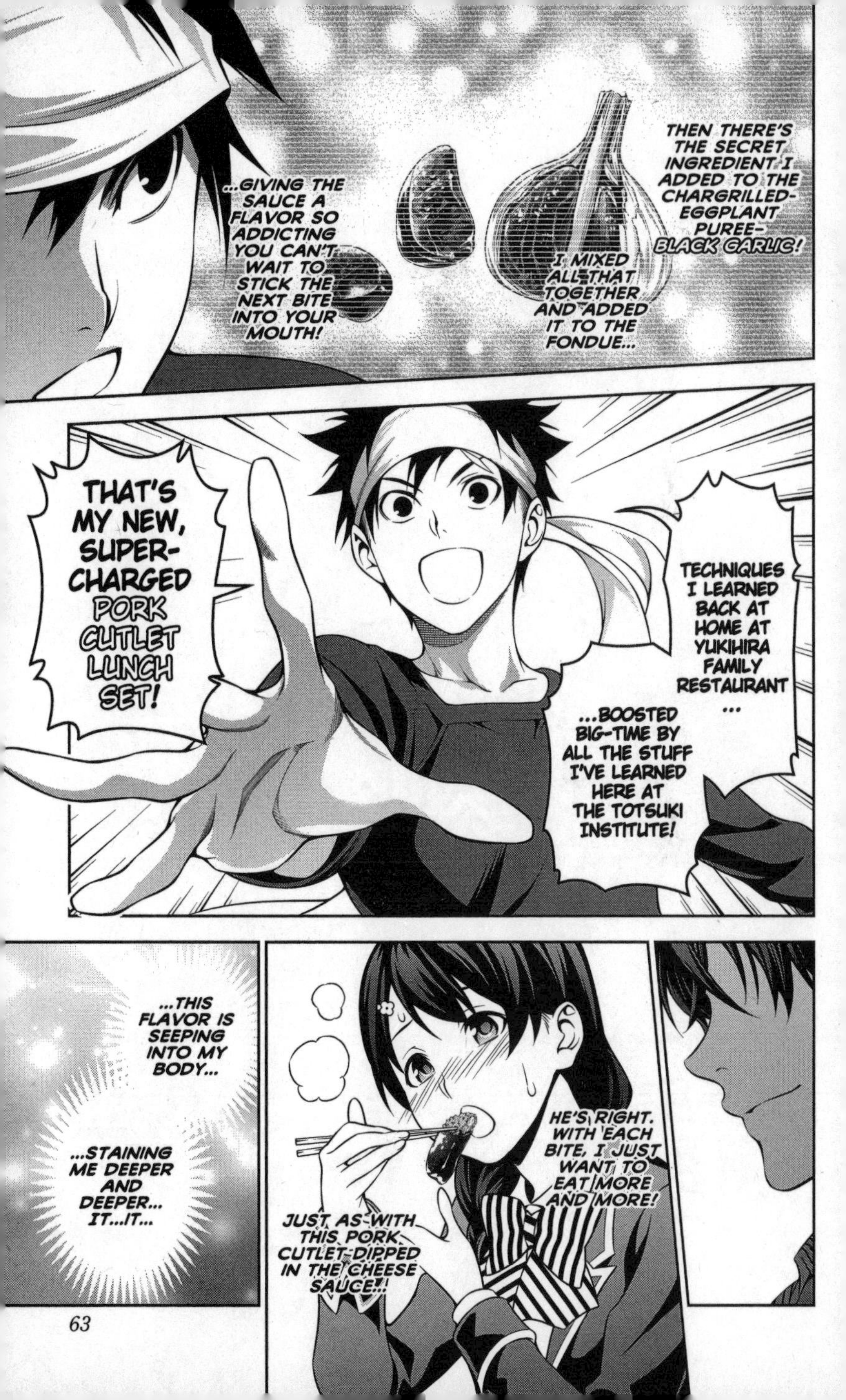
THEN THERE'S THE SECRET INGREDIENT I ADDED TO THE CHARGRILLED-EGGPLANT PUREE— BLACK GARLIC!
I MIXED ALL THAT TOGETHER AND ADDED IT TO THE FONDUE...
...GIVING THE SAUCE A FLAVOR SO ADDICTING YOU CAN'T WAIT TO STICK THE NEXT BITE INTO YOUR MOUTH!
TECHNIQUES I LEARNED BACK AT HOME AT YUKIHIRA FAMILY RESTAURANT...
...BOOSTED BIG-TIME BY ALL THE STUFF I'VE LEARNED HERE AT THE TOTSUKI INSTITUTE!
THAT'S MY NEW, SUPER-CHARGED PORK CUTLET LUNCH SET!
HE'S RIGHT. WITH EACH BITE, I JUST WANT TO EAT MORE AND MORE!
JUST AS WITH THIS PORK CUTLET DIPPED IN THE CHEESE SAUCE...!
...THIS FLAVOR IS SEEPING INTO MY BODY...
...STAINING ME DEEPER AND DEEPER... IT...IT...

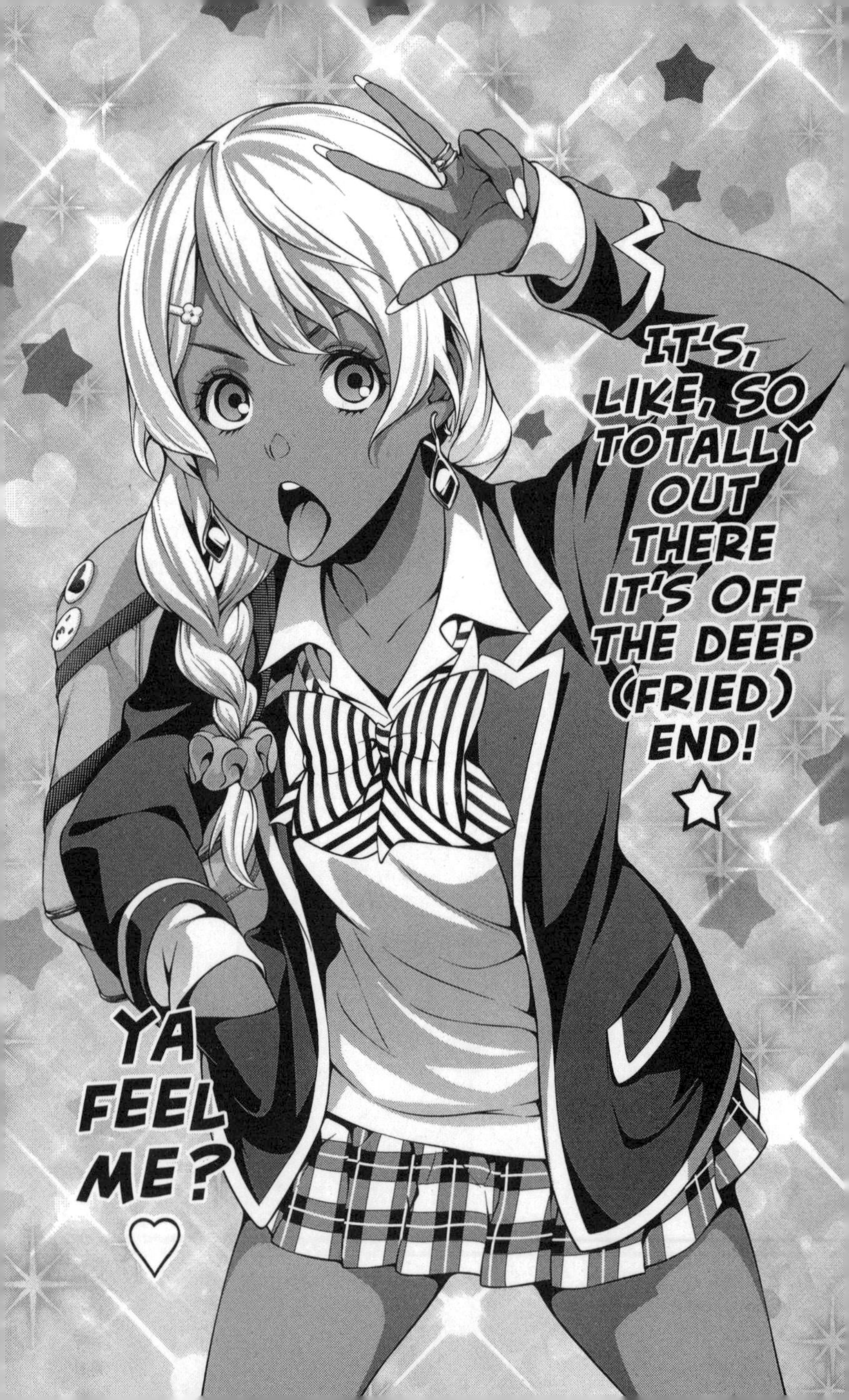
IT'S, LIKE, SO TOTALLY OUT THERE IT'S OFF THE DEEP (FRIED) END! ☆
YA FEEL ME? ♡

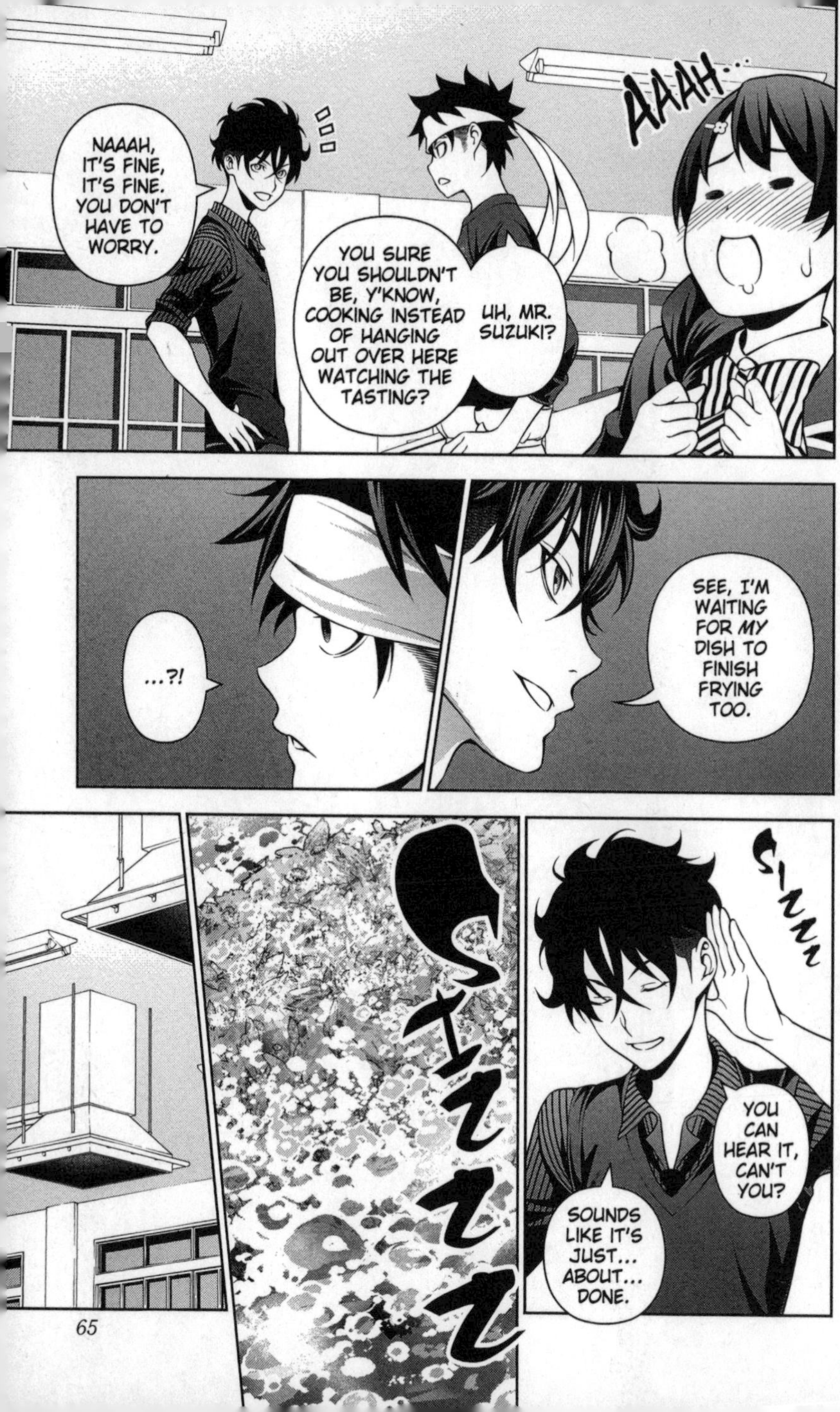
AAAH...
UH, MR. SUZUKI?
YOU SURE YOU SHOULDN'T BE, Y'KNOW, COOKING INSTEAD OF HANGING OUT OVER HERE WATCHING THE TASTING?
NAAAH, IT'S FINE, IT'S FINE. YOU DON'T HAVE TO WORRY.
SEE, I'M WAITING FOR *MY* DISH TO FINISH FRYING TOO.
...?!
SIZZZZ
YOU CAN HEAR IT, CAN'T YOU?
SOUNDS LIKE IT'S JUST... ABOUT... DONE.

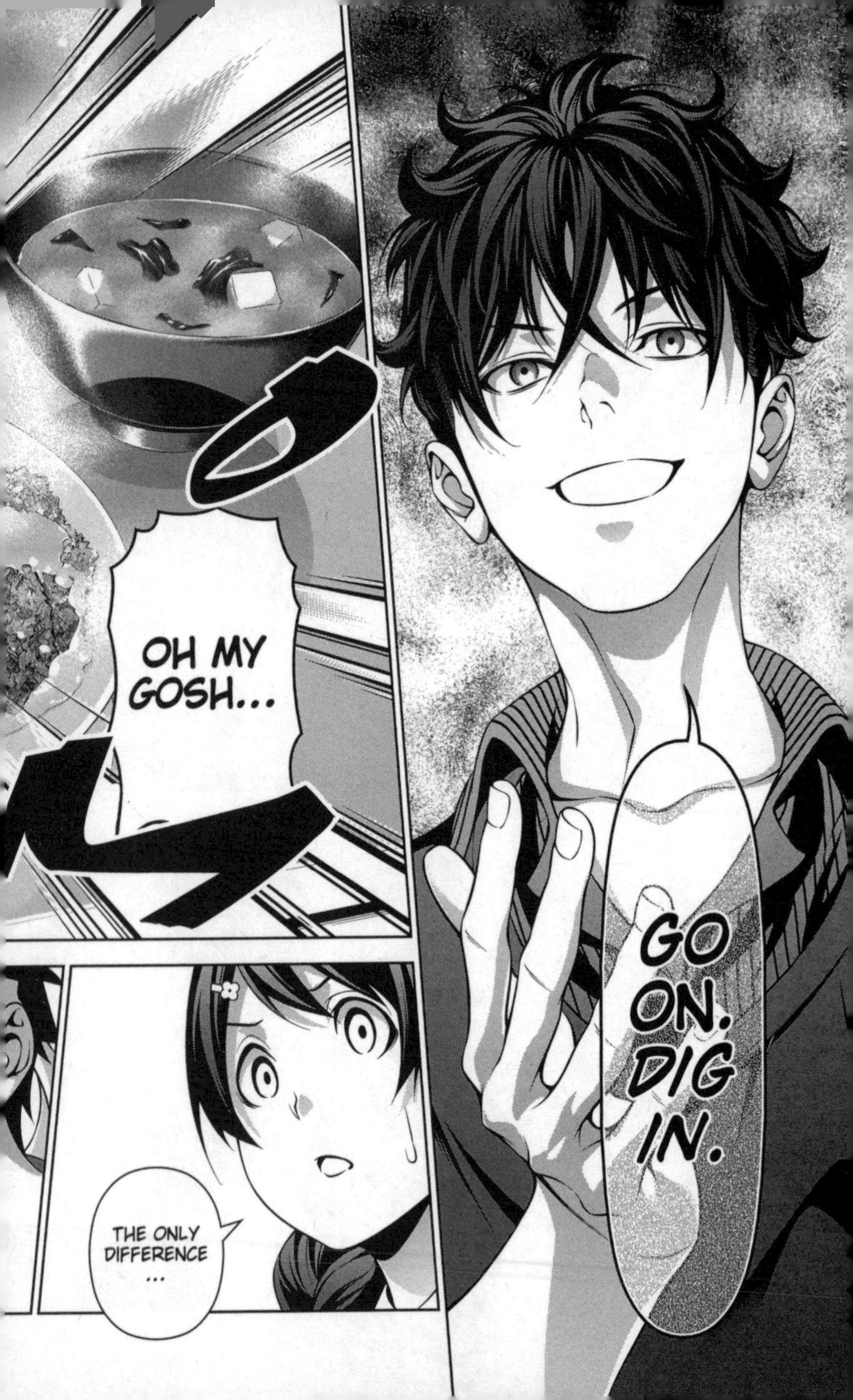
GO ON. DIG IN.
OH MY GOSH...
THE ONLY DIFFERENCE
...

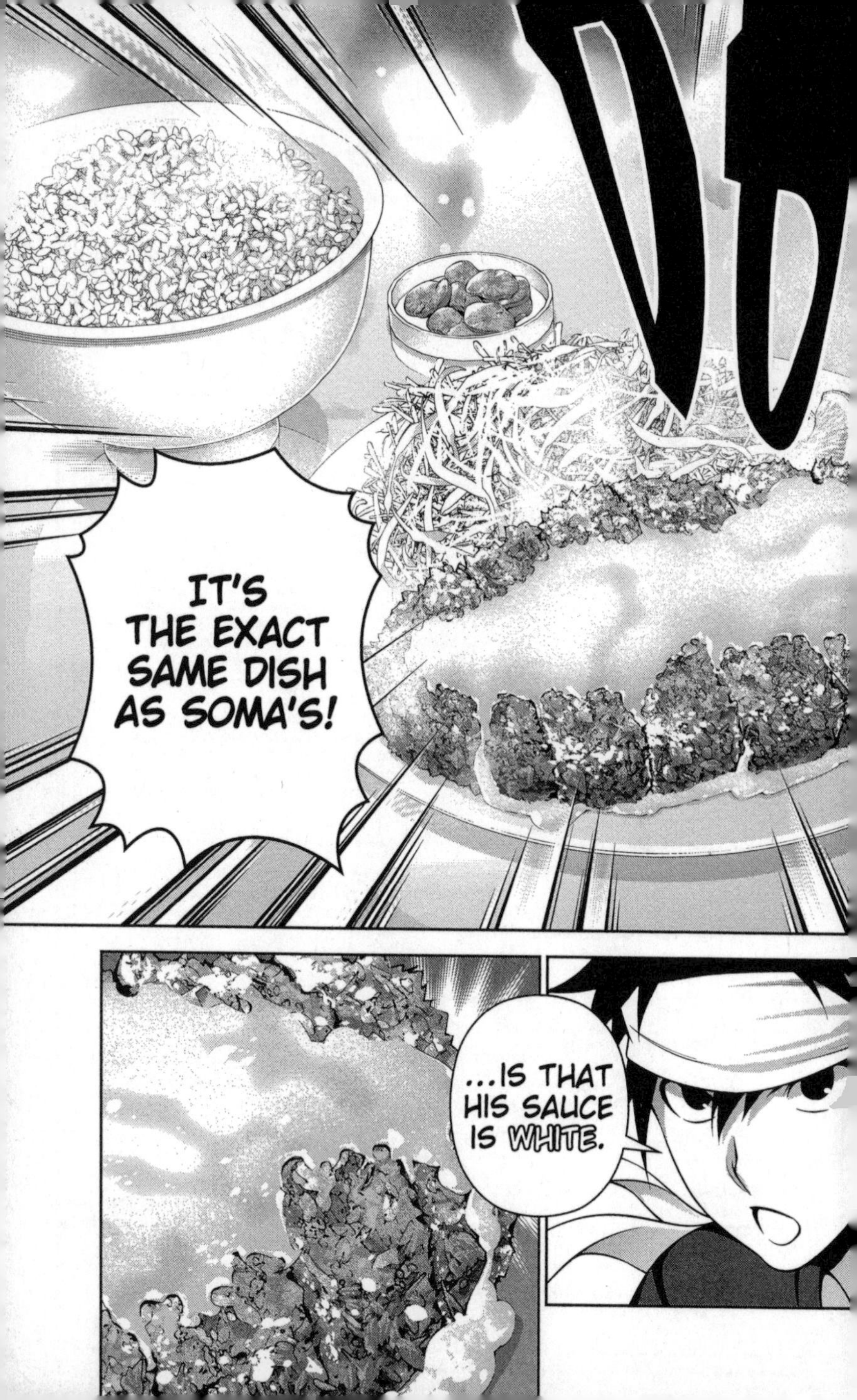
IT'S THE EXACT SAME DISH AS SOMA'S!
...IS THAT HIS SAUCE IS WHITE.

ARTIST: YUTO TSUKUDA RECIPE BY: YUKI MORISAKI

VOLUME 32 SPECIAL SUPPLEMENT!

PRACTICAL RECIPE #1

SOMA'S DEEP-FRIED PORK CUTLET WITH FONDUE LUNCH SET

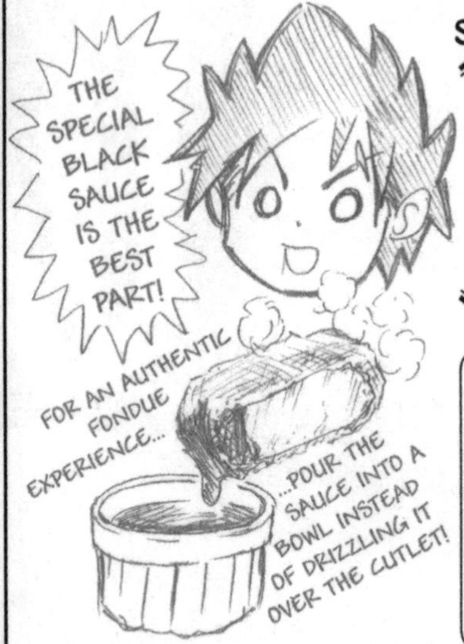
THE SPECIAL BLACK SAUCE IS THE BEST PART!
FOR AN AUTHENTIC FONDUE EXPERIENCE...
...POUR THE SAUCE INTO A BOWL INSTEAD OF DRIZZLING IT OVER THE CUTLET!

● INGREDIENTS ●
(SERVES 2)

2 SLICES PORK LOIN
FLOUR, SOFT *PANKO* BREADCRUMBS, EGGS, SALT, PEPPER, VEGETABLE OIL

★**CHEESE FONDUE SAUCE**

- 1 EGGPLANT
- 4 TABLESPOONS WATER
- 100 CC MILK
- 4 CLOVES STORE-BOUGHT BLACK GARLIC
- 50 GRAMS SHREDDED CHEESE
- 1 TABLESPOON EACH BUTTER, FLOUR

* SHREDDED CABBAGE, STEAMED RICE, MISO SOUP AND PICKLED VEGETABLES, IF DESIRED

1. TRIM THE PORK-LOIN SLICES AND SPRINKLE THEM WITH SALT AND PEPPER. TO MAKE THE BREADING, COAT SLICES THOROUGHLY WITH FLOUR, BEATEN EGG AND PANKO CRUMBS, IN THAT ORDER.

2. PUT THE BREADED PORK LOINS IN A COLD FRYING PAN AND THEN POUR IN VEGETABLE OIL UNTIL THEY ARE JUST COVERED. TURN THE HEAT ON TO LOW AND HEAT FOR 10 MINUTES.

3. FLIP THE PORK LOINS OVER AND HEAT FOR ANOTHER 5 MINUTES AND THEN TAKE THEM OUT OF THE FRYING PAN AND SET ASIDE.

4. HEAT THE OIL IN THE PAN TO 355°F. PUT THE PORK LOINS BACK IN AND DEEP-FRY UNTIL THEY ARE GOLDEN BROWN.

5. MAKE THE CHEESE FONDUE SAUCE. CUT THE STEM OFF OF THE EGGPLANT AND SLICE IT IN HALF VERTICALLY. PLACE THE EGGPLANT CUT-EDGE DOWN ON A BAKING SHEET AND BAKE IN AN OVEN UNTIL TENDER. CHOP THE EGGPLANT INTO CHUNKS AND PUT IT IN A FOOD PROCESSOR WITH THE BLACK GARLIC AND WATER. BLEND UNTIL IT'S A SMOOTH PASTE.

6. PUT THE BUTTER IN A PAN ON MEDIUM HEAT UNTIL IT MELTS. SPRINKLE IN THE FLOUR AND BLEND INTO A PASTE. SLOWLY POUR IN THE MILK AND MIX UNTIL SMOOTH USING A WHISK.

7. SPRINKLE THE SHREDDED CHEESE INTO THE PAN FROM (6) AND STIR IT UNTIL MELTED. ADD THE PASTE FROM (5) AND MIX UNTIL THOROUGHLY COMBINED. SEASON TO TASTE WITH SALT AND PEPPER. POUR THE SAUCE INTO A SMALL BOWL AND PLATE IT NEXT TO THE DEEP-FRIED PORK LOIN. GARNISH WITH SHREDDED CABBAGE AND PLATE WITH STEAMED RICE, PICKLED VEGETABLES AND A BOWL OF MISO SOUP.

***MIXING THE SAUCE IN WITH THE RICE AND MAKING IT INTO A GRATIN IS ALSO REALLY TASTY!**

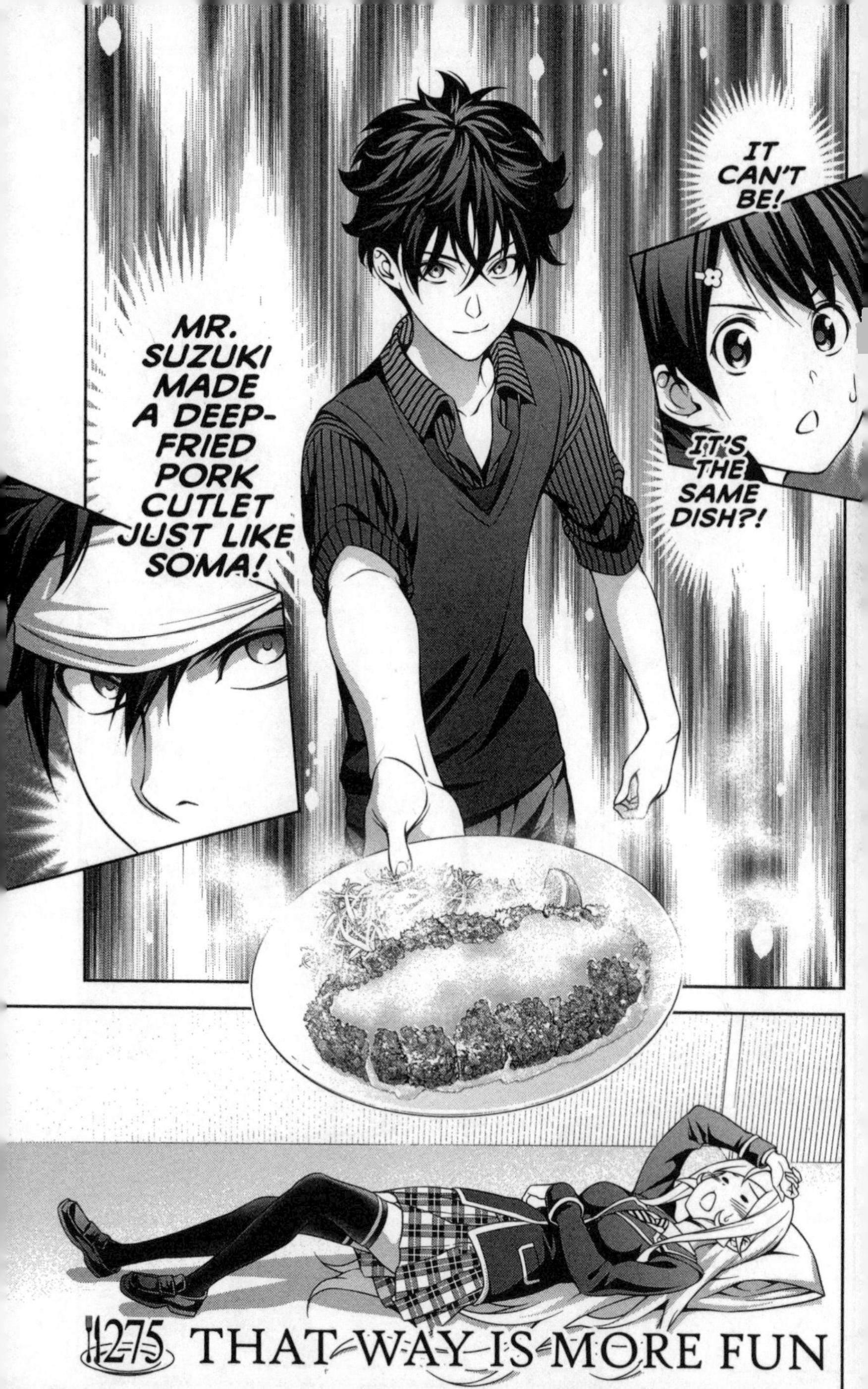
IT CAN'T BE!
IT'S THE SAME DISH?!
MR. SUZUKI MADE A DEEP-FRIED PORK CUTLET JUST LIKE SOMA!

275 THAT WAY IS MORE FUN

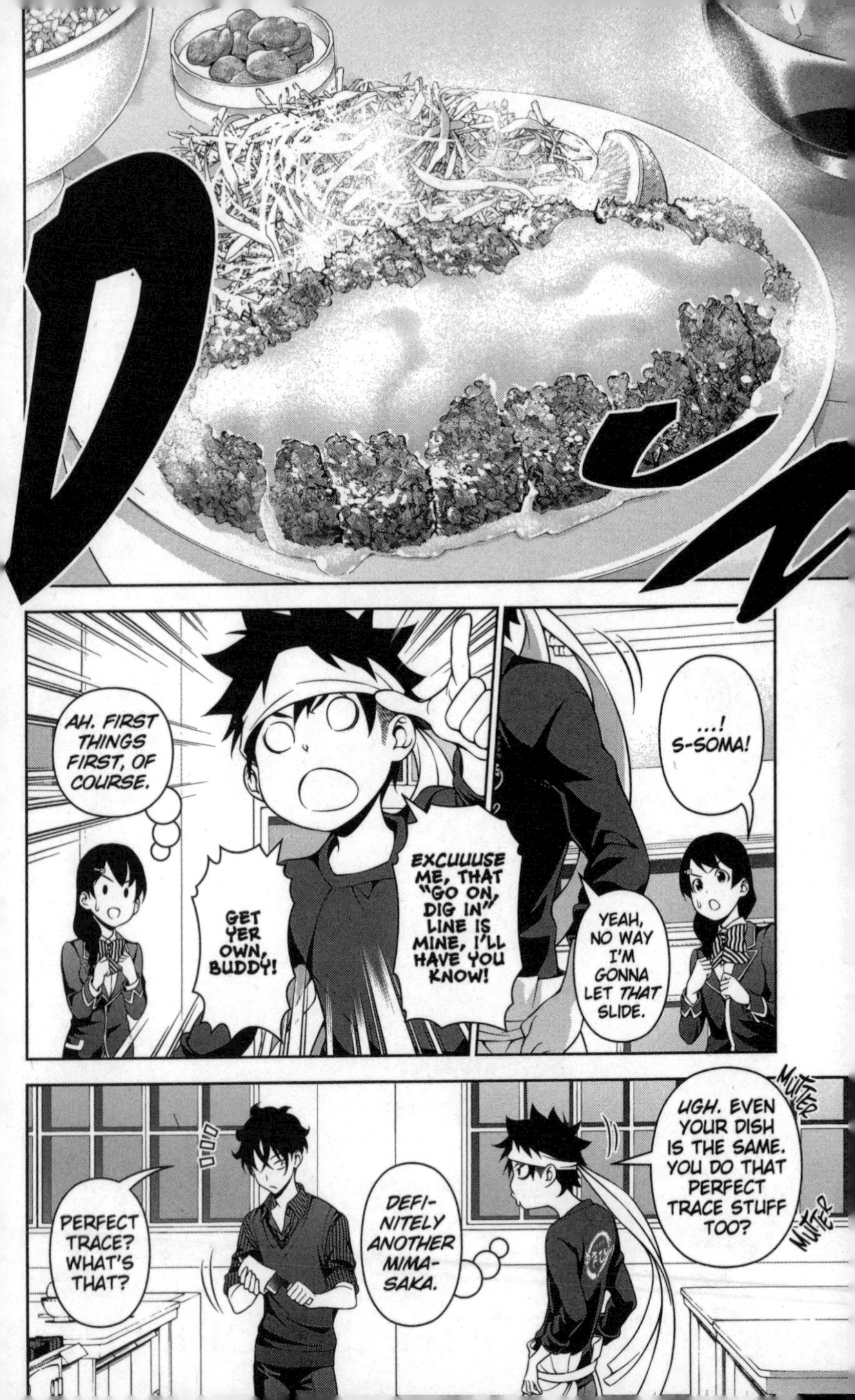
...! S-SOMA!
YEAH, NO WAY I'M GONNA LET *THAT* SLIDE.
EXCUUUSE ME, THAT "GO ON, DIG IN" LINE IS MINE, I'LL HAVE YOU KNOW!
GET YER OWN, BUDDY!
AH. FIRST THINGS FIRST, OF COURSE.
MUTTER
MUTTER
UGH. EVEN YOUR DISH IS THE SAME. YOU DO THAT PERFECT TRACE STUFF TOO?
DEFI-NITELY ANOTHER MIMA-SAKA.
PERFECT TRACE? WHAT'S THAT?

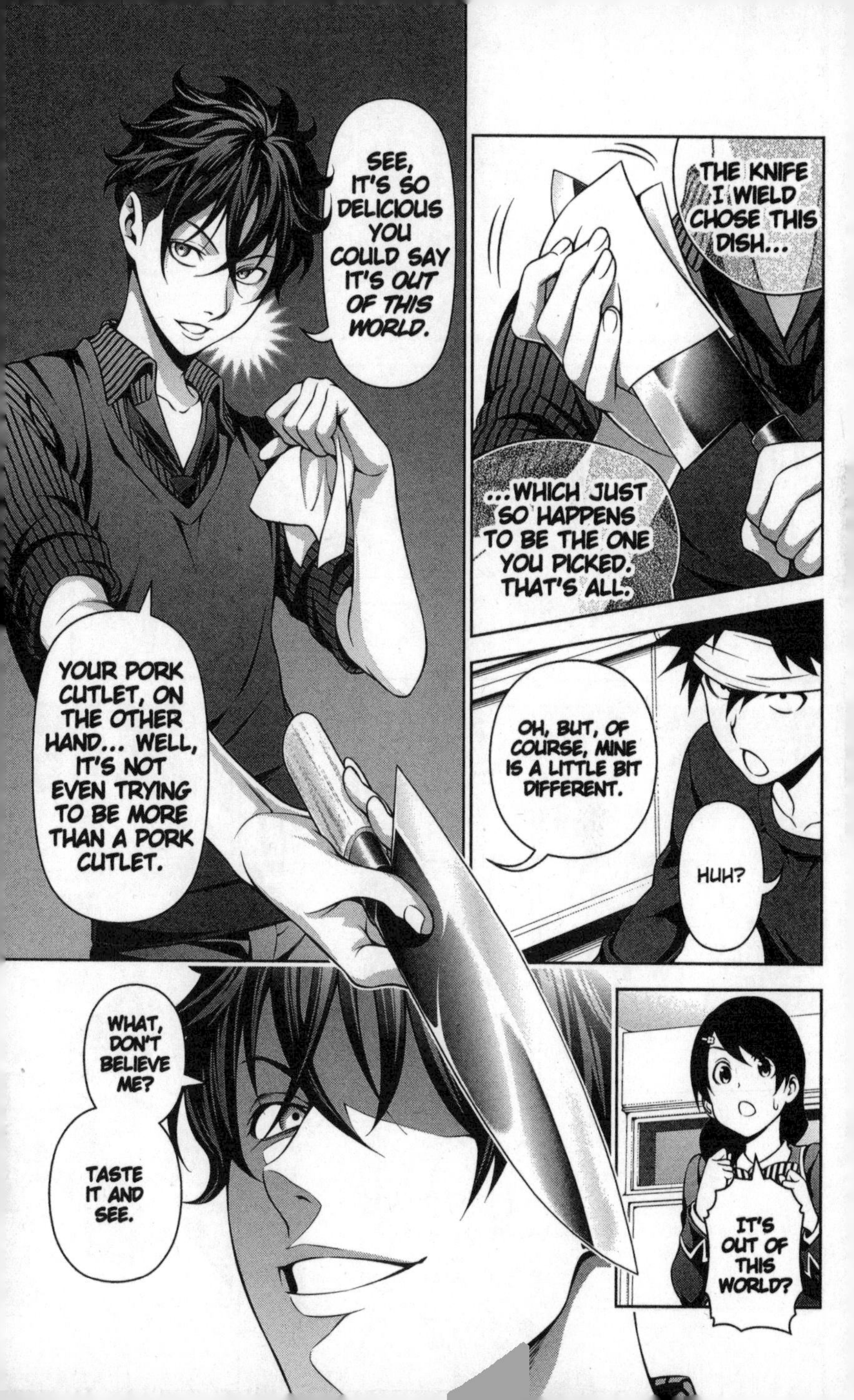
THE KNIFE I WIELD CHOSE THIS DISH...
...WHICH JUST SO HAPPENS TO BE THE ONE YOU PICKED. THAT'S ALL.
OH, BUT, OF COURSE, MINE IS A LITTLE BIT DIFFERENT.
HUH?
SEE, IT'S SO DELICIOUS YOU COULD SAY IT'S OUT OF THIS WORLD.
YOUR PORK CUTLET, ON THE OTHER HAND... WELL, IT'S NOT EVEN TRYING TO BE MORE THAN A PORK CUTLET.
IT'S OUT OF THIS WORLD?
WHAT, DON'T BELIEVE ME?
TASTE IT AND SEE.

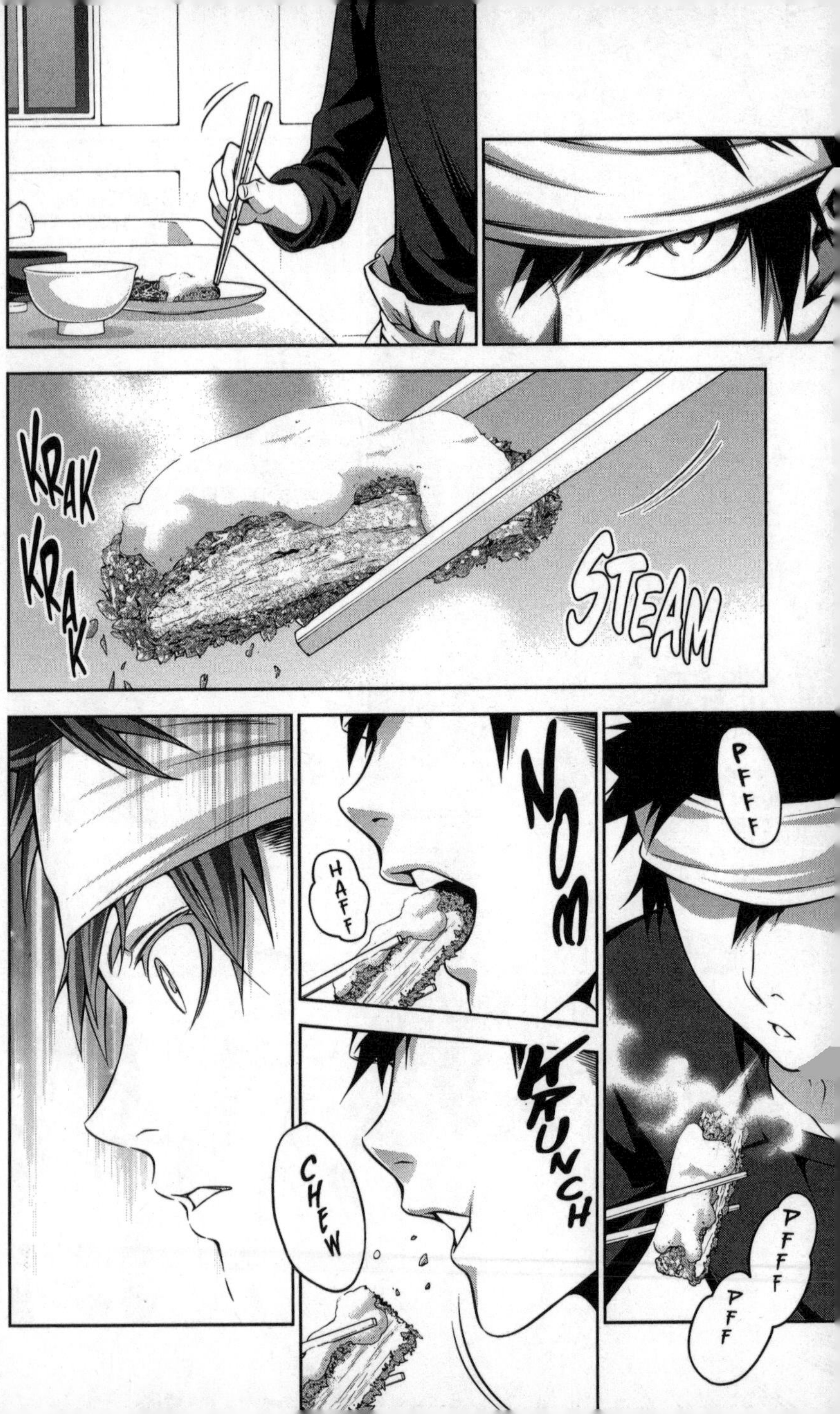
STEAM
KRAK KRAK KRAK
PFFF
PFFF
PFF
NOM
HAFF
KRUNCH
CHEW

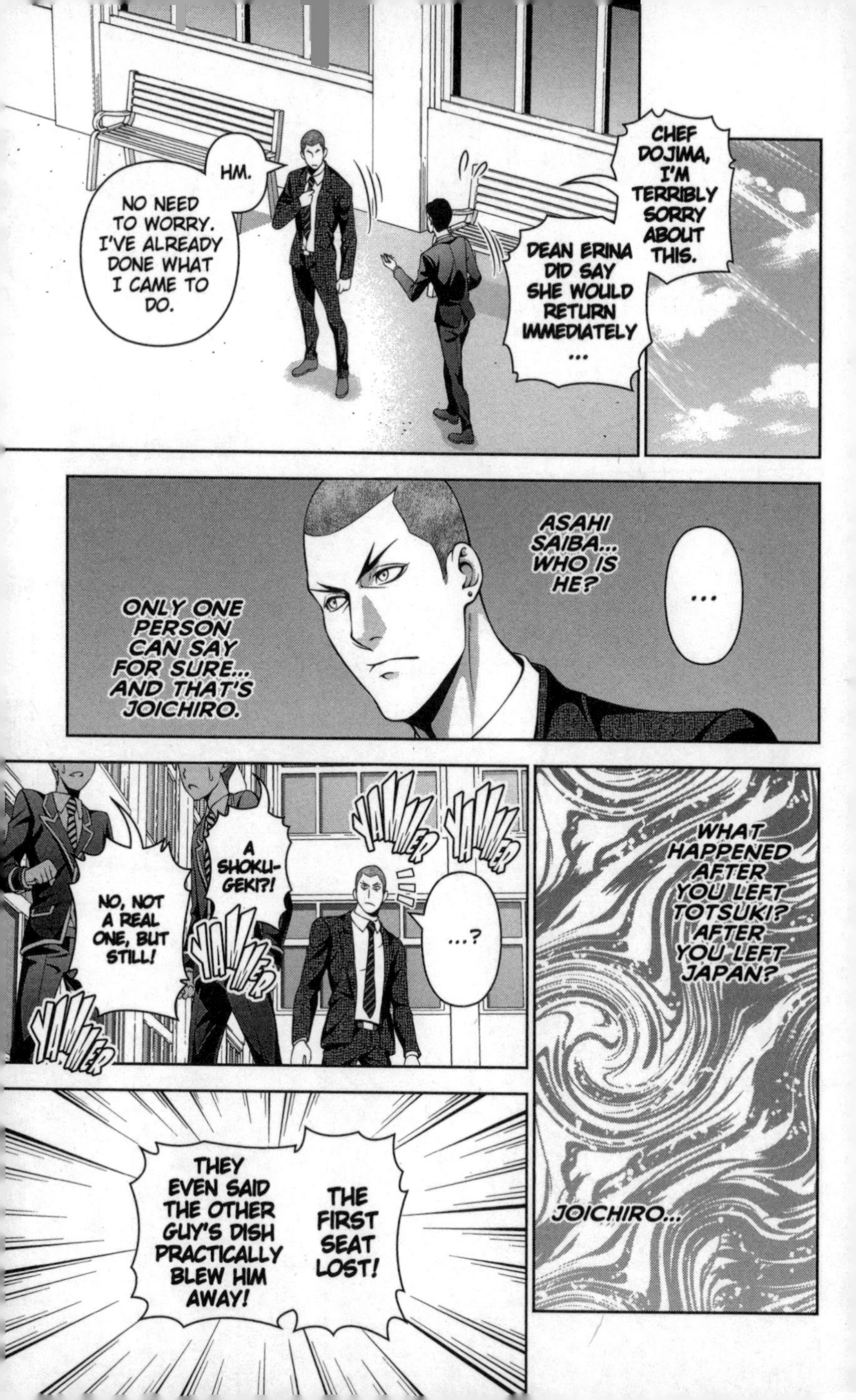

CHEF DOJIMA, I'M TERRIBLY SORRY ABOUT THIS.
DEAN ERINA DID SAY SHE WOULD RETURN IMMEDIATELY...
HM.
NO NEED TO WORRY. I'VE ALREADY DONE WHAT I CAME TO DO.
...
ASAHI SAIBA... WHO IS HE?
ONLY ONE PERSON CAN SAY FOR SURE... AND THAT'S JOICHIRO.
WHAT HAPPENED AFTER YOU LEFT TOTSUKI? AFTER YOU LEFT JAPAN?
JOICHIRO...
YAMMER YAMMER
...?
A SHOKUGEKI?!
NO, NOT A REAL ONE, BUT STILL!
YAMMER
YAMMER
THE FIRST SEAT LOST!
THEY EVEN SAID THE OTHER GUY'S DISH PRACTICALLY BLEW HIM AWAY!

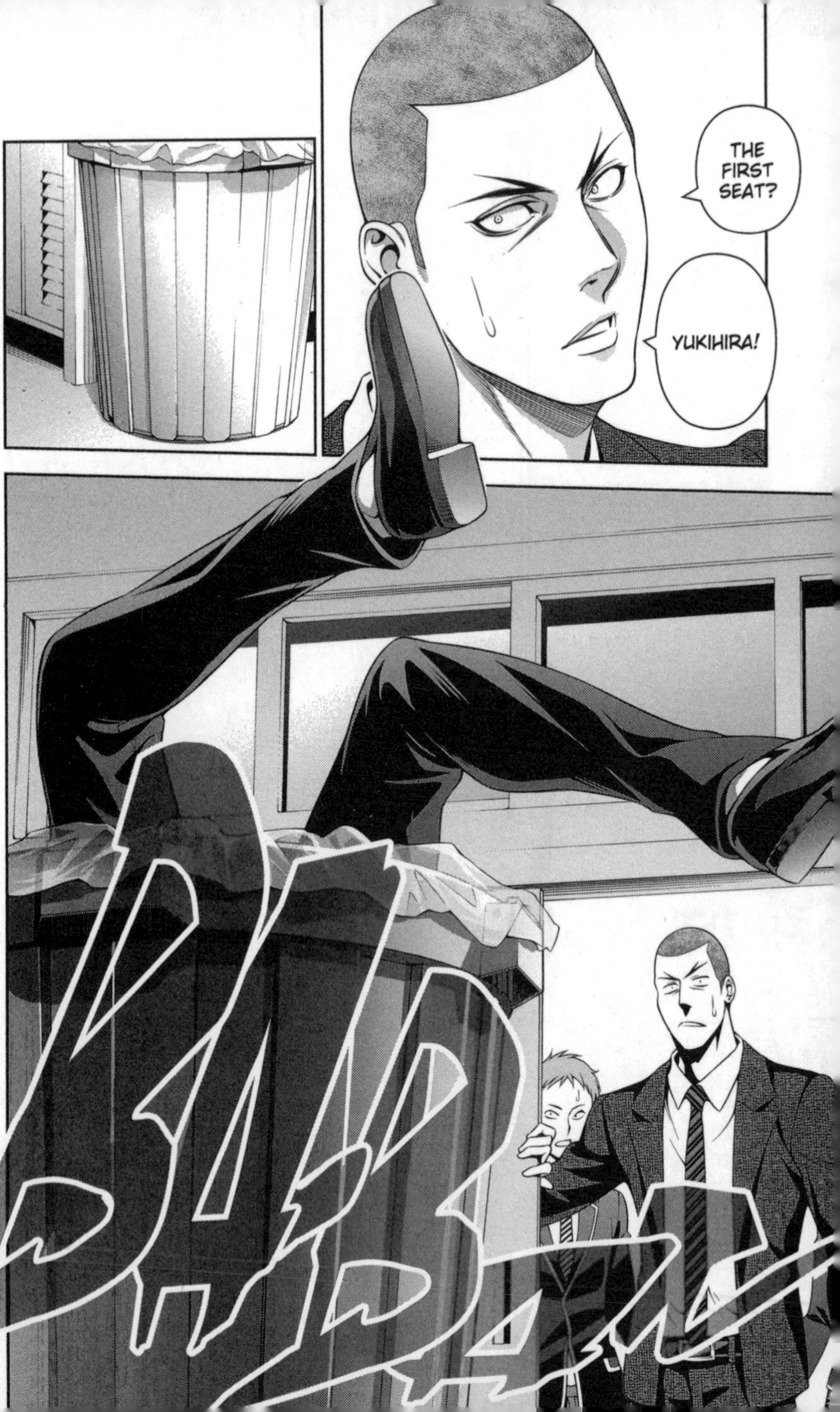
THE FIRST SEAT?
YUKIHIRA!

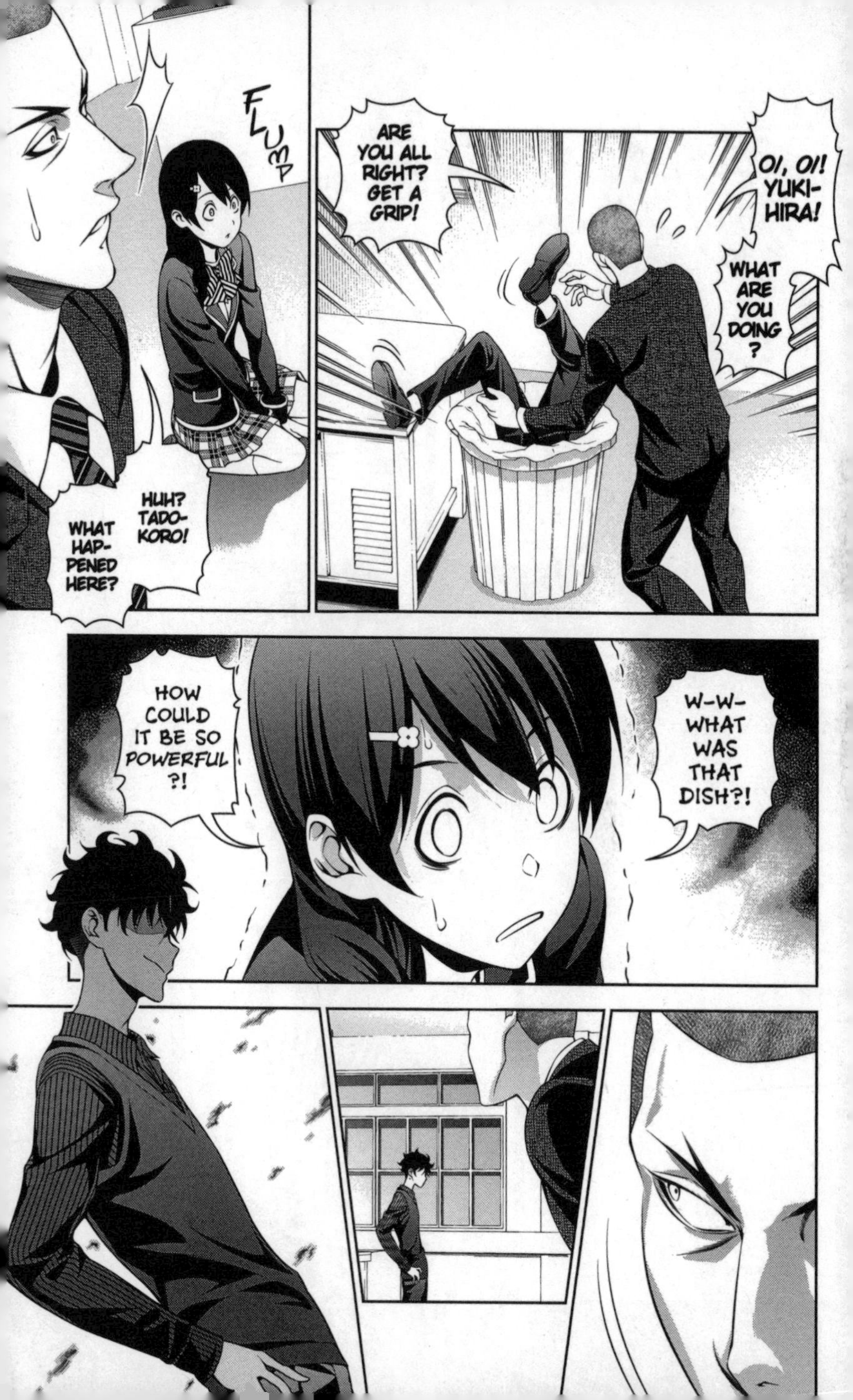
OI, OI! YUKIHIRA!
WHAT ARE YOU DOING?
ARE YOU ALL RIGHT? GET A GRIP!
FLUMP
HUH? TADOKORO!
WHAT HAPPENED HERE?
W-W-WHAT WAS THAT DISH?!
HOW COULD IT BE SO POWERFUL?!

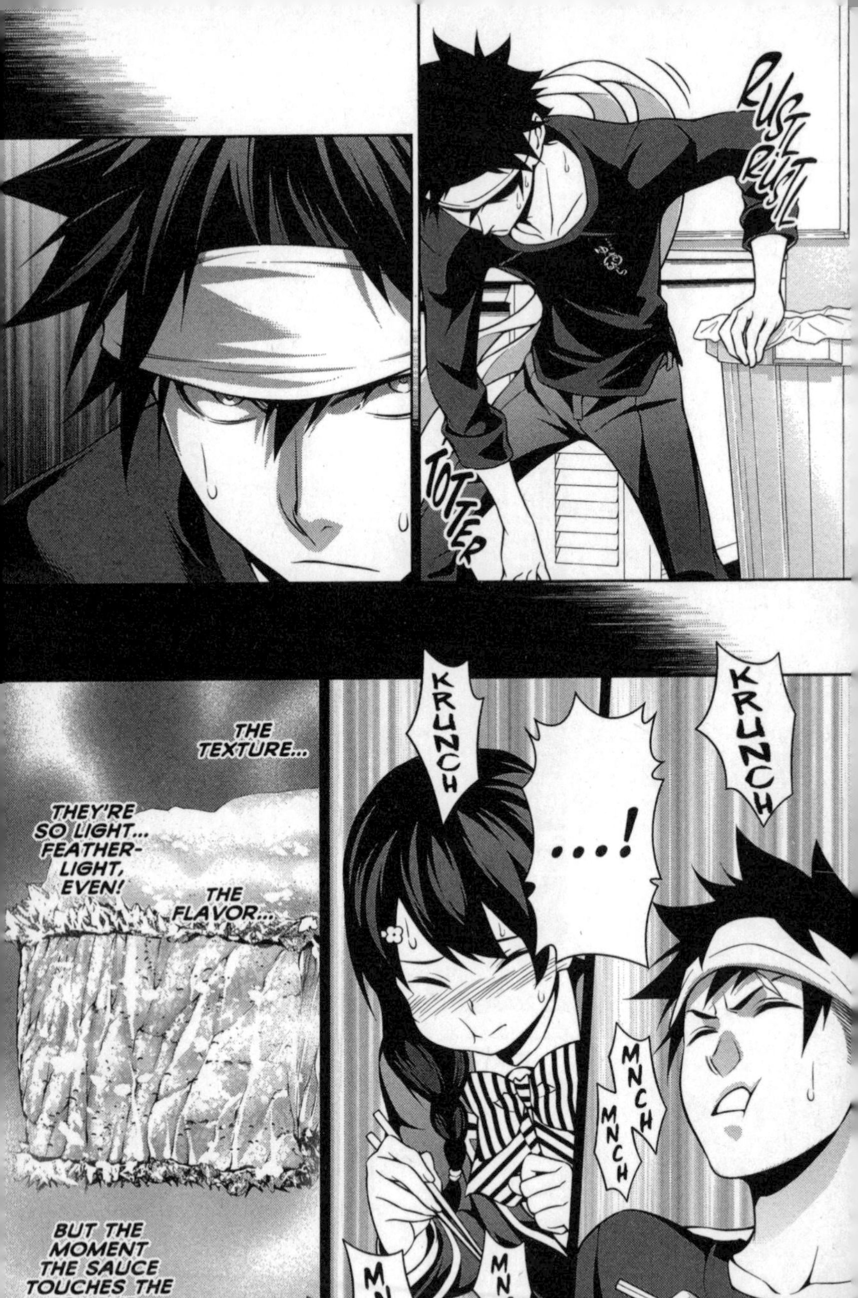
RUSTL RUSTL
TOTTER
KRUNCH
KRUNCH
...!
MNCH MNCH MNCH
THE TEXTURE...
THEY'RE SO LIGHT... FEATHER-LIGHT, EVEN!
THE FLAVOR...
BUT THE MOMENT THE SAUCE TOUCHES THE TONGUE...

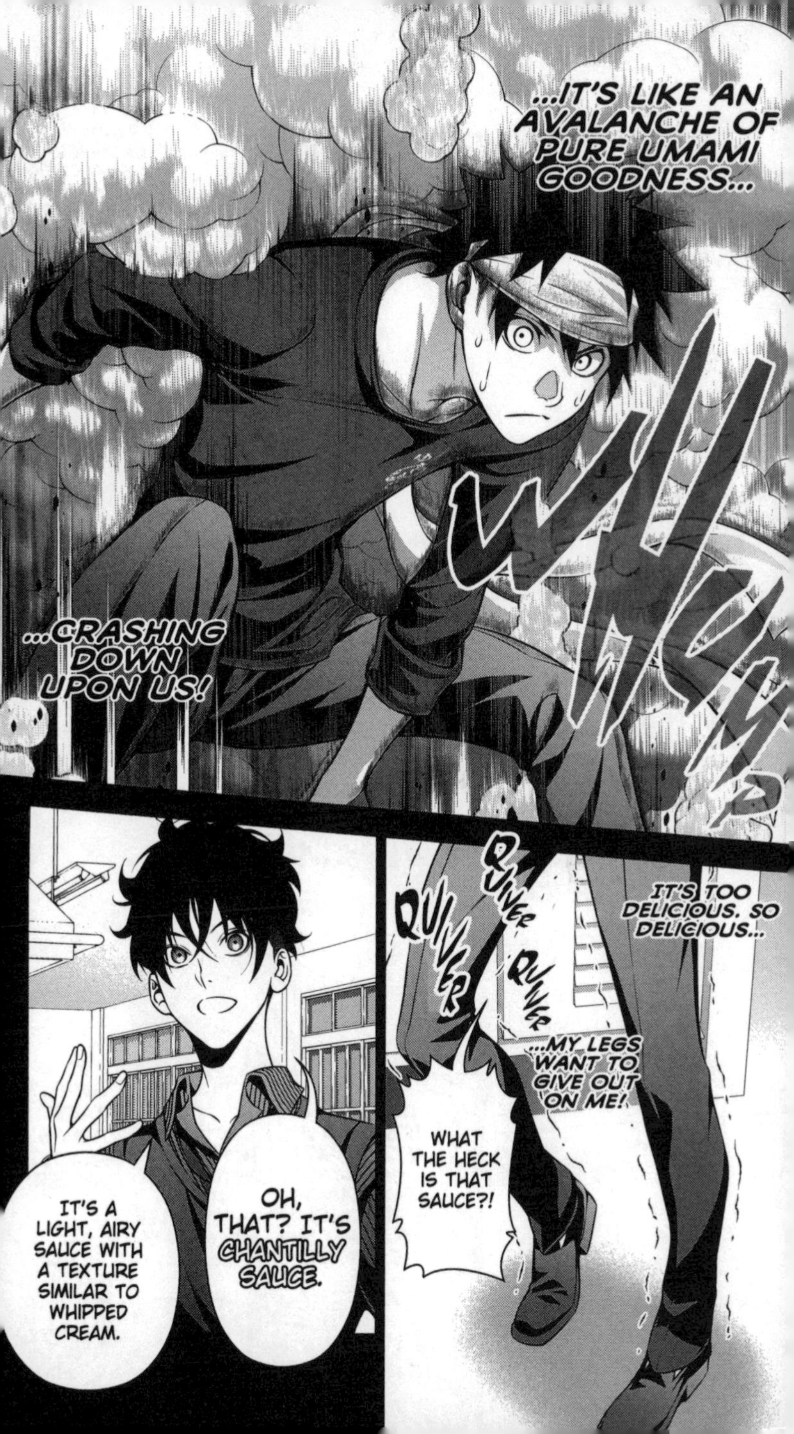
...IT'S LIKE AN AVALANCHE OF PURE UMAMI GOODNESS...
...CRASHING DOWN UPON US!
QUIVER
QUIVER
QUIVER
QUIVER
IT'S TOO DELICIOUS. SO DELICIOUS...
...MY LEGS WANT TO GIVE OUT ON ME!
WHAT THE HECK IS THAT SAUCE?!
OH, THAT? IT'S CHANTILLY SAUCE.
IT'S A LIGHT, AIRY SAUCE WITH A TEXTURE SIMILAR TO WHIPPED CREAM.

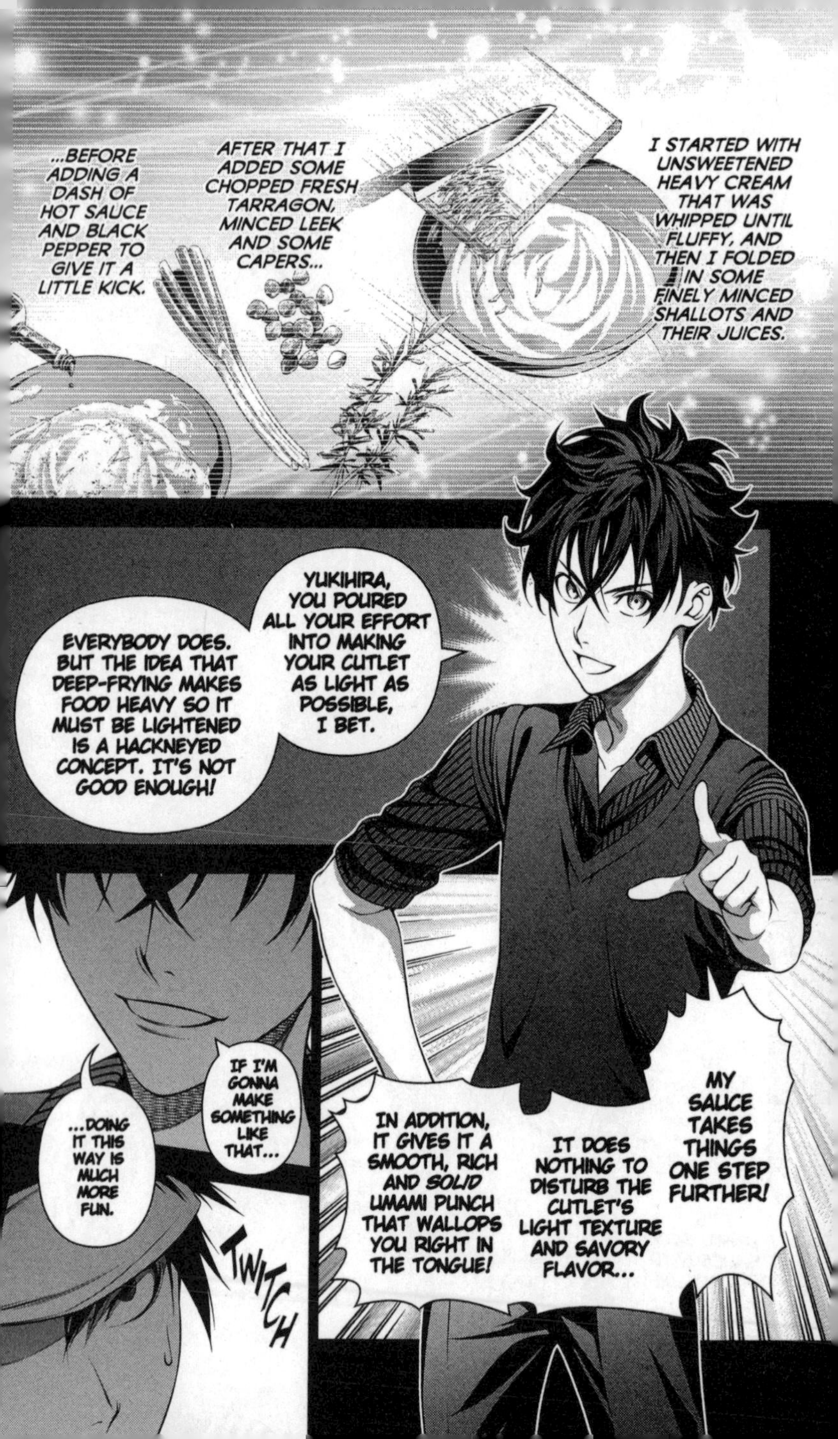

I STARTED WITH UNSWEETENED HEAVY CREAM THAT WAS WHIPPED UNTIL FLUFFY, AND THEN I FOLDED IN SOME FINELY MINCED SHALLOTS AND THEIR JUICES.
AFTER THAT I ADDED SOME CHOPPED FRESH TARRAGON, MINCED LEEK AND SOME CAPERS...
...BEFORE ADDING A DASH OF HOT SAUCE AND BLACK PEPPER TO GIVE IT A LITTLE KICK.
YUKIHIRA, YOU POURED ALL YOUR EFFORT INTO MAKING YOUR CUTLET AS LIGHT AS POSSIBLE, I BET.
EVERYBODY DOES. BUT THE IDEA THAT DEEP-FRYING MAKES FOOD HEAVY SO IT MUST BE LIGHTENED IS A HACKNEYED CONCEPT. IT'S NOT GOOD ENOUGH!
MY SAUCE TAKES THINGS ONE STEP FURTHER!
IT DOES NOTHING TO DISTURB THE CUTLET'S LIGHT TEXTURE AND SAVORY FLAVOR...
IN ADDITION, IT GIVES IT A SMOOTH, RICH AND *SOLID* UMAMI PUNCH THAT WALLOPS YOU RIGHT IN THE TONGUE!
IF I'M GONNA MAKE SOMETHING LIKE THAT...
...DOING IT THIS WAY IS MUCH MORE FUN.
TWITCH

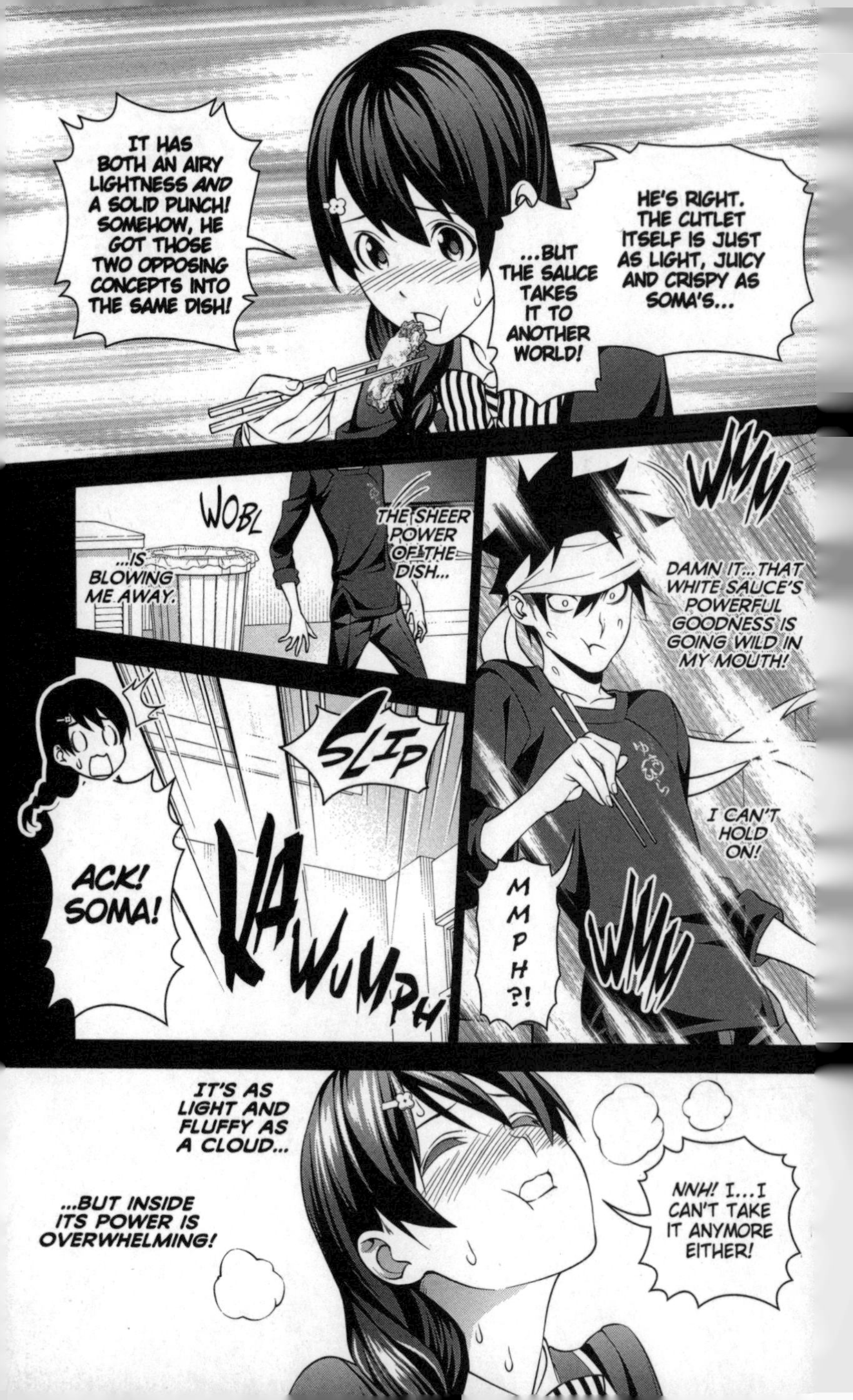
HE'S RIGHT. THE CUTLET ITSELF IS JUST AS LIGHT, JUICY AND CRISPY AS SOMA'S...
...BUT THE SAUCE TAKES IT TO ANOTHER WORLD!
IT HAS BOTH AN AIRY LIGHTNESS AND A SOLID PUNCH! SOMEHOW, HE GOT THOSE TWO OPPOSING CONCEPTS INTO THE SAME DISH!
WMM
DAMN IT... THAT WHITE SAUCE'S POWERFUL GOODNESS IS GOING WILD IN MY MOUTH!
I CAN'T HOLD ON!
WMM
MMPH?!
THE SHEER POWER OF THE DISH...
WOBL
...IS BLOWING ME AWAY.
SLIP
KAWUMPH
ACK! SOMA!
NNH! I... I CAN'T TAKE IT ANYMORE EITHER!
IT'S AS LIGHT AND FLUFFY AS A CLOUD...
...BUT INSIDE ITS POWER IS OVERWHELMING!

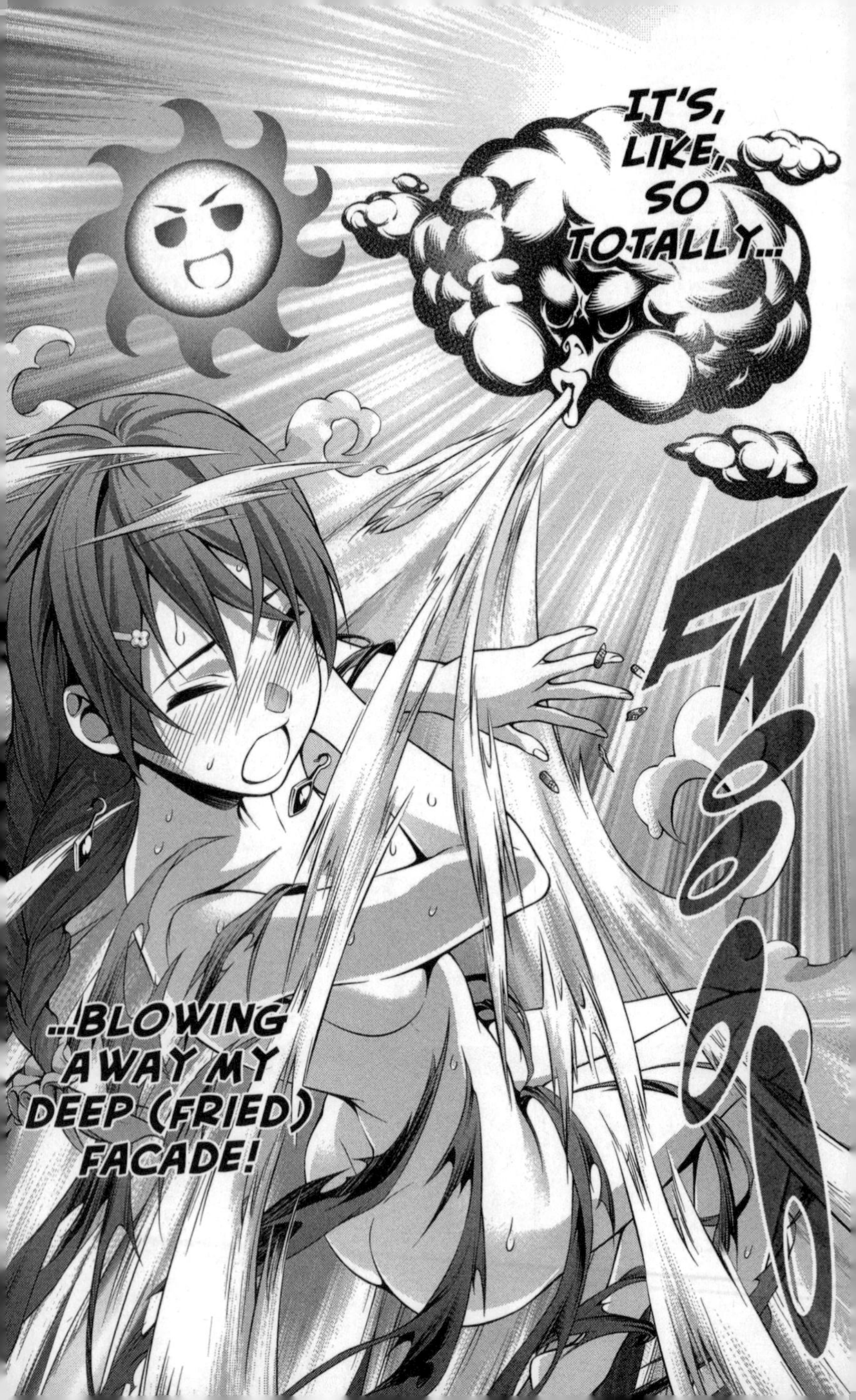
IT'S, LIKE, SO TOTALLY...
...BLOWING AWAY MY DEEP (FRIED) FACADE!

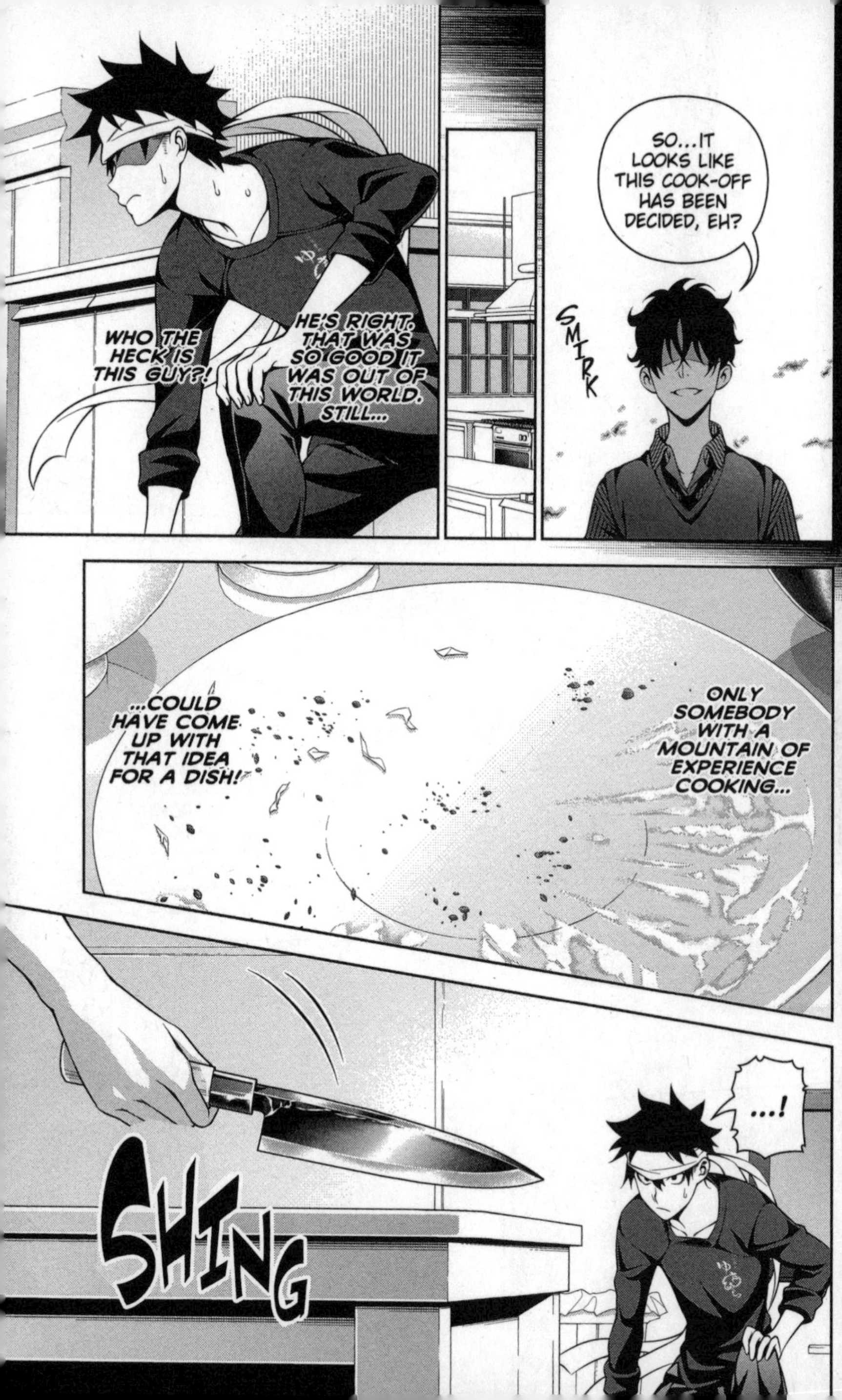

SO...IT LOOKS LIKE THIS COOK-OFF HAS BEEN DECIDED, EH?
SMIRK
HE'S RIGHT. THAT WAS SO GOOD IT WAS OUT OF THIS WORLD. STILL...
WHO THE HECK IS THIS GUY?!
ONLY SOMEBODY WITH A MOUNTAIN OF EXPERIENCE COOKING...
...COULD HAVE COME UP WITH THAT IDEA FOR A DISH!
...!
SHING

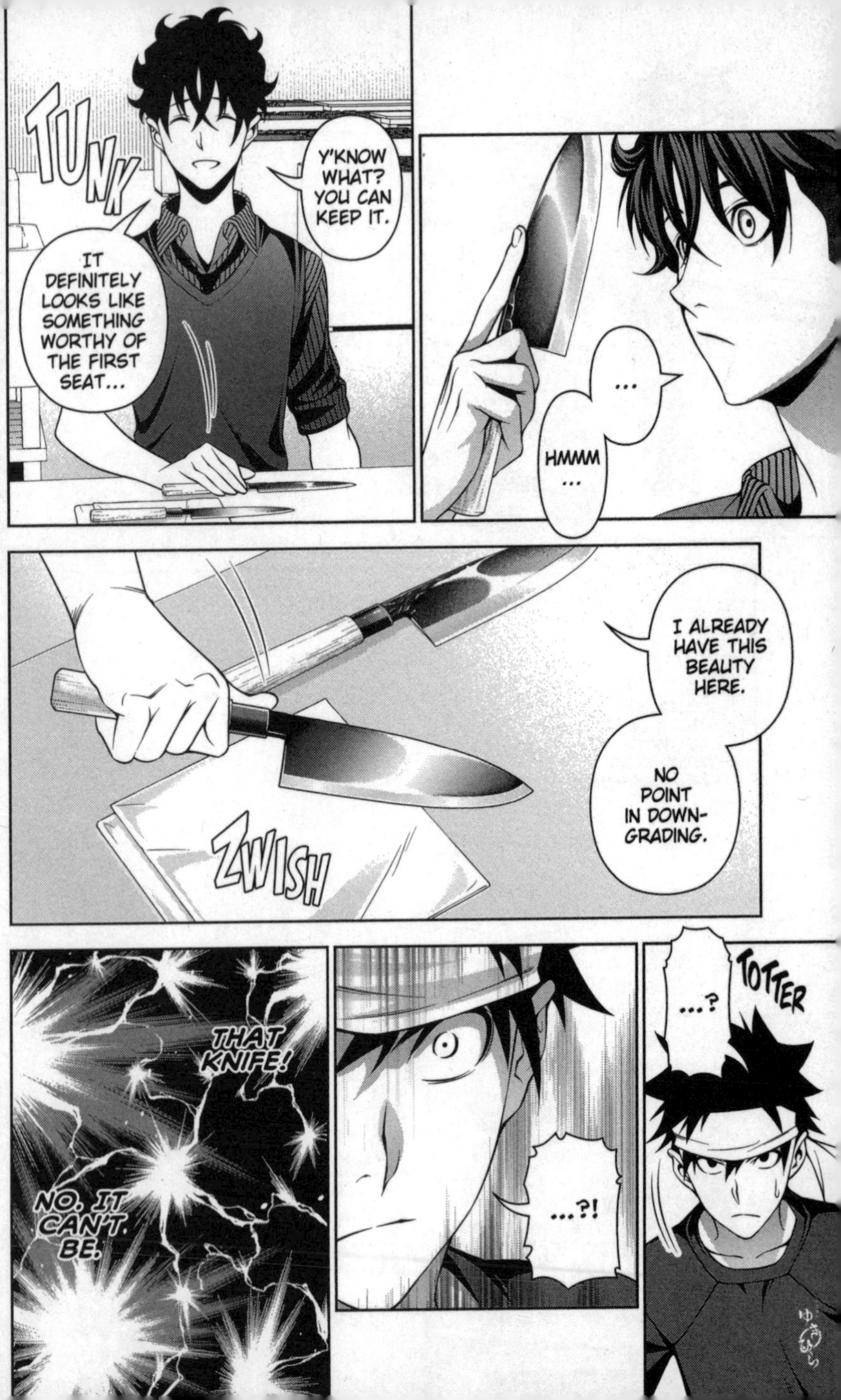
...
HMMM...
Y'KNOW WHAT? YOU CAN KEEP IT.
TUNK
IT DEFINITELY LOOKS LIKE SOMETHING WORTHY OF THE FIRST SEAT...
I ALREADY HAVE THIS BEAUTY HERE.
NO POINT IN DOWN-GRADING.
ZWISH
TOTTER
...?
...?!
THAT KNIFE!
NO. IT CAN'T BE.

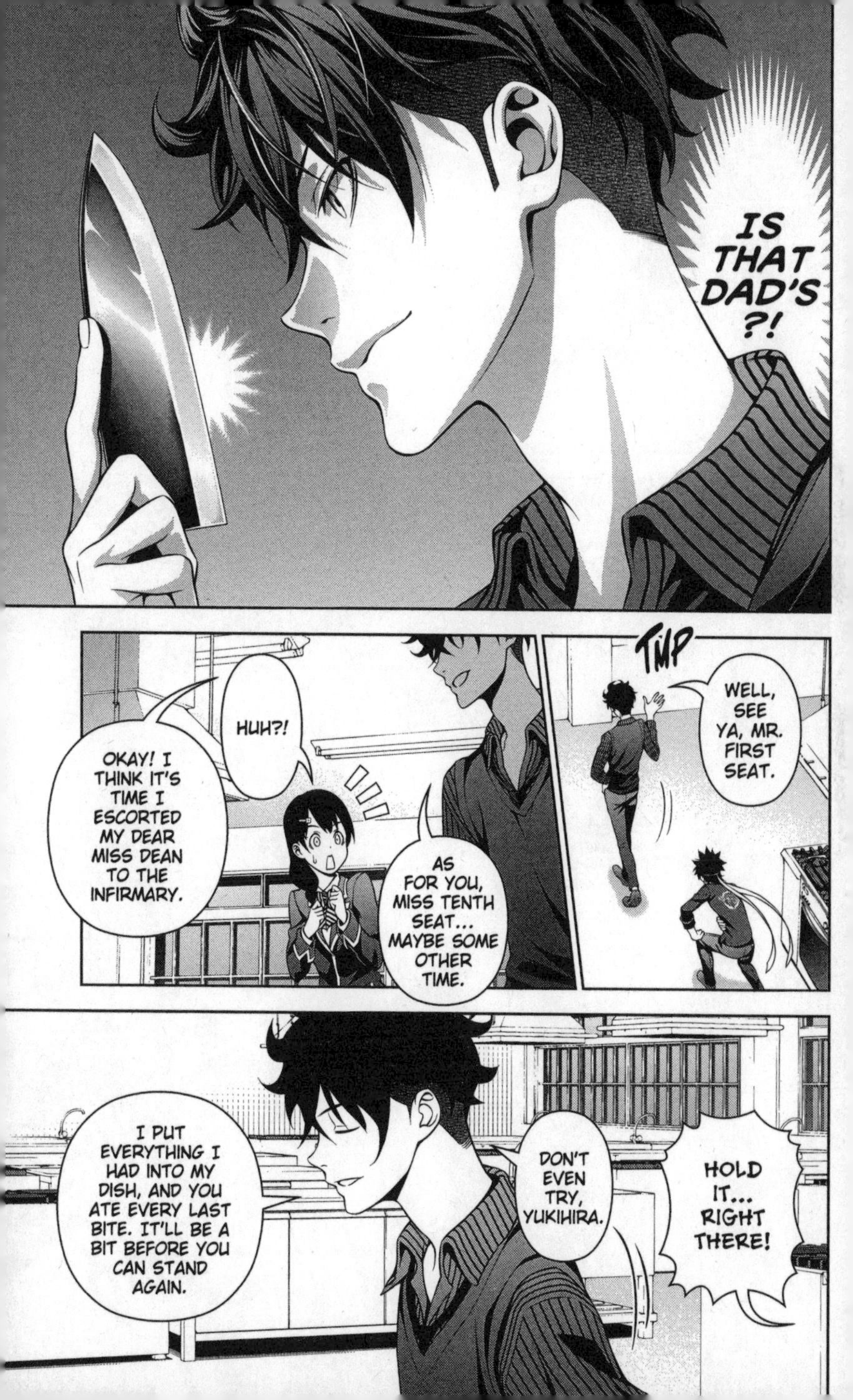
IS THAT DAD'S ?!
TMP
WELL, SEE YA, MR. FIRST SEAT.
HUH?!
AS FOR YOU, MISS TENTH SEAT... MAYBE SOME OTHER TIME.
OKAY! I THINK IT'S TIME I ESCORTED MY DEAR MISS DEAN TO THE INFIRMARY.
HOLD IT... RIGHT THERE!
DON'T EVEN TRY, YUKIHIRA.
I PUT EVERYTHING I HAD INTO MY DISH, AND YOU ATE EVERY LAST BITE. IT'LL BE A BIT BEFORE YOU CAN STAND AGAIN.

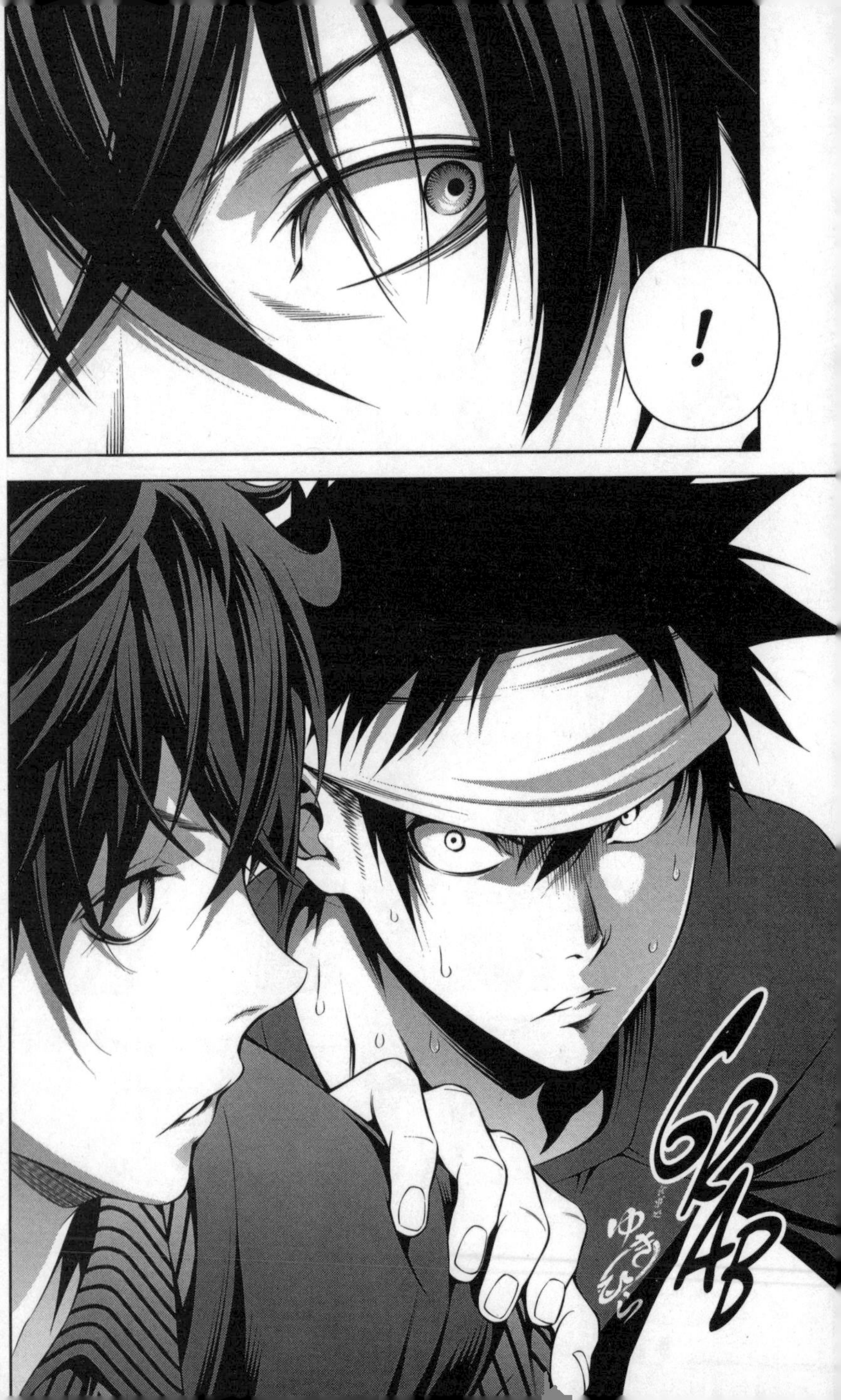
!
GRAB
ゆきひら

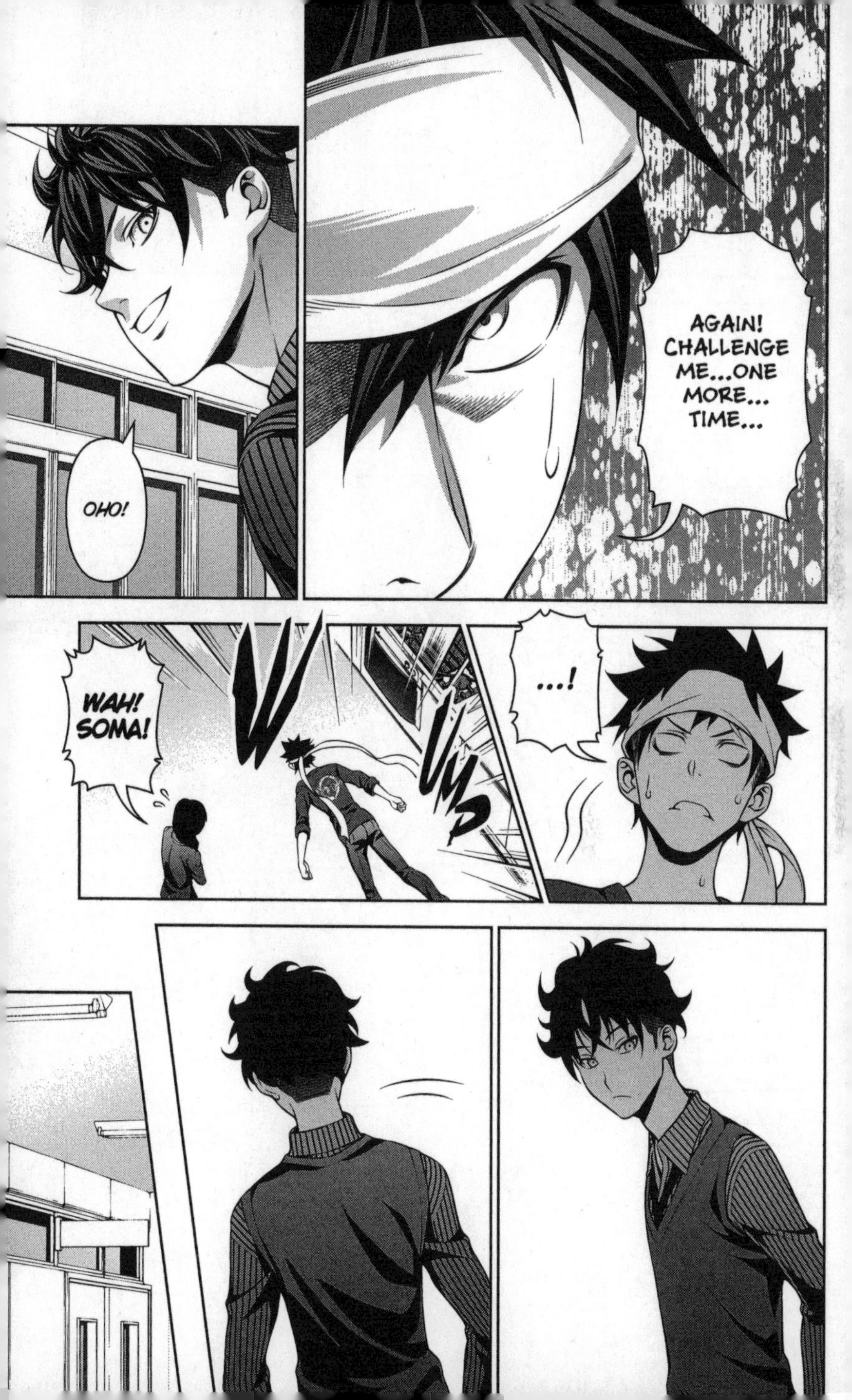
AGAIN! CHALLENGE ME...ONE MORE... TIME...
OHO!
...!
WAH! SOMA!

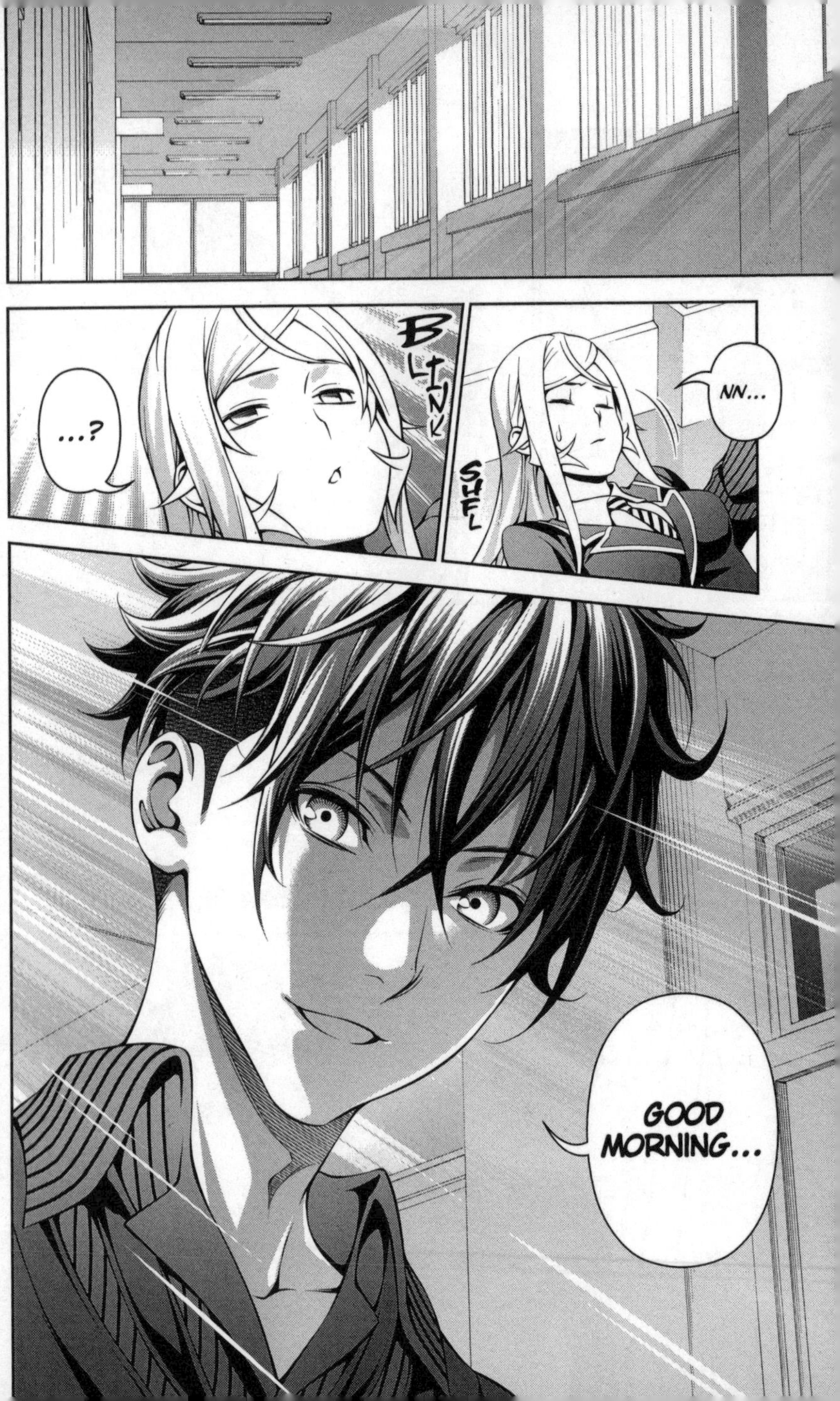
NN...
SHFL
BLINK
...?
GOOD MORNING...

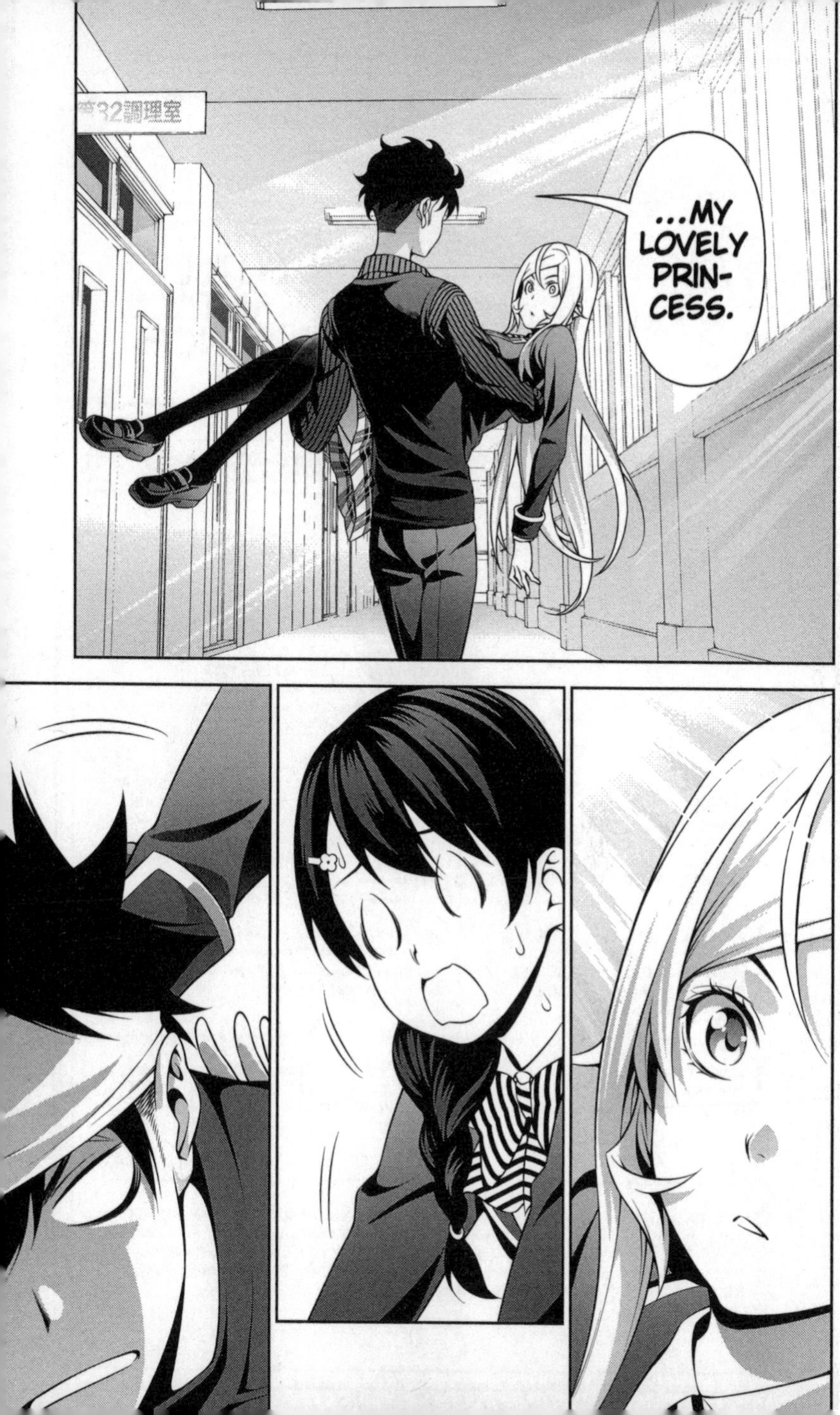
...MY LOVELY PRIN- CESS.
32調理室

ARTIST: YUTO TSUKUDA RECIPE BY: YUKI MORISAKI

VOLUME 32 SPECIAL SUPPLEMENT!

PRACTICAL RECIPE #2

DEEP-FRIED PORK CUTLET WITH CHANTILLY SAUCE LUNCH SET

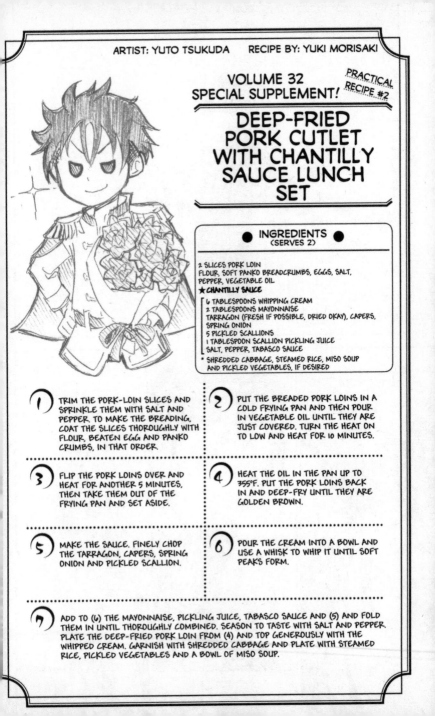

INGREDIENTS
(SERVES 2)

2 SLICES PORK LOIN
FLOUR, SOFT PANKO BREADCRUMBS, EGGS, SALT, PEPPER, VEGETABLE OIL

★CHANTILLY SAUCE

- 6 TABLESPOONS WHIPPING CREAM
- 2 TABLESPOONS MAYONNAISE
- TARRAGON (FRESH IF POSSIBLE, DRIED OKAY), CAPERS, SPRING ONION
- 5 PICKLED SCALLIONS
- 1 TABLESPOON SCALLION PICKLING JUICE
- SALT, PEPPER, TABASCO SAUCE

* SHREDDED CABBAGE, STEAMED RICE, MISO SOUP AND PICKLED VEGETABLES, IF DESIRED

1. TRIM THE PORK-LOIN SLICES AND SPRINKLE THEM WITH SALT AND PEPPER. TO MAKE THE BREADING, COAT THE SLICES THOROUGHLY WITH FLOUR, BEATEN EGG AND PANKO CRUMBS, IN THAT ORDER.
2. PUT THE BREADED PORK LOINS IN A COLD FRYING PAN AND THEN POUR IN VEGETABLE OIL UNTIL THEY ARE JUST COVERED. TURN THE HEAT ON TO LOW AND HEAT FOR 10 MINUTES.
3. FLIP THE PORK LOINS OVER AND HEAT FOR ANOTHER 5 MINUTES, THEN TAKE THEM OUT OF THE FRYING PAN AND SET ASIDE.
4. HEAT THE OIL IN THE PAN UP TO 355°F. PUT THE PORK LOINS BACK IN AND DEEP-FRY UNTIL THEY ARE GOLDEN BROWN.
5. MAKE THE SAUCE. FINELY CHOP THE TARRAGON, CAPERS, SPRING ONION AND PICKLED SCALLION.
6. POUR THE CREAM INTO A BOWL AND USE A WHISK TO WHIP IT UNTIL SOFT PEAKS FORM.
7. ADD TO (6) THE MAYONNAISE, PICKLING JUICE, TABASCO SAUCE AND (5) AND FOLD THEM IN UNTIL THOROUGHLY COMBINED. SEASON TO TASTE WITH SALT AND PEPPER. PLATE THE DEEP-FRIED PORK LOIN FROM (4) AND TOP GENEROUSLY WITH THE WHIPPED CREAM. GARNISH WITH SHREDDED CABBAGE AND PLATE WITH STEAMED RICE, PICKLED VEGETABLES AND A BOWL OF MISO SOUP.

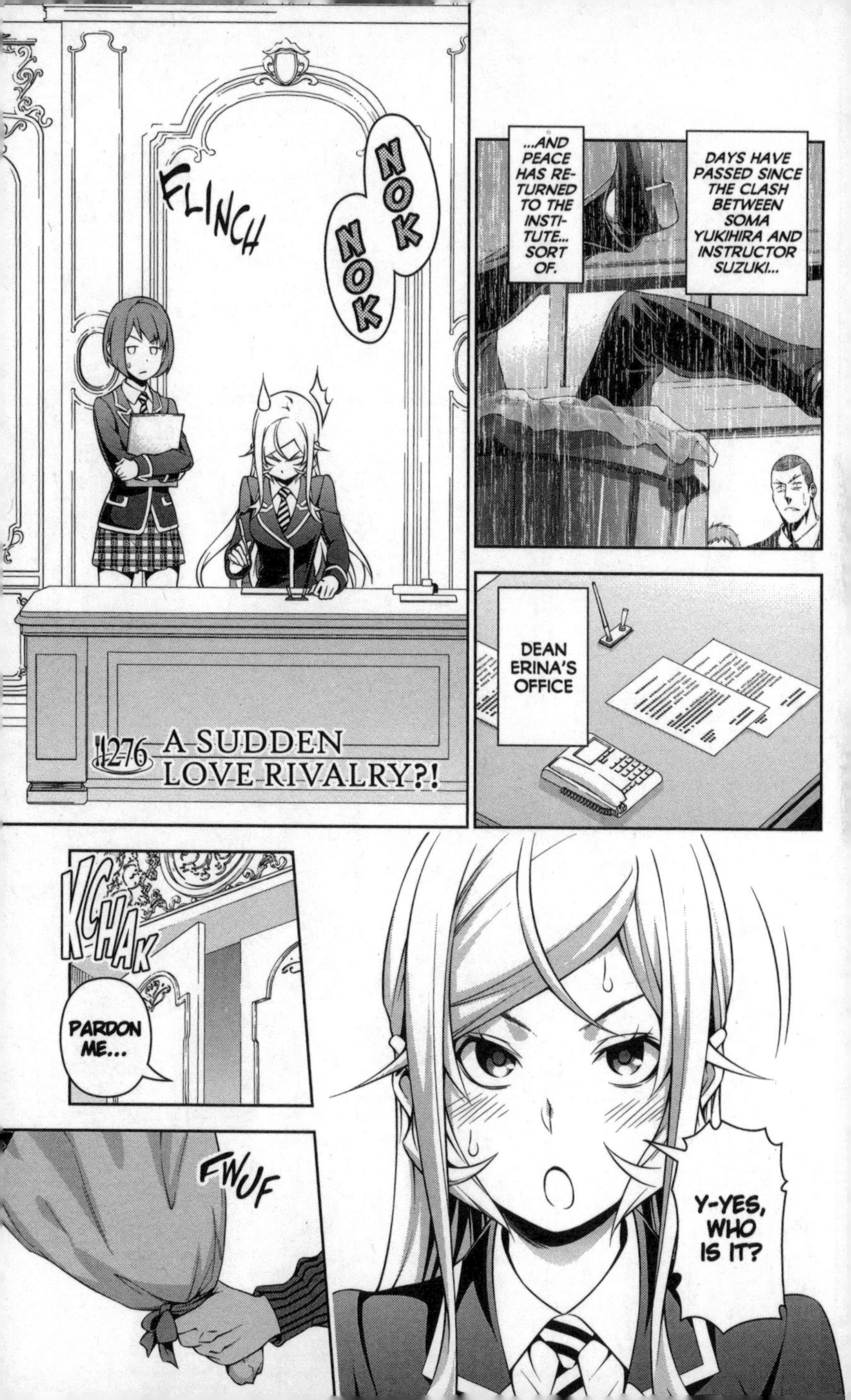
DAYS HAVE PASSED SINCE THE CLASH BETWEEN SOMA YUKIHIRA AND INSTRUCTOR SUZUKI...
...AND PEACE HAS RETURNED TO THE INSTITUTE... SORT OF.
DEAN ERINA'S OFFICE
NOK NOK
FLINCH
276 A SUDDEN LOVE RIVALRY?!
Y-YES, WHO IS IT?
KCHAK
PARDON ME...
FWUF

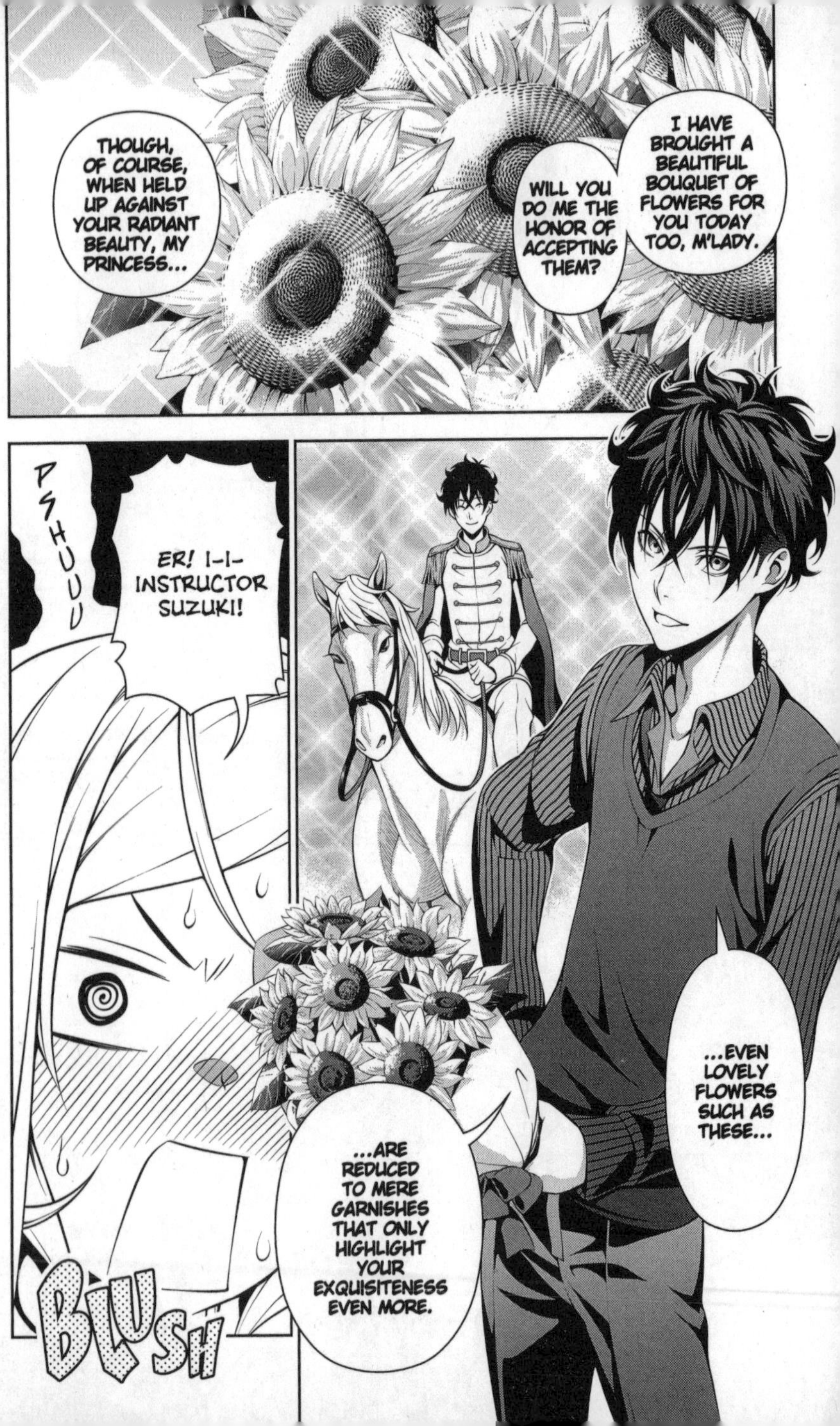
I HAVE BROUGHT A BEAUTIFUL BOUQUET OF FLOWERS FOR YOU TODAY TOO, M'LADY.
WILL YOU DO ME THE HONOR OF ACCEPTING THEM?
THOUGH, OF COURSE, WHEN HELD UP AGAINST YOUR RADIANT BEAUTY, MY PRINCESS...
...EVEN LOVELY FLOWERS SUCH AS THESE...
...ARE REDUCED TO MERE GARNISHES THAT ONLY HIGHLIGHT YOUR EXQUISITENESS EVEN MORE.
PSHUUU
ER! I-I-INSTRUCTOR SUZUKI!
BLUSH

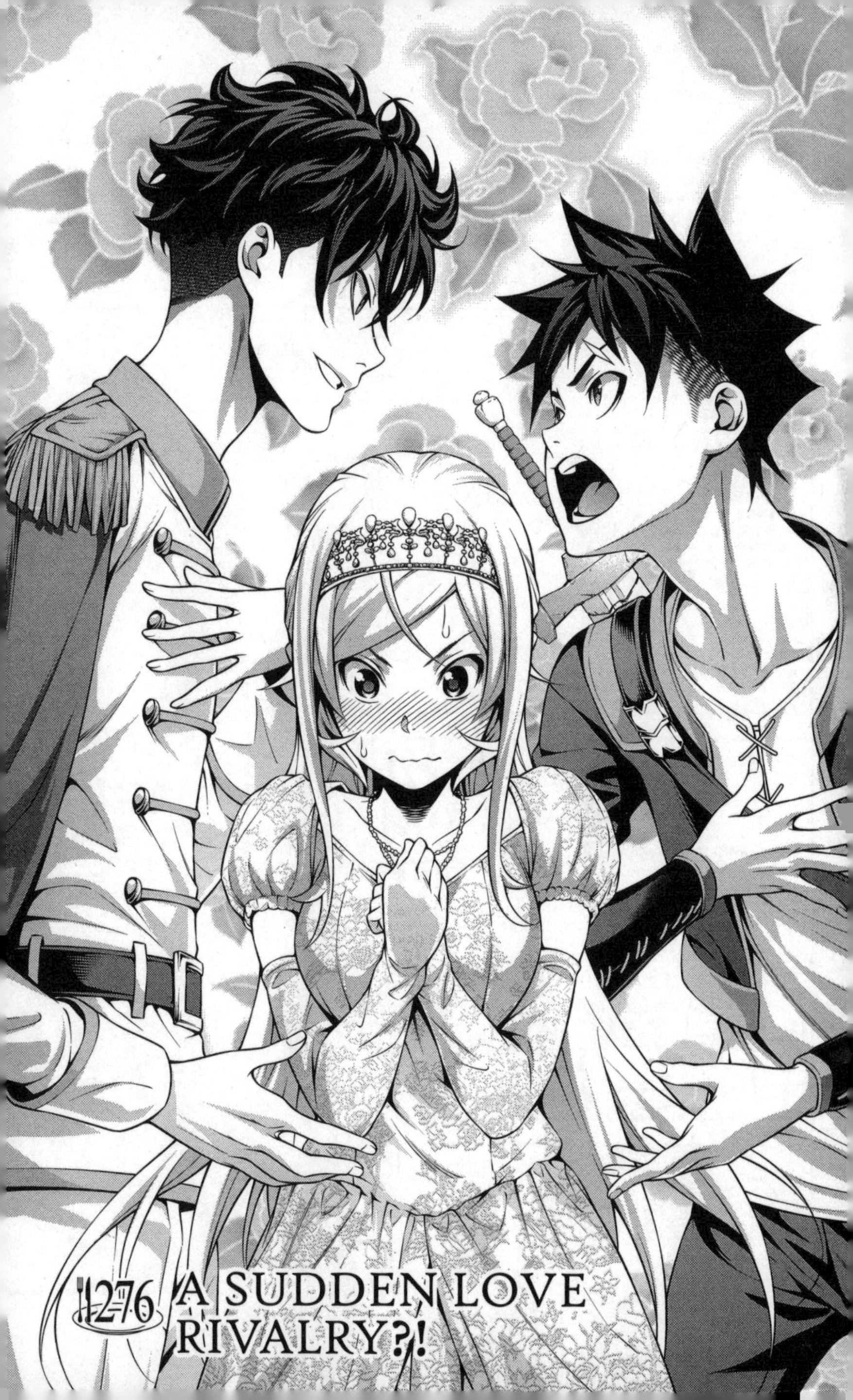
276
A SUDDEN LOVE RIVALRY?!

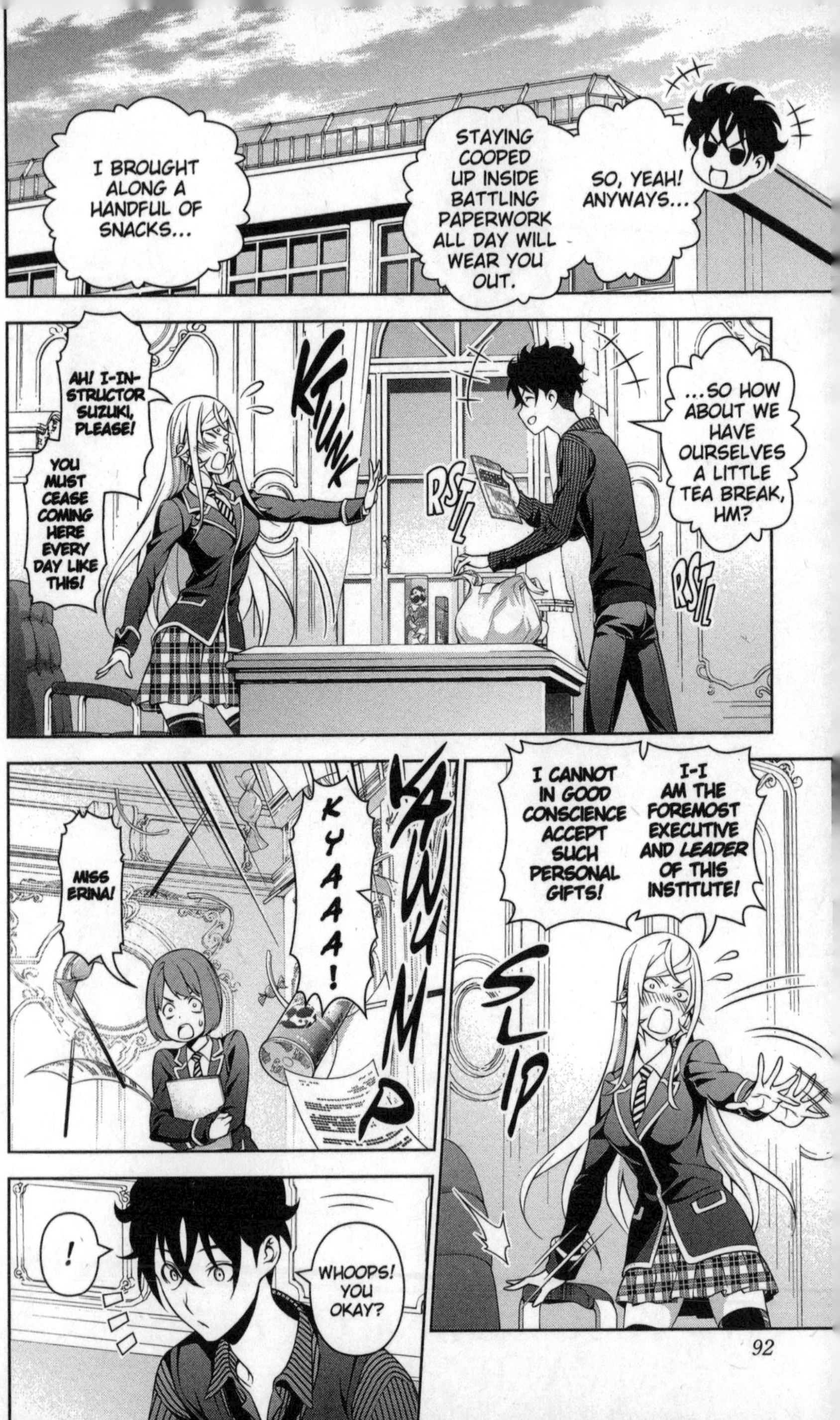

SO, YEAH! ANYWAYS...
STAYING COOPED UP INSIDE BATTLING PAPERWORK ALL DAY WILL WEAR YOU OUT.
I BROUGHT ALONG A HANDFUL OF SNACKS...
...SO HOW ABOUT WE HAVE OURSELVES A LITTLE TEA BREAK, HM?
RSTL
RSTL
KRUNK
AH! I-INSTRUCTOR SUZUKI, PLEASE!
YOU MUST CEASE COMING HERE EVERY DAY LIKE THIS!
I-I AM THE FOREMOST EXECUTIVE AND LEADER OF THIS INSTITUTE!
I CANNOT IN GOOD CONSCIENCE ACCEPT SUCH PERSONAL GIFTS!
SLIP
KAWUMP
KYAAAA!
MISS ERINA!
WHOOPS! YOU OKAY?
!

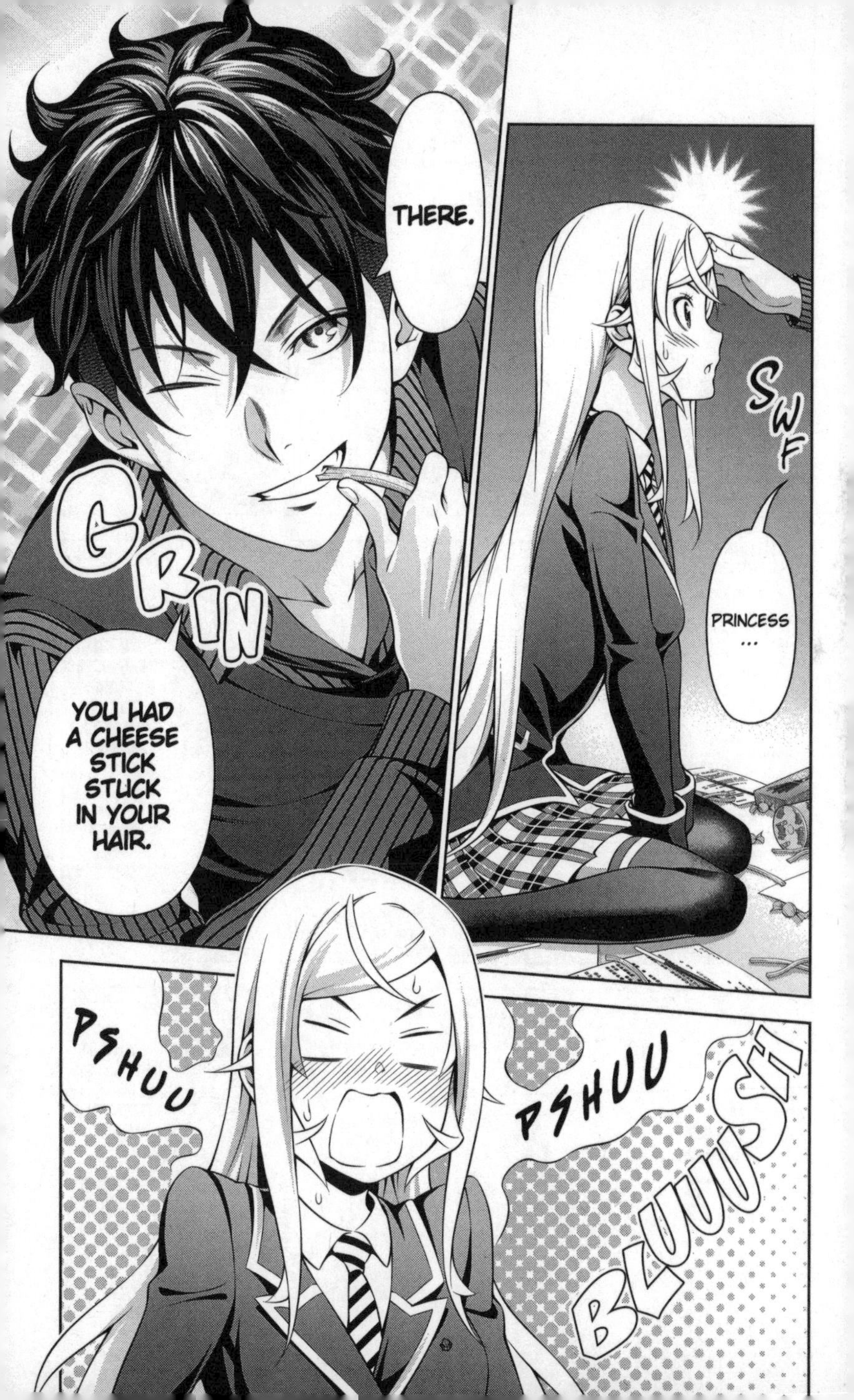
SWF
PRINCESS ...
THERE.
GRIN
YOU HAD A CHEESE STICK STUCK IN YOUR HAIR.
BLUUUSH
PSHUU
PSHUU

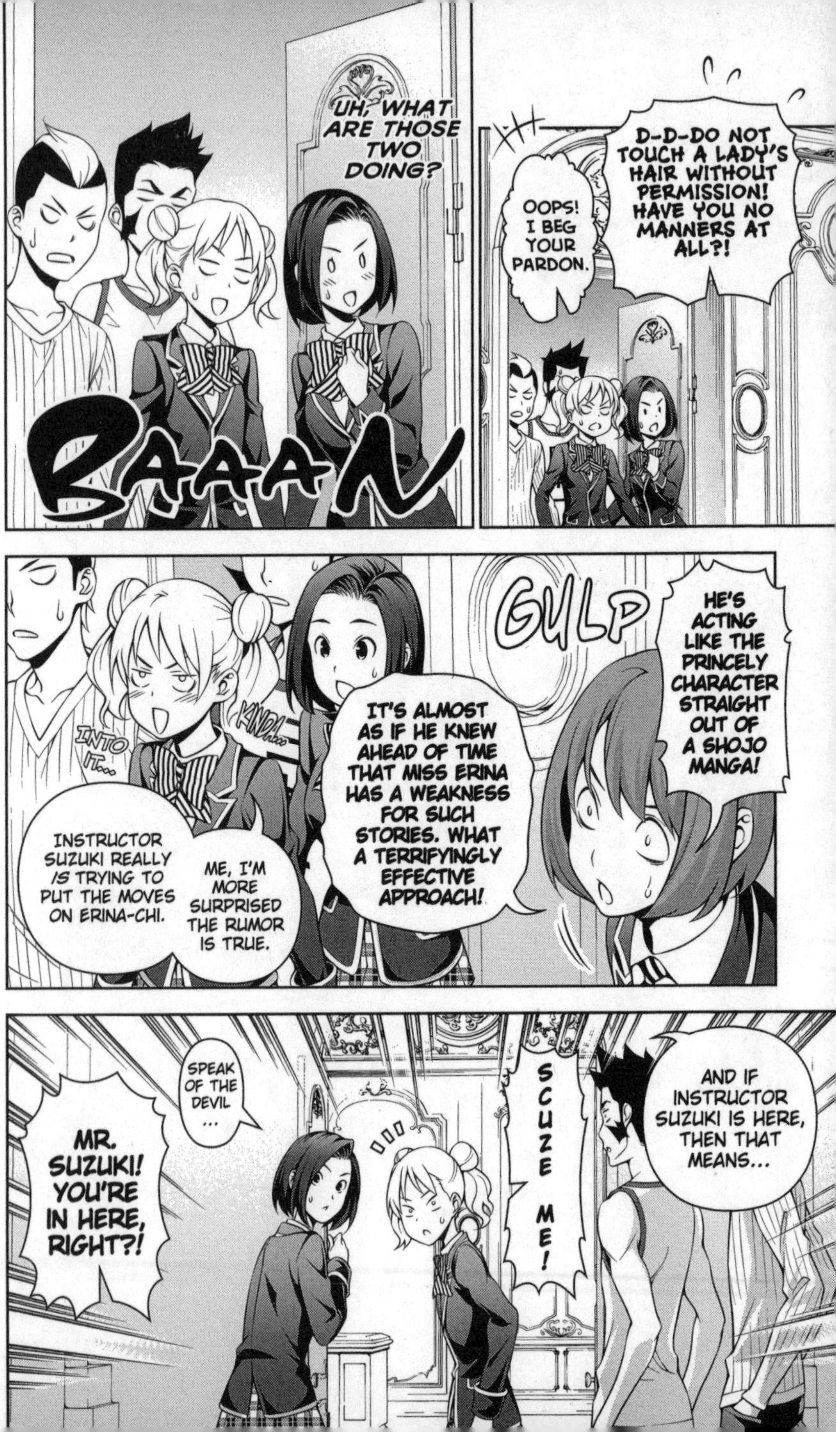
D-D-DO NOT TOUCH A LADY'S HAIR WITHOUT PERMISSION! HAVE YOU NO MANNERS AT ALL?!
OOPS! I BEG YOUR PARDON.
UH, WHAT ARE THOSE TWO DOING?
BAAAN
HE'S ACTING LIKE THE PRINCELY CHARACTER STRAIGHT OUT OF A SHOJO MANGA!
GULP
IT'S ALMOST AS IF HE KNEW AHEAD OF TIME THAT MISS ERINA HAS A WEAKNESS FOR SUCH STORIES. WHAT A TERRIFYINGLY EFFECTIVE APPROACH!
KINDA...
INTO IT...
ME, I'M MORE SURPRISED THE RUMOR IS TRUE.
INSTRUCTOR SUZUKI REALLY IS TRYING TO PUT THE MOVES ON ERINA-CHI.
AND IF INSTRUCTOR SUZUKI IS HERE, THEN THAT MEANS...
SCUZE ME!
SPEAK OF THE DEVIL...
MR. SUZUKI! YOU'RE IN HERE, RIGHT?!

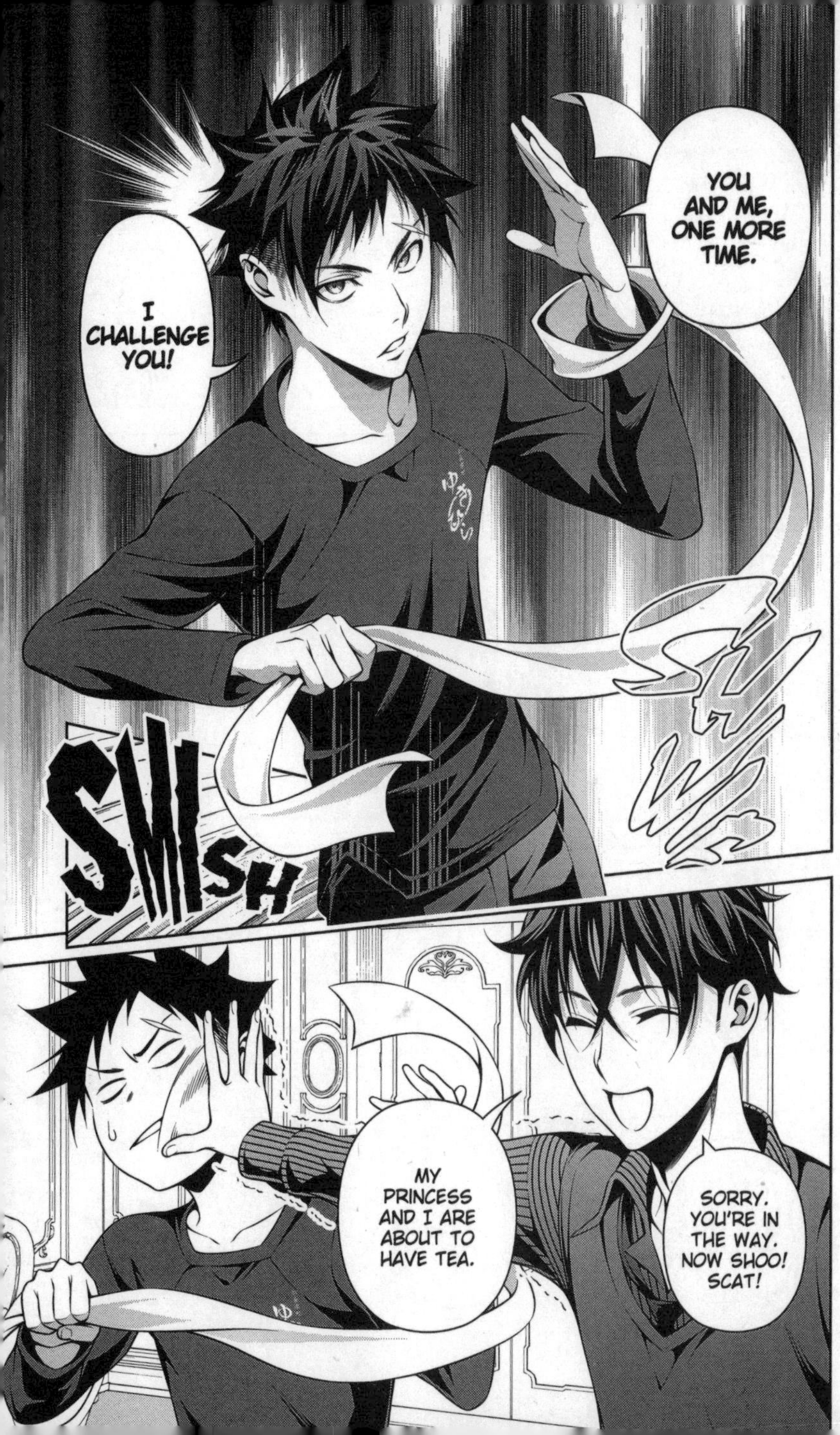
YOU AND ME, ONE MORE TIME.
I CHALLENGE YOU!
SMISH
SORRY. YOU'RE IN THE WAY. NOW SHOO! SCAT!
MY PRINCESS AND I ARE ABOUT TO HAVE TEA.

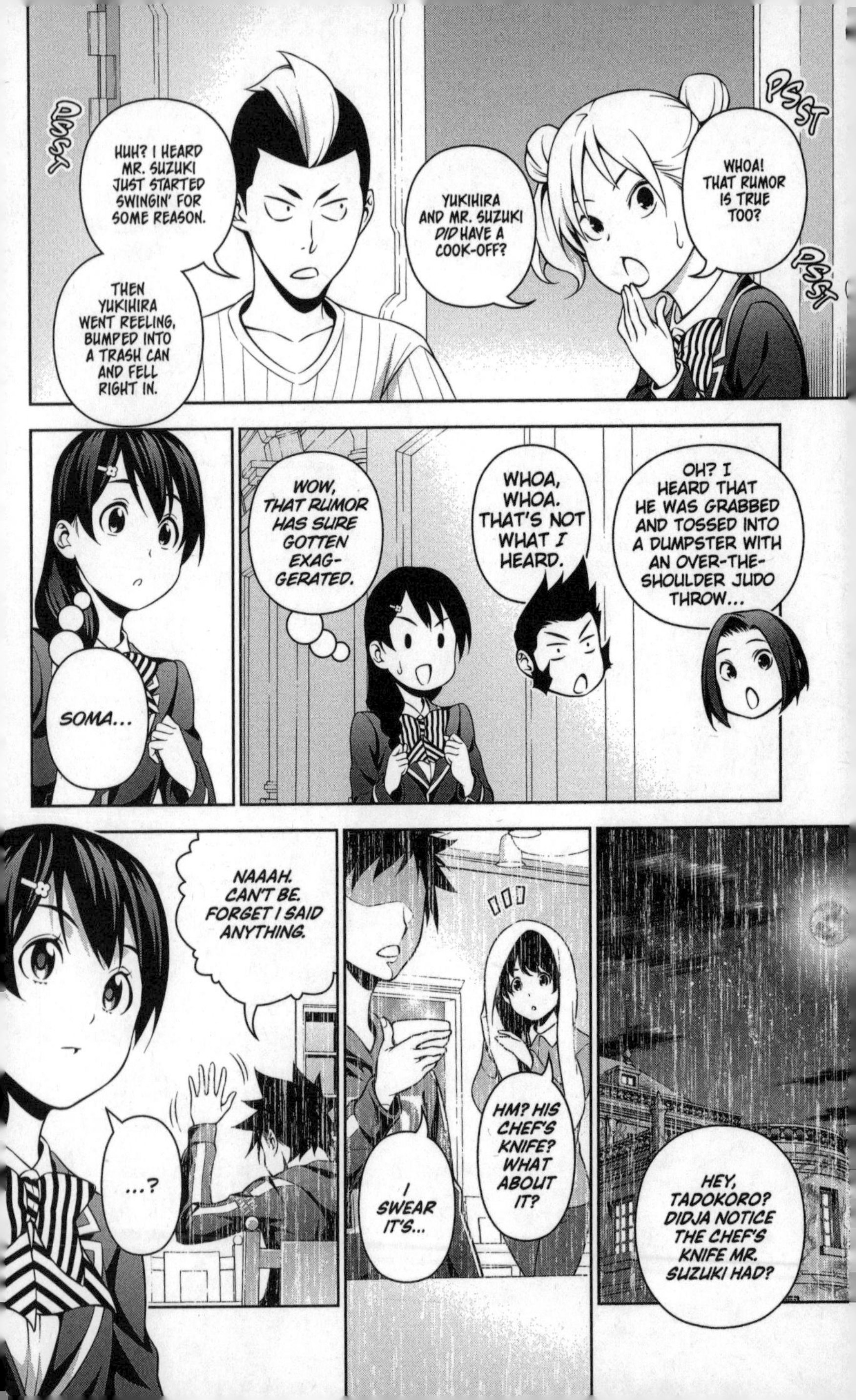
PSST
WHOA! THAT RUMOR IS TRUE TOO?
PSST
YUKIHIRA AND MR. SUZUKI *DID* HAVE A COOK-OFF?
PSST
HUH? I HEARD MR. SUZUKI JUST STARTED SWINGIN' FOR SOME REASON.
THEN YUKIHIRA WENT REELING, BUMPED INTO A TRASH CAN AND FELL RIGHT IN.
OH? I HEARD THAT HE WAS GRABBED AND TOSSED INTO A DUMPSTER WITH AN OVER-THE-SHOULDER JUDO THROW...
WHOA, WHOA. THAT'S NOT WHAT *I* HEARD.
WOW, THAT RUMOR HAS SURE GOTTEN EXAG-GERATED.
SOMA...
HEY, TADOKORO? DIDJA NOTICE THE CHEF'S KNIFE MR. SUZUKI HAD?
HM? HIS CHEF'S KNIFE? WHAT ABOUT IT?
I SWEAR IT'S...
NAAAH. CAN'T BE. FORGET I SAID ANYTHING.
...?

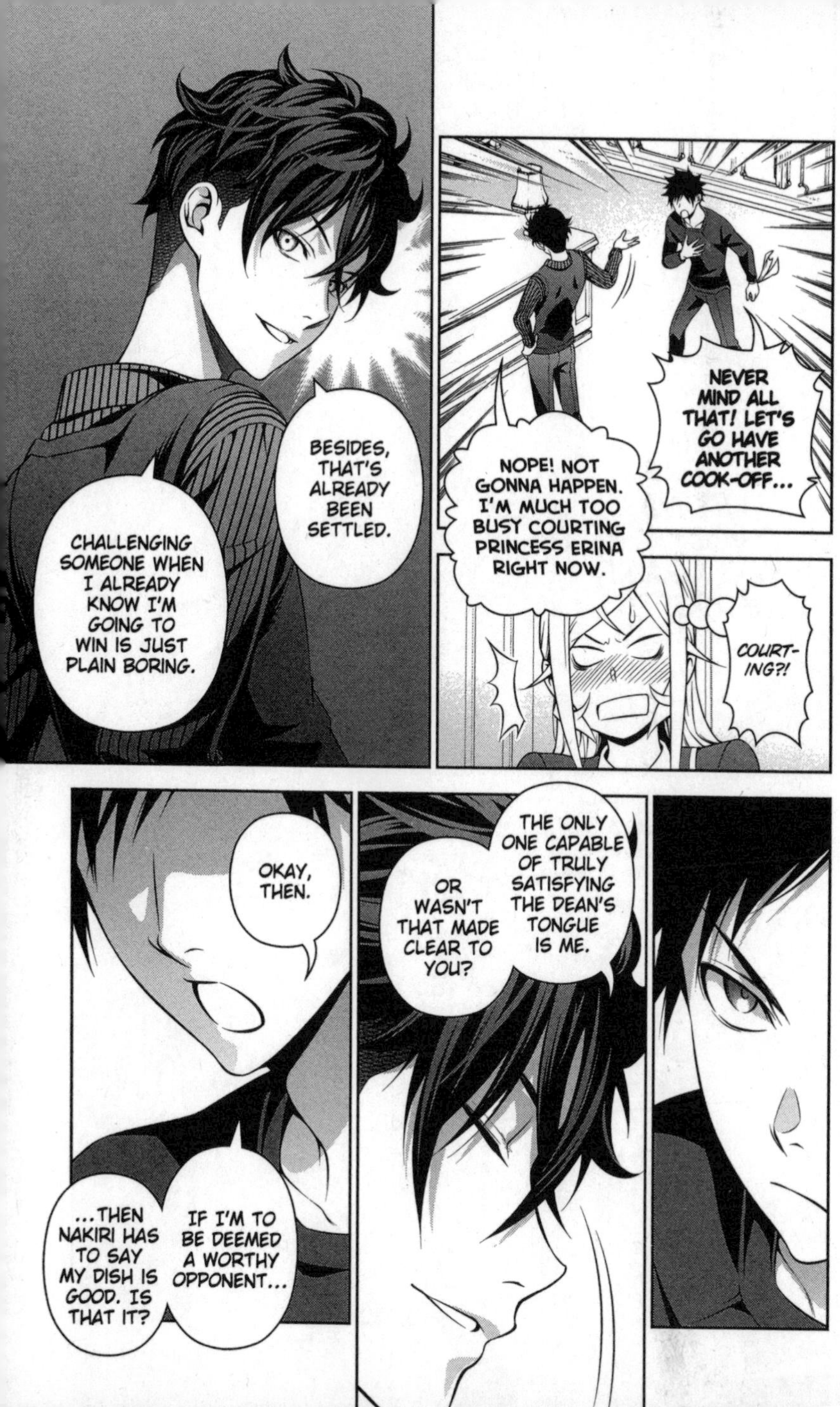
NEVER MIND ALL THAT! LET'S GO HAVE ANOTHER COOK-OFF...
NOPE! NOT GONNA HAPPEN. I'M MUCH TOO BUSY COURTING PRINCESS ERINA RIGHT NOW.
COURTING?!
BESIDES, THAT'S ALREADY BEEN SETTLED.
CHALLENGING SOMEONE WHEN I ALREADY KNOW I'M GOING TO WIN IS JUST PLAIN BORING.
THE ONLY ONE CAPABLE OF TRULY SATISFYING THE DEAN'S TONGUE IS ME.
OR WASN'T THAT MADE CLEAR TO YOU?
OKAY, THEN.
IF I'M TO BE DEEMED A WORTHY OPPONENT...
...THEN NAKIRI HAS TO SAY MY DISH IS GOOD. IS THAT IT?

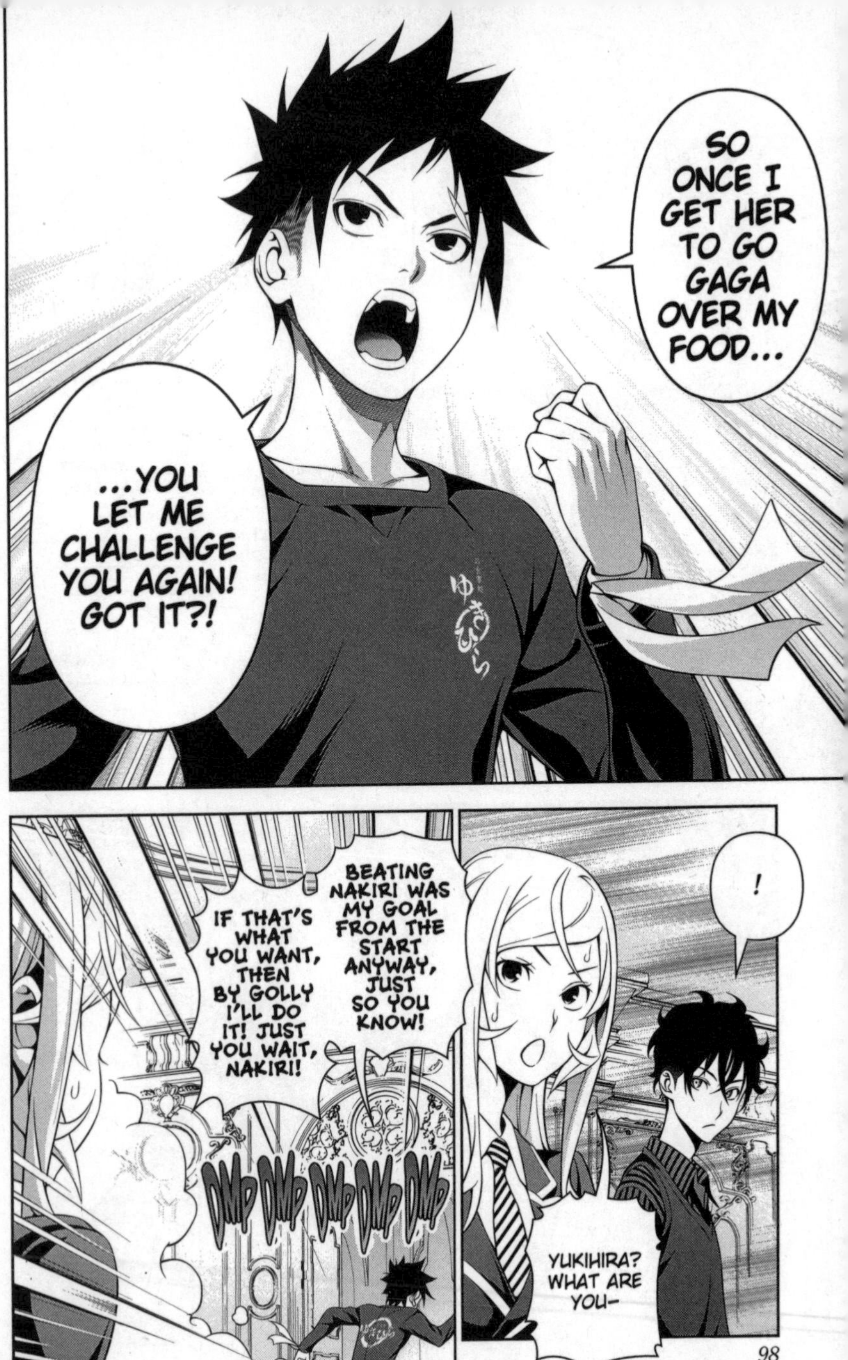
SO ONCE I GET HER TO GO GAGA OVER MY FOOD...
...YOU LET ME CHALLENGE YOU AGAIN! GOT IT?!
!
YUKIHIRA? WHAT ARE YOU-
BEATING NAKIRI WAS MY GOAL FROM THE START ANYWAY, JUST SO YOU KNOW!
IF THAT'S WHAT YOU WANT, THEN BY GOLLY I'LL DO IT! JUST YOU WAIT, NAKIRI!
DMP DMP DMP DMP DMP

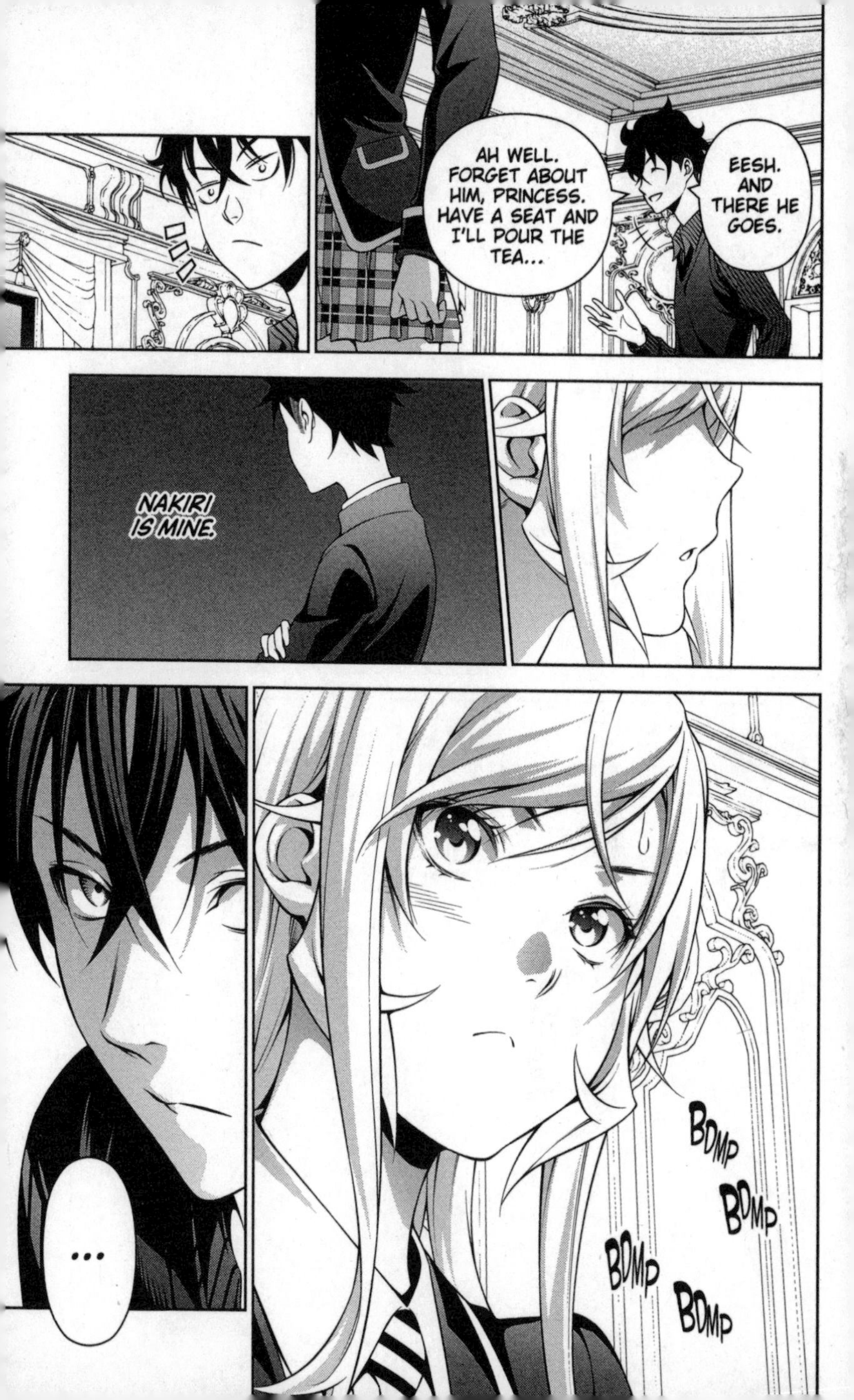
EESH. AND THERE HE GOES.
AH WELL. FORGET ABOUT HIM, PRINCESS. HAVE A SEAT AND I'LL POUR THE TEA...
NAKIRI IS MINE.
BDMP
BDMP
BDMP
BDMP
...

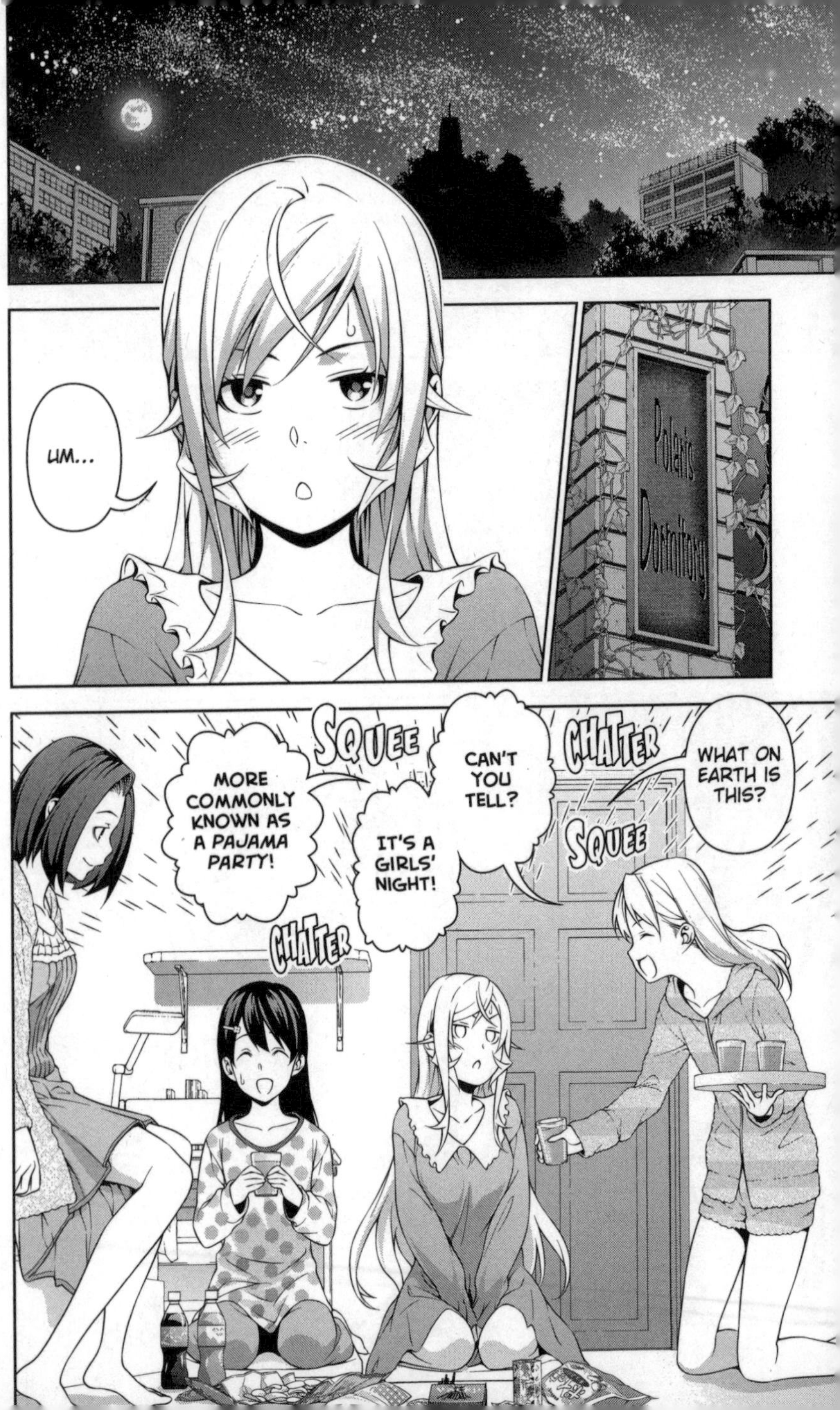
Polaris Dormitory
UM...
WHAT ON EARTH IS THIS?
CHATTER
SQUEE
CAN'T YOU TELL?
IT'S A GIRLS' NIGHT!
SQUEE
MORE COMMONLY KNOWN AS A PAJAMA PARTY!
CHATTER

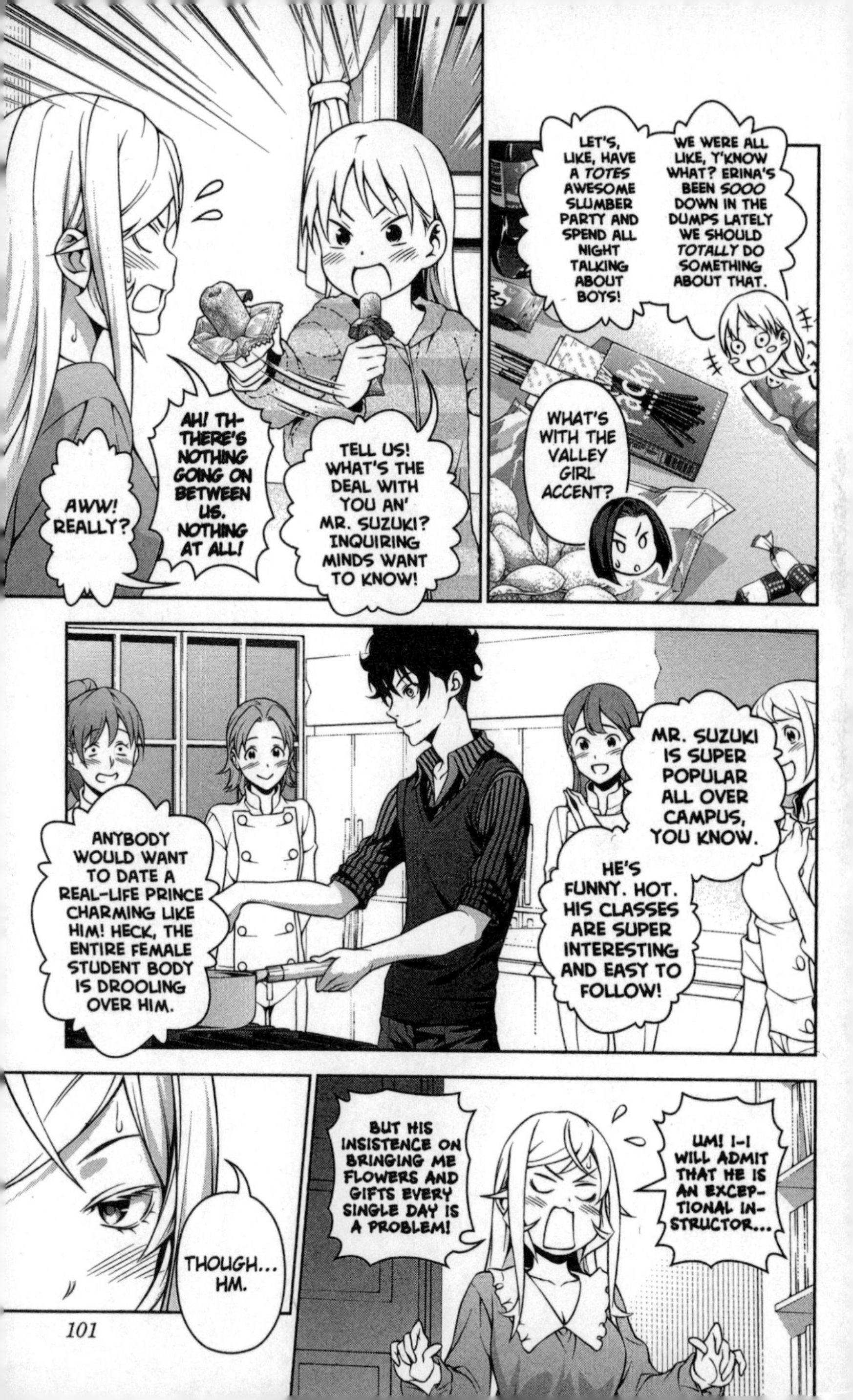
WE WERE ALL LIKE, Y'KNOW WHAT? ERINA'S BEEN *SOOO* DOWN IN THE DUMPS LATELY WE SHOULD *TOTALLY* DO SOMETHING ABOUT THAT.
LET'S, LIKE, HAVE A *TOTES* AWESOME SLUMBER PARTY AND SPEND ALL NIGHT TALKING ABOUT BOYS!
WHAT'S WITH THE VALLEY GIRL ACCENT?
TELL US! WHAT'S THE DEAL WITH YOU AN' MR. SUZUKI? INQUIRING MINDS WANT TO KNOW!
AH! TH-THERE'S NOTHING GOING ON BETWEEN US. NOTHING AT ALL!
AWW! REALLY?
MR. SUZUKI IS SUPER POPULAR ALL OVER CAMPUS, YOU KNOW.
HE'S FUNNY. HOT. HIS CLASSES ARE SUPER INTERESTING AND EASY TO FOLLOW!
ANYBODY WOULD WANT TO DATE A REAL-LIFE PRINCE CHARMING LIKE HIM! HECK, THE ENTIRE FEMALE STUDENT BODY IS DROOLING OVER HIM.
UM! I-I WILL ADMIT THAT HE IS AN EXCEPTIONAL INSTRUCTOR...
BUT HIS INSISTENCE ON BRINGING ME FLOWERS AND GIFTS EVERY SINGLE DAY IS A PROBLEM!
THOUGH... HM.

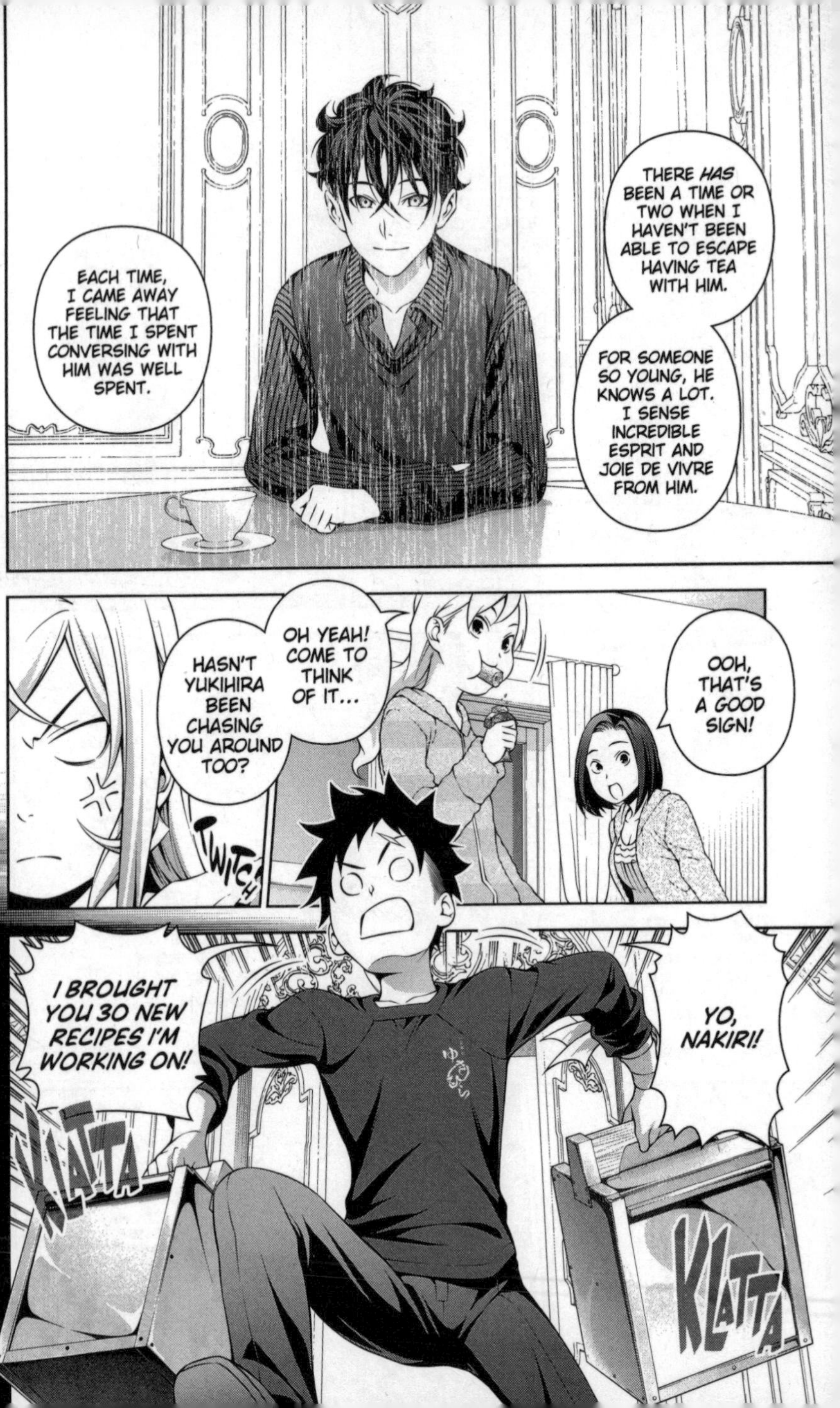
THERE *HAS* BEEN A TIME OR TWO WHEN I HAVEN'T BEEN ABLE TO ESCAPE HAVING TEA WITH HIM.
FOR SOMEONE SO YOUNG, HE KNOWS A LOT. I SENSE INCREDIBLE ESPRIT AND JOIE DE VIVRE FROM HIM.
EACH TIME, I CAME AWAY FEELING THAT THE TIME I SPENT CONVERSING WITH HIM WAS WELL SPENT.
OOH, THAT'S A GOOD SIGN!
OH YEAH! COME TO THINK OF IT...
HASN'T YUKIHIRA BEEN CHASING YOU AROUND TOO?
TWITCH
YO, NAKIRI!
I BROUGHT YOU 30 NEW RECIPES I'M WORKING ON!
KLATTA
KLATTA

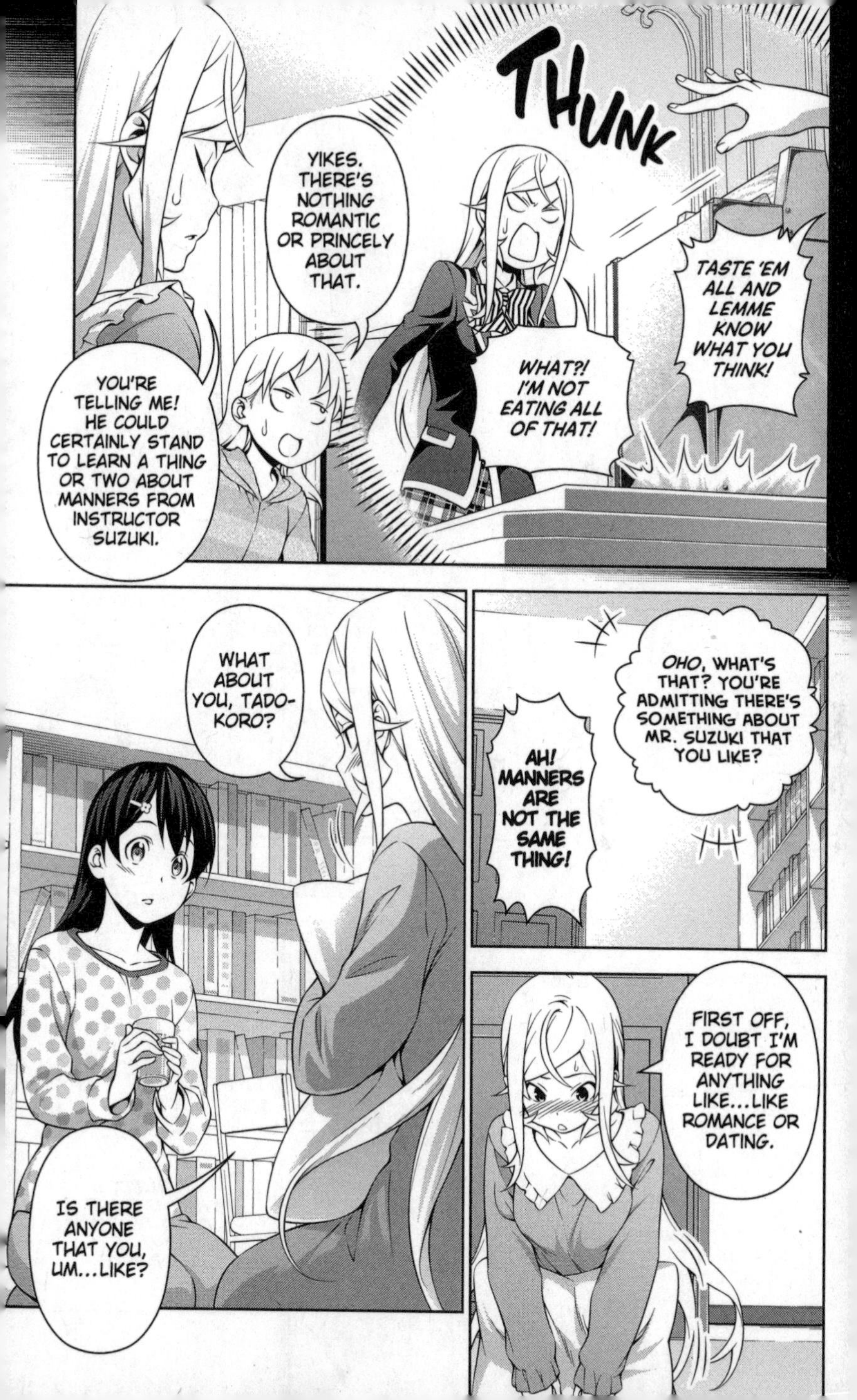
THUNK
TASTE 'EM ALL AND LEMME KNOW WHAT YOU THINK!
WHAT?! I'M NOT EATING ALL OF THAT!
YIKES. THERE'S NOTHING ROMANTIC OR PRINCELY ABOUT THAT.
YOU'RE TELLING ME! HE COULD CERTAINLY STAND TO LEARN A THING OR TWO ABOUT MANNERS FROM INSTRUCTOR SUZUKI.
OHO, WHAT'S THAT? YOU'RE ADMITTING THERE'S SOMETHING ABOUT MR. SUZUKI THAT YOU LIKE?
AH! MANNERS ARE NOT THE SAME THING!
WHAT ABOUT YOU, TADO-KORO?
IS THERE ANYONE THAT YOU, UM...LIKE?
FIRST OFF, I DOUBT I'M READY FOR ANYTHING LIKE...LIKE ROMANCE OR DATING.

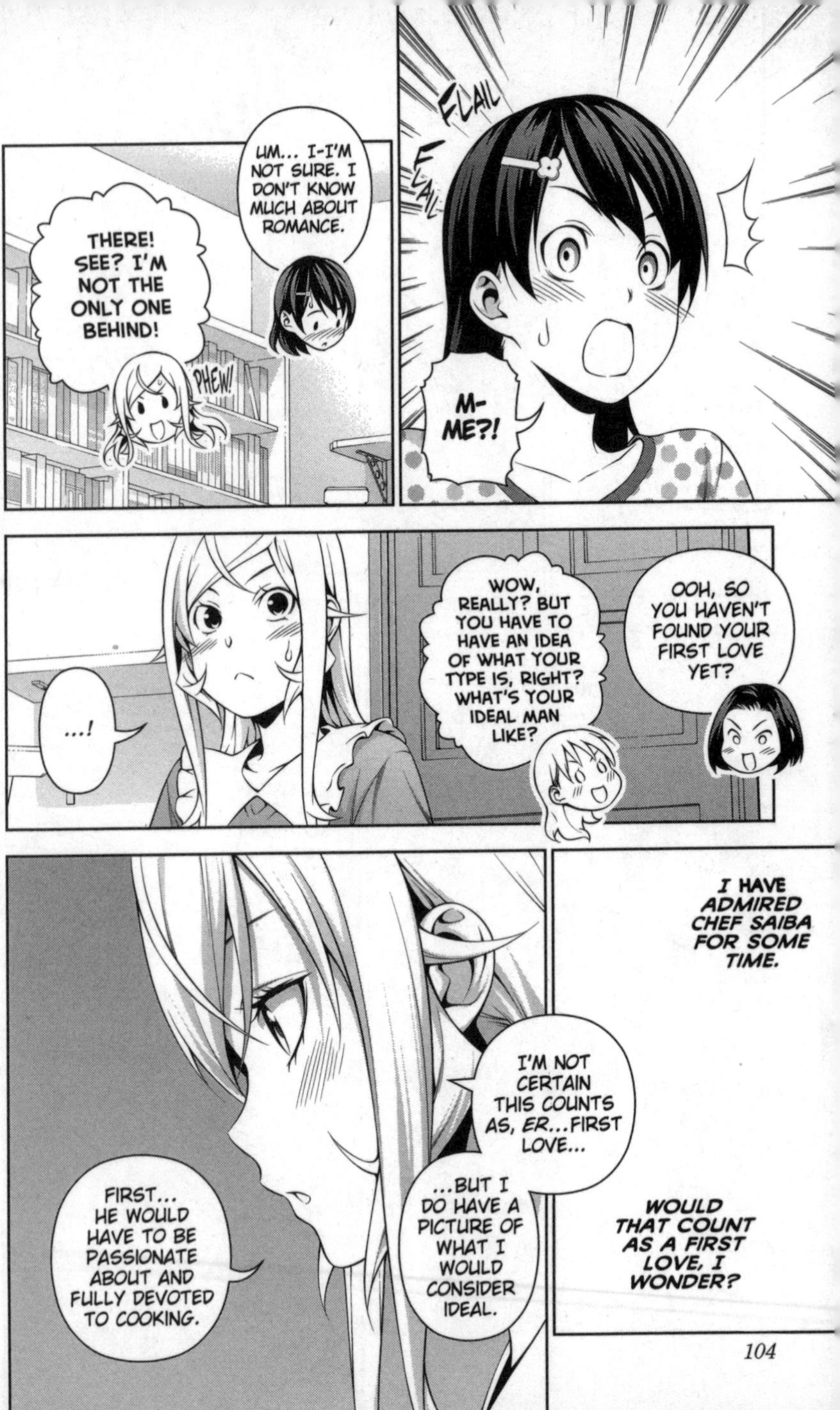
FLAIL
FLAIL
M-ME?!
UM... I-I'M NOT SURE. I DON'T KNOW MUCH ABOUT ROMANCE.
THERE! SEE? I'M NOT THE ONLY ONE BEHIND!
PHEW!
OOH, SO YOU HAVEN'T FOUND YOUR FIRST LOVE YET?
WOW, REALLY? BUT YOU HAVE TO HAVE AN IDEA OF WHAT YOUR TYPE IS, RIGHT? WHAT'S YOUR IDEAL MAN LIKE?
...!
I HAVE ADMIRED CHEF SAIBA FOR SOME TIME.
WOULD THAT COUNT AS A FIRST LOVE, I WONDER?
I'M NOT CERTAIN THIS COUNTS AS, ER...FIRST LOVE...
...BUT I DO HAVE A PICTURE OF WHAT I WOULD CONSIDER IDEAL.
FIRST... HE WOULD HAVE TO BE PASSIONATE ABOUT AND FULLY DEVOTED TO COOKING.

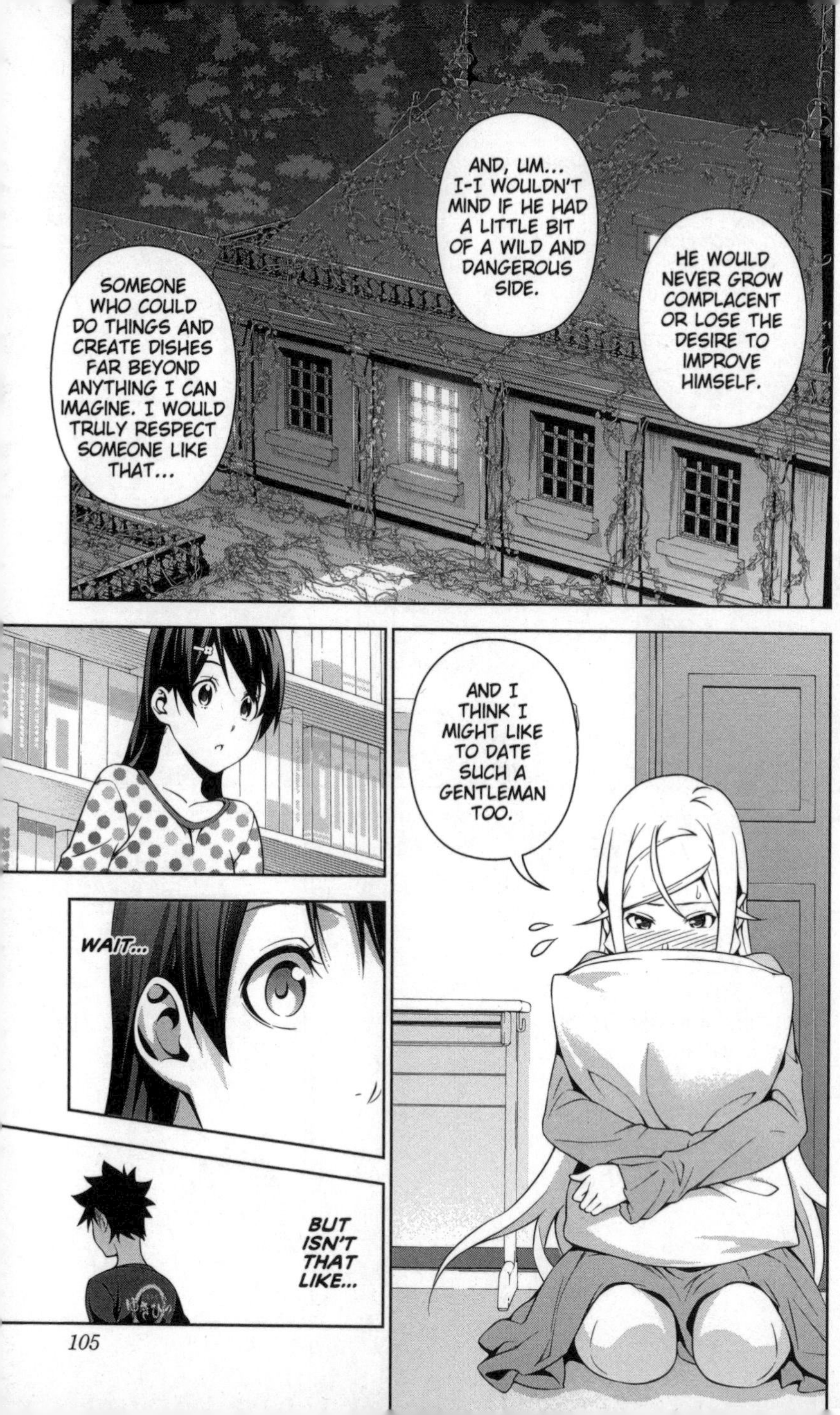
HE WOULD NEVER GROW COMPLACENT OR LOSE THE DESIRE TO IMPROVE HIMSELF.
AND, UM... I-I WOULDN'T MIND IF HE HAD A LITTLE BIT OF A WILD AND DANGEROUS SIDE.
SOMEONE WHO COULD DO THINGS AND CREATE DISHES FAR BEYOND ANYTHING I CAN IMAGINE. I WOULD TRULY RESPECT SOMEONE LIKE THAT...
AND I THINK I MIGHT LIKE TO DATE SUCH A GENTLEMAN TOO.
WAIT...
BUT ISN'T THAT LIKE...

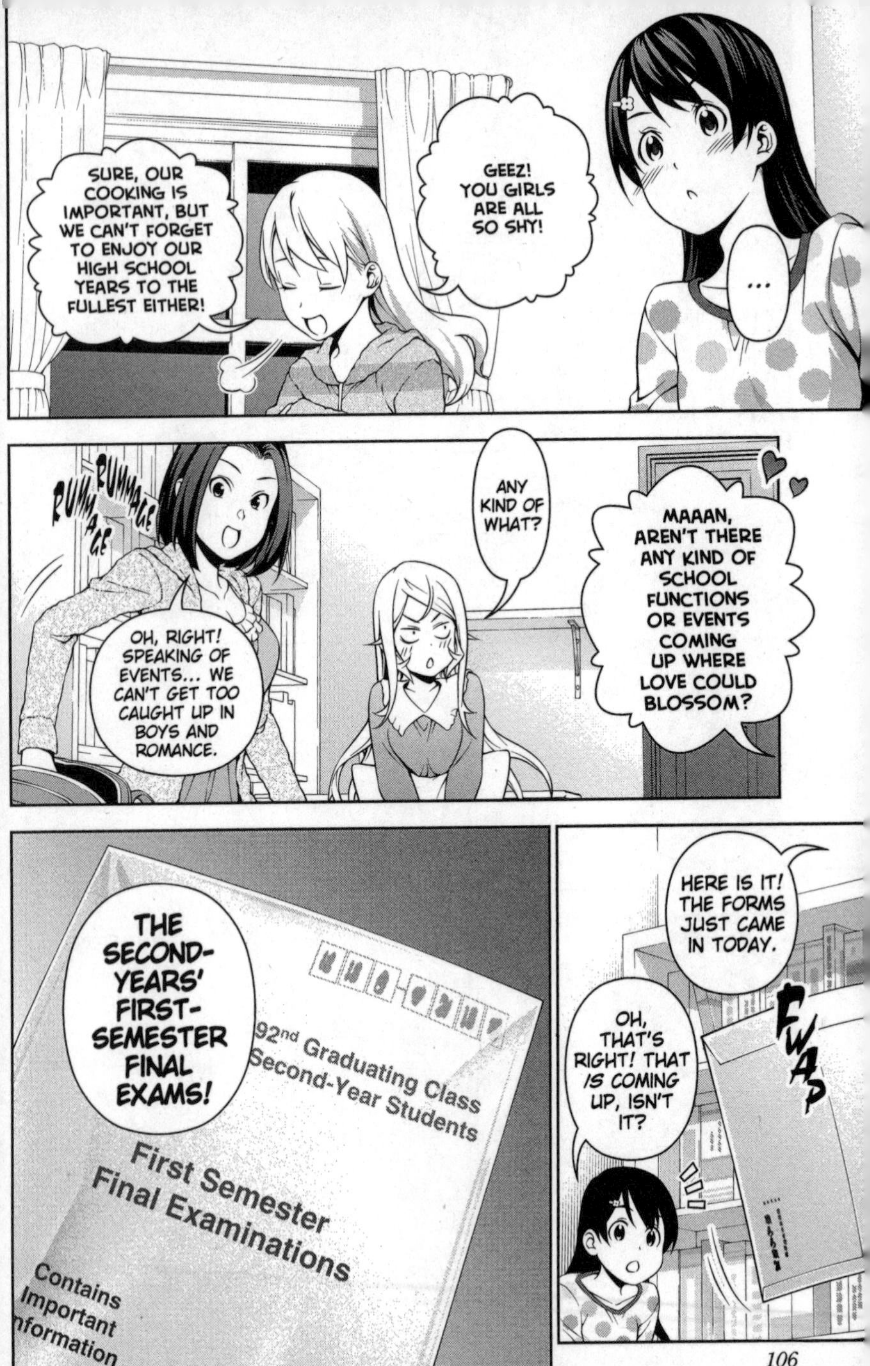
...
GEEZ! YOU GIRLS ARE ALL SO SHY!
SURE, OUR COOKING IS IMPORTANT, BUT WE CAN'T FORGET TO ENJOY OUR HIGH SCHOOL YEARS TO THE FULLEST EITHER!
MAAAN, AREN'T THERE ANY KIND OF SCHOOL FUNCTIONS OR EVENTS COMING UP WHERE LOVE COULD BLOSSOM?
ANY KIND OF WHAT?
RUMMAGE RUMMAGE
OH, RIGHT! SPEAKING OF EVENTS... WE CAN'T GET TOO CAUGHT UP IN BOYS AND ROMANCE.
HERE IS IT! THE FORMS JUST CAME IN TODAY.
FWAP
OH, THAT'S RIGHT! THAT *IS* COMING UP, ISN'T IT?
THE SECOND-YEARS' FIRST-SEMESTER FINAL EXAMS!
92nd Graduating Class
Second-Year Students
First Semester
Final Examinations
Contains
Important
nformation

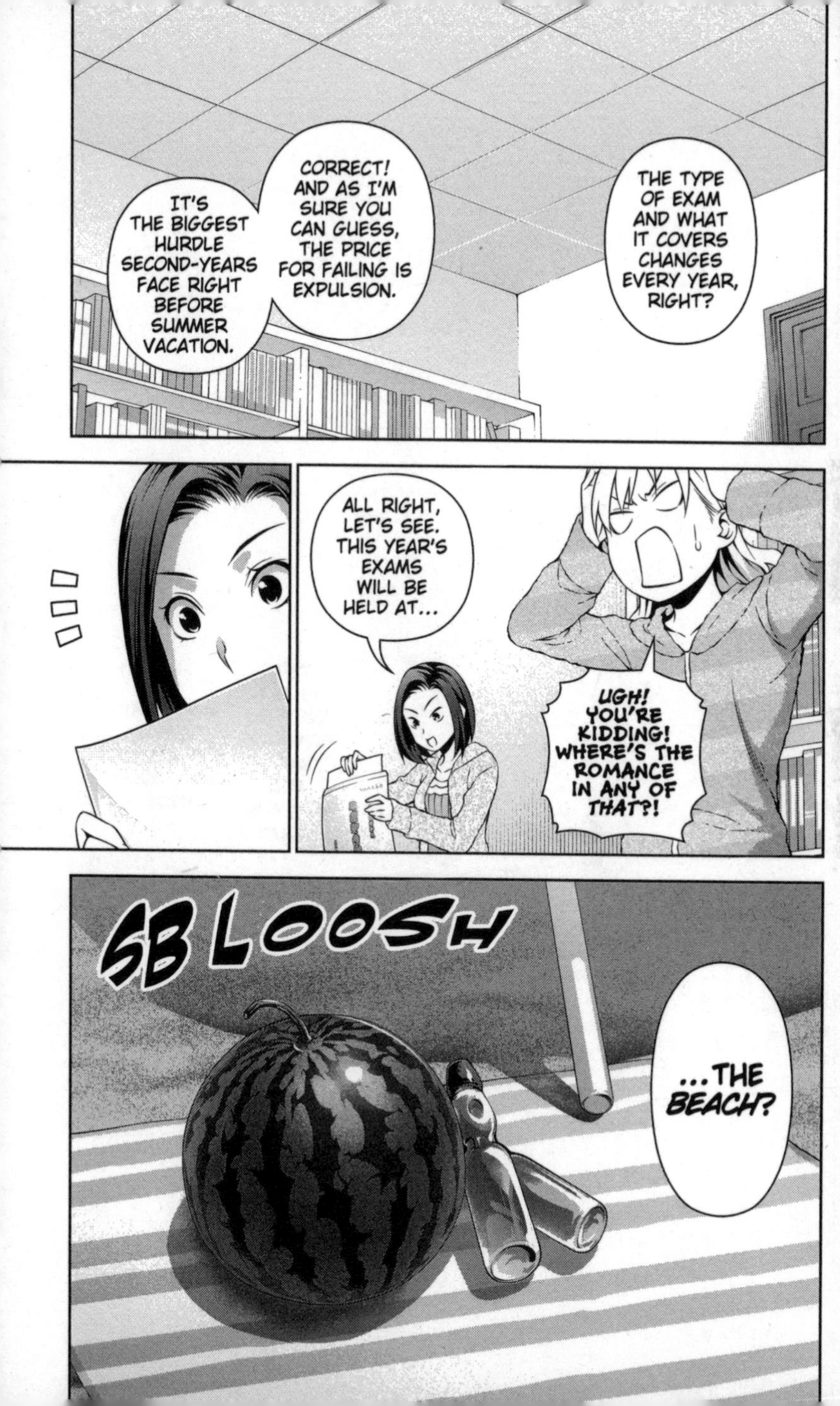
THE TYPE OF EXAM AND WHAT IT COVERS CHANGES EVERY YEAR, RIGHT?
CORRECT! AND AS I'M SURE YOU CAN GUESS, THE PRICE FOR FAILING IS EXPULSION.
IT'S THE BIGGEST HURDLE SECOND-YEARS FACE RIGHT BEFORE SUMMER VACATION.
UGH! YOU'RE KIDDING! WHERE'S THE ROMANCE IN ANY OF THAT?!
ALL RIGHT, LET'S SEE. THIS YEAR'S EXAMS WILL BE HELD AT...
SBLOOSH
...THE BEACH?

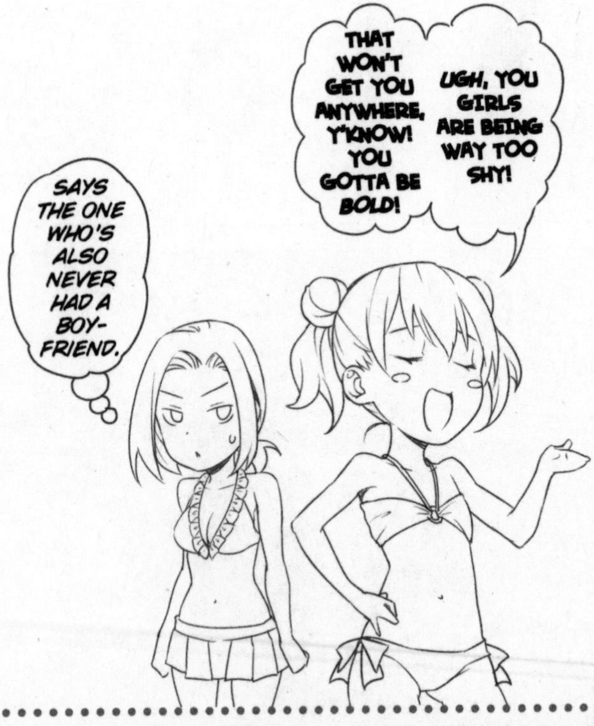
UGH, YOU GIRLS ARE BEING WAY TOO SHY!
THAT WON'T GET YOU ANYWHERE, Y'KNOW! YOU GOTTA BE BOLD!
SAYS THE ONE WHO'S ALSO NEVER HAD A BOY-FRIEND.

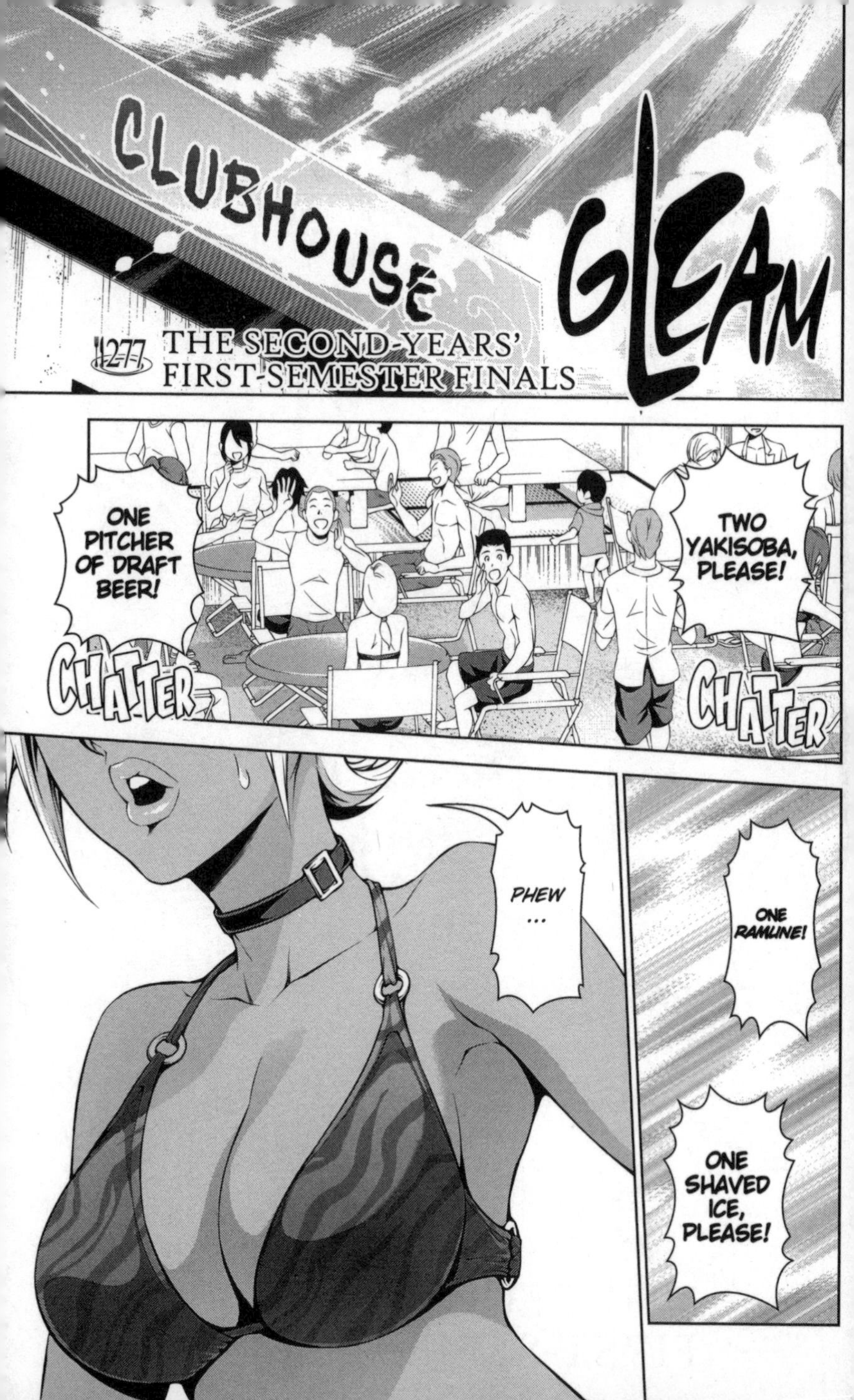
GLEAM
CLUBHOUSE
277 THE SECOND-YEARS' FIRST-SEMESTER FINALS
TWO YAKISOBA, PLEASE!
CHATTER
ONE PITCHER OF DRAFT BEER!
CHATTER
ONE RAMUNE!
ONE SHAVED ICE, PLEASE!
PHEW ...

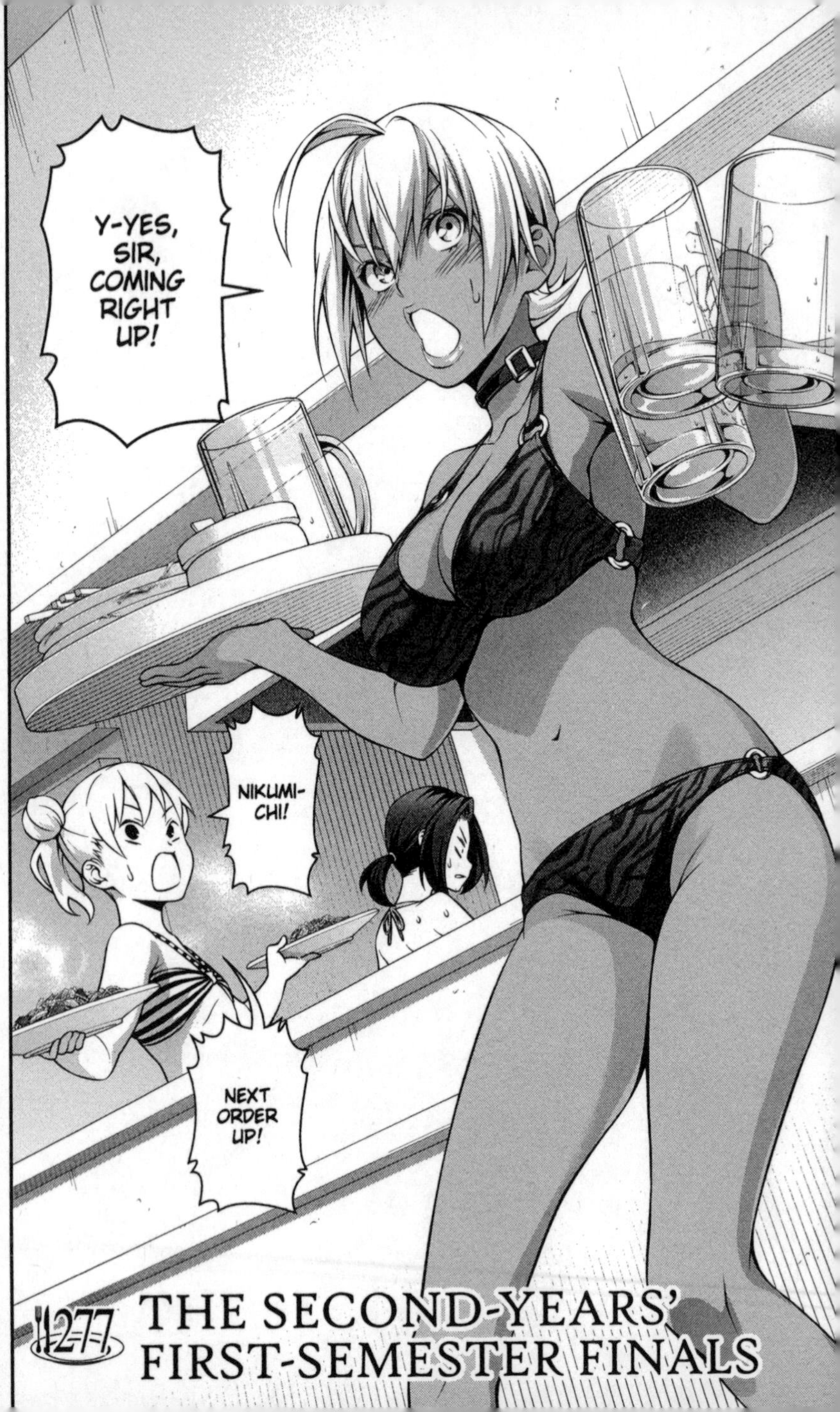
Y-YES, SIR, COMING RIGHT UP!
NIKUMI-CHI!
NEXT ORDER UP!

277 THE SECOND-YEARS' FIRST-SEMESTER FINALS

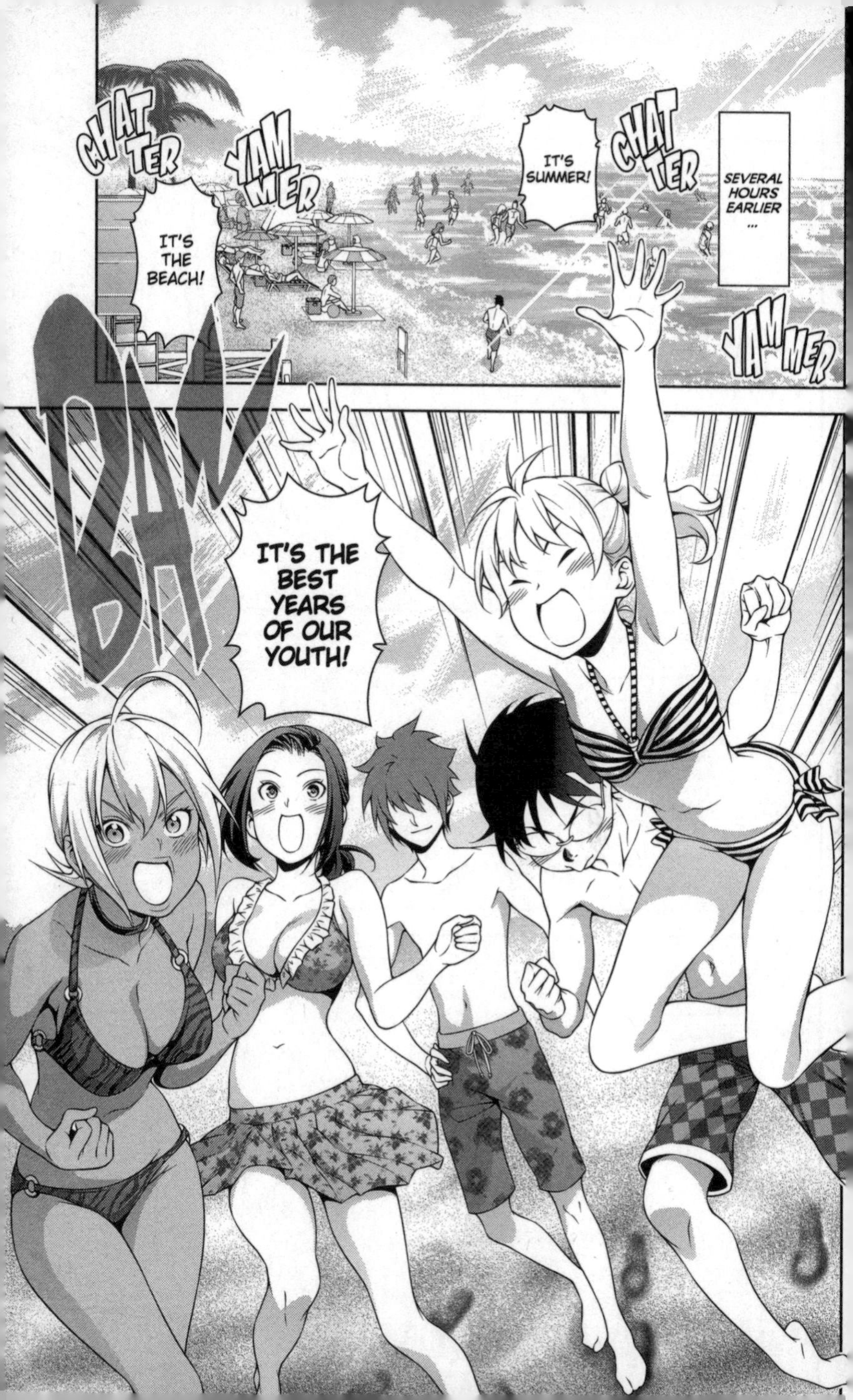
SEVERAL HOURS EARLIER ...
YAMMER
CHATTER
IT'S SUMMER!
YAMMER
CHATTER
IT'S THE BEACH!
IT'S THE BEST YEARS OF OUR YOUTH!

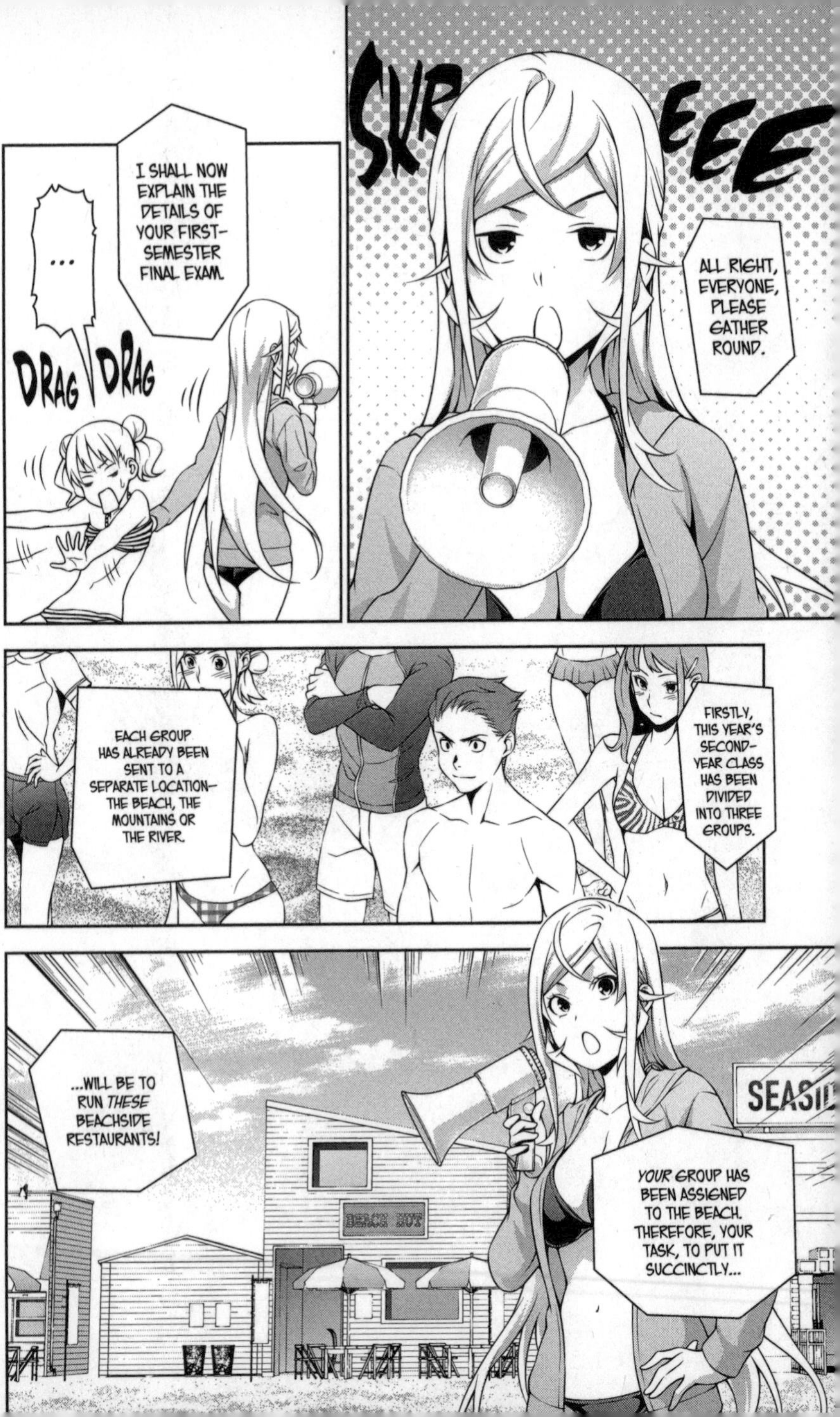
SKR
EEE
ALL RIGHT, EVERYONE, PLEASE GATHER ROUND.
I SHALL NOW EXPLAIN THE DETAILS OF YOUR FIRST-SEMESTER FINAL EXAM.
...
DRAG DRAG
FIRSTLY, THIS YEAR'S SECOND-YEAR CLASS HAS BEEN DIVIDED INTO THREE GROUPS.
EACH GROUP HAS ALREADY BEEN SENT TO A SEPARATE LOCATION— THE BEACH, THE MOUNTAINS OR THE RIVER.
SEASID
YOUR GROUP HAS BEEN ASSIGNED TO THE BEACH. THEREFORE, YOUR TASK, TO PUT IT SUCCINCTLY...
...WILL BE TO RUN THESE BEACHSIDE RESTAURANTS!

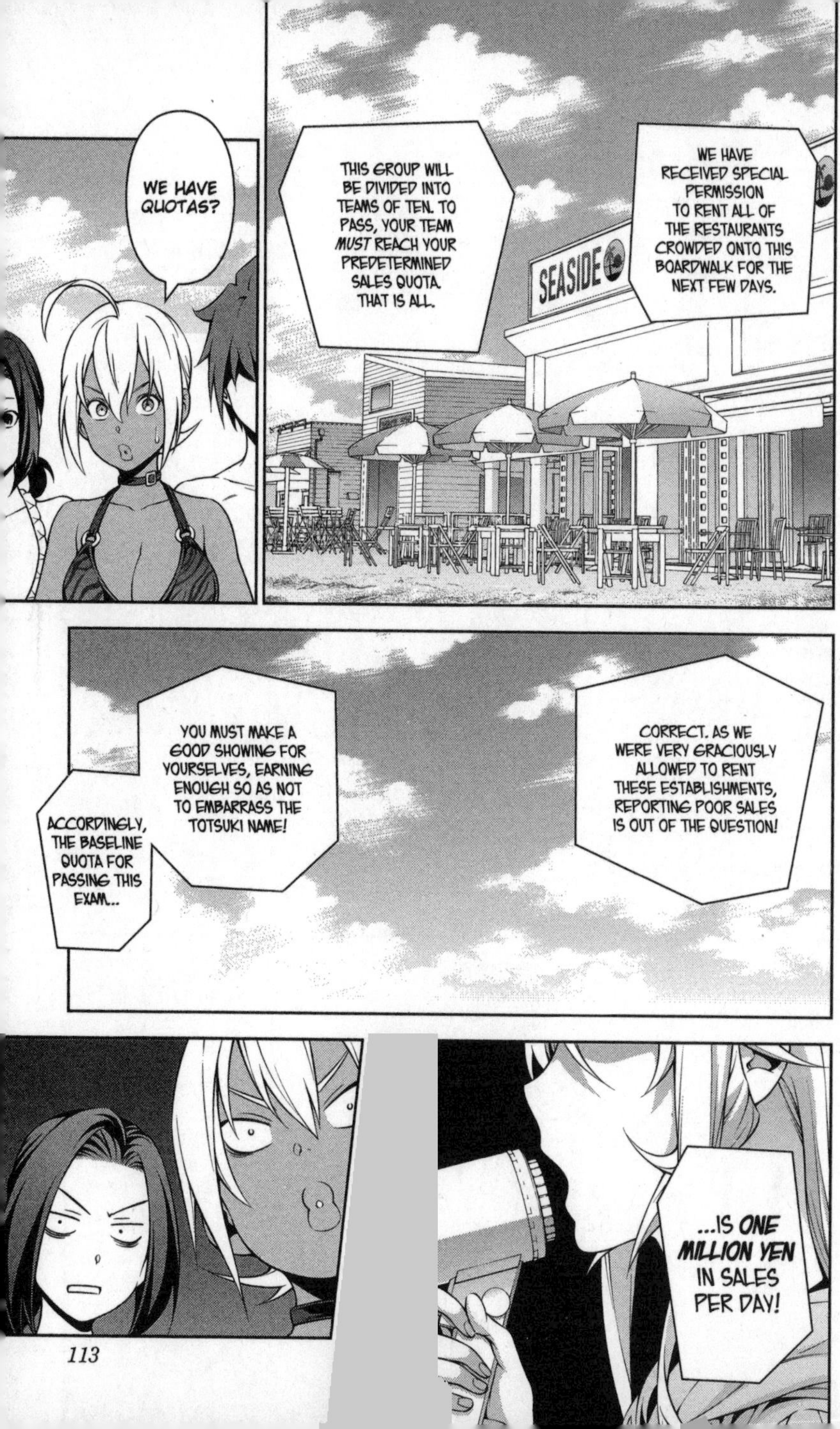
WE HAVE RECEIVED SPECIAL PERMISSION TO RENT ALL OF THE RESTAURANTS CROWDED ONTO THIS BOARDWALK FOR THE NEXT FEW DAYS.
SEASIDE
THIS GROUP WILL BE DIVIDED INTO TEAMS OF TEN. TO PASS, YOUR TEAM *MUST* REACH YOUR PREDETERMINED SALES QUOTA. THAT IS ALL.
WE HAVE QUOTAS?
CORRECT. AS WE WERE VERY GRACIOUSLY ALLOWED TO RENT THESE ESTABLISHMENTS, REPORTING POOR SALES IS OUT OF THE QUESTION!
YOU MUST MAKE A GOOD SHOWING FOR YOURSELVES, EARNING ENOUGH SO AS NOT TO EMBARRASS THE TOTSUKI NAME!
ACCORDINGLY, THE BASELINE QUOTA FOR PASSING THIS EXAM...
...IS ***ONE MILLION YEN*** IN SALES PER DAY!

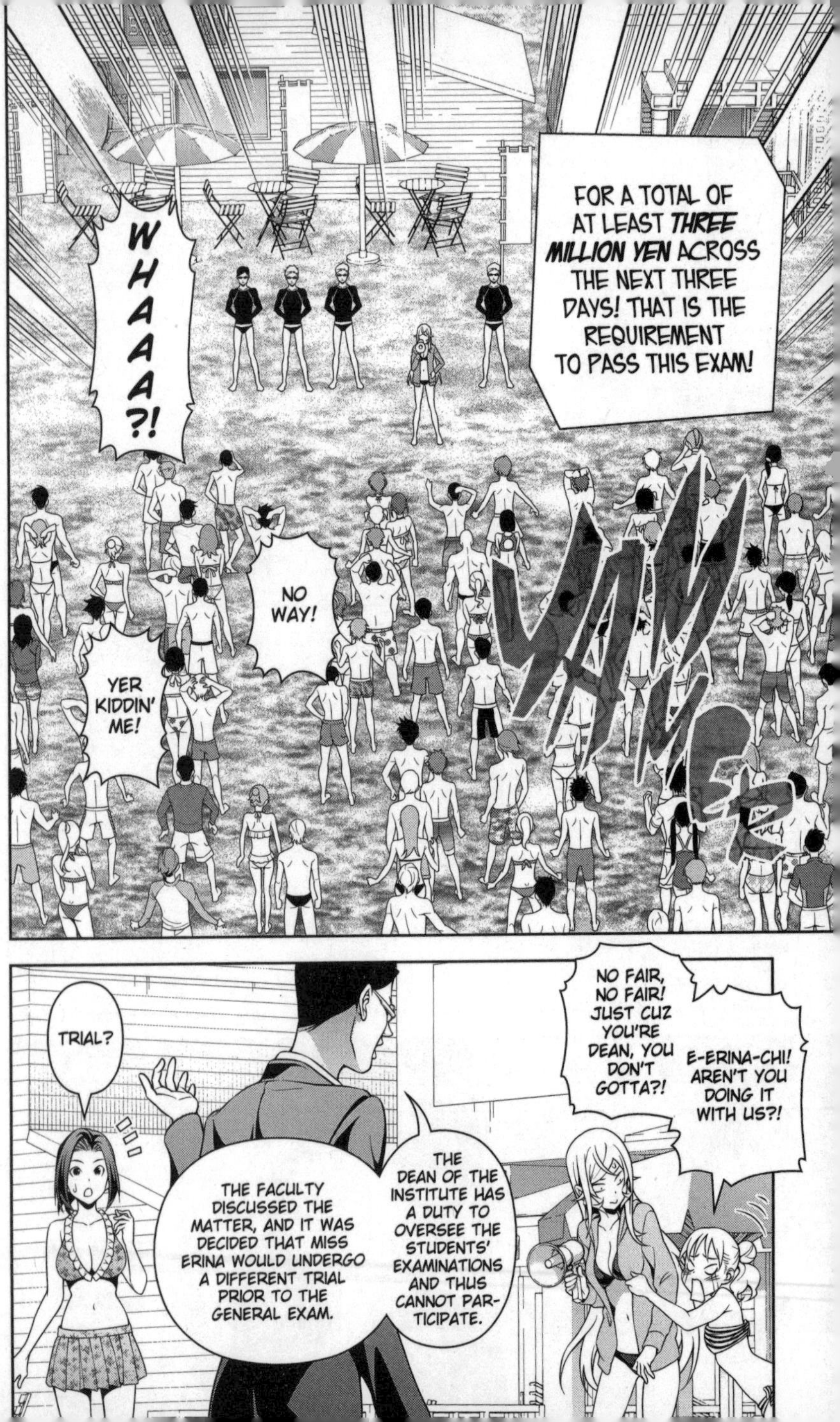
FOR A TOTAL OF AT LEAST THREE MILLION YEN ACROSS THE NEXT THREE DAYS! THAT IS THE REQUIREMENT TO PASS THIS EXAM!
WHAAAA?!
NO WAY!
YER KIDDIN' ME!
E-ERINA-CHI! AREN'T YOU DOING IT WITH US?!
NO FAIR, NO FAIR! JUST CUZ YOU'RE DEAN, YOU DON'T GOTTA?!
THE DEAN OF THE INSTITUTE HAS A DUTY TO OVERSEE THE STUDENTS' EXAMINATIONS AND THUS CANNOT PARTICIPATE.
THE FACULTY DISCUSSED THE MATTER, AND IT WAS DECIDED THAT MISS ERINA WOULD UNDERGO A DIFFERENT TRIAL PRIOR TO THE GENERAL EXAM.
TRIAL?

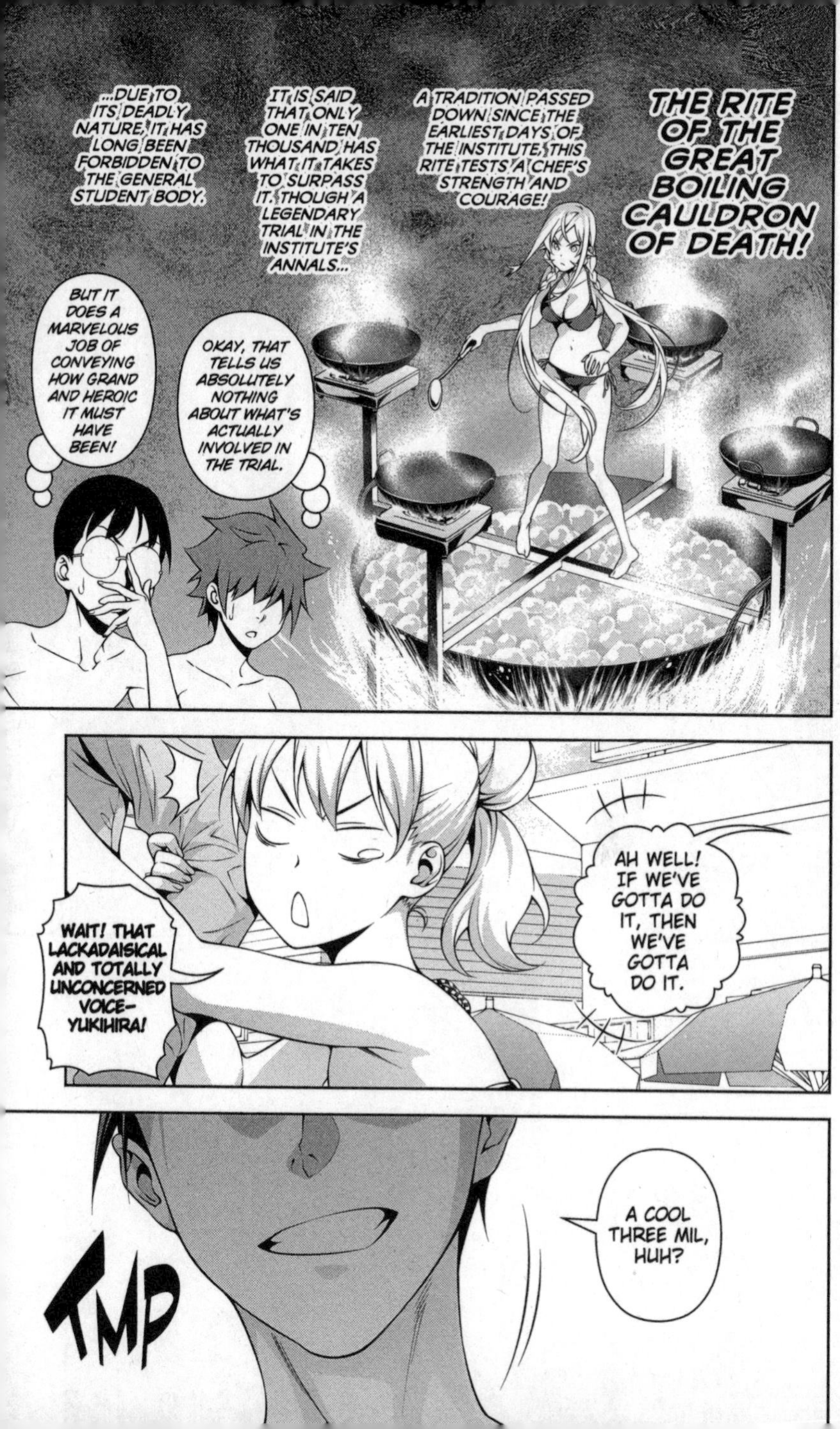
THE RITE OF THE GREAT BOILING CAULDRON OF DEATH!
A TRADITION PASSED DOWN SINCE THE EARLIEST DAYS OF THE INSTITUTE, THIS RITE TESTS A CHEF'S STRENGTH AND COURAGE!
IT IS SAID THAT ONLY ONE IN TEN THOUSAND HAS WHAT IT TAKES TO SURPASS IT. THOUGH A LEGENDARY TRIAL IN THE INSTITUTE'S ANNALS...
...DUE TO ITS DEADLY NATURE, IT HAS LONG BEEN FORBIDDEN TO THE GENERAL STUDENT BODY.
OKAY, THAT TELLS US ABSOLUTELY NOTHING ABOUT WHAT'S ACTUALLY INVOLVED IN THE TRIAL.
BUT IT DOES A MARVELOUS JOB OF CONVEYING HOW GRAND AND HEROIC IT MUST HAVE BEEN!
AH WELL! IF WE'VE GOTTA DO IT, THEN WE'VE GOTTA DO IT.
WAIT! THAT LACKADAISICAL AND TOTALLY UNCONCERNED VOICE- YUKIHIRA!
A COOL THREE MIL, HUH?
TMP

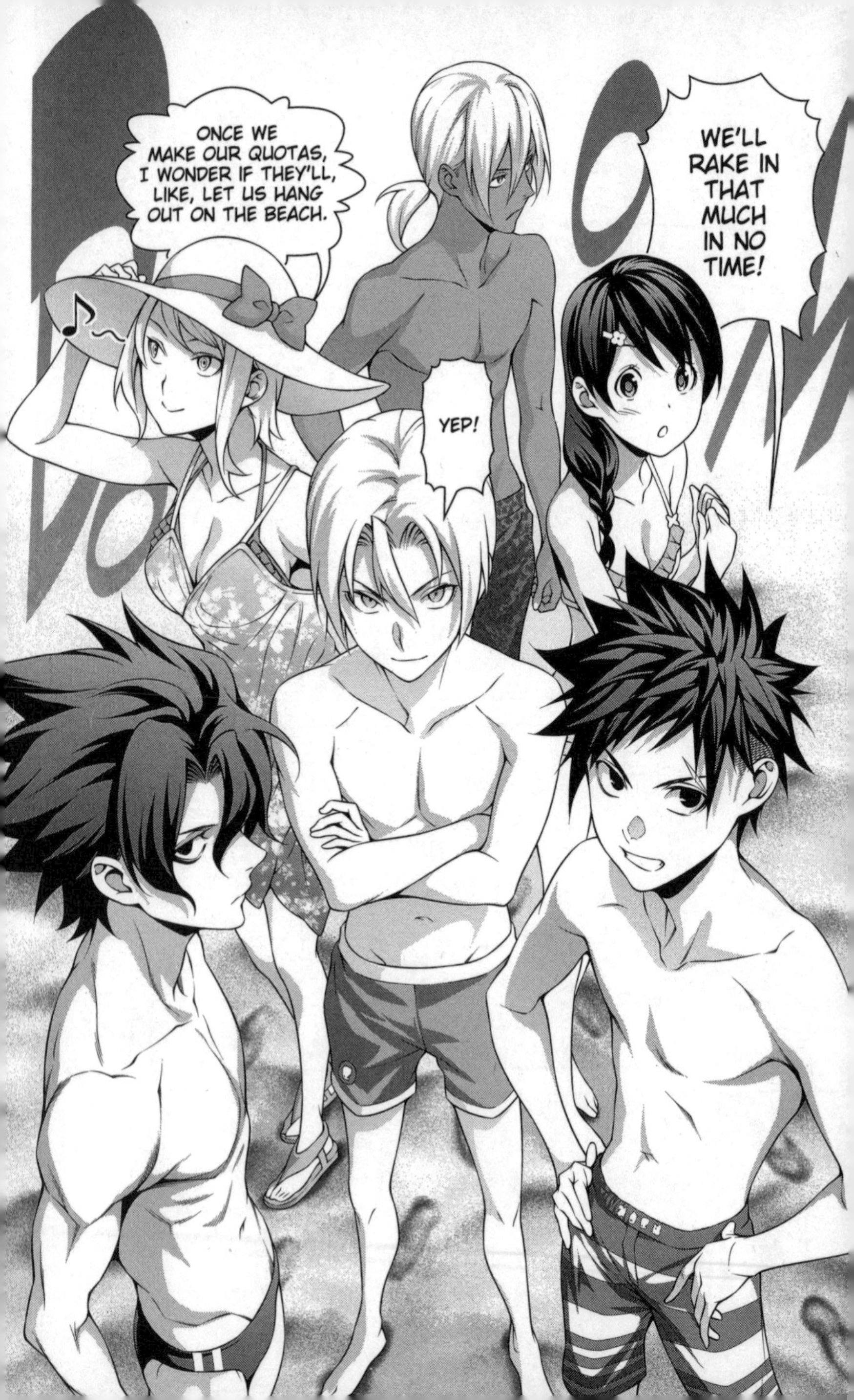
WE'LL RAKE IN THAT MUCH IN NO TIME!
ONCE WE MAKE OUR QUOTAS, I WONDER IF THEY'LL, LIKE, LET US HANG OUT ON THE BEACH.
YEP!

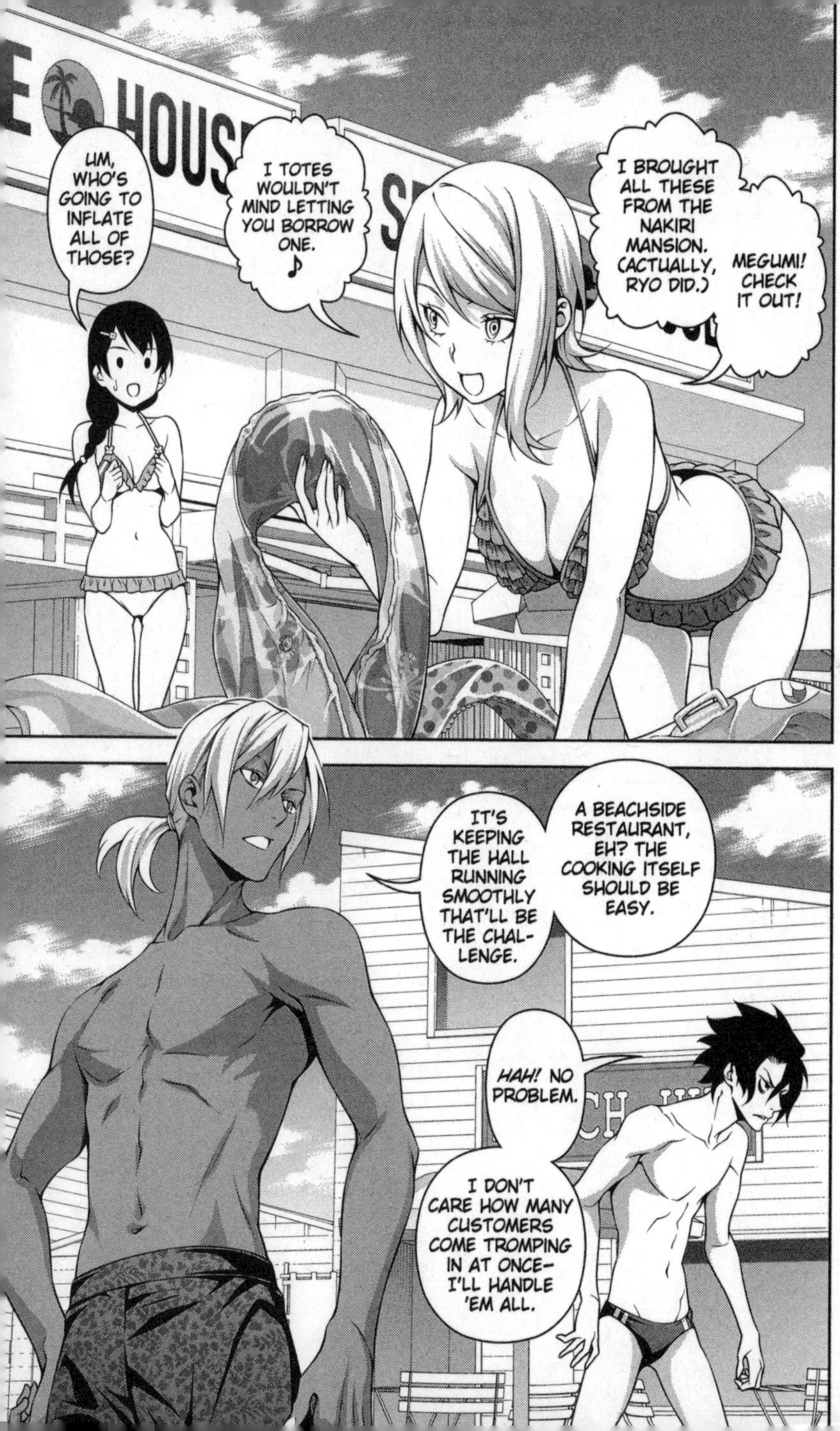
MEGUMI! CHECK IT OUT!
I BROUGHT ALL THESE FROM THE NAKIRI MANSION. (ACTUALLY, RYO DID.)
I TOTES WOULDN'T MIND LETTING YOU BORROW ONE. ♪
UM, WHO'S GOING TO INFLATE ALL OF THOSE?
A BEACHSIDE RESTAURANT, EH? THE COOKING ITSELF SHOULD BE EASY.
IT'S KEEPING THE HALL RUNNING SMOOTHLY THAT'LL BE THE CHAL-LENGE.
HAH! NO PROBLEM.
I DON'T CARE HOW MANY CUSTOMERS COME TROMPING IN AT ONCE-I'LL HANDLE 'EM ALL.

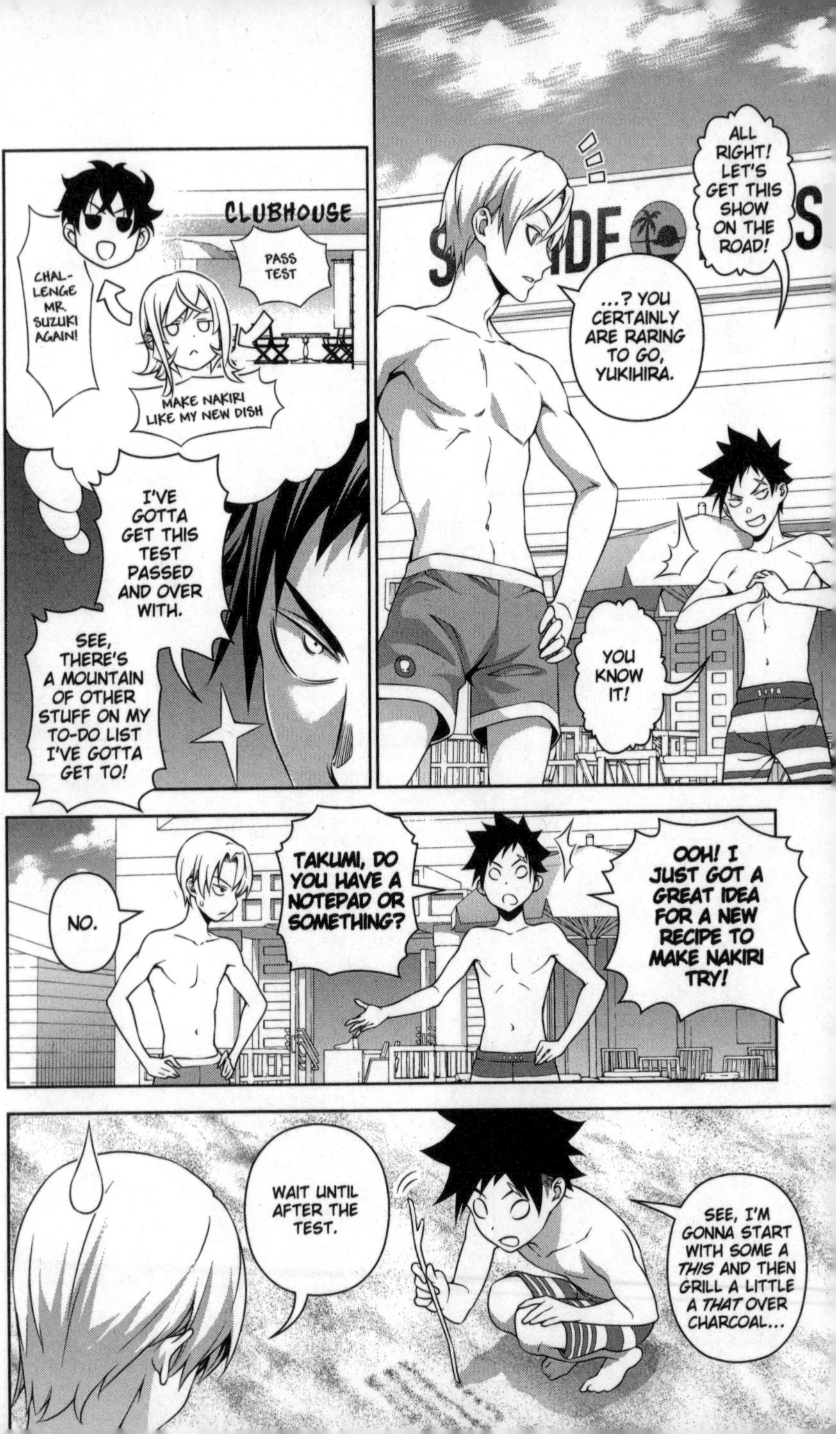
ALL RIGHT! LET'S GET THIS SHOW ON THE ROAD!
...? YOU CERTAINLY ARE RARING TO GO, YUKIHIRA.
YOU KNOW IT!
CLUBHOUSE
PASS TEST
CHAL-LENGE MR. SUZUKI AGAIN!
MAKE NAKIRI LIKE MY NEW DISH
I'VE GOTTA GET THIS TEST PASSED AND OVER WITH.
SEE, THERE'S A MOUNTAIN OF OTHER STUFF ON MY TO-DO LIST I'VE GOTTA GET TO!
OOH! I JUST GOT A GREAT IDEA FOR A NEW RECIPE TO MAKE NAKIRI TRY!
TAKUMI, DO YOU HAVE A NOTEPAD OR SOMETHING?
NO.
SEE, I'M GONNA START WITH SOME A *THIS* AND THEN GRILL A LITTLE A *THAT* OVER CHARCOAL...
WAIT UNTIL AFTER THE TEST.

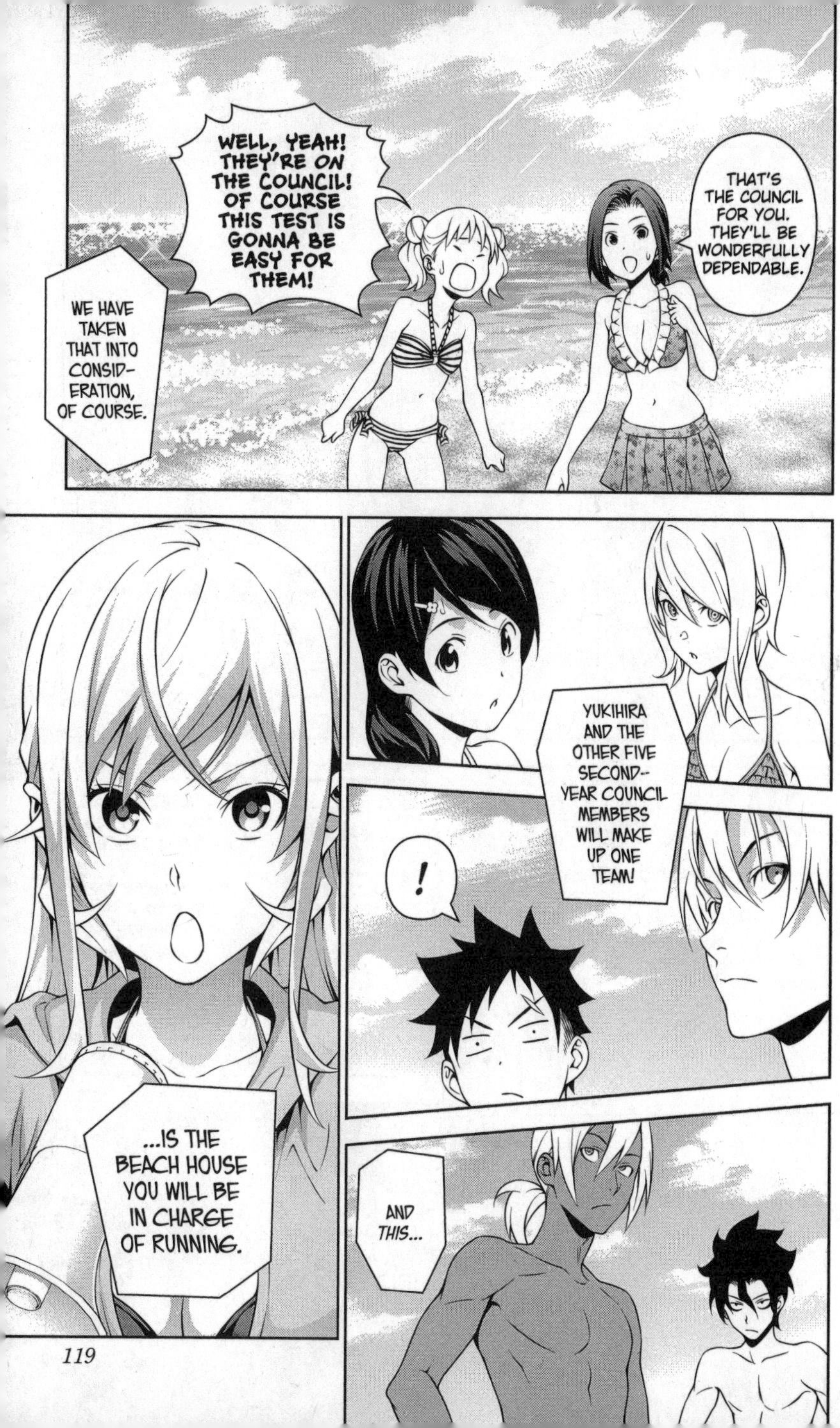
THAT'S THE COUNCIL FOR YOU. THEY'LL BE WONDERFULLY DEPENDABLE.
WELL, YEAH! THEY'RE ON THE COUNCIL! OF COURSE THIS TEST IS GONNA BE EASY FOR THEM!
WE HAVE TAKEN THAT INTO CONSID-ERATION, OF COURSE.
YUKIHIRA AND THE OTHER FIVE SECOND-YEAR COUNCIL MEMBERS WILL MAKE UP ONE TEAM!
!
AND THIS...
...IS THE BEACH HOUSE YOU WILL BE IN CHARGE OF RUNNING.

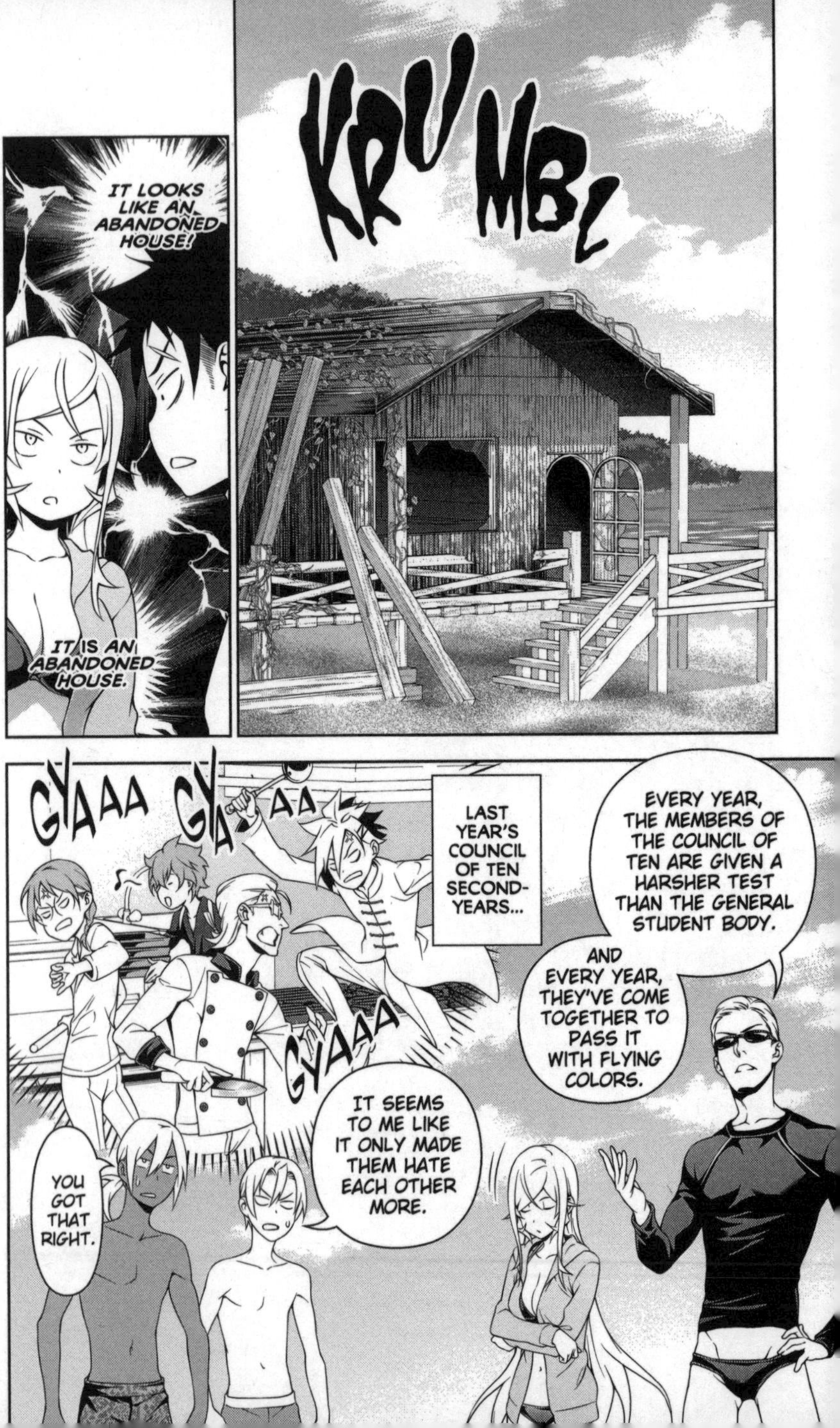
KRUMBL
IT LOOKS LIKE AN ABANDONED HOUSE!
IT IS AN ABANDONED HOUSE.
EVERY YEAR, THE MEMBERS OF THE COUNCIL OF TEN ARE GIVEN A HARSHER TEST THAN THE GENERAL STUDENT BODY.
AND EVERY YEAR, THEY'VE COME TOGETHER TO PASS IT WITH FLYING COLORS.
LAST YEAR'S COUNCIL OF TEN SECOND-YEARS...
GYAAA GYAAA
GYAAA
IT SEEMS TO ME LIKE IT ONLY MADE THEM HATE EACH OTHER MORE.
YOU GOT THAT RIGHT.

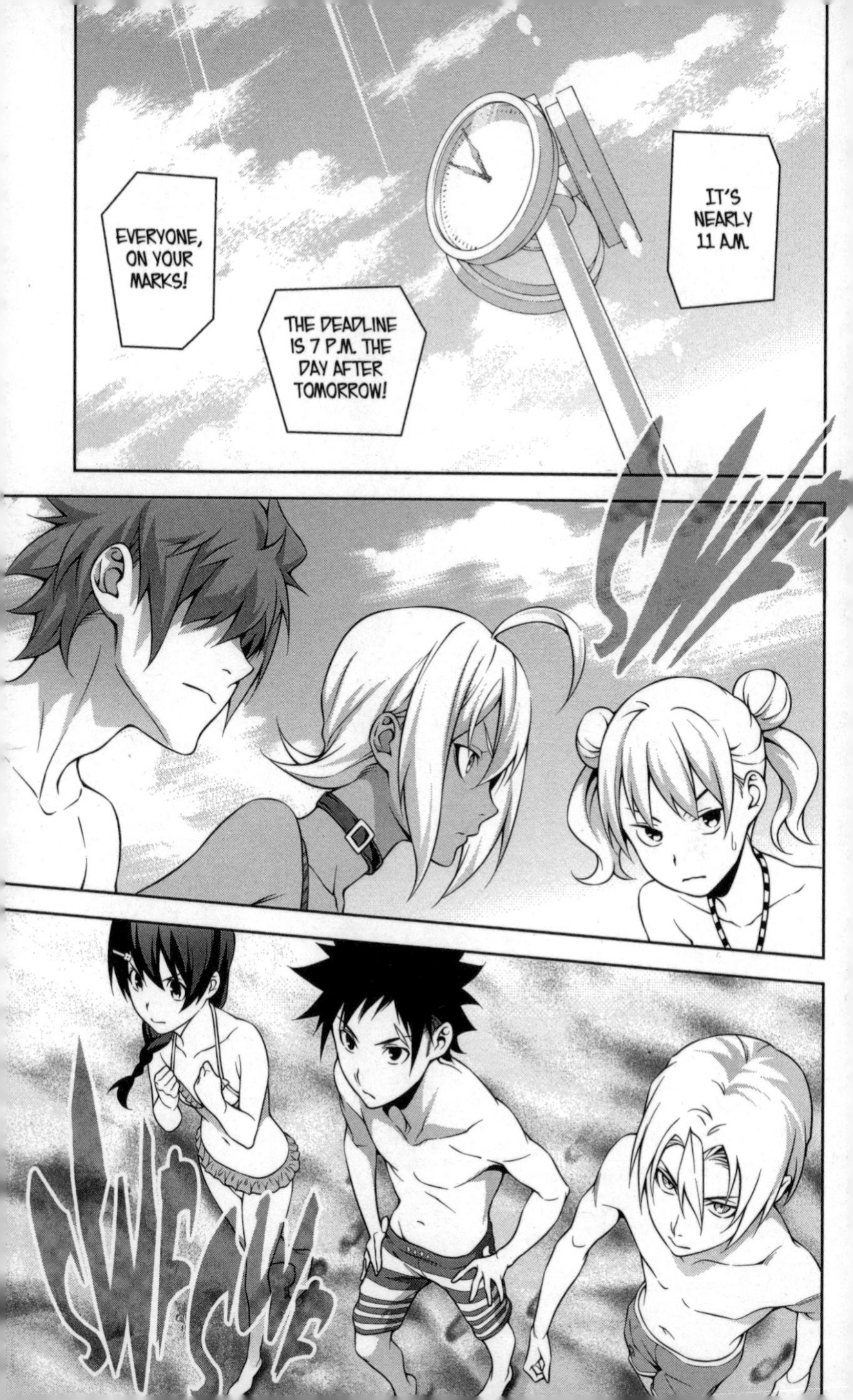
IT'S NEARLY 11 A.M.
EVERYONE, ON YOUR MARKS!
THE DEADLINE IS 7 P.M. THE DAY AFTER TOMORROW!

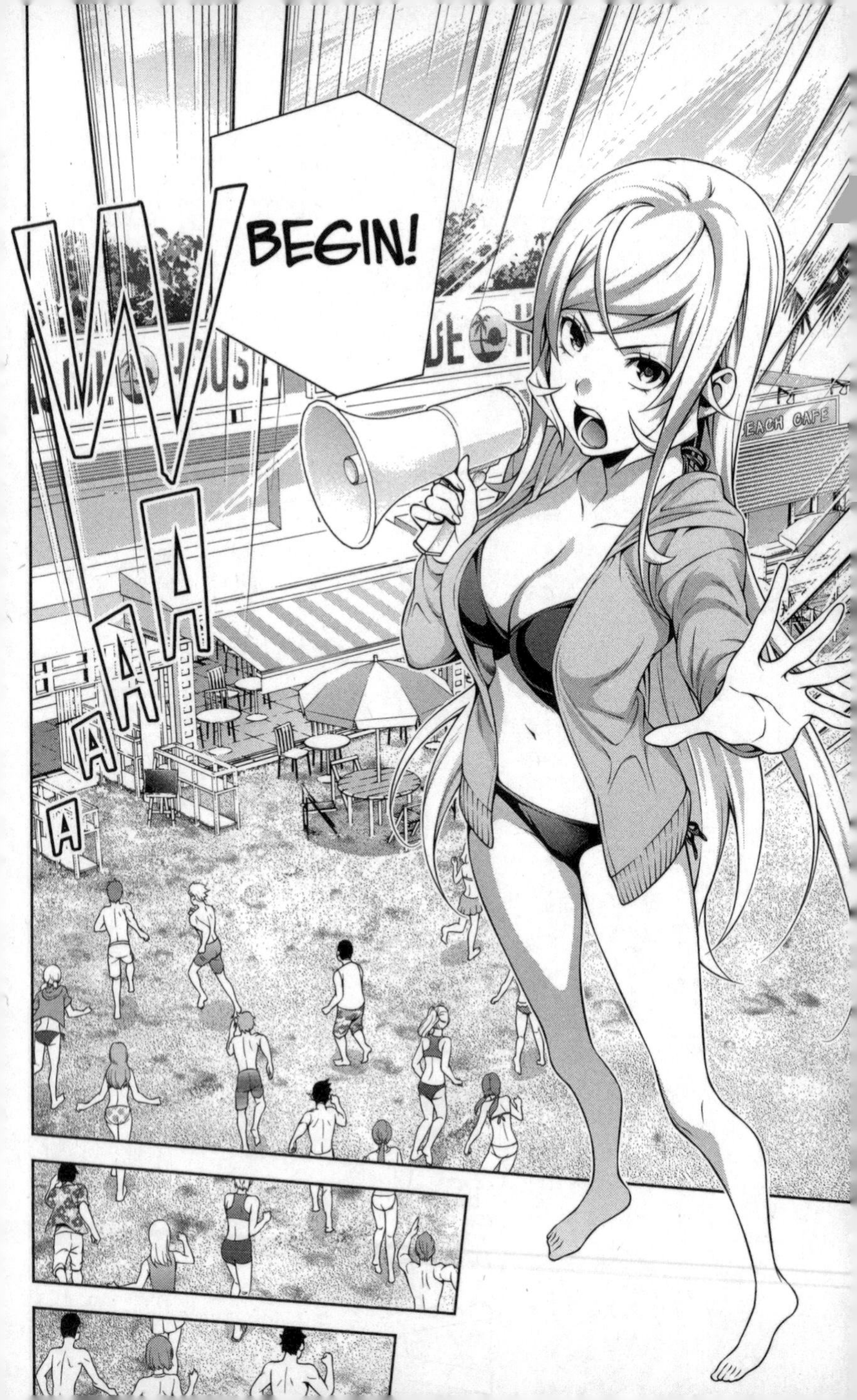

BEGIN!
WWAAAA

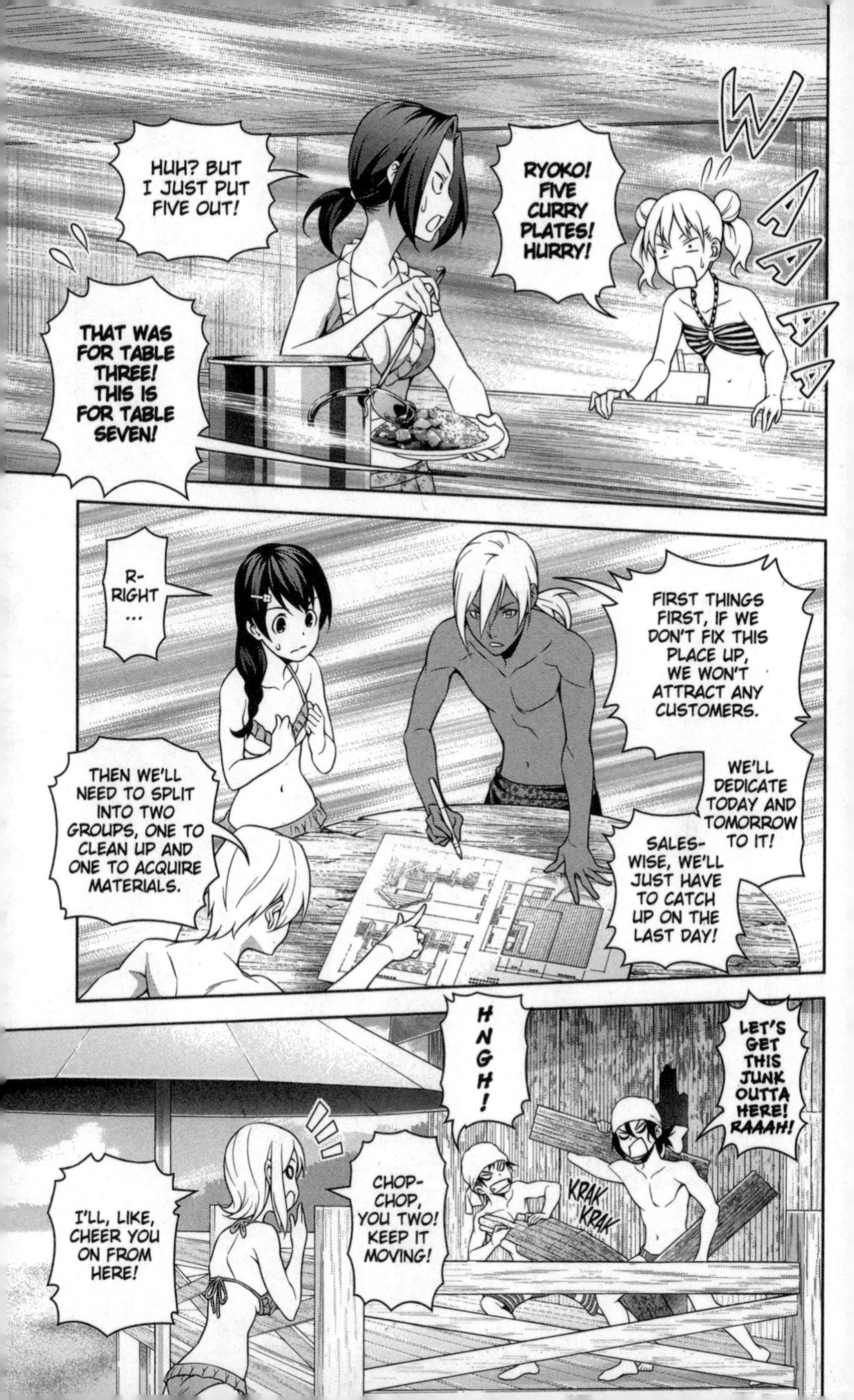
WAAAA
RYOKO! FIVE CURRY PLATES! HURRY!
HUH? BUT I JUST PUT FIVE OUT!
THAT WAS FOR TABLE THREE! THIS IS FOR TABLE SEVEN!
FIRST THINGS FIRST, IF WE DON'T FIX THIS PLACE UP, WE WON'T ATTRACT ANY CUSTOMERS.
WE'LL DEDICATE TODAY AND TOMORROW TO IT!
SALES-WISE, WE'LL JUST HAVE TO CATCH UP ON THE LAST DAY!
R-RIGHT...
THEN WE'LL NEED TO SPLIT INTO TWO GROUPS, ONE TO CLEAN UP AND ONE TO ACQUIRE MATERIALS.
LET'S GET THIS JUNK OUTTA HERE! RAAAH!
HNGH!
KRAK KRAK
CHOP-CHOP, YOU TWO! KEEP IT MOVING!
I'LL, LIKE, CHEER YOU ON FROM HERE!

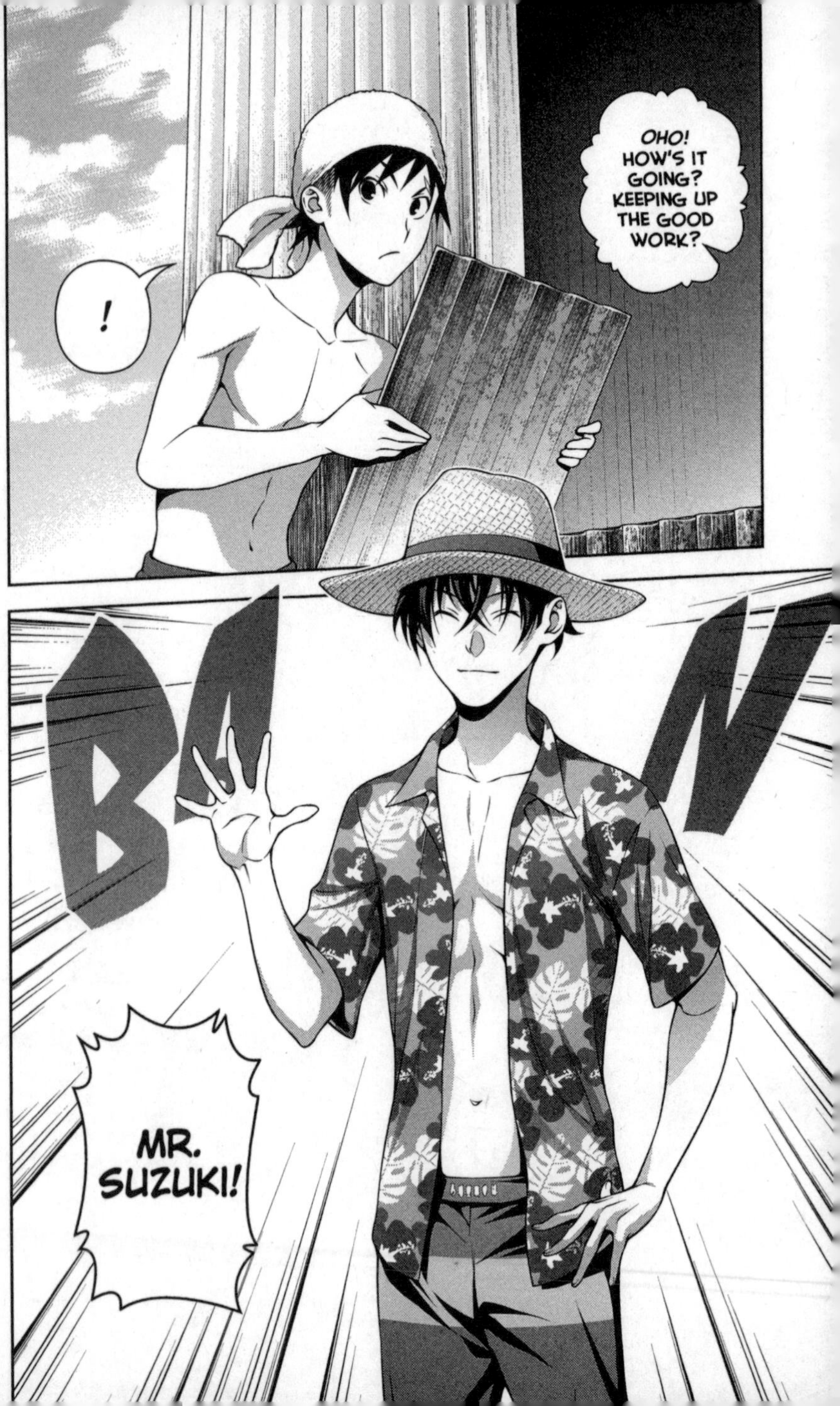
OHO! HOW'S IT GOING? KEEPING UP THE GOOD WORK?
!
BAN
MR. SUZUKI!

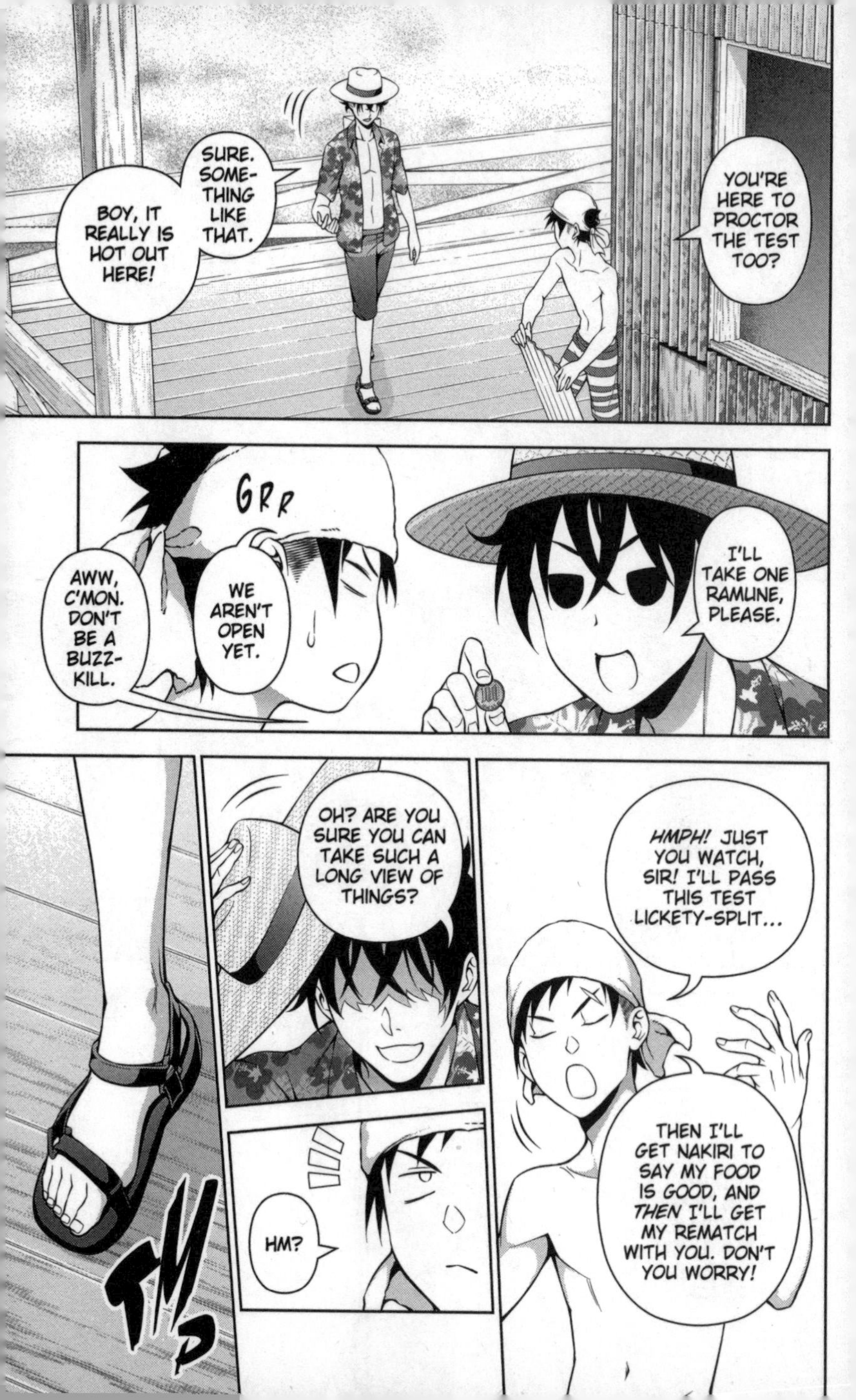
YOU'RE HERE TO PROCTOR THE TEST TOO?
SURE. SOMETHING LIKE THAT.
BOY, IT REALLY IS HOT OUT HERE!
I'LL TAKE ONE RAMUNE, PLEASE.
GRR
WE AREN'T OPEN YET.
AWW, C'MON. DON'T BE A BUZZKILL.
HMPH! JUST YOU WATCH, SIR! I'LL PASS THIS TEST LICKETY-SPLIT...
THEN I'LL GET NAKIRI TO SAY MY FOOD IS GOOD, AND *THEN* I'LL GET MY REMATCH WITH YOU. DON'T YOU WORRY!
OH? ARE YOU SURE YOU CAN TAKE SUCH A LONG VIEW OF THINGS?
HM?
TMP

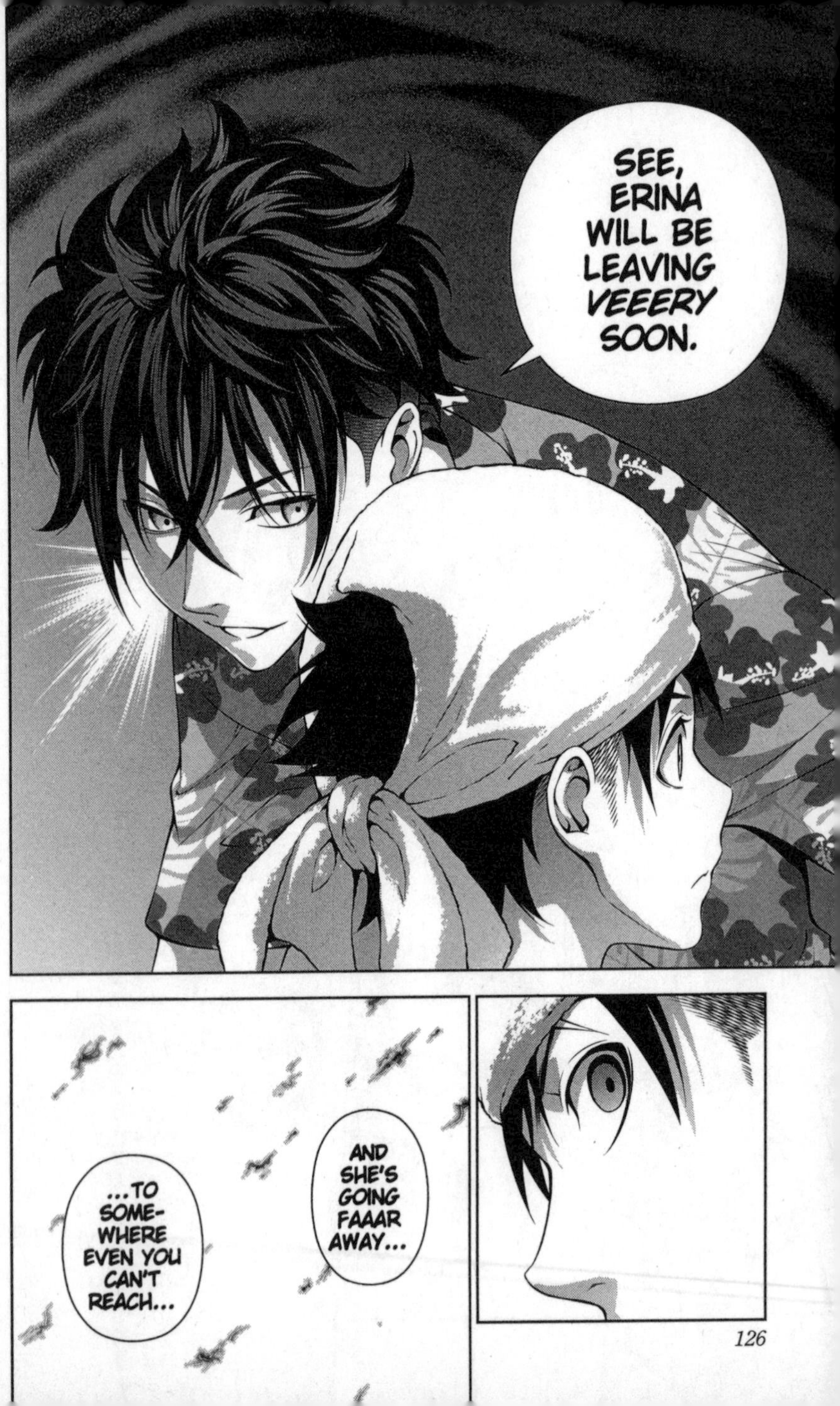
SEE, ERINA WILL BE LEAVING VEEERY SOON.
AND SHE'S GOING FAAAR AWAY...
...TO SOME-WHERE EVEN YOU CAN'T REACH...

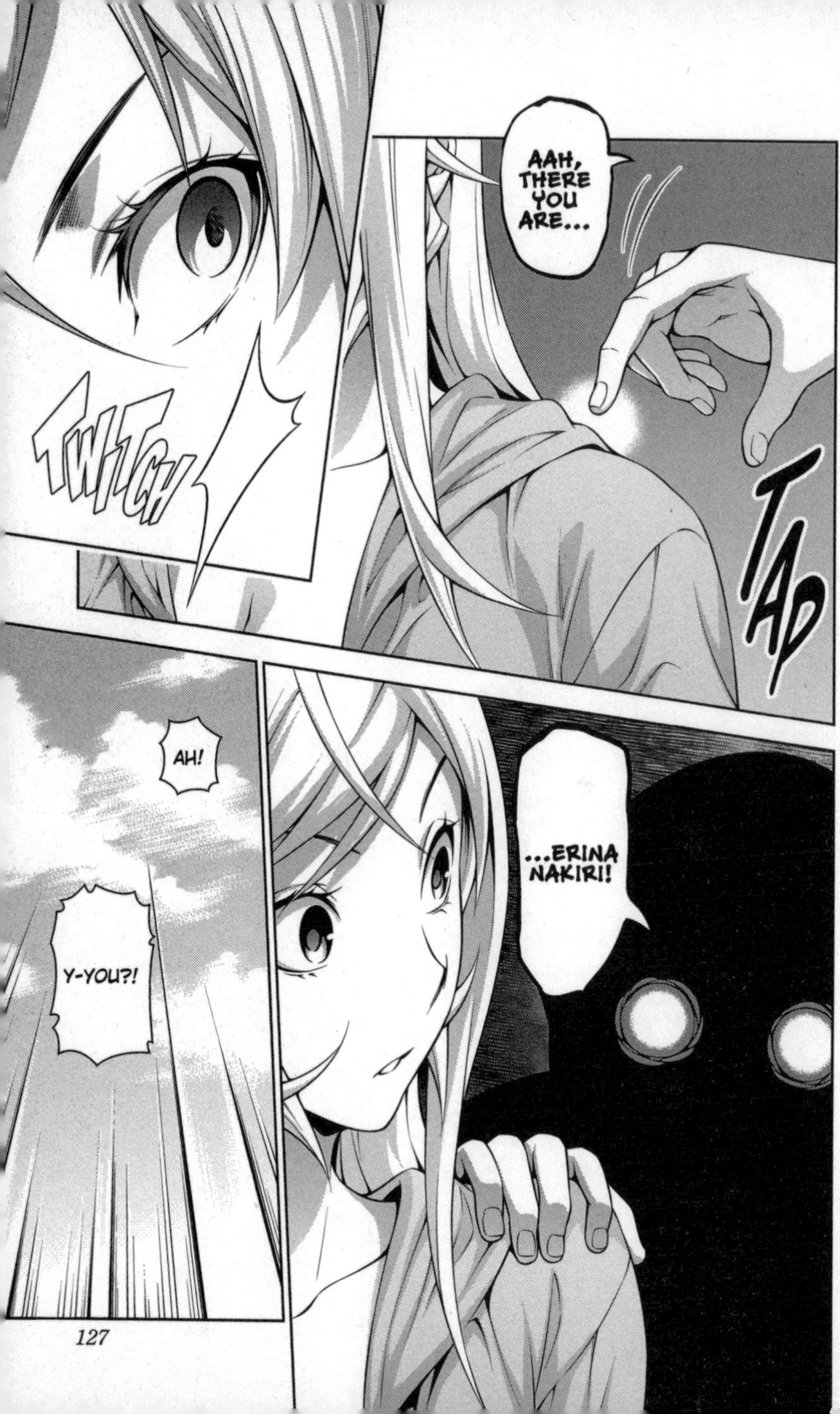
AAH, THERE YOU ARE...
TAP
TWITCH
...ERINA NAKIRI!
AH!
Y-YOU?!

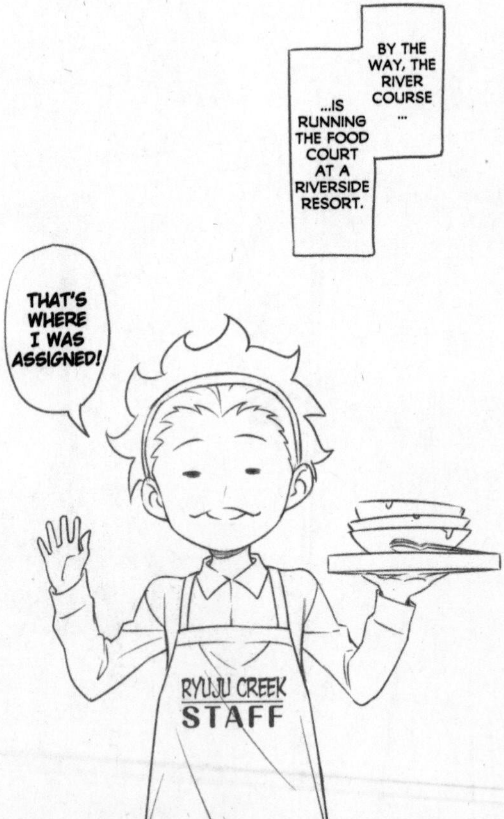
BY THE WAY, THE RIVER COURSE ...
...IS RUNNING THE FOOD COURT AT A RIVERSIDE RESORT.
THAT'S WHERE I WAS ASSIGNED!
RYUJU CREEK
STAFF

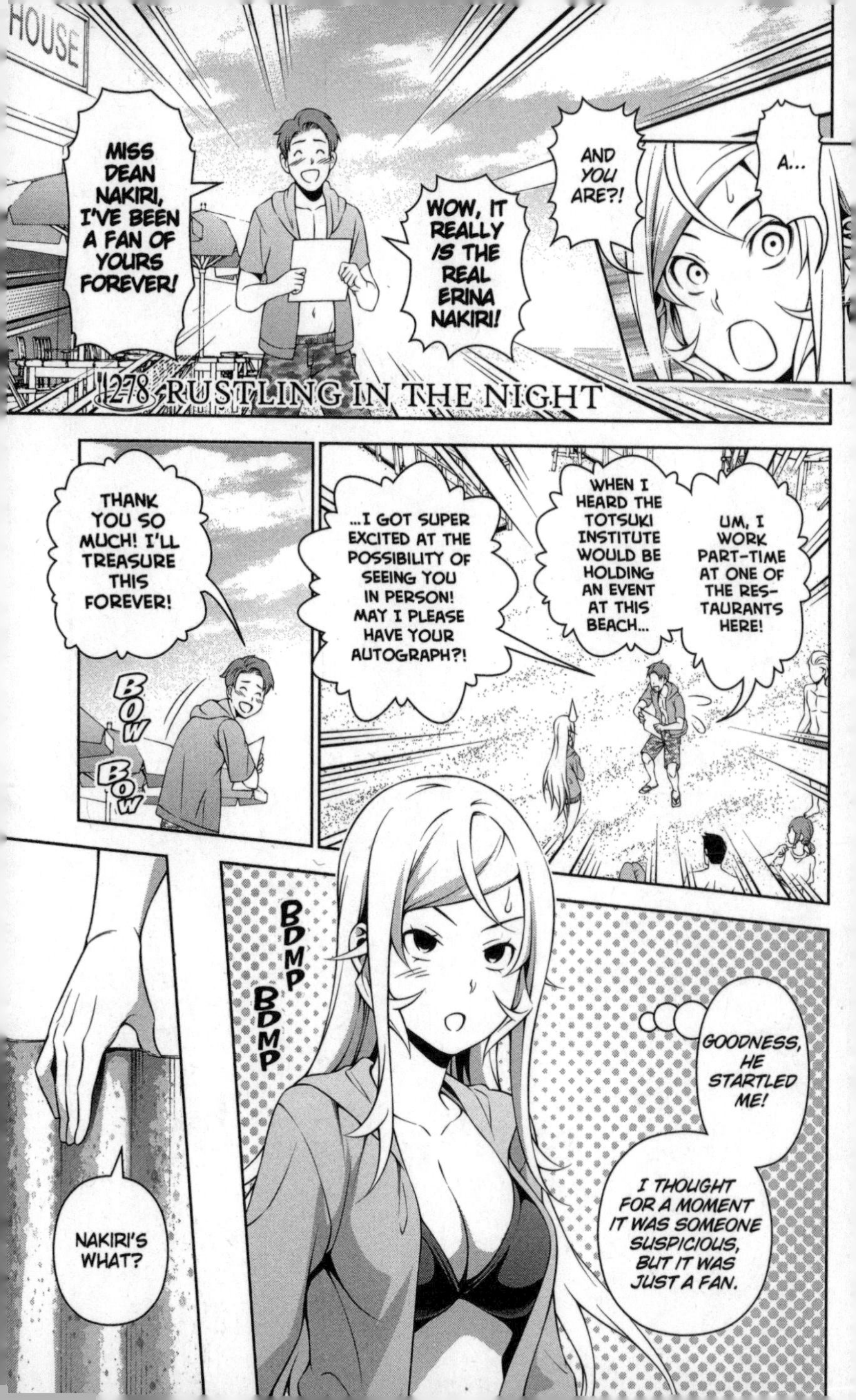
A...
AND YOU ARE?!
WOW, IT REALLY IS THE REAL ERINA NAKIRI!
MISS DEAN NAKIRI, I'VE BEEN A FAN OF YOURS FOREVER!
HOUSE
1278 RUSTLING IN THE NIGHT
UM, I WORK PART-TIME AT ONE OF THE RES-TAURANTS HERE!
WHEN I HEARD THE TOTSUKI INSTITUTE WOULD BE HOLDING AN EVENT AT THIS BEACH...
...I GOT SUPER EXCITED AT THE POSSIBILITY OF SEEING YOU IN PERSON! MAY I PLEASE HAVE YOUR AUTOGRAPH?!
THANK YOU SO MUCH! I'LL TREASURE THIS FOREVER!
BOW
BOW
BDMP
BDMP
GOODNESS, HE STARTLED ME!
I THOUGHT FOR A MOMENT IT WAS SOMEONE SUSPICIOUS, BUT IT WAS JUST A FAN.
NAKIRI'S WHAT?

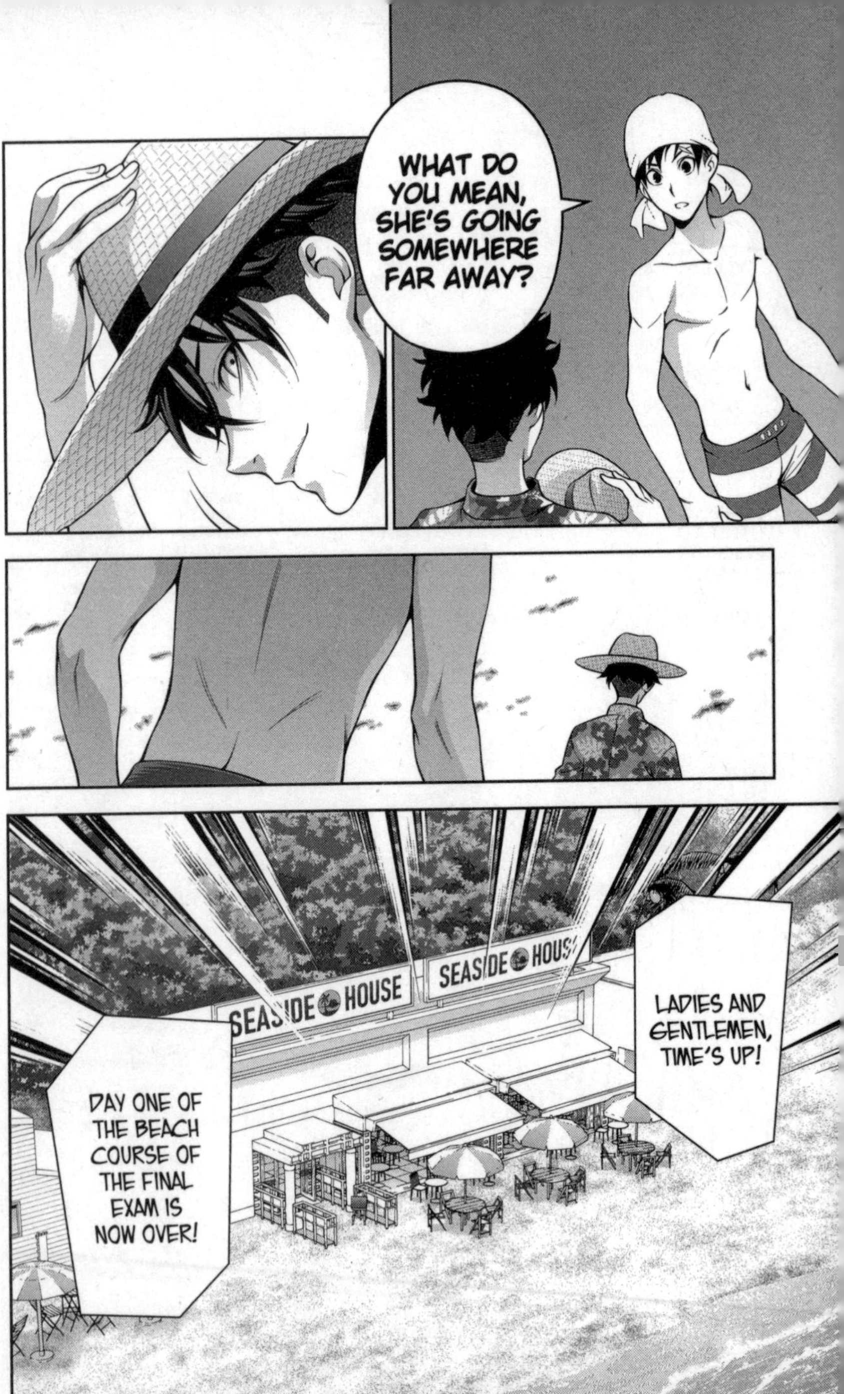
WHAT DO YOU MEAN, SHE'S GOING SOMEWHERE FAR AWAY?
SEASIDE HOUSE
SEASIDE HOUSE
LADIES AND GENTLEMEN, TIME'S UP!
DAY ONE OF THE BEACH COURSE OF THE FINAL EXAM IS NOW OVER!

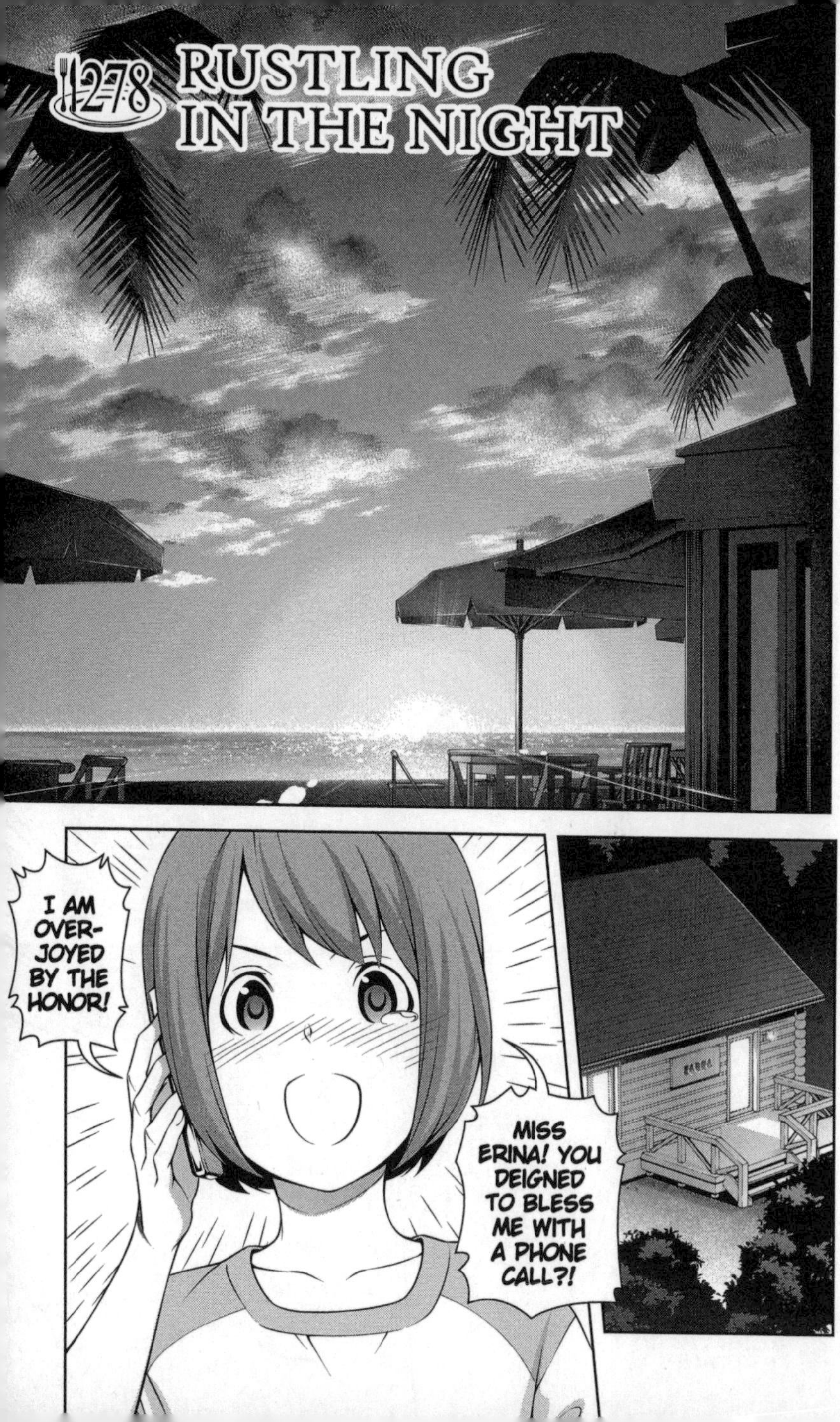
278 RUSTLING IN THE NIGHT
MISS ERINA! YOU DEIGNED TO BLESS ME WITH A PHONE CALL?!
I AM OVERJOYED BY THE HONOR!

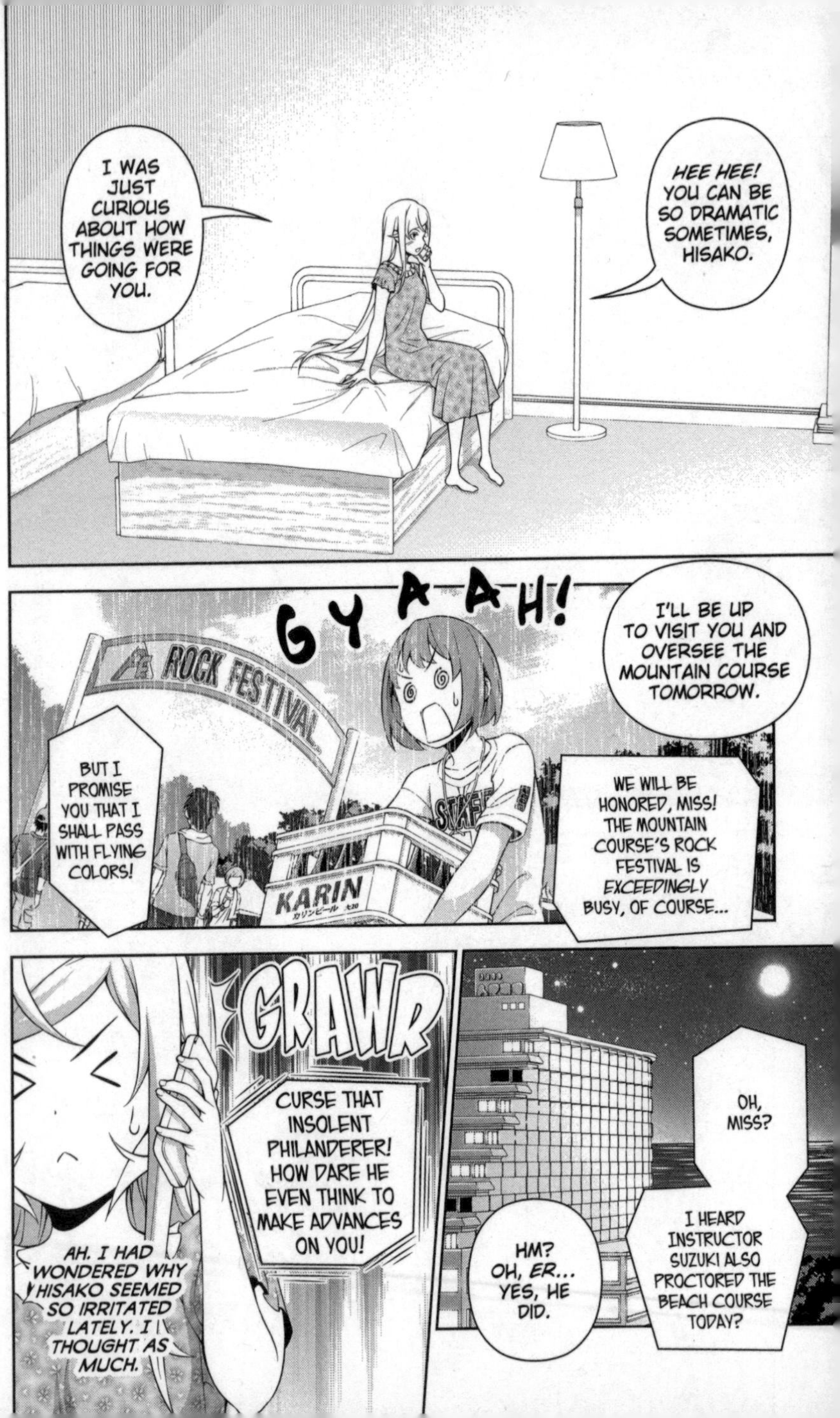

HEE HEE! YOU CAN BE SO DRAMATIC SOMETIMES, HISAKO.
I WAS JUST CURIOUS ABOUT HOW THINGS WERE GOING FOR YOU.
I'LL BE UP TO VISIT YOU AND OVERSEE THE MOUNTAIN COURSE TOMORROW.
GYAAAH!
ROCK FESTIVAL
WE WILL BE HONORED, MISS! THE MOUNTAIN COURSE'S ROCK FESTIVAL IS EXCEEDINGLY BUSY, OF COURSE...
BUT I PROMISE YOU THAT I SHALL PASS WITH FLYING COLORS!
KARIN
OH, MISS?
I HEARD INSTRUCTOR SUZUKI ALSO PROCTORED THE BEACH COURSE TODAY?
HM? OH, ER... YES, HE DID.
GRAWR
CURSE THAT INSOLENT PHILANDERER! HOW DARE HE EVEN THINK TO MAKE ADVANCES ON YOU!
AH. I HAD WONDERED WHY HISAKO SEEMED SO IRRITATED LATELY. I THOUGHT AS MUCH.

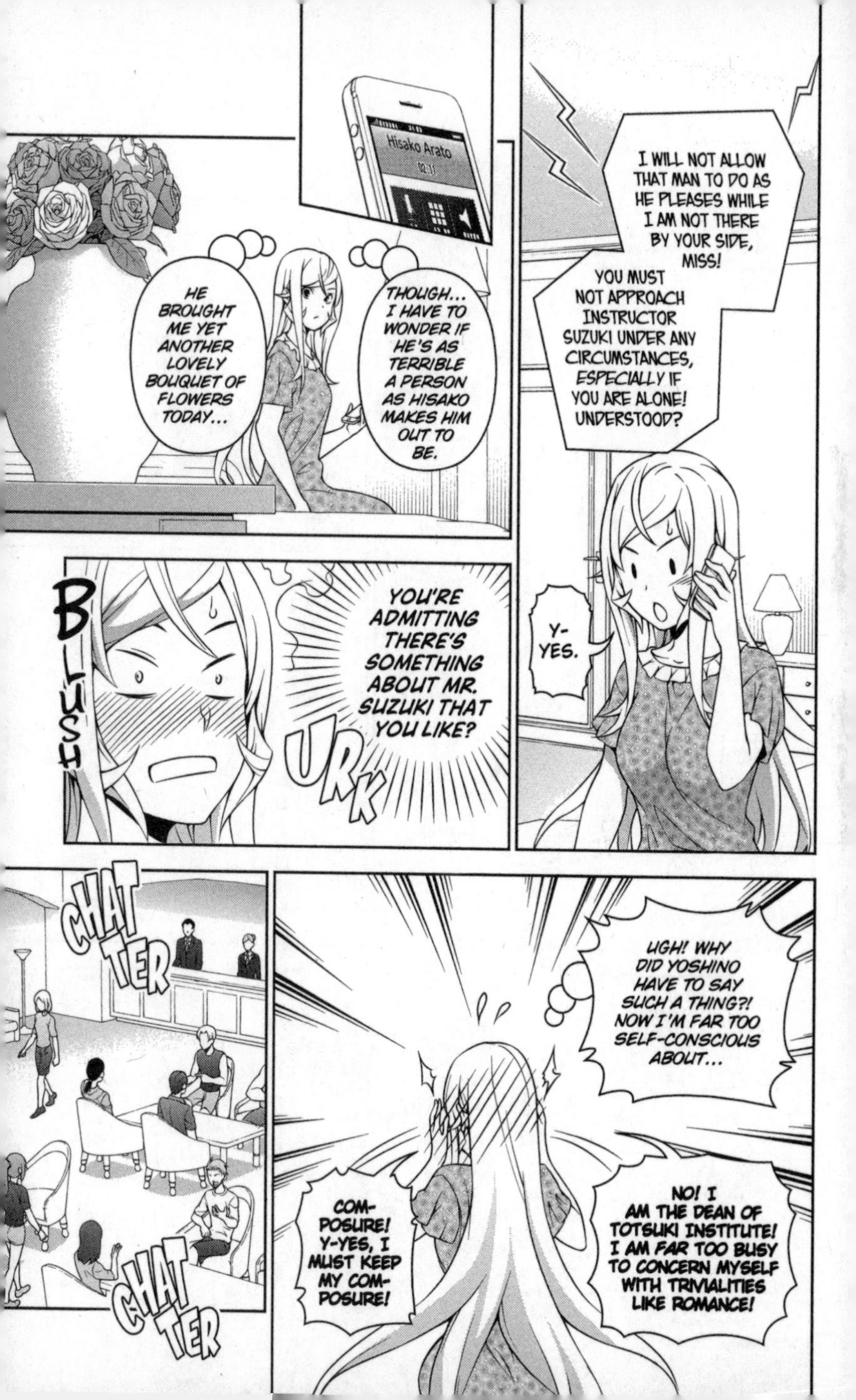
I WILL NOT ALLOW THAT MAN TO DO AS HE PLEASES WHILE I AM NOT THERE BY YOUR SIDE, MISS!
YOU MUST NOT APPROACH INSTRUCTOR SUZUKI UNDER ANY CIRCUMSTANCES, ESPECIALLY IF YOU ARE ALONE! UNDERSTOOD?
Y-YES.
Hisako Arato
02:11
THOUGH... I HAVE TO WONDER IF HE'S AS TERRIBLE A PERSON AS HISAKO MAKES HIM OUT TO BE.
HE BROUGHT ME YET ANOTHER LOVELY BOUQUET OF FLOWERS TODAY...
YOU'RE ADMITTING THERE'S SOMETHING ABOUT MR. SUZUKI THAT YOU LIKE?
URK
BLUSH
UGH! WHY DID YOSHINO HAVE TO SAY SUCH A THING?! NOW I'M FAR TOO SELF-CONSCIOUS ABOUT...
NO! I AM THE DEAN OF TOTSUKI INSTITUTE! I AM FAR TOO BUSY TO CONCERN MYSELF WITH TRIVIALITIES LIKE ROMANCE!
COM-POSURE! Y-YES, I MUST KEEP MY COM-POSURE!
CHATTER
CHATTER

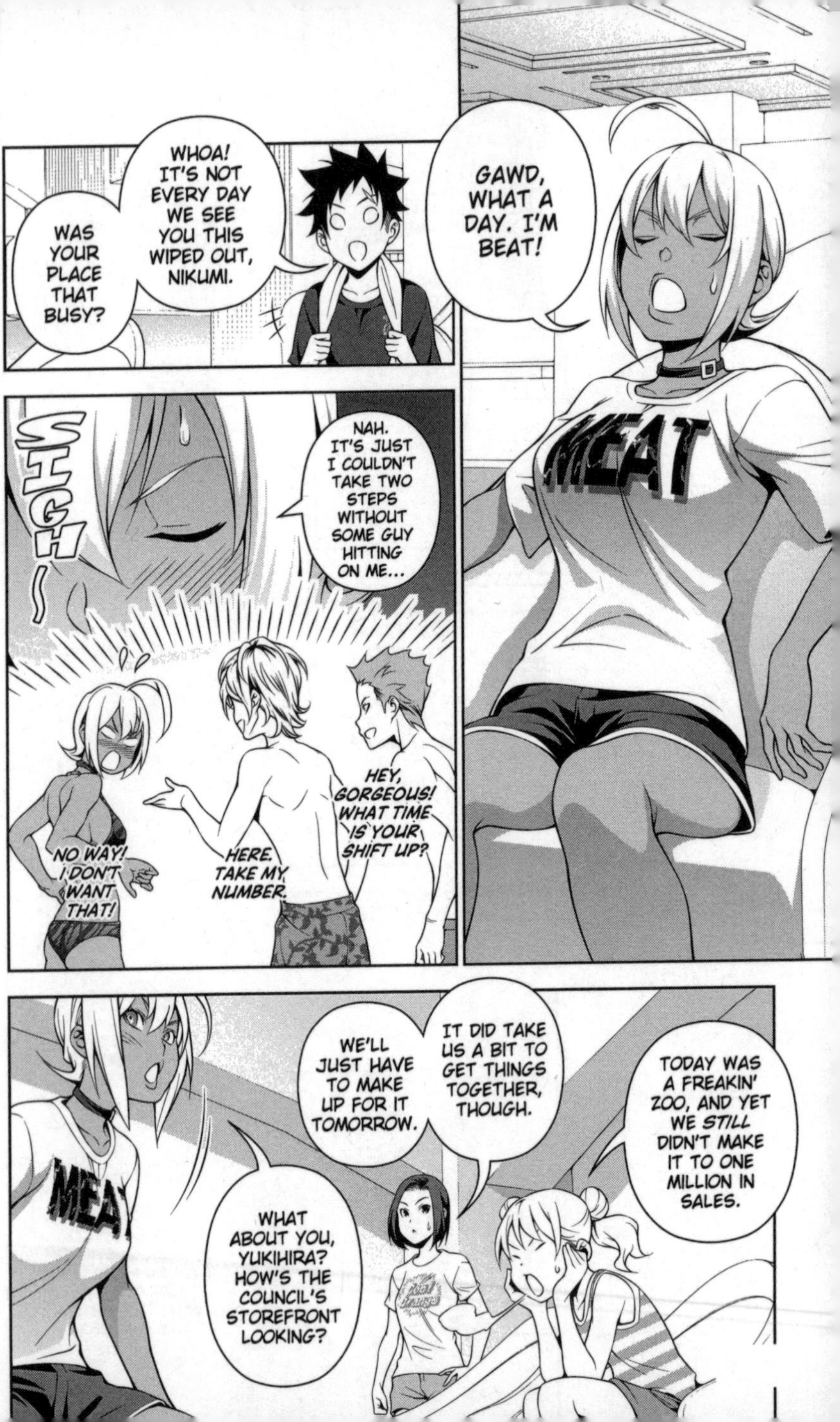
GAWD, WHAT A DAY. I'M BEAT!
WHOA! IT'S NOT EVERY DAY WE SEE YOU THIS WIPED OUT, NIKUMI.
WAS YOUR PLACE THAT BUSY?
NAH. IT'S JUST I COULDN'T TAKE TWO STEPS WITHOUT SOME GUY HITTING ON ME...
SIGH~
HEY, GORGEOUS! WHAT TIME IS YOUR SHIFT UP?
HERE. TAKE MY NUMBER.
NO WAY! I DON'T WANT THAT!
TODAY WAS A FREAKIN' ZOO, AND YET WE *STILL* DIDN'T MAKE IT TO ONE MILLION IN SALES.
IT DID TAKE US A BIT TO GET THINGS TOGETHER, THOUGH.
WE'LL JUST HAVE TO MAKE UP FOR IT TOMORROW.
WHAT ABOUT YOU, YUKIHIRA? HOW'S THE COUNCIL'S STOREFRONT LOOKING?

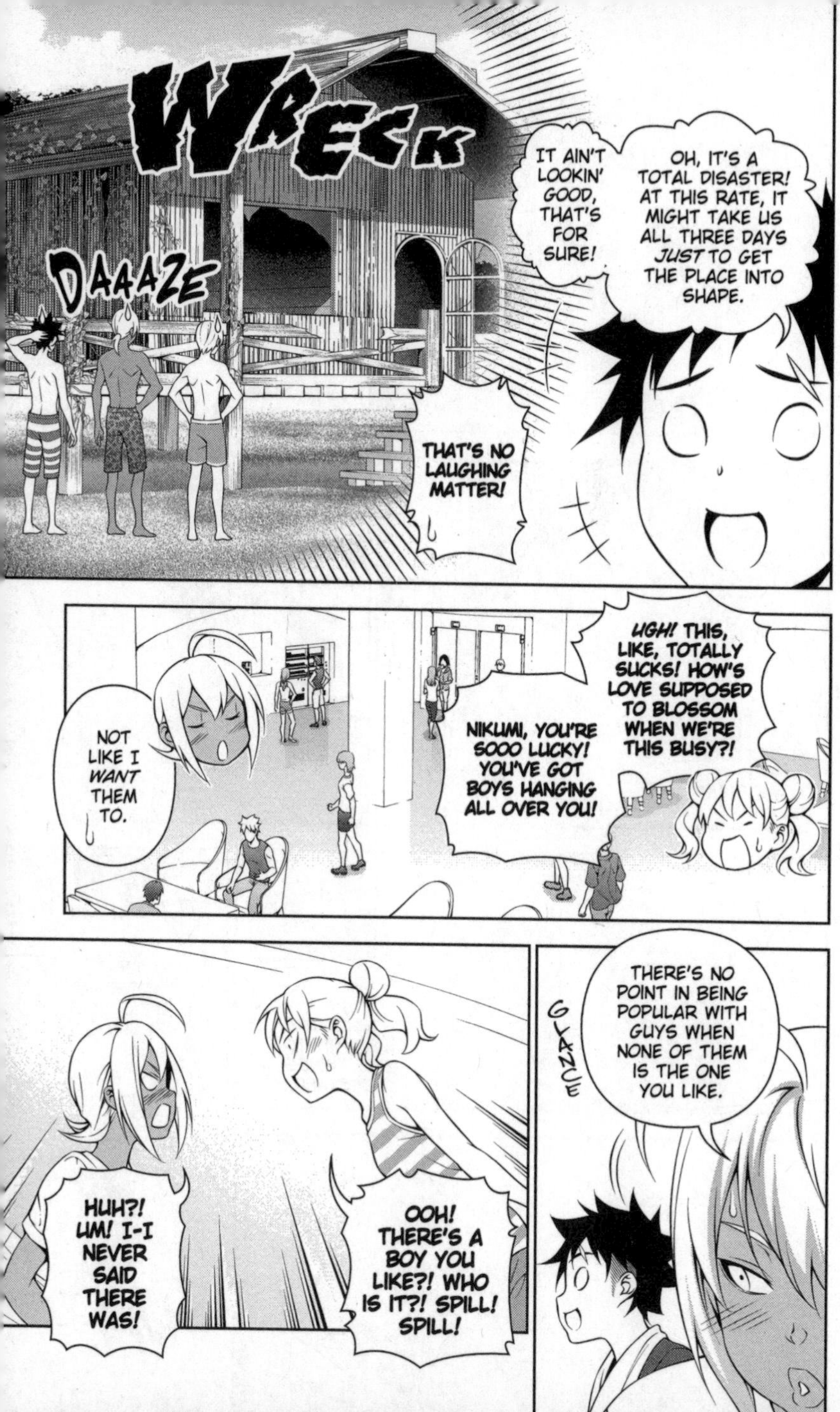
OH, IT'S A TOTAL DISASTER! AT THIS RATE, IT MIGHT TAKE US ALL THREE DAYS *JUST* TO GET THE PLACE INTO SHAPE.
IT AIN'T LOOKIN' GOOD, THAT'S FOR SURE!
WRECK
THAT'S NO LAUGHING MATTER!
DAAAZE
UGH! THIS, LIKE, TOTALLY SUCKS! HOW'S LOVE SUPPOSED TO BLOSSOM WHEN WE'RE THIS BUSY?!
NIKUMI, YOU'RE SOOO LUCKY! YOU'VE GOT BOYS HANGING ALL OVER YOU!
NOT LIKE I *WANT* THEM TO.
THERE'S NO POINT IN BEING POPULAR WITH GUYS WHEN NONE OF THEM IS THE ONE YOU LIKE.
GLANCE
OOH! THERE'S A BOY YOU LIKE?! WHO IS IT?! SPILL! SPILL!
HUH?! UM! I-I NEVER SAID THERE WAS!

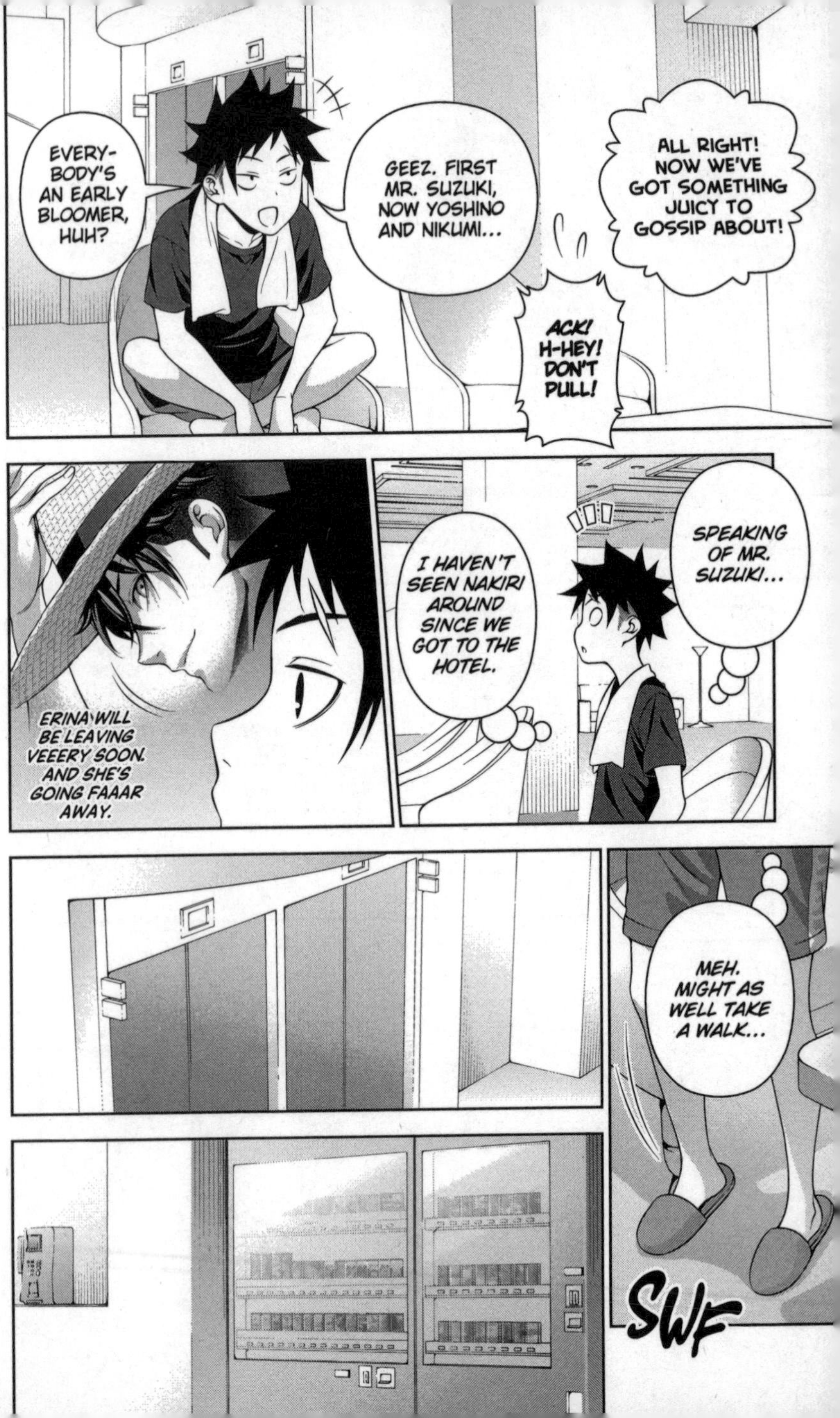
ALL RIGHT! NOW WE'VE GOT SOMETHING JUICY TO GOSSIP ABOUT!
ACK! H-HEY! DON'T PULL!
GEEZ. FIRST MR. SUZUKI, NOW YOSHINO AND NIKUMI...
EVERY-BODY'S AN EARLY BLOOMER, HUH?
SPEAKING OF MR. SUZUKI...
I HAVEN'T SEEN NAKIRI AROUND SINCE WE GOT TO THE HOTEL.
ERINA WILL BE LEAVING VEEERY SOON. AND SHE'S GOING FAAAR AWAY.
MEH. MIGHT AS WELL TAKE A WALK...
SWF

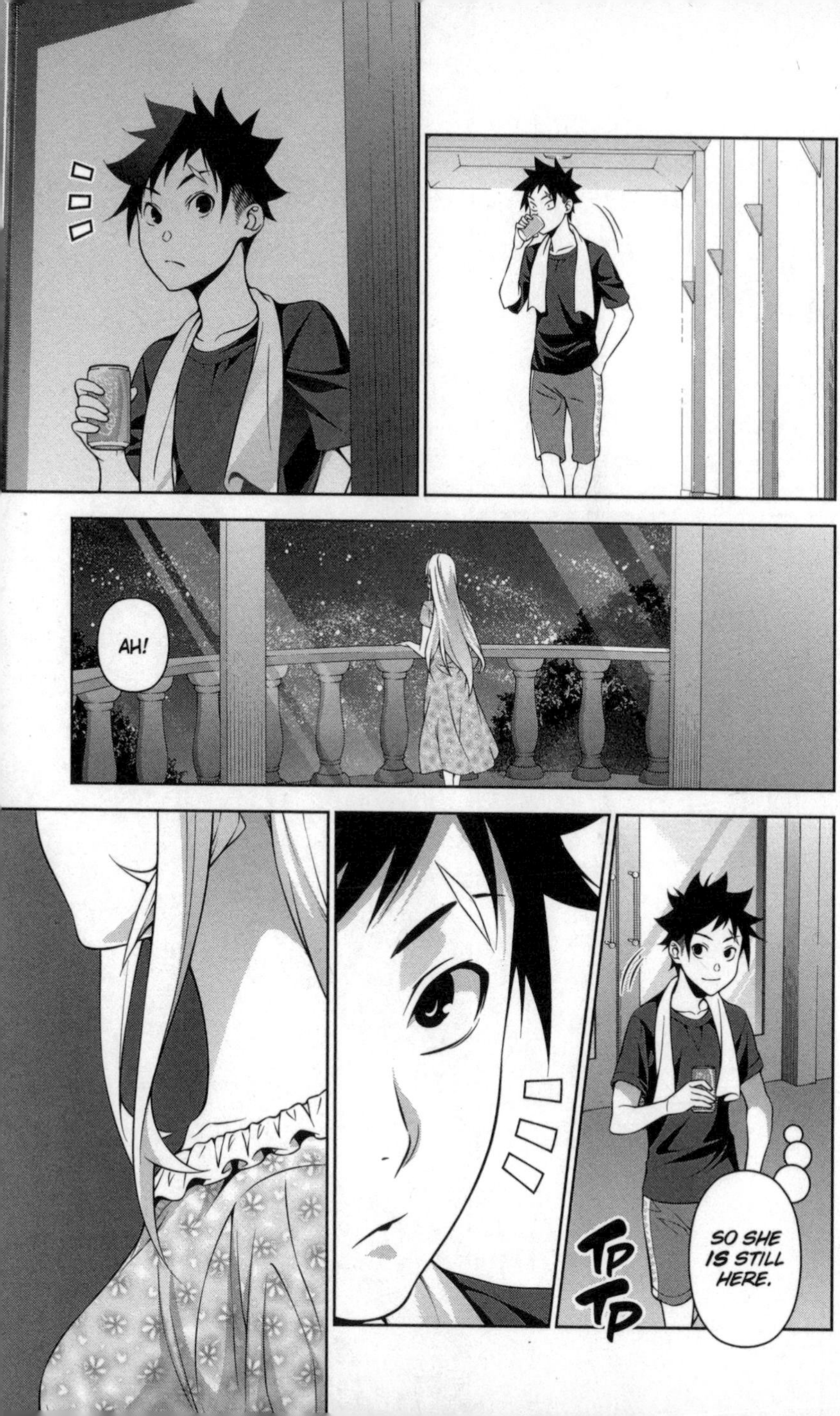
AH!
SO SHE IS STILL HERE.
TP TP

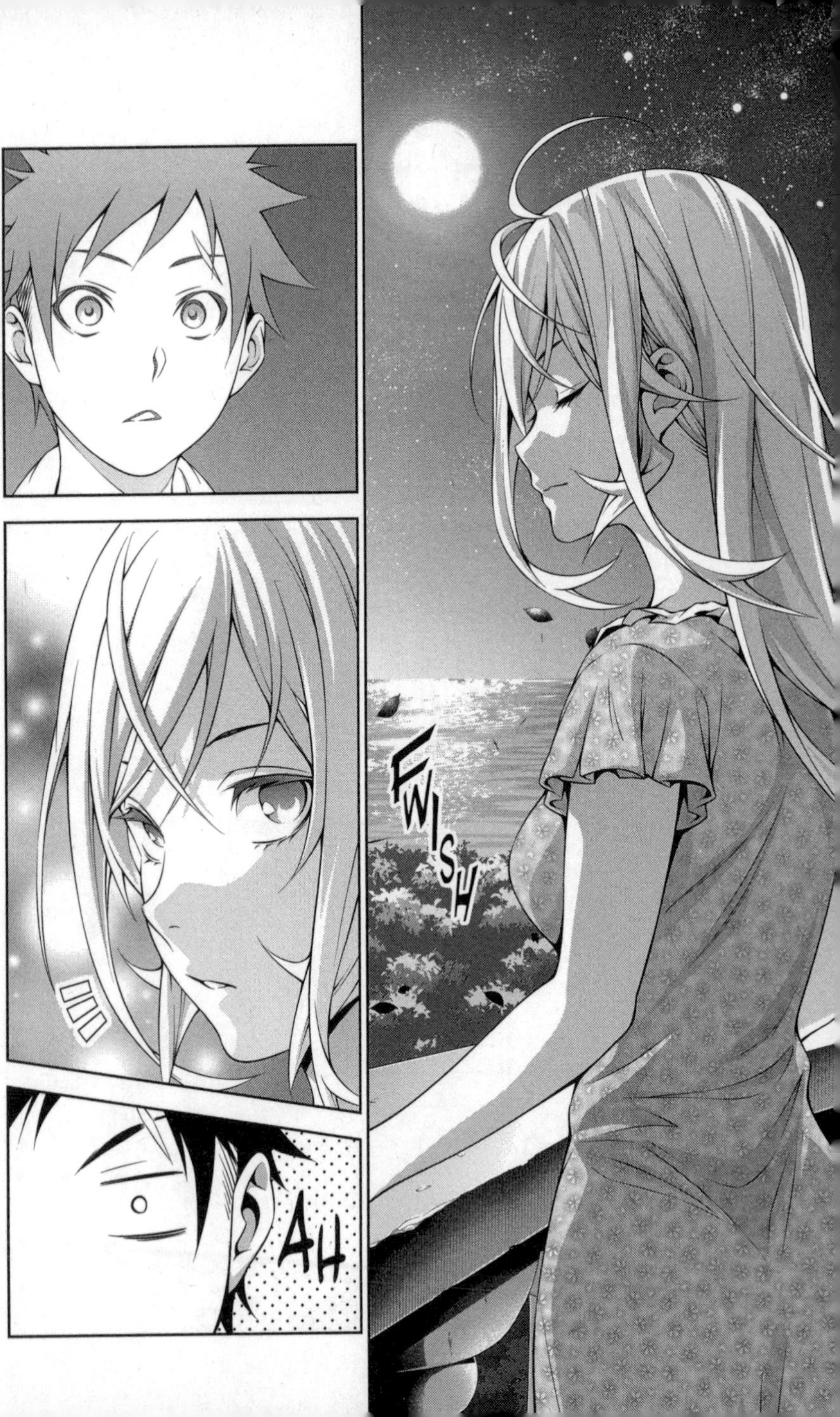
FWISH
AH

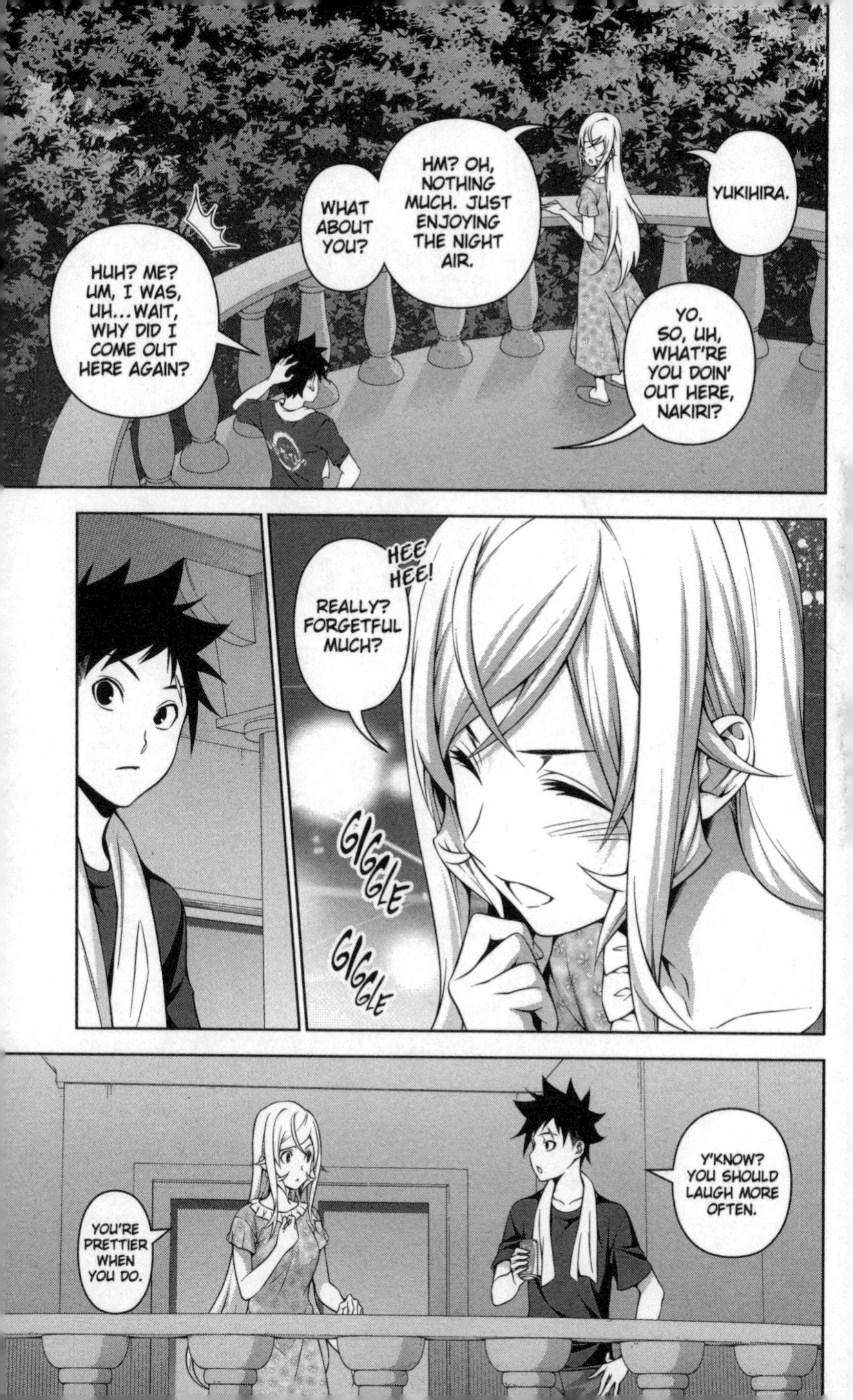
YUKIHIRA.
YO. SO, UH, WHAT'RE YOU DOIN' OUT HERE, NAKIRI?
HM? OH, NOTHING MUCH. JUST ENJOYING THE NIGHT AIR.
WHAT ABOUT YOU?
HUH? ME? UM, I WAS, UH...WAIT, WHY DID I COME OUT HERE AGAIN?
HEE HEE!
REALLY? FORGETFUL MUCH?
GIGGLE
GIGGLE
Y'KNOW? YOU SHOULD LAUGH MORE OFTEN.
YOU'RE PRETTIER WHEN YOU DO.

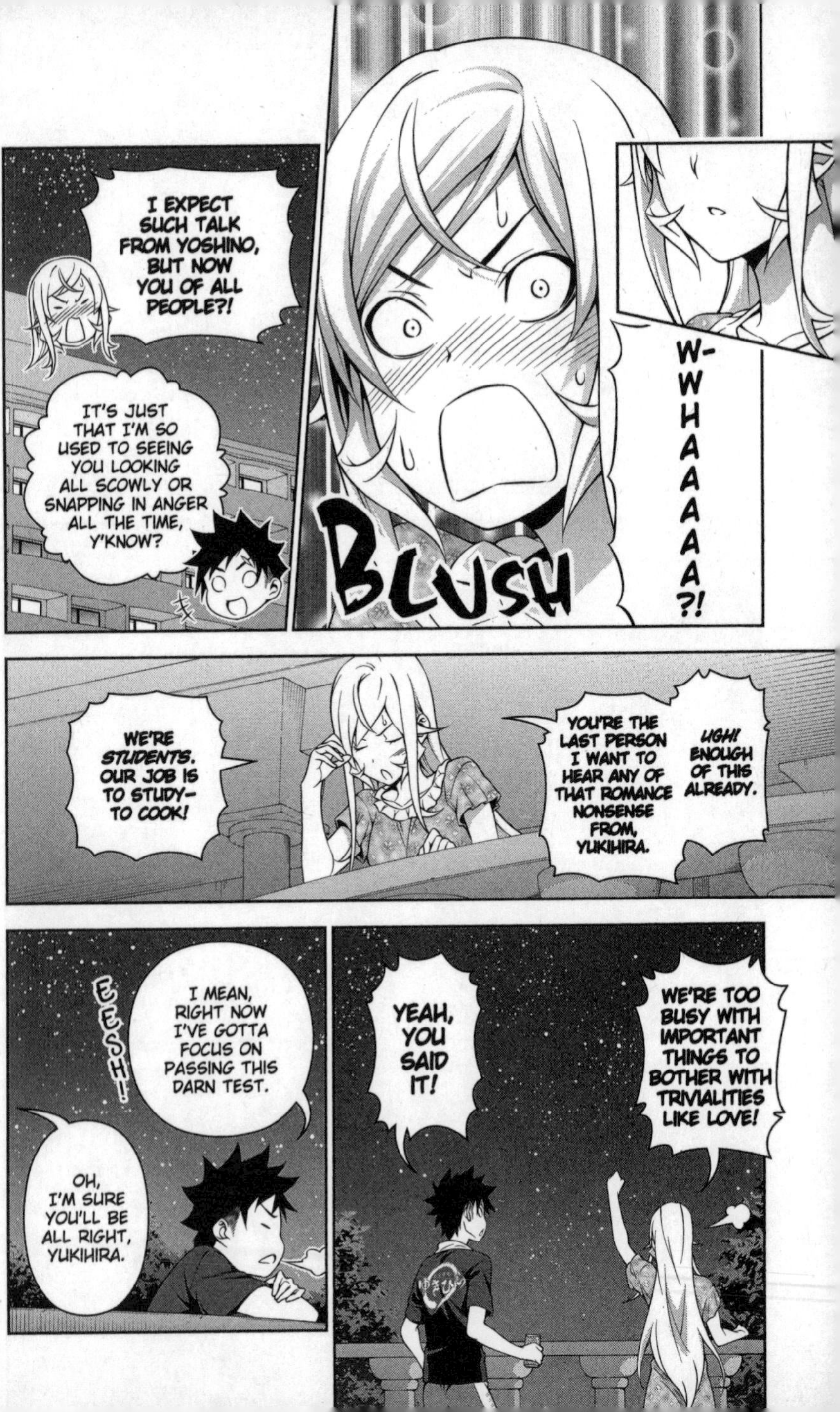
W-WHAAAAAA?!
BLUSH
I EXPECT SUCH TALK FROM YOSHINO, BUT NOW YOU OF ALL PEOPLE?!
IT'S JUST THAT I'M SO USED TO SEEING YOU LOOKING ALL SCOWLY OR SNAPPING IN ANGER ALL THE TIME, Y'KNOW?
UGH! ENOUGH OF THIS ALREADY.
YOU'RE THE LAST PERSON I WANT TO HEAR ANY OF THAT ROMANCE NONSENSE FROM, YUKIHIRA.
WE'RE STUDENTS. OUR JOB IS TO STUDY– TO COOK!
WE'RE TOO BUSY WITH IMPORTANT THINGS TO BOTHER WITH TRIVIALITIES LIKE LOVE!
YEAH, YOU SAID IT!
I MEAN, RIGHT NOW I'VE GOTTA FOCUS ON PASSING THIS DARN TEST.
EESH!
OH, I'M SURE YOU'LL BE ALL RIGHT, YUKIHIRA.

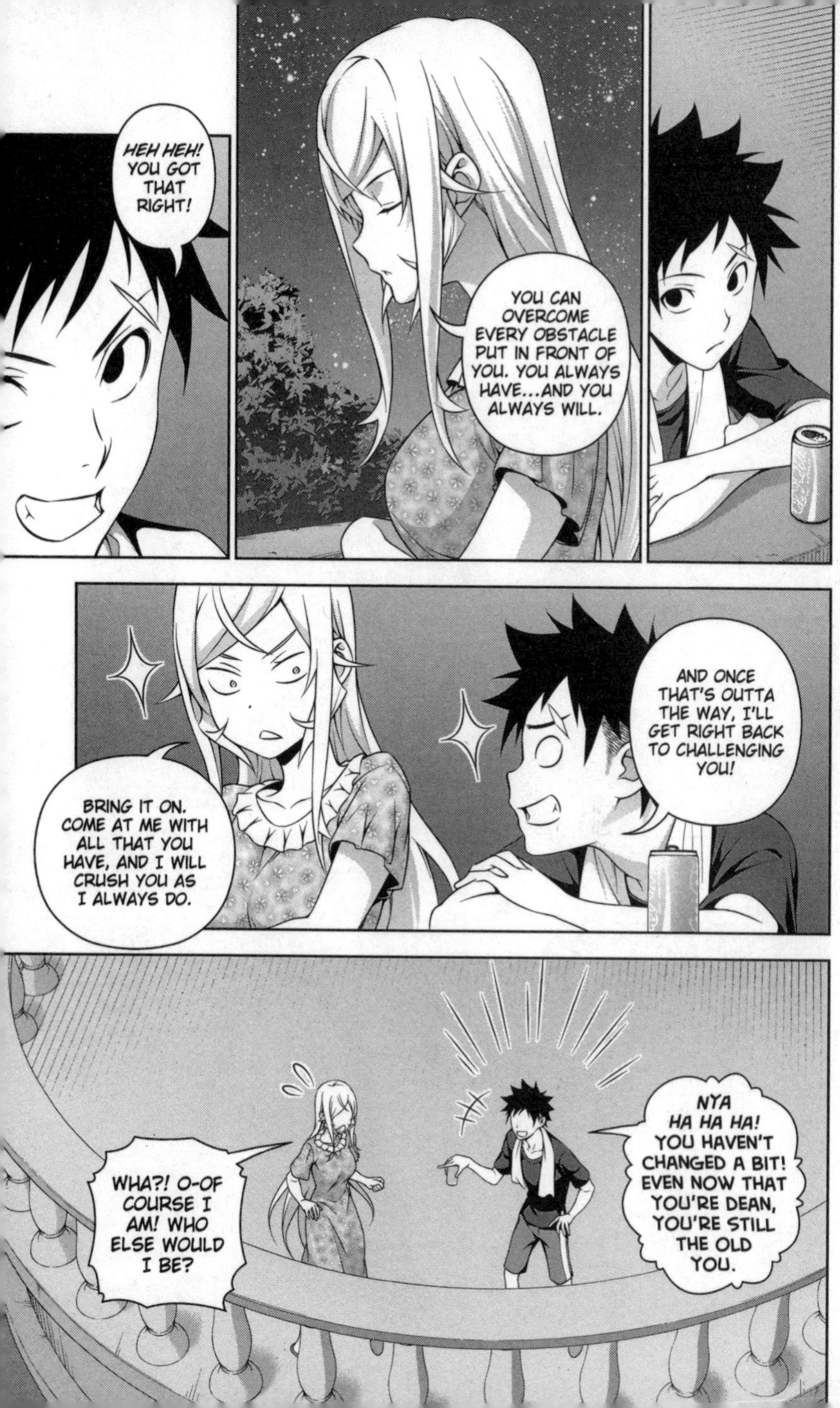
YOU CAN OVERCOME EVERY OBSTACLE PUT IN FRONT OF YOU. YOU ALWAYS HAVE...AND YOU ALWAYS WILL.
HEH HEH! YOU GOT THAT RIGHT!
AND ONCE THAT'S OUTTA THE WAY, I'LL GET RIGHT BACK TO CHALLENGING YOU!
BRING IT ON. COME AT ME WITH ALL THAT YOU HAVE, AND I WILL CRUSH YOU AS I ALWAYS DO.
NYA HA HA HA! YOU HAVEN'T CHANGED A BIT! EVEN NOW THAT YOU'RE DEAN, YOU'RE STILL THE OLD YOU.
WHA?! O-OF COURSE I AM! WHO ELSE WOULD I BE?

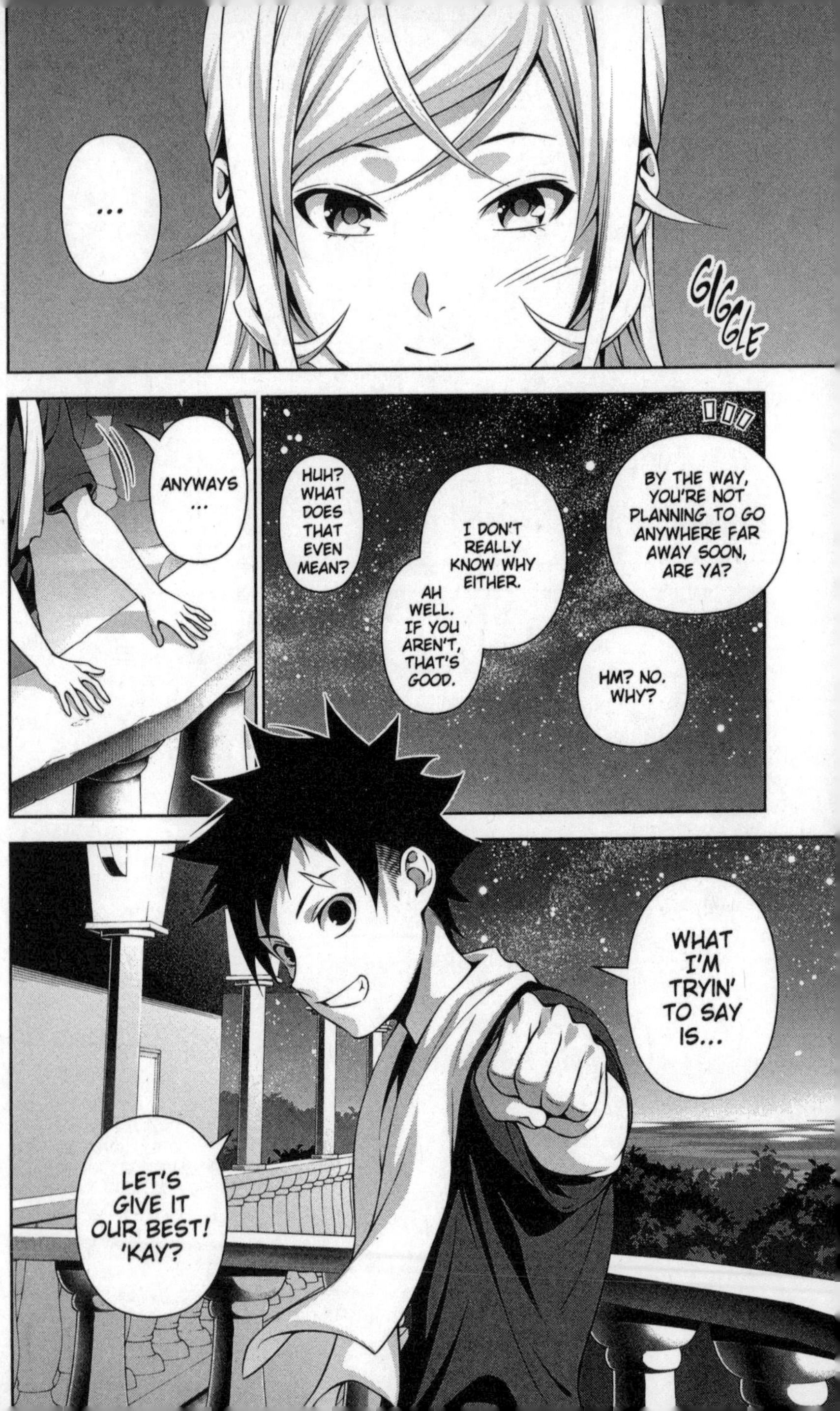
...
GIGGLE
BY THE WAY, YOU'RE NOT PLANNING TO GO ANYWHERE FAR AWAY SOON, ARE YA?
HM? NO. WHY?
I DON'T REALLY KNOW WHY EITHER.
AH WELL. IF YOU AREN'T, THAT'S GOOD.
HUH? WHAT DOES THAT EVEN MEAN?
ANYWAYS ...
WHAT I'M TRYIN' TO SAY IS...
LET'S GIVE IT OUR BEST! 'KAY?

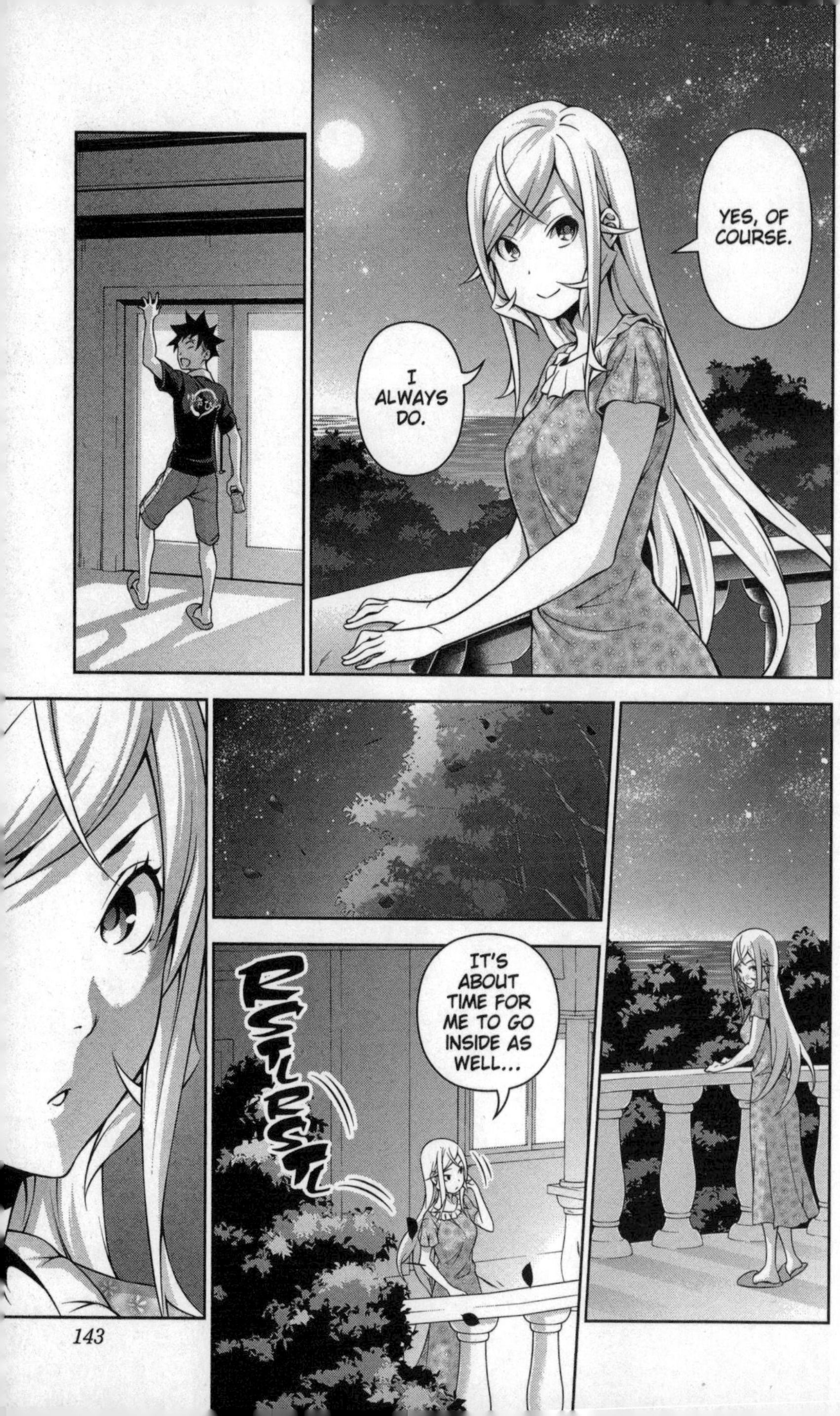
YES, OF COURSE.
I ALWAYS DO.
IT'S ABOUT TIME FOR ME TO GO INSIDE AS WELL...
RSTL RSTL

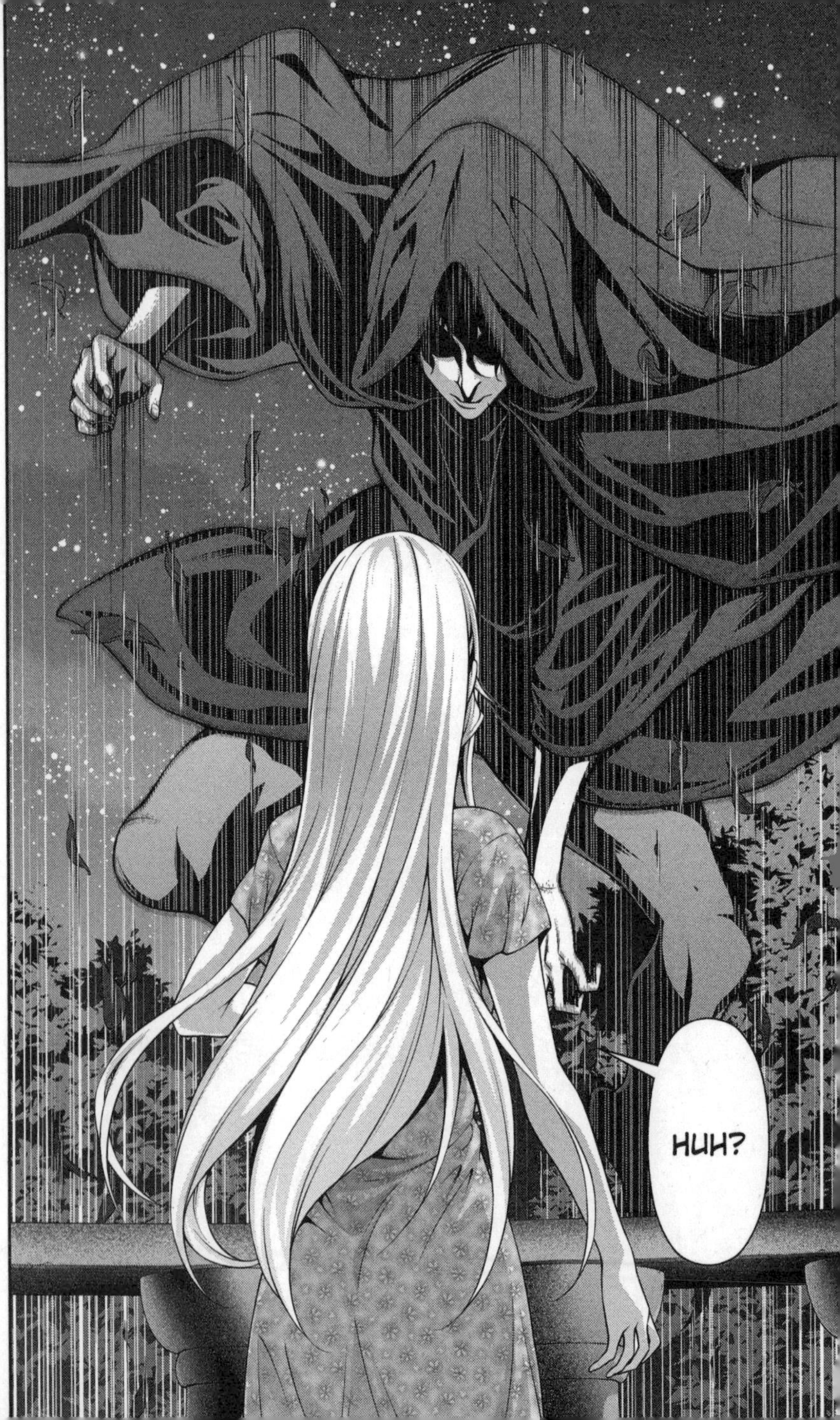
HUH?

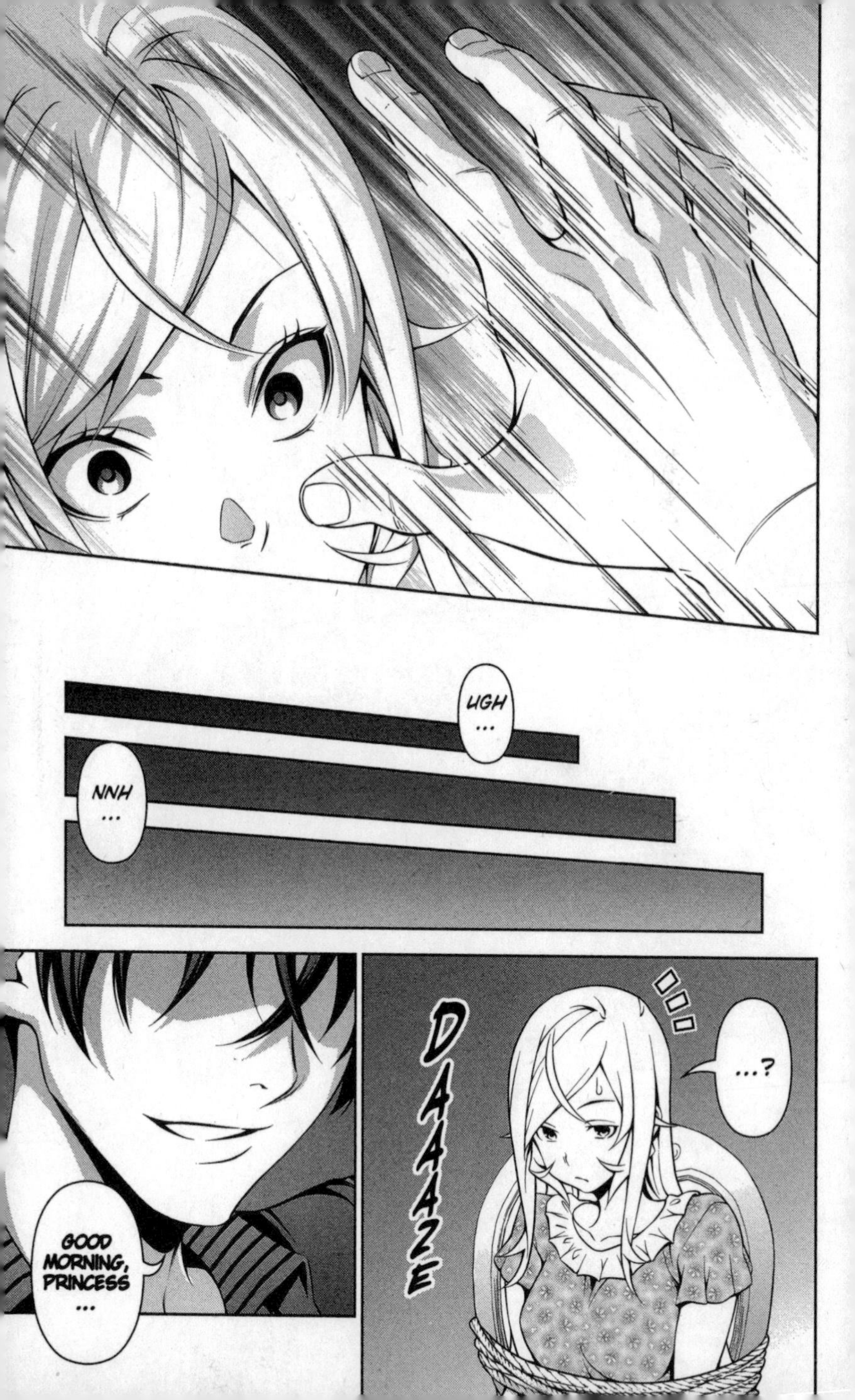
UGH ...
NNH ...
...?
DAAAAZE
GOOD MORNING, PRINCESS ...

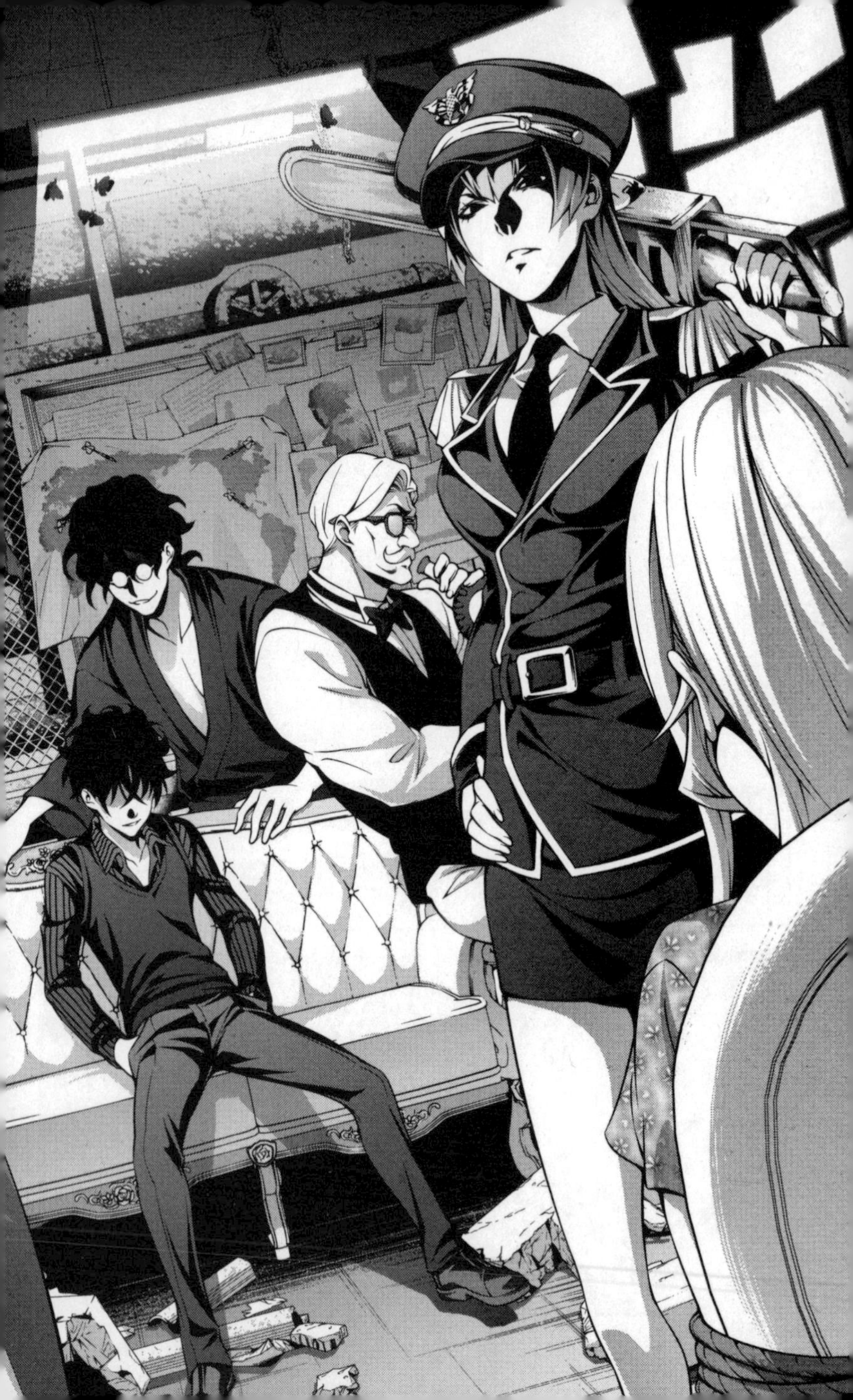

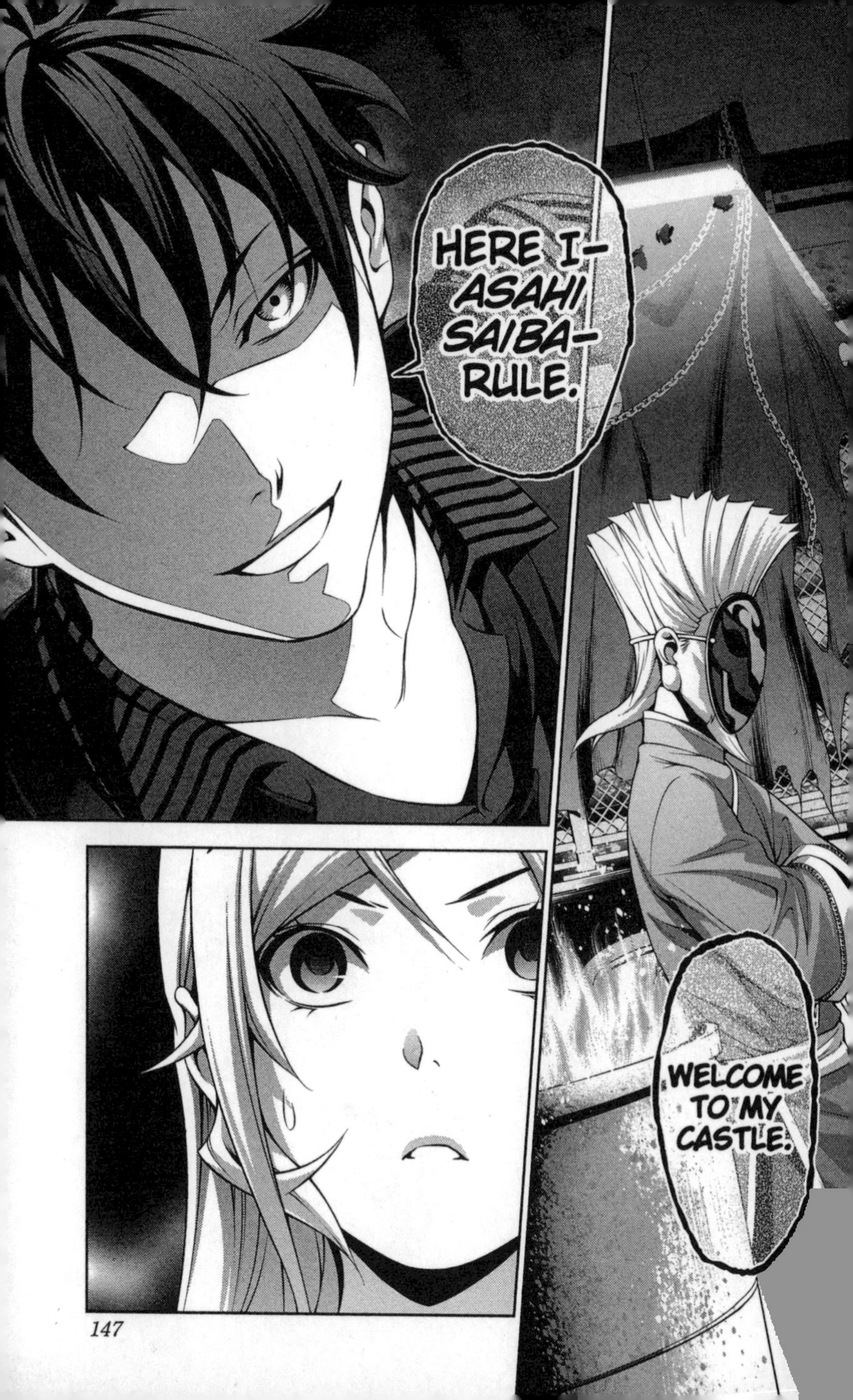
HERE I-ASAHI SAIBA-RULE.
WELCOME TO MY CASTLE.

279 SIGNAL THE COUNTERATTACK

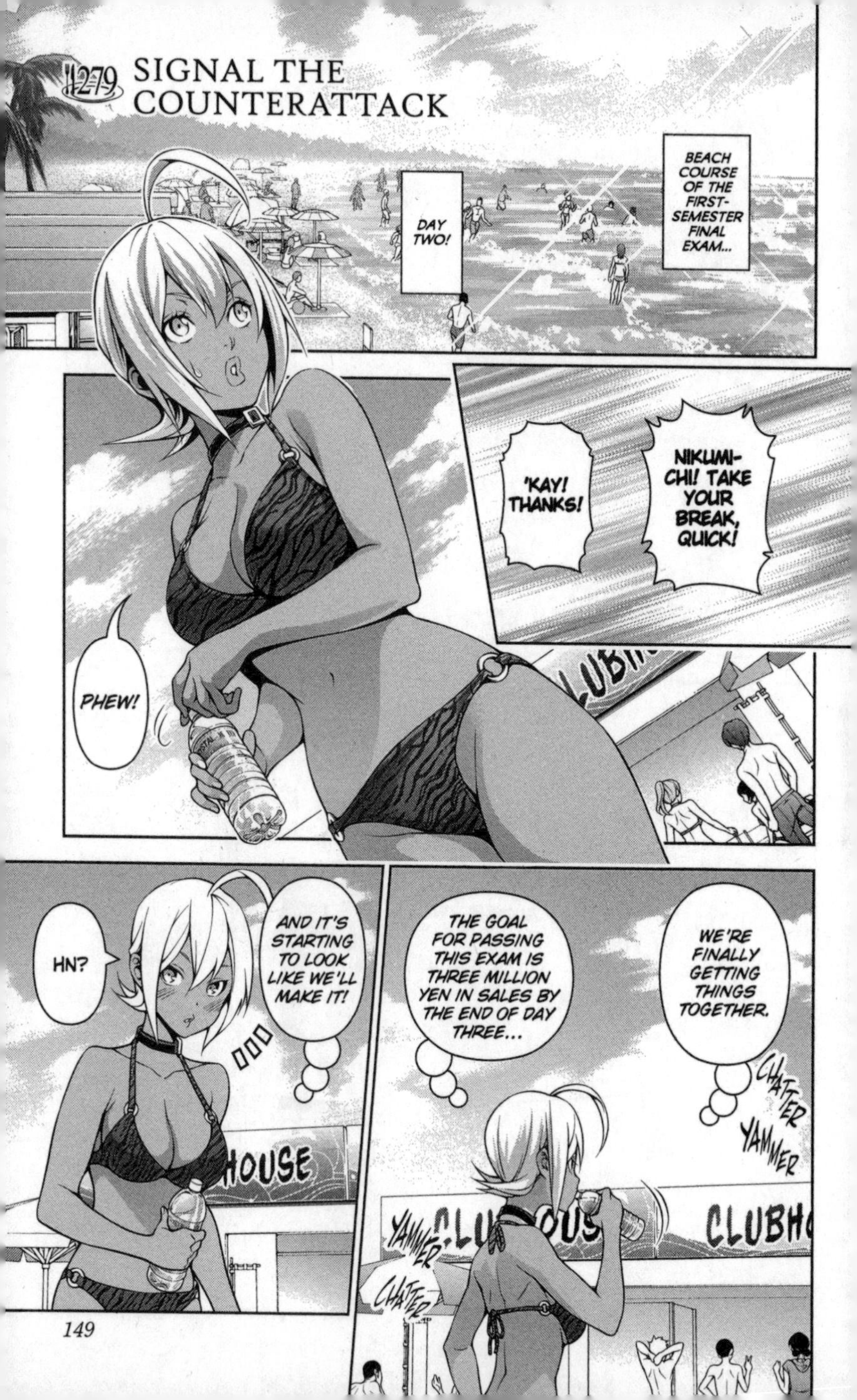
BEACH COURSE OF THE FIRST-SEMESTER FINAL EXAM...
DAY TWO!
NIKUMI-CHI! TAKE YOUR BREAK, QUICK!
'KAY! THANKS!
PHEW!
WE'RE FINALLY GETTING THINGS TOGETHER.
THE GOAL FOR PASSING THIS EXAM IS THREE MILLION YEN IN SALES BY THE END OF DAY THREE...
CHATTER
YAMMER
YAMMER
CHATTER
AND IT'S STARTING TO LOOK LIKE WE'LL MAKE IT!
HN?
HOUSE

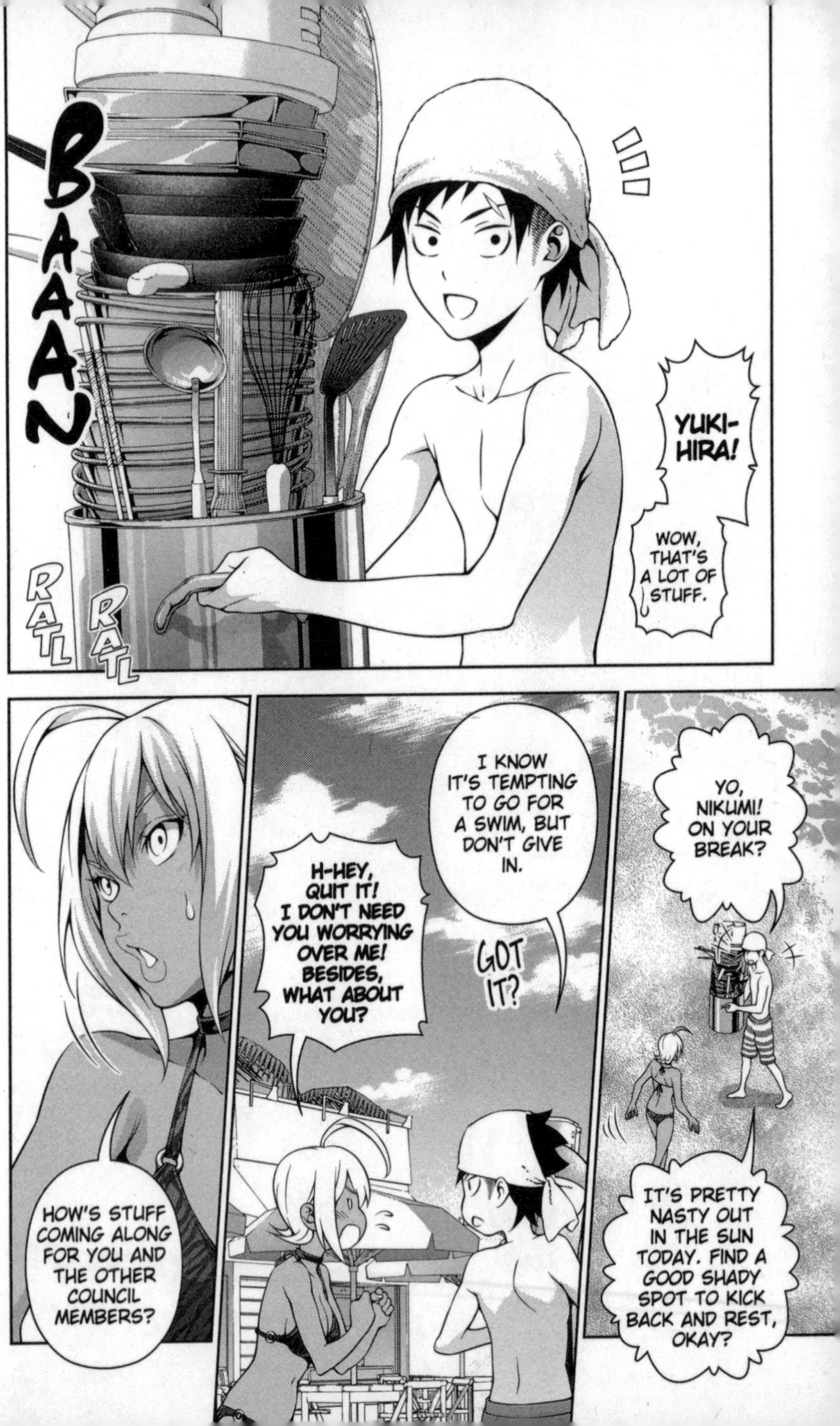
YUKI-HIRA!
WOW, THAT'S A LOT OF STUFF.
BAAAN
RATL
RATL
YO, NIKUMI! ON YOUR BREAK?
IT'S PRETTY NASTY OUT IN THE SUN TODAY. FIND A GOOD SHADY SPOT TO KICK BACK AND REST, OKAY?
I KNOW IT'S TEMPTING TO GO FOR A SWIM, BUT DON'T GIVE IN.
GOT IT?
H-HEY, QUIT IT! I DON'T NEED YOU WORRYING OVER ME! BESIDES, WHAT ABOUT YOU?
HOW'S STUFF COMING ALONG FOR YOU AND THE OTHER COUNCIL MEMBERS?

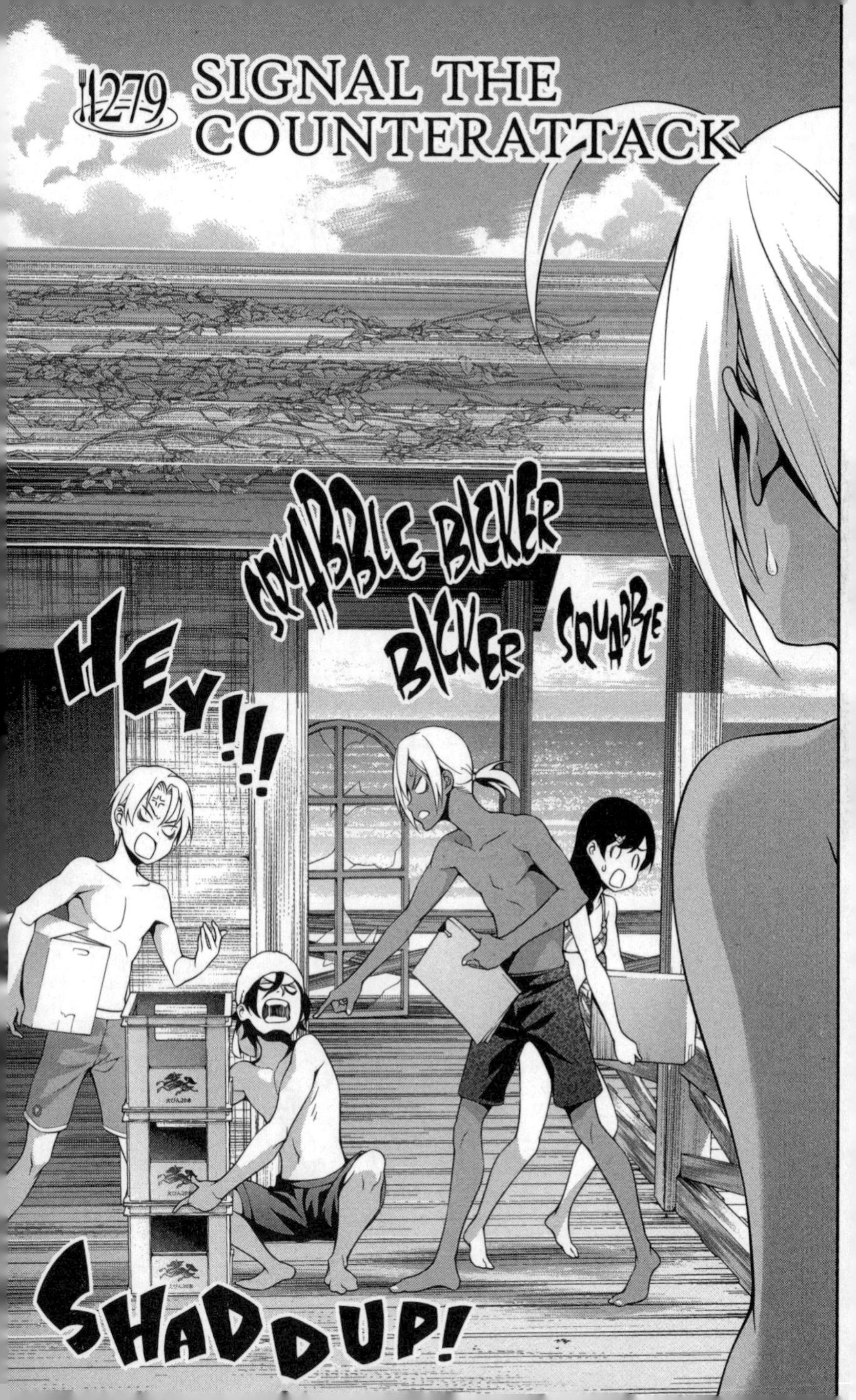

279
SIGNAL THE COUNTERATTACK
SQUABBLE BICKER
BICKER
SQUABBLE
HEY!!!
SHADDUP!

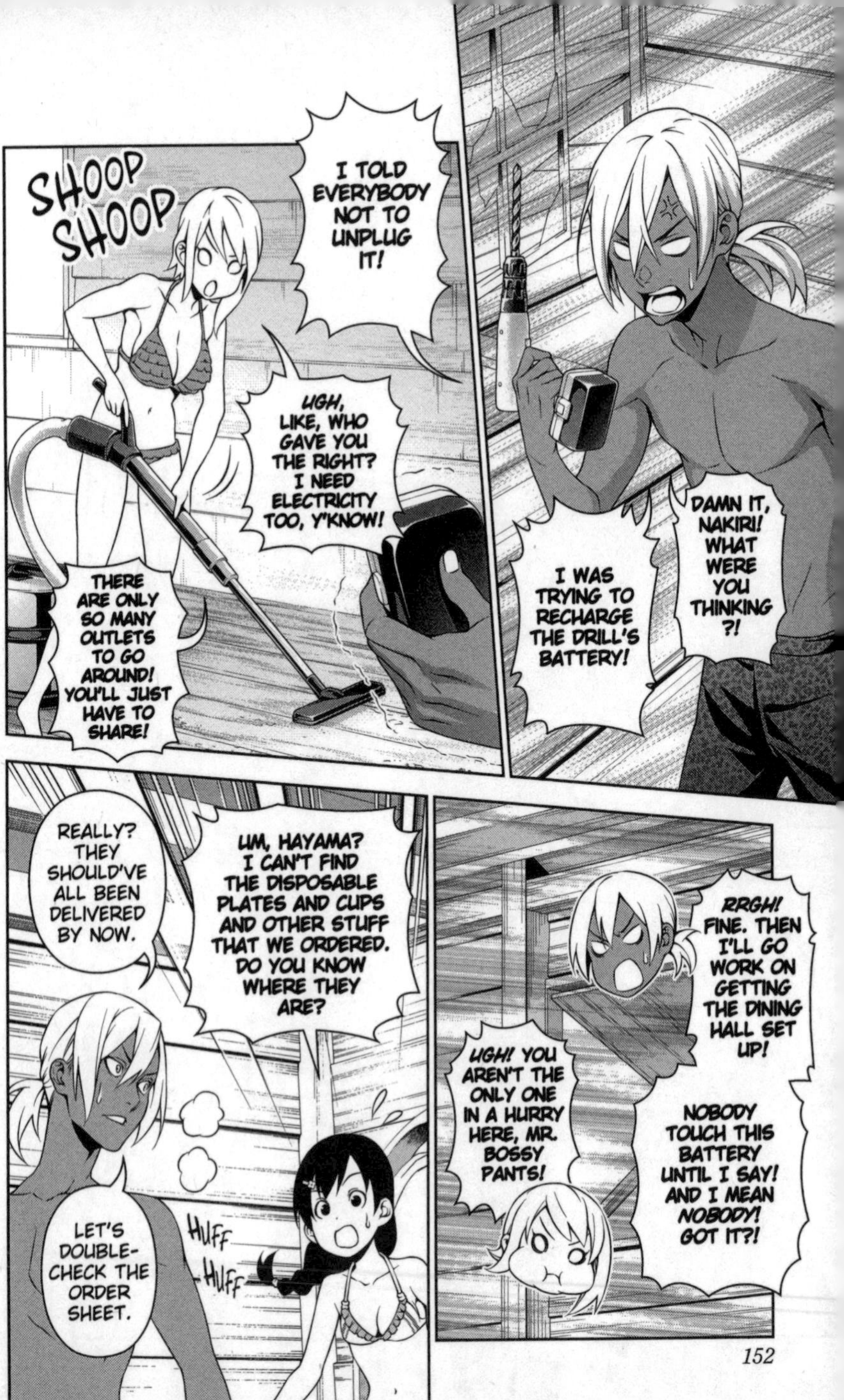
DAMN IT, NAKIRI! WHAT WERE YOU THINKING?!
I WAS TRYING TO RECHARGE THE DRILL'S BATTERY!
I TOLD EVERYBODY NOT TO UNPLUG IT!
SHOOP SHOOP
UGH, LIKE, WHO GAVE YOU THE RIGHT? I NEED ELECTRICITY TOO, Y'KNOW!
THERE ARE ONLY SO MANY OUTLETS TO GO AROUND! YOU'LL JUST HAVE TO SHARE!
RRGH! FINE. THEN I'LL GO WORK ON GETTING THE DINING HALL SET UP!
NOBODY TOUCH THIS BATTERY UNTIL I SAY! AND I MEAN NOBODY! GOT IT?!
UGH! YOU AREN'T THE ONLY ONE IN A HURRY HERE, MR. BOSSY PANTS!
UM, HAYAMA? I CAN'T FIND THE DISPOSABLE PLATES AND CUPS AND OTHER STUFF THAT WE ORDERED. DO YOU KNOW WHERE THEY ARE?
HUFF HUFF
REALLY? THEY SHOULD'VE ALL BEEN DELIVERED BY NOW.
LET'S DOUBLE-CHECK THE ORDER SHEET.

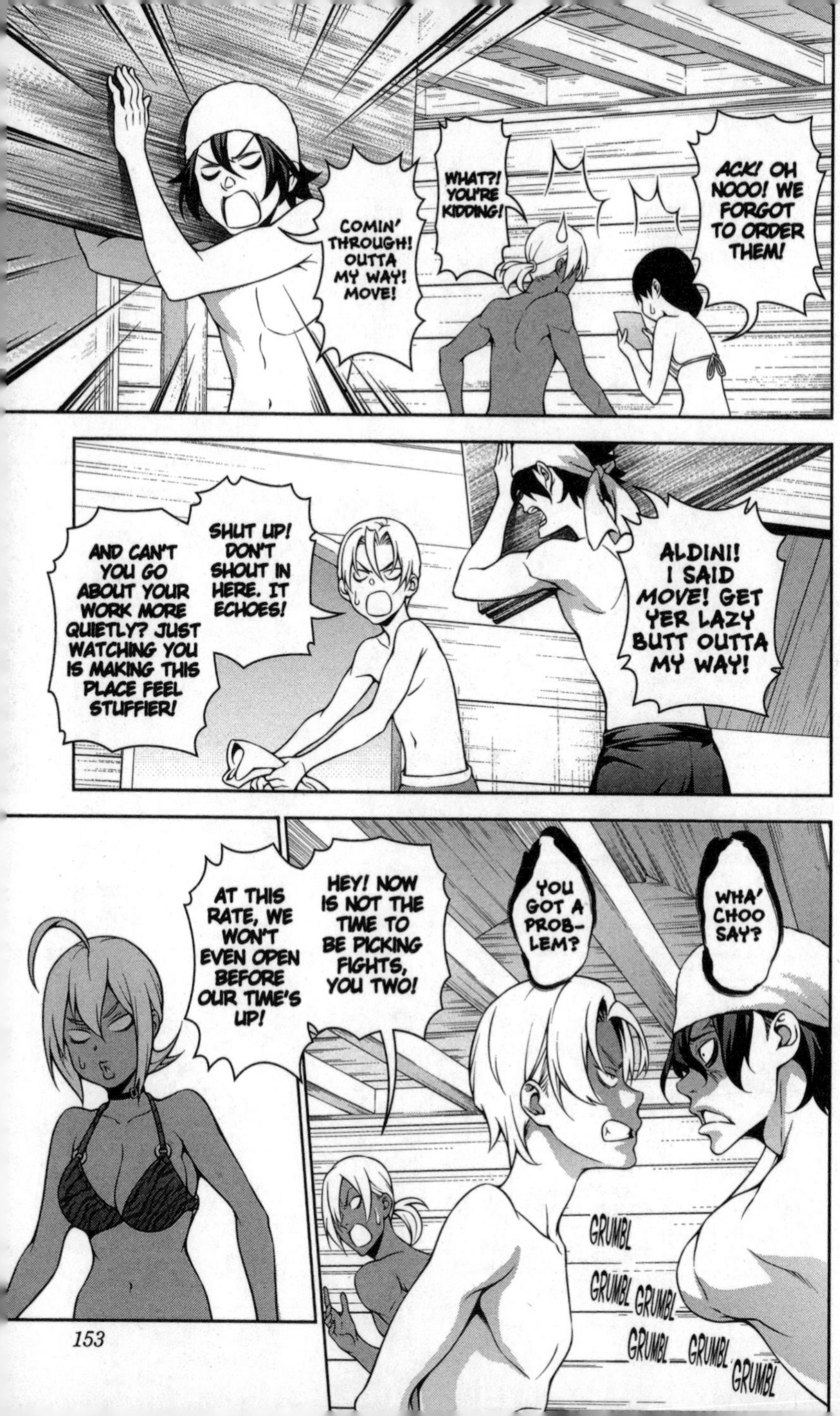
ACK! OH NOOO! WE FORGOT TO ORDER THEM!
WHAT?! YOU'RE KIDDING!
COMIN' THROUGH! OUTTA MY WAY! MOVE!
ALDINI! I SAID MOVE! GET YER LAZY BUTT OUTTA MY WAY!
SHUT UP! DON'T SHOUT IN HERE. IT ECHOES!
AND CAN'T YOU GO ABOUT YOUR WORK MORE QUIETLY? JUST WATCHING YOU IS MAKING THIS PLACE FEEL STUFFIER!
WHA' CHOO SAY?
YOU GOT A PROB-LEM?
HEY! NOW IS NOT THE TIME TO BE PICKING FIGHTS, YOU TWO!
AT THIS RATE, WE WON'T EVEN OPEN BEFORE OUR TIME'S UP!
GRUMBL
GRUMBL GRUMBL
GRUMBL GRUMBL GRUMBL

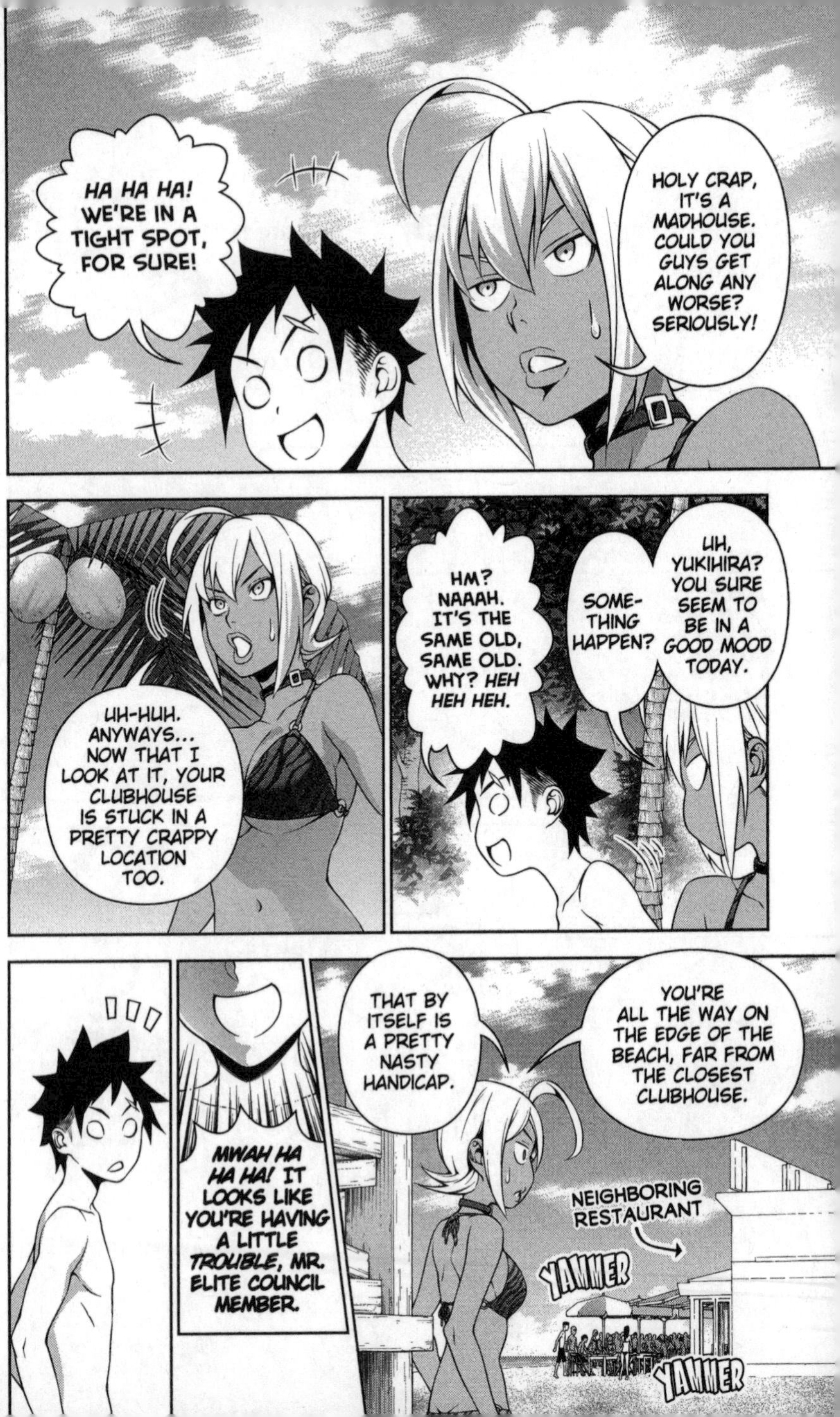
HOLY CRAP, IT'S A MADHOUSE. COULD YOU GUYS GET ALONG ANY WORSE? SERIOUSLY!
HA HA HA! WE'RE IN A TIGHT SPOT, FOR SURE!
UH, YUKIHIRA? YOU SURE SEEM TO BE IN A GOOD MOOD TODAY.
SOME-THING HAPPEN?
HM? NAAAH. IT'S THE SAME OLD, SAME OLD. WHY? HEH HEH HEH.
UH-HUH. ANYWAYS... NOW THAT I LOOK AT IT, YOUR CLUBHOUSE IS STUCK IN A PRETTY CRAPPY LOCATION TOO.
YOU'RE ALL THE WAY ON THE EDGE OF THE BEACH, FAR FROM THE CLOSEST CLUBHOUSE.
THAT BY ITSELF IS A PRETTY NASTY HANDICAP.
NEIGHBORING RESTAURANT
YAMMER
YAMMER
MWAH HA HA HA! IT LOOKS LIKE YOU'RE HAVING A LITTLE TROUBLE, MR. ELITE COUNCIL MEMBER.

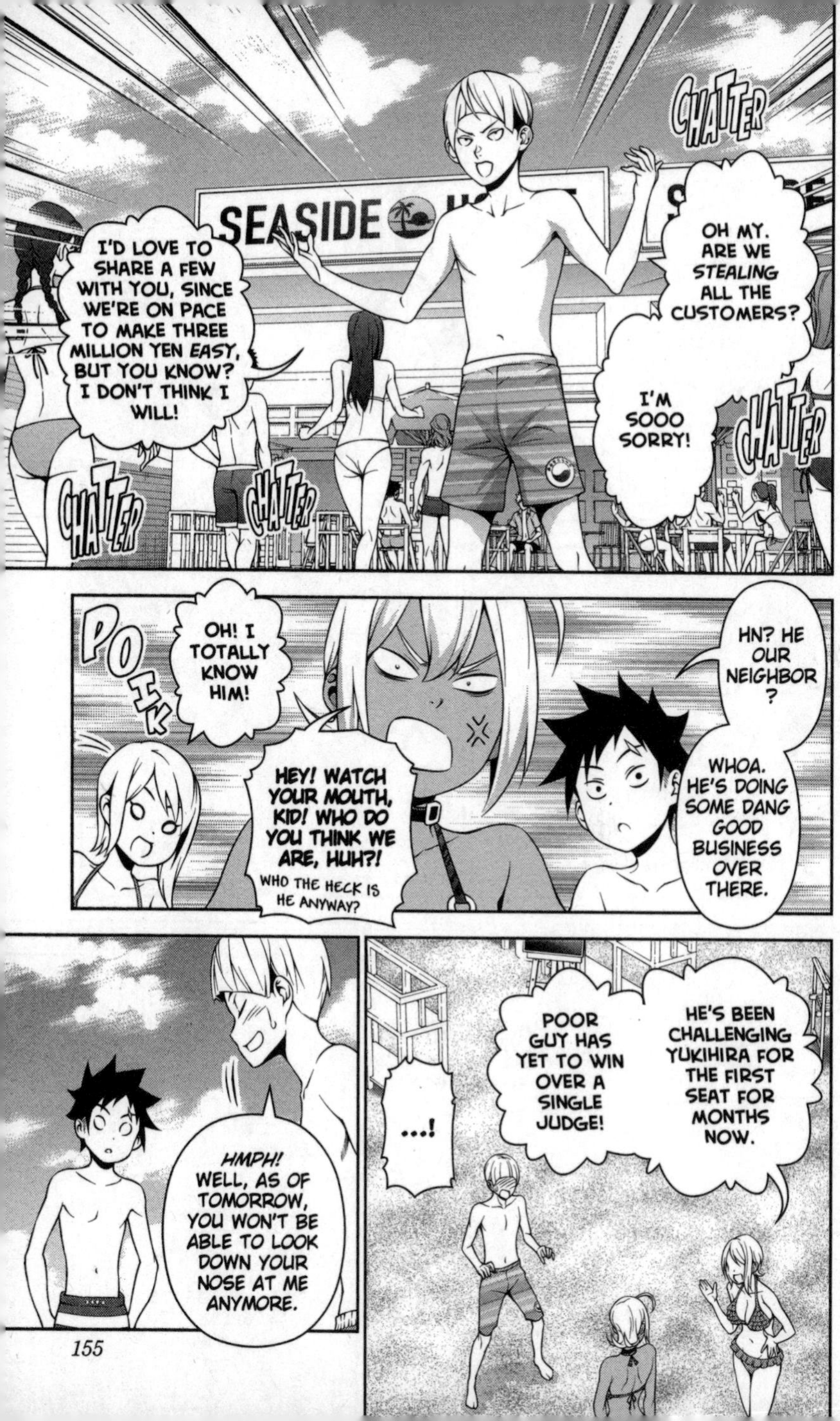
CHATTER
OH MY. ARE WE STEALING ALL THE CUSTOMERS?
I'M SOOO SORRY!
CHATTER
SEASIDE
I'D LOVE TO SHARE A FEW WITH YOU, SINCE WE'RE ON PACE TO MAKE THREE MILLION YEN *EASY*, BUT YOU KNOW? I DON'T THINK I WILL!
CHATTER
CHATTER
HN? HE OUR NEIGHBOR?
WHOA. HE'S DOING SOME DANG GOOD BUSINESS OVER THERE.
HEY! WATCH YOUR MOUTH, KID! WHO DO YOU THINK WE ARE, HUH?!
WHO THE HECK IS HE ANYWAY?
OH! I TOTALLY KNOW HIM!
POIK
HE'S BEEN CHALLENGING YUKIHIRA FOR THE FIRST SEAT FOR MONTHS NOW.
POOR GUY HAS YET TO WIN OVER A SINGLE JUDGE!
...!
HMPH! WELL, AS OF TOMORROW, YOU WON'T BE ABLE TO LOOK DOWN YOUR NOSE AT ME ANYMORE.

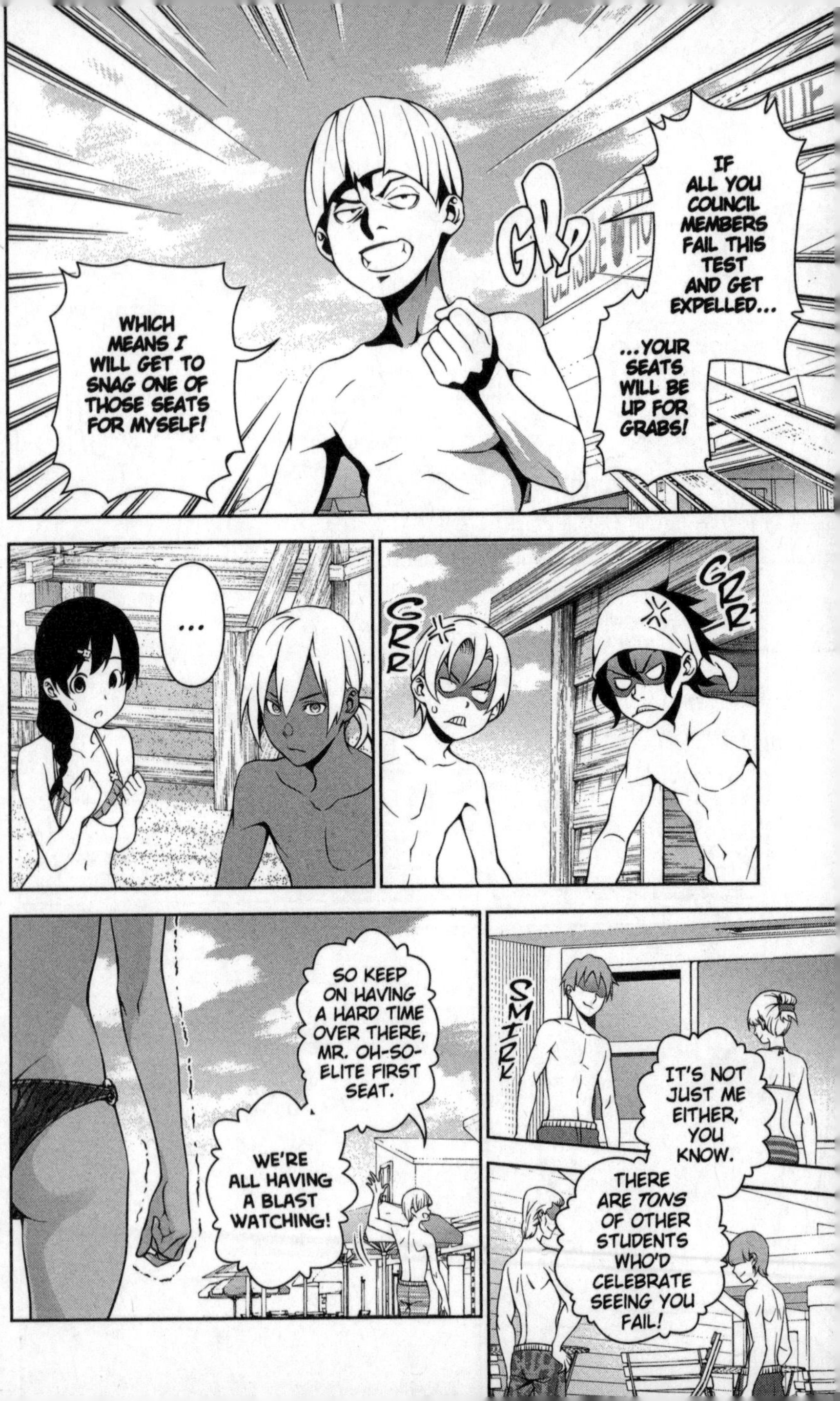
IF ALL YOU COUNCIL MEMBERS FAIL THIS TEST AND GET EXPELLED...
...YOUR SEATS WILL BE UP FOR GRABS!
GRR
WHICH MEANS I WILL GET TO SNAG ONE OF THOSE SEATS FOR MYSELF!
GRR
GRR
...
SMIRK
IT'S NOT JUST ME EITHER, YOU KNOW.
THERE ARE *TONS* OF OTHER STUDENTS WHO'D CELEBRATE SEEING YOU FAIL!
SO KEEP ON HAVING A HARD TIME OVER THERE, MR. OH-SO-ELITE FIRST SEAT.
WE'RE ALL HAVING A BLAST WATCHING!

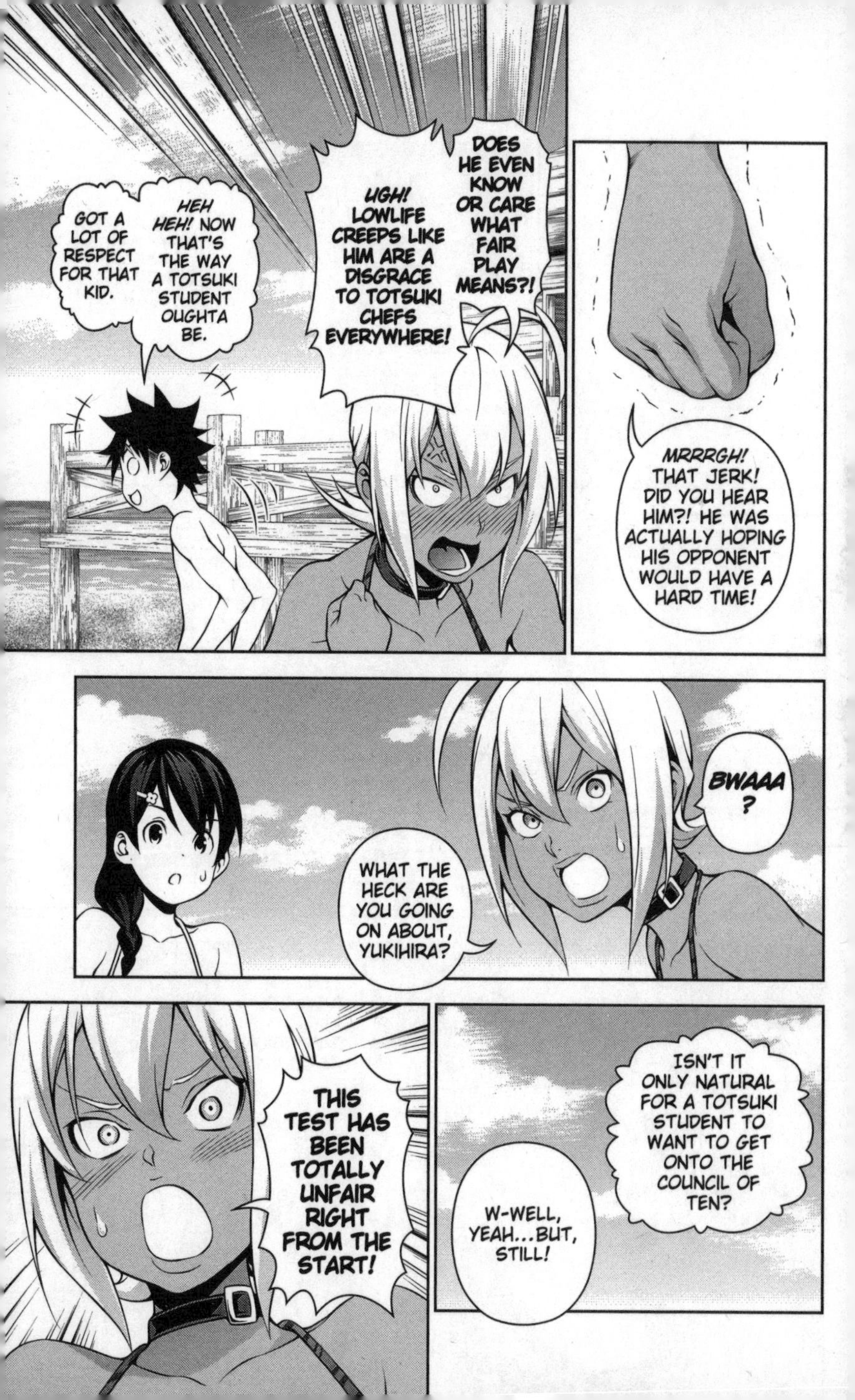
MRRRGH! THAT JERK! DID YOU HEAR HIM?! HE WAS ACTUALLY HOPING HIS OPPONENT WOULD HAVE A HARD TIME!
DOES HE EVEN KNOW OR CARE WHAT FAIR PLAY MEANS?!
UGH! LOWLIFE CREEPS LIKE HIM ARE A DISGRACE TO TOTSUKI CHEFS EVERYWHERE!
HEH HEH! NOW THAT'S THE WAY A TOTSUKI STUDENT OUGHTA BE.
GOT A LOT OF RESPECT FOR THAT KID.
BWAAA ?
WHAT THE HECK ARE YOU GOING ON ABOUT, YUKIHIRA?
ISN'T IT ONLY NATURAL FOR A TOTSUKI STUDENT TO WANT TO GET ONTO THE COUNCIL OF TEN?
W-WELL, YEAH...BUT, STILL!
THIS TEST HAS BEEN TOTALLY UNFAIR RIGHT FROM THE START!

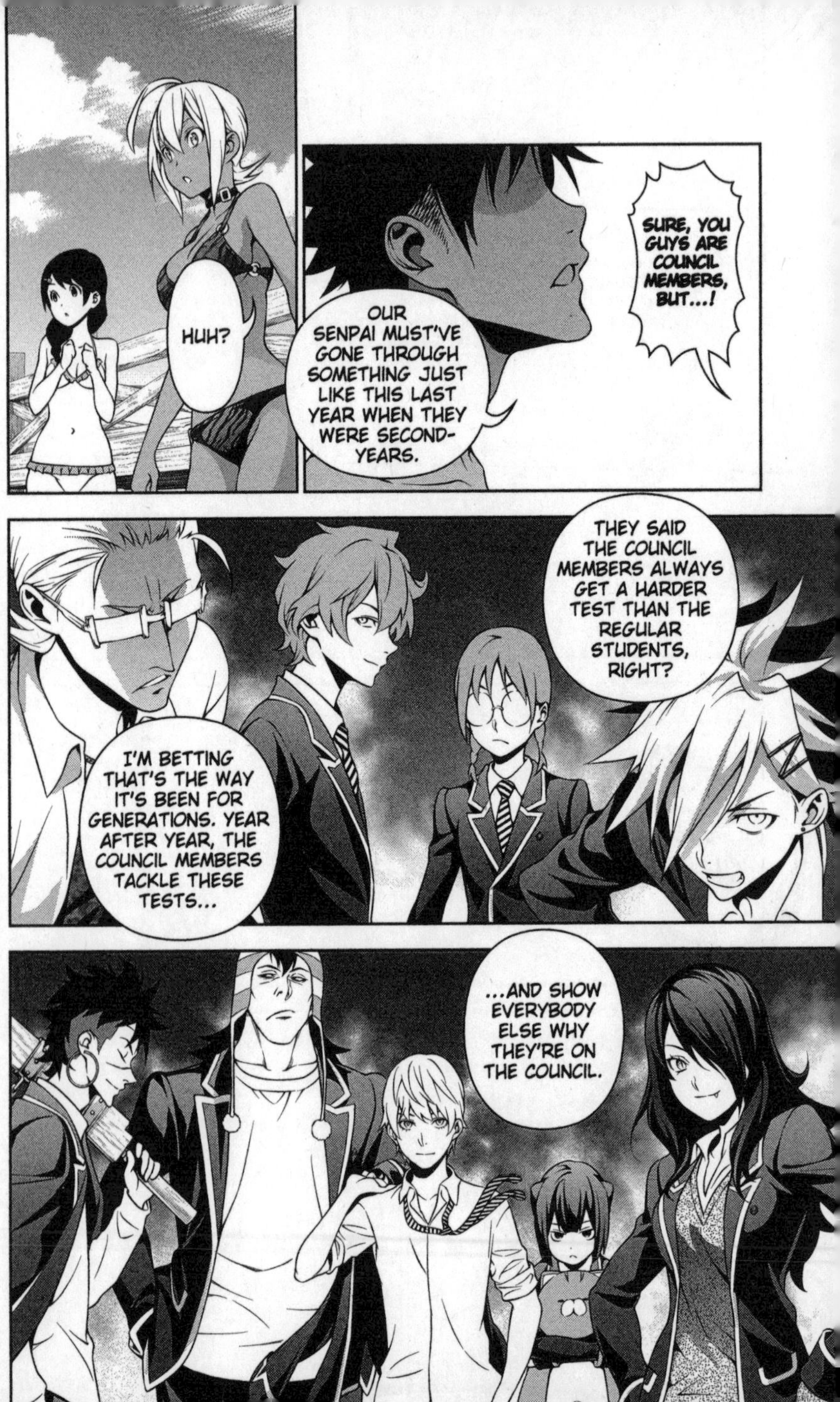
SURE, YOU GUYS ARE COUNCIL MEMBERS, BUT...!
OUR SENPAI MUST'VE GONE THROUGH SOMETHING JUST LIKE THIS LAST YEAR WHEN THEY WERE SECOND-YEARS.
HUH?
THEY SAID THE COUNCIL MEMBERS ALWAYS GET A HARDER TEST THAN THE REGULAR STUDENTS, RIGHT?
I'M BETTING THAT'S THE WAY IT'S BEEN FOR GENERATIONS. YEAR AFTER YEAR, THE COUNCIL MEMBERS TACKLE THESE TESTS...
...AND SHOW EVERYBODY ELSE WHY THEY'RE ON THE COUNCIL.

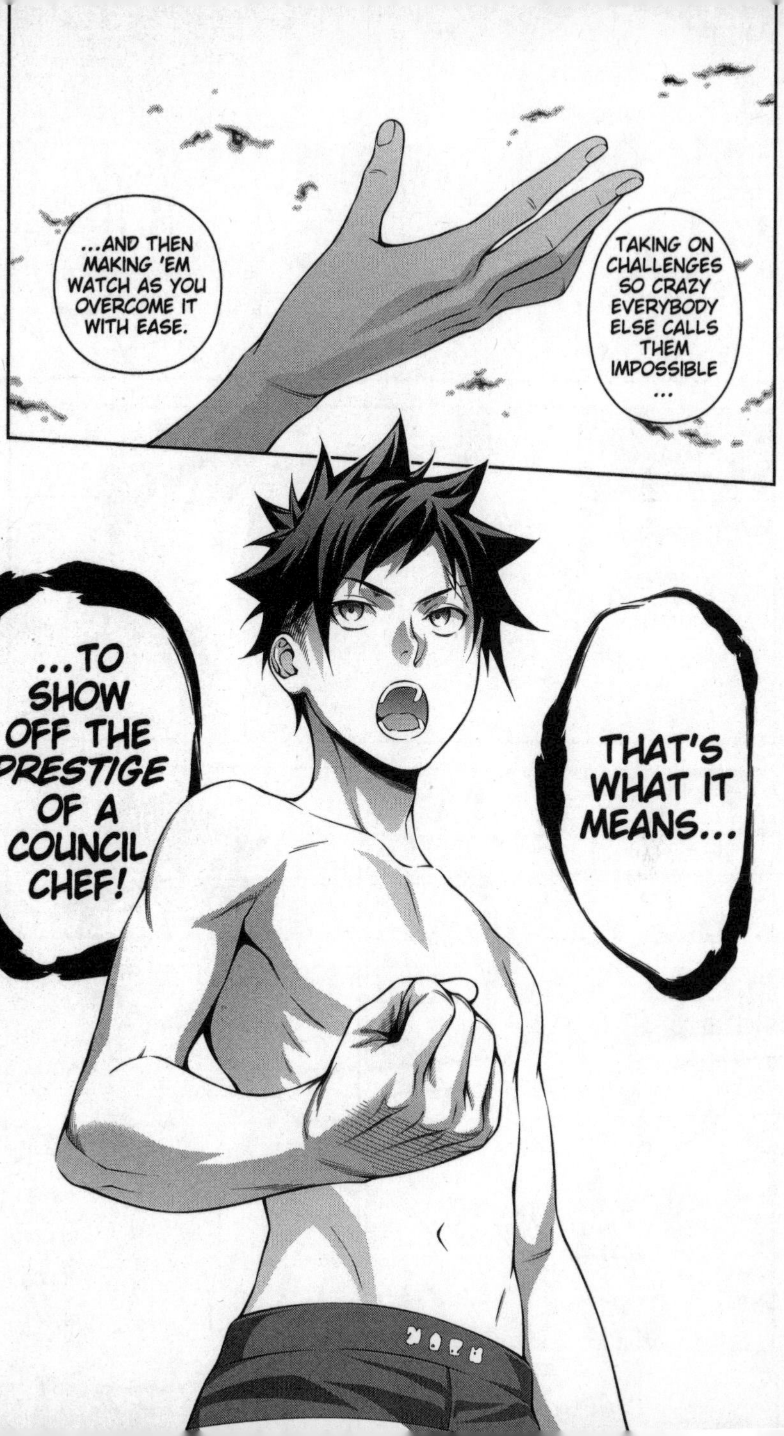
TAKING ON CHALLENGES SO CRAZY EVERYBODY ELSE CALLS THEM IMPOSSIBLE ...
...AND THEN MAKING 'EM WATCH AS YOU OVERCOME IT WITH EASE.
THAT'S WHAT IT MEANS...
...TO SHOW OFF THE *PRESTIGE* OF A COUNCIL CHEF!

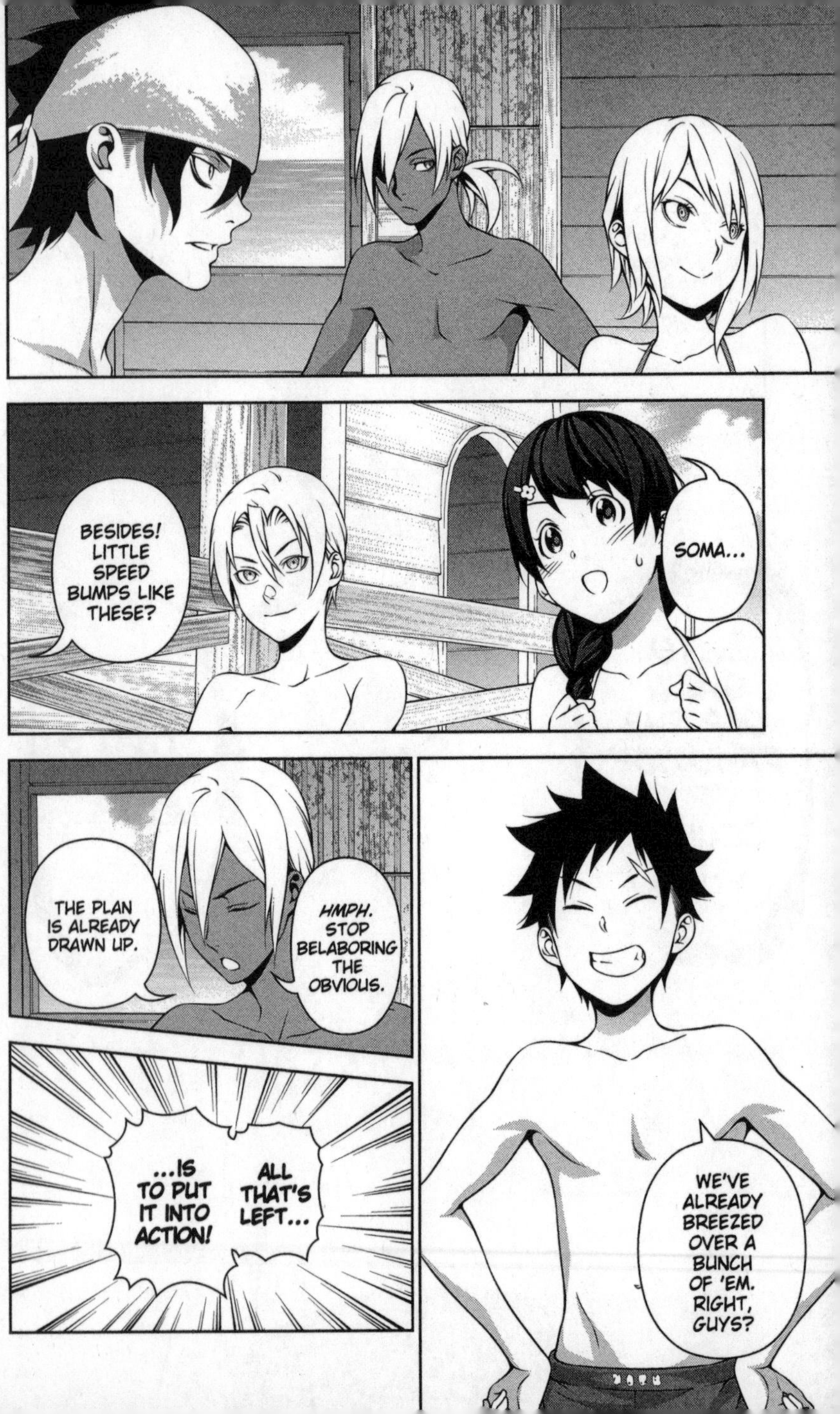
SOMA...
BESIDES! LITTLE SPEED BUMPS LIKE THESE?
WE'VE ALREADY BREEZED OVER A BUNCH OF 'EM. RIGHT, GUYS?
HMPH. STOP BELABORING THE OBVIOUS.
THE PLAN IS ALREADY DRAWN UP.
ALL THAT'S LEFT...
...IS TO PUT IT INTO ACTION!

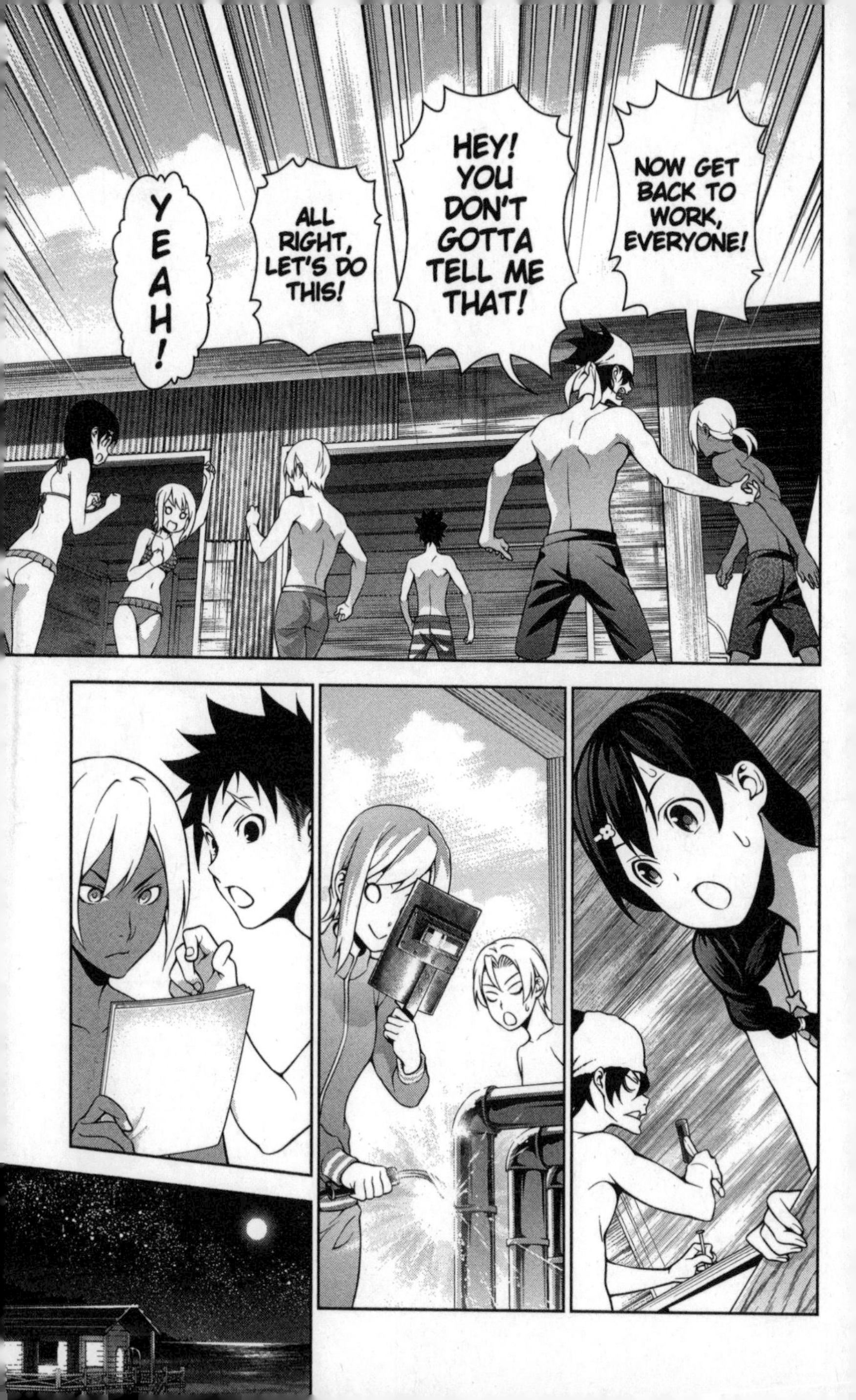
NOW GET BACK TO WORK, EVERYONE!
HEY! YOU DON'T GOTTA TELL ME THAT!
ALL RIGHT, LET'S DO THIS!
YEAH!

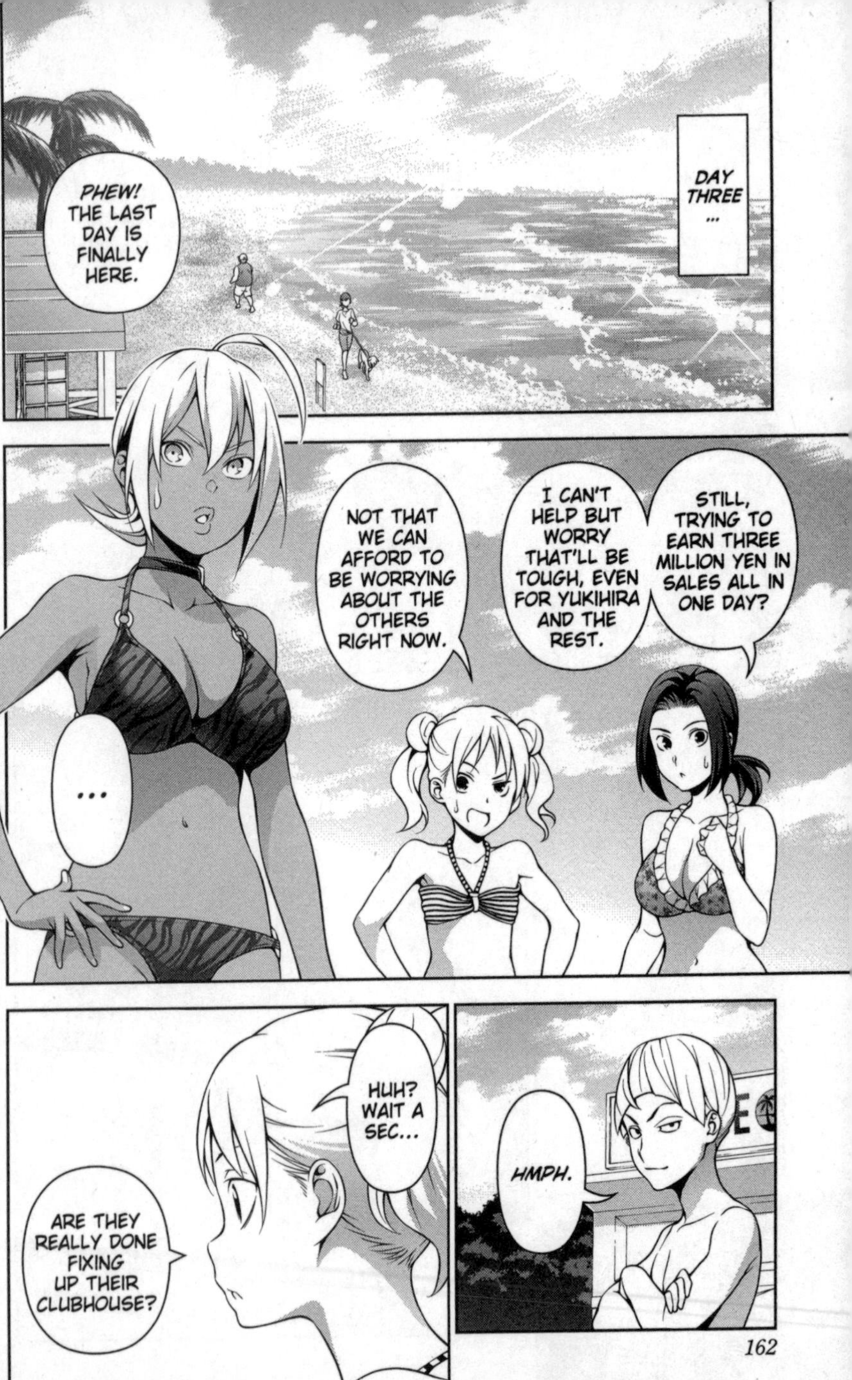
DAY THREE ...
PHEW! THE LAST DAY IS FINALLY HERE.
STILL, TRYING TO EARN THREE MILLION YEN IN SALES ALL IN ONE DAY?
I CAN'T HELP BUT WORRY THAT'LL BE TOUGH, EVEN FOR YUKIHIRA AND THE REST.
NOT THAT WE CAN AFFORD TO BE WORRYING ABOUT THE OTHERS RIGHT NOW.
...
HMPH.
HUH? WAIT A SEC...
ARE THEY REALLY DONE FIXING UP THEIR CLUBHOUSE?

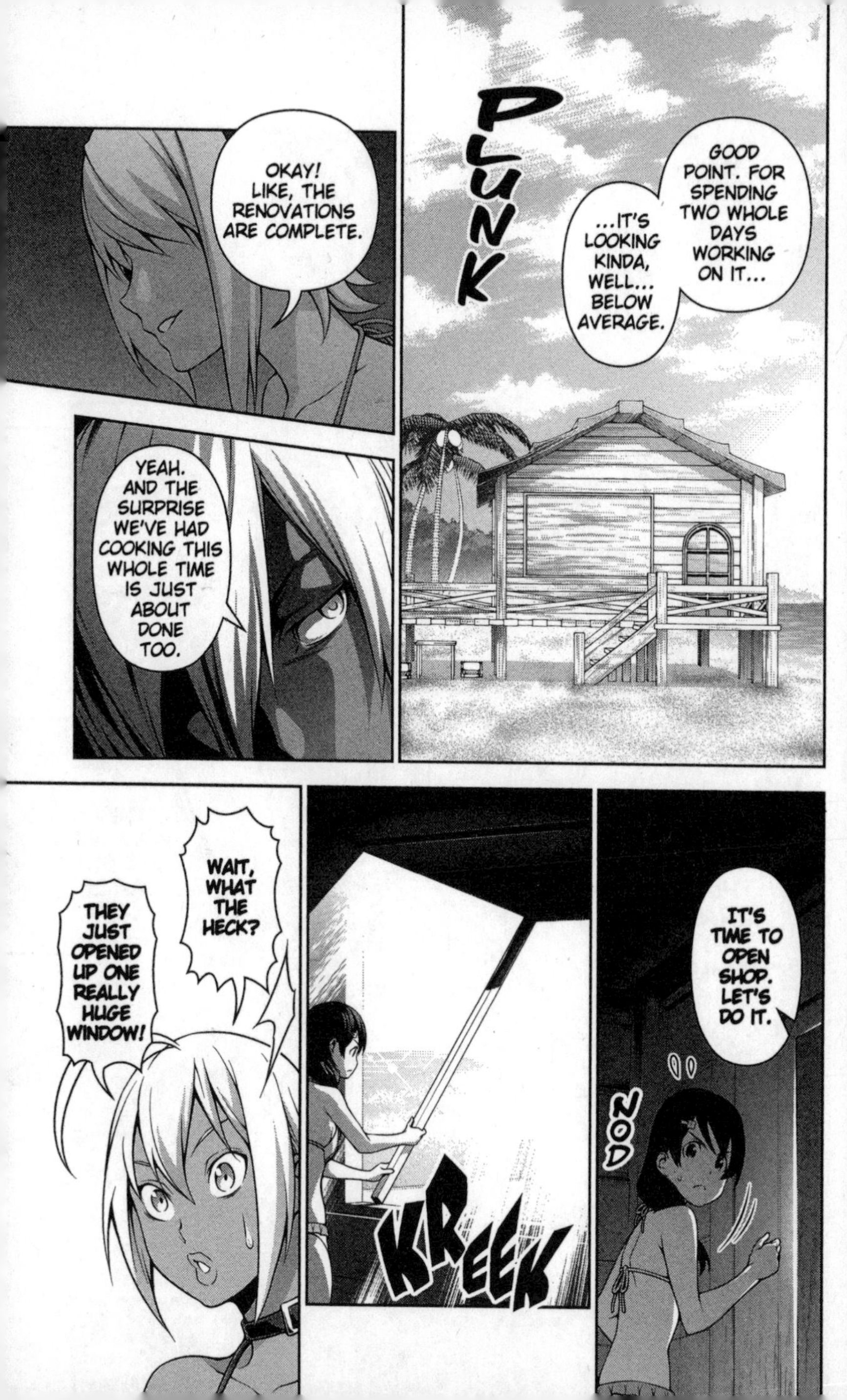
GOOD POINT. FOR SPENDING TWO WHOLE DAYS WORKING ON IT...
...IT'S LOOKING KINDA, WELL... BELOW AVERAGE.
PLUNK
OKAY! LIKE, THE RENOVATIONS ARE COMPLETE.
YEAH. AND THE SURPRISE WE'VE HAD COOKING THIS WHOLE TIME IS JUST ABOUT DONE TOO.
IT'S TIME TO OPEN SHOP. LET'S DO IT.
NOD
KREEK
WAIT, WHAT THE HECK?
THEY JUST OPENED UP ONE REALLY HUGE WINDOW!

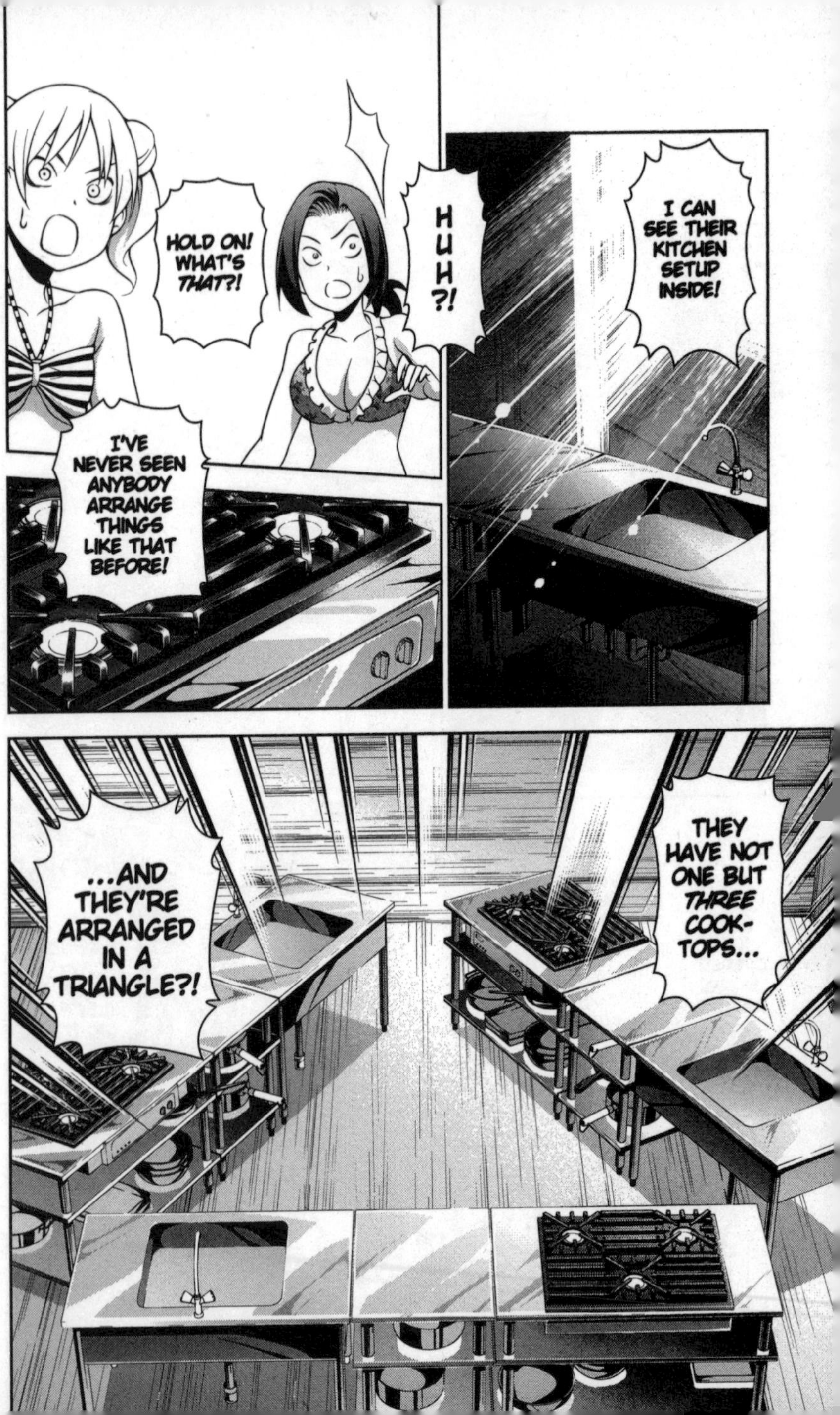
I CAN SEE THEIR KITCHEN SETUP INSIDE!
HUH?!
HOLD ON! WHAT'S *THAT*?!
I'VE NEVER SEEN ANYBODY ARRANGE THINGS LIKE THAT BEFORE!
THEY HAVE NOT ONE BUT *THREE* COOK-TOPS...
...AND THEY'RE ARRANGED IN A TRIANGLE?!

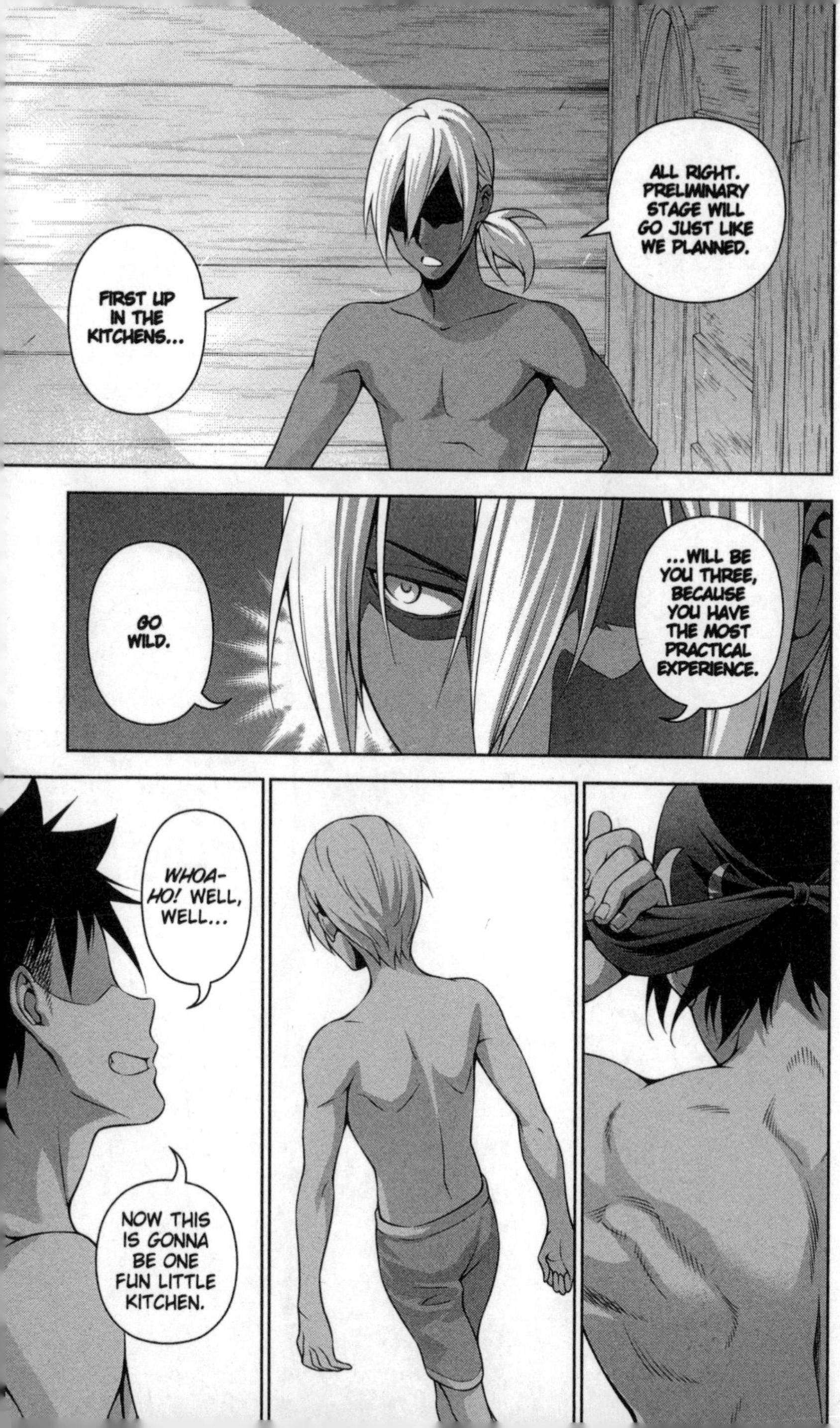
ALL RIGHT. PRELIMINARY STAGE WILL GO JUST LIKE WE PLANNED.
FIRST UP IN THE KITCHENS...
...WILL BE YOU THREE, BECAUSE YOU HAVE THE MOST PRACTICAL EXPERIENCE.
GO WILD.
WHOA-HO! WELL, WELL...
NOW THIS IS GONNA BE ONE FUN LITTLE KITCHEN.

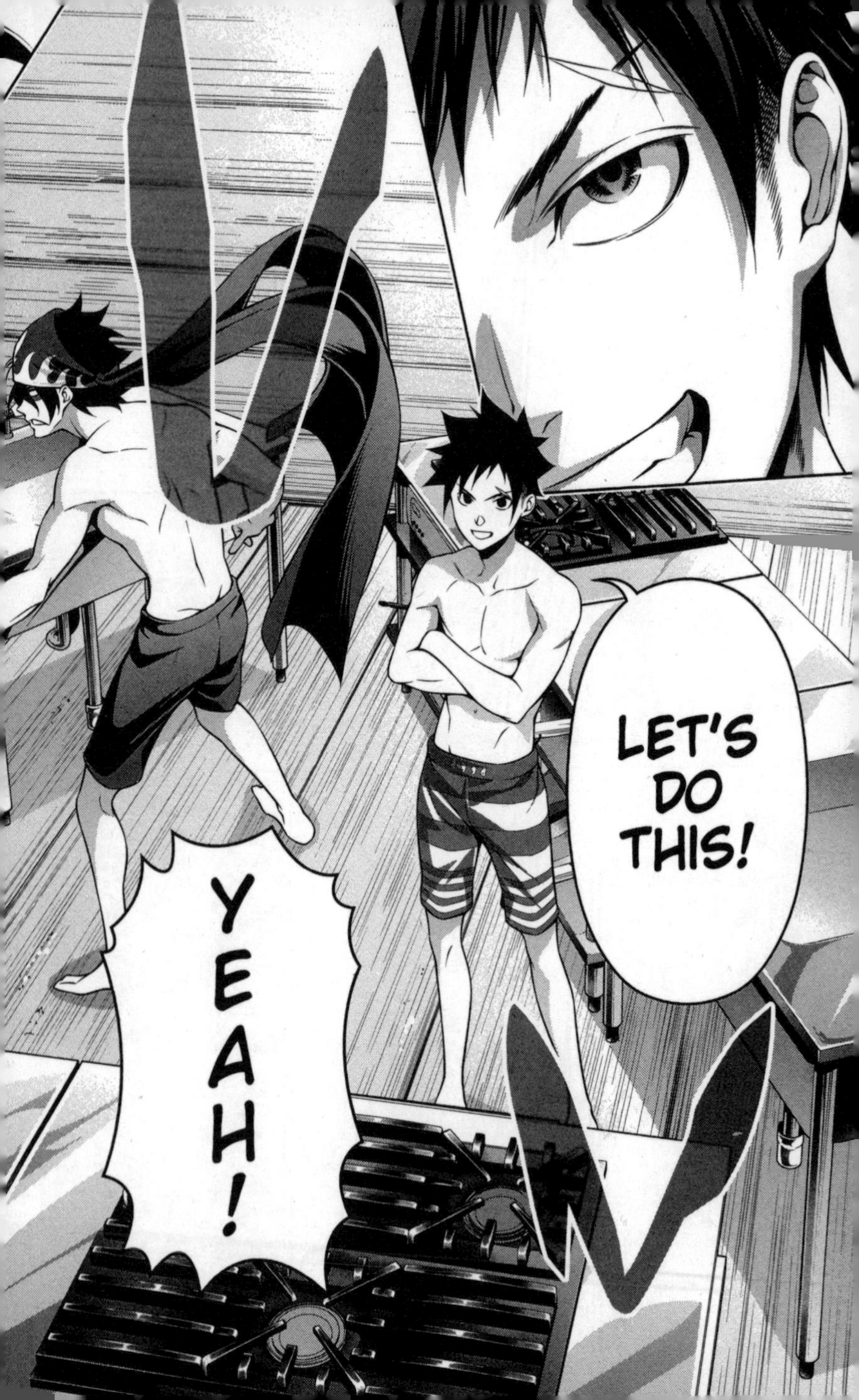
LET'S DO THIS!
YEAH!

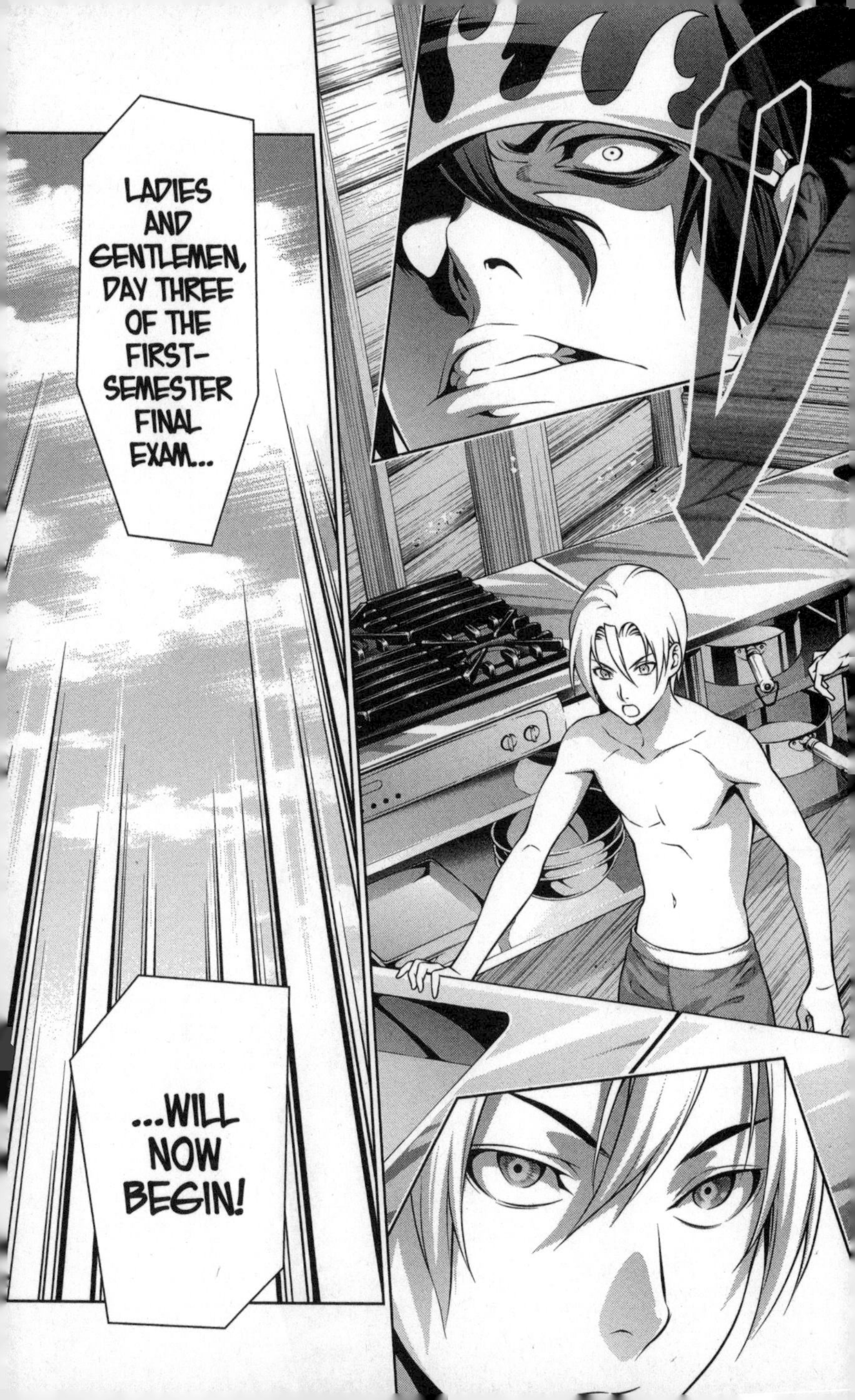
LADIES AND GENTLEMEN, DAY THREE OF THE FIRST-SEMESTER FINAL EXAM...
...WILL NOW BEGIN!

COMMANDER

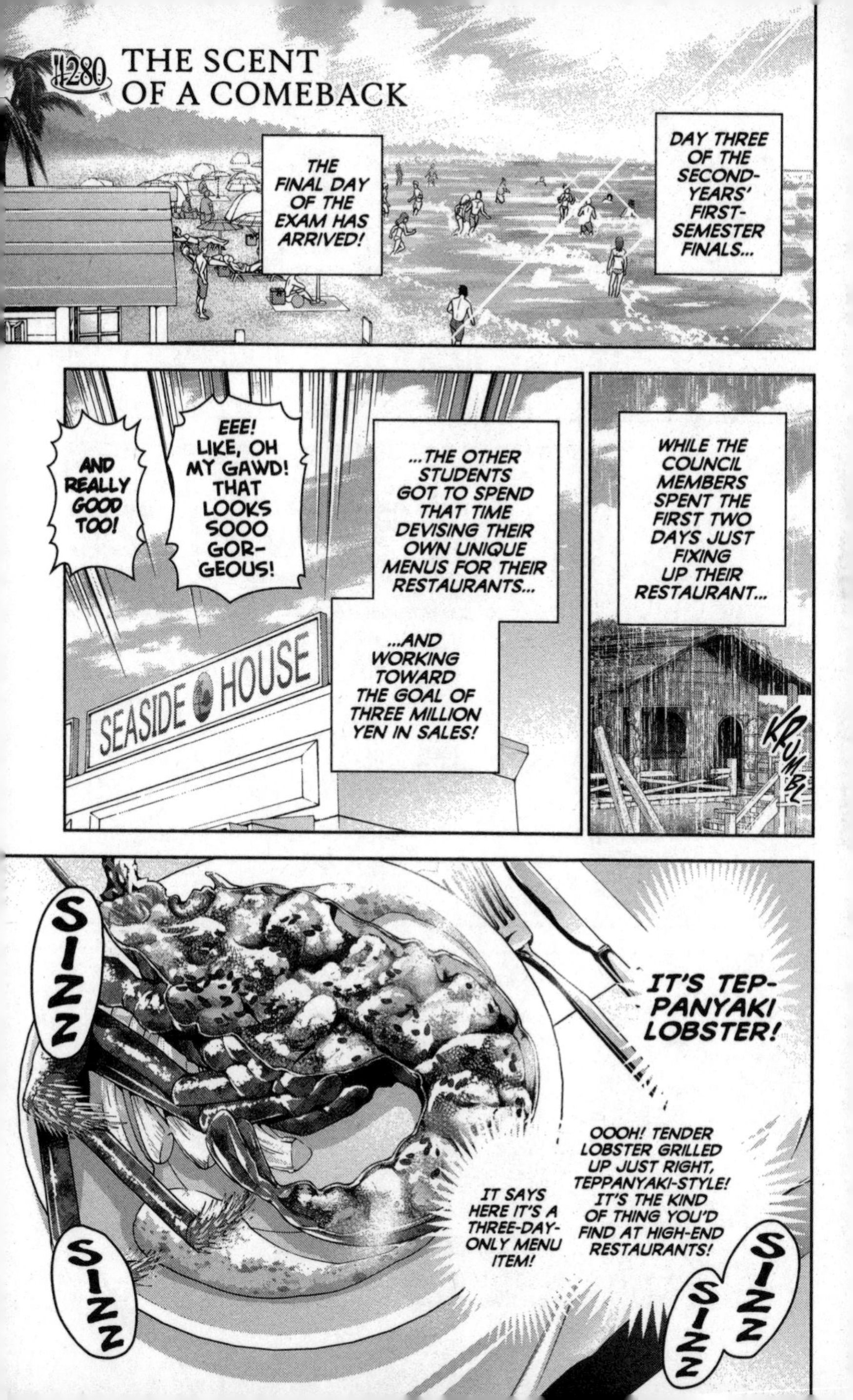
#280 THE SCENT OF A COMEBACK
DAY THREE OF THE SECOND-YEARS' FIRST-SEMESTER FINALS...
THE FINAL DAY OF THE EXAM HAS ARRIVED!
WHILE THE COUNCIL MEMBERS SPENT THE FIRST TWO DAYS JUST FIXING UP THEIR RESTAURANT...
KRUMBL
...THE OTHER STUDENTS GOT TO SPEND THAT TIME DEVISING THEIR OWN UNIQUE MENUS FOR THEIR RESTAURANTS...
EEE! LIKE, OH MY GAWD! THAT LOOKS SOOO GOR-GEOUS!
AND REALLY GOOD TOO!
...AND WORKING TOWARD THE GOAL OF THREE MILLION YEN IN SALES!
SEASIDE HOUSE
IT'S TEP-PANYAKI LOBSTER!
SIZZ
SIZZ
OOOH! TENDER LOBSTER GRILLED UP JUST RIGHT, TEPPANYAKI-STYLE! IT'S THE KIND OF THING YOU'D FIND AT HIGH-END RESTAURANTS!
IT SAYS HERE IT'S A THREE-DAY-ONLY MENU ITEM!
SIZZ
SIZZ

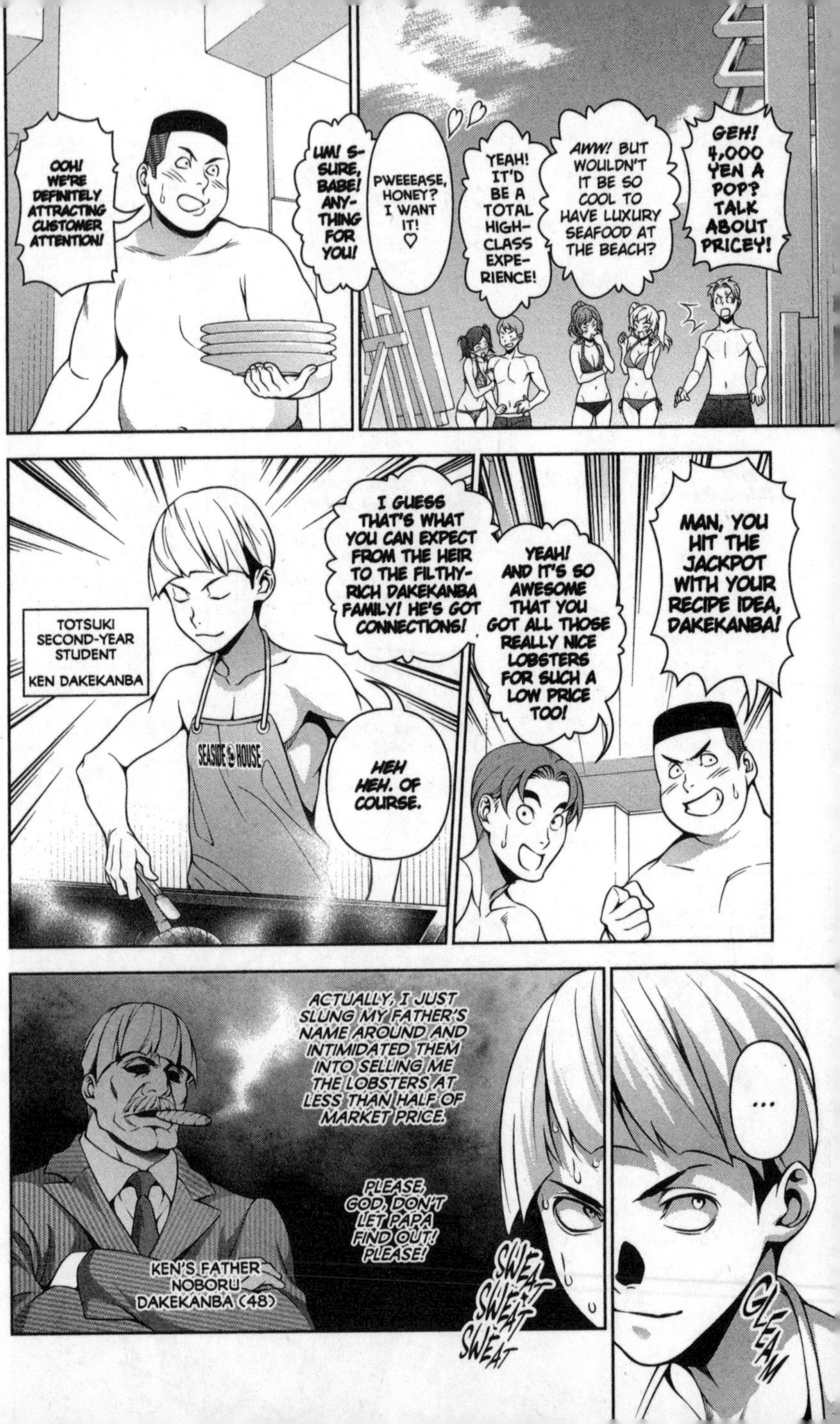

GEH! 4,000 YEN A POP? TALK ABOUT PRICEY!
AWW! BUT WOULDN'T IT BE SO COOL TO HAVE LUXURY SEAFOOD AT THE BEACH?
YEAH! IT'D BE A TOTAL HIGH-CLASS EXPERIENCE!
PWEEEASE, HONEY? I WANT IT! ♡
UM! S-SURE, BABE! ANYTHING FOR YOU!
OOH! WE'RE DEFINITELY ATTRACTING CUSTOMER ATTENTION!
MAN, YOU HIT THE JACKPOT WITH YOUR RECIPE IDEA, DAKEKANBA!
YEAH! AND IT'S SO AWESOME THAT YOU GOT ALL THOSE REALLY NICE LOBSTERS FOR SUCH A LOW PRICE TOO!
I GUESS THAT'S WHAT YOU CAN EXPECT FROM THE HEIR TO THE FILTHY-RICH DAKEKANBA FAMILY! HE'S GOT CONNECTIONS!
TOTSUKI SECOND-YEAR STUDENT
KEN DAKEKANBA
SEASIDE HOUSE
HEH HEH. OF COURSE.
...
GLEAM
ACTUALLY, I JUST SLUNG MY FATHER'S NAME AROUND AND INTIMIDATED THEM INTO SELLING ME THE LOBSTERS AT LESS THAN HALF OF MARKET PRICE.
PLEASE, GOD, DON'T LET PAPA FIND OUT! PLEASE!
KEN'S FATHER NOBORU DAKEKANBA (48)
SWEAT SWEAT SWEAT

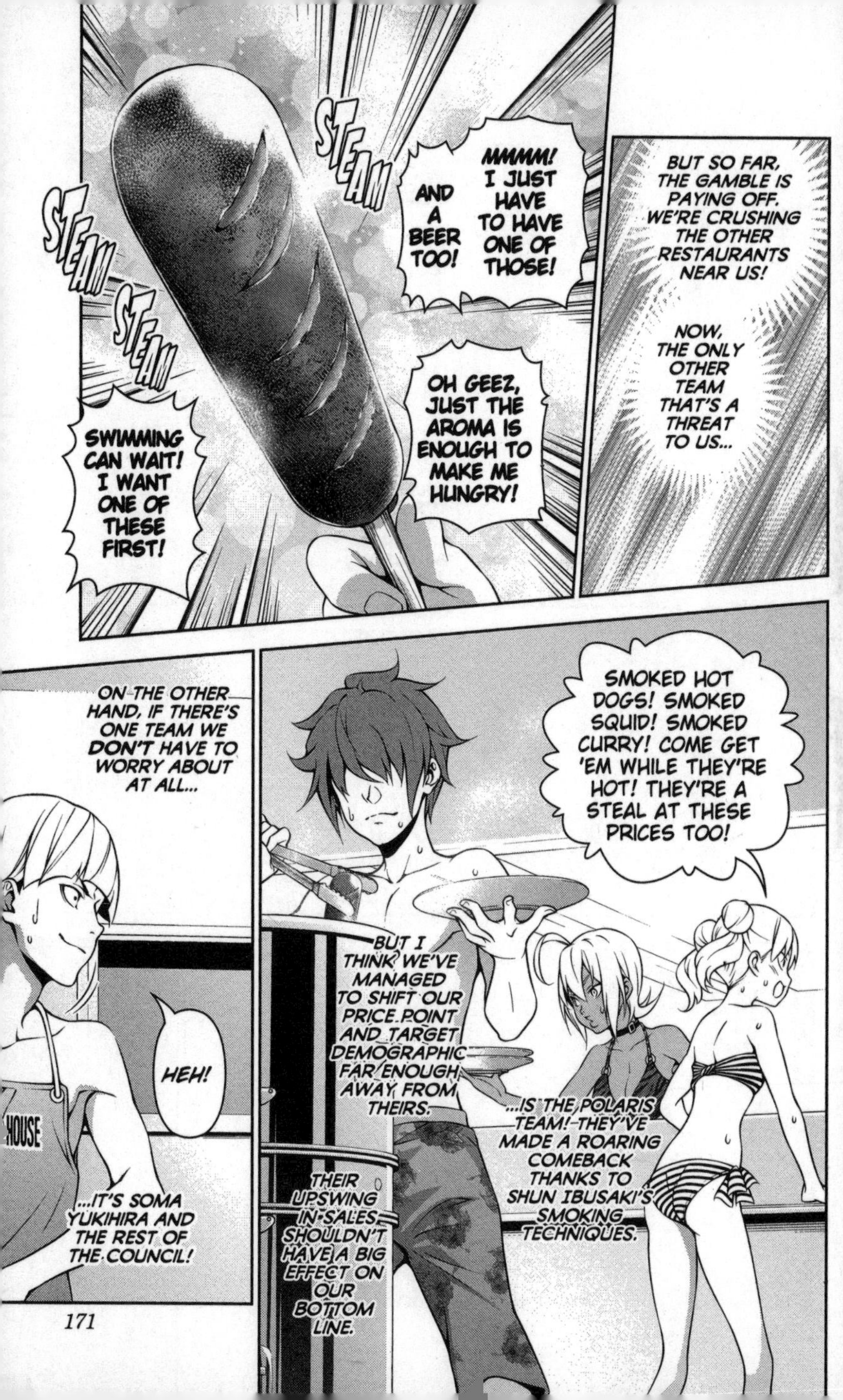
BUT SO FAR, THE GAMBLE IS PAYING OFF. WE'RE CRUSHING THE OTHER RESTAURANTS NEAR US!
NOW, THE ONLY OTHER TEAM THAT'S A THREAT TO US...
MMMM! I JUST HAVE TO HAVE ONE OF THOSE!
AND A BEER TOO!
STEAM
STEAM
STEAM
OH GEEZ, JUST THE AROMA IS ENOUGH TO MAKE ME HUNGRY!
SWIMMING CAN WAIT! I WANT ONE OF THESE FIRST!
SMOKED HOT DOGS! SMOKED SQUID! SMOKED CURRY! COME GET 'EM WHILE THEY'RE HOT! THEY'RE A STEAL AT THESE PRICES TOO!
...IS THE POLARIS TEAM! THEY'VE MADE A ROARING COMEBACK THANKS TO SHUN IBUSAKI'S SMOKING TECHNIQUES.
BUT I THINK WE'VE MANAGED TO SHIFT OUR PRICE POINT AND TARGET DEMOGRAPHIC FAR ENOUGH AWAY FROM THEIRS.
THEIR UPSWING IN SALES SHOULDN'T HAVE A BIG EFFECT ON OUR BOTTOM LINE.
ON THE OTHER HAND, IF THERE'S ONE TEAM WE DON'T HAVE TO WORRY ABOUT AT ALL...
HEH!
...IT'S SOMA YUKIHIRA AND THE REST OF THE COUNCIL!
HOUSE

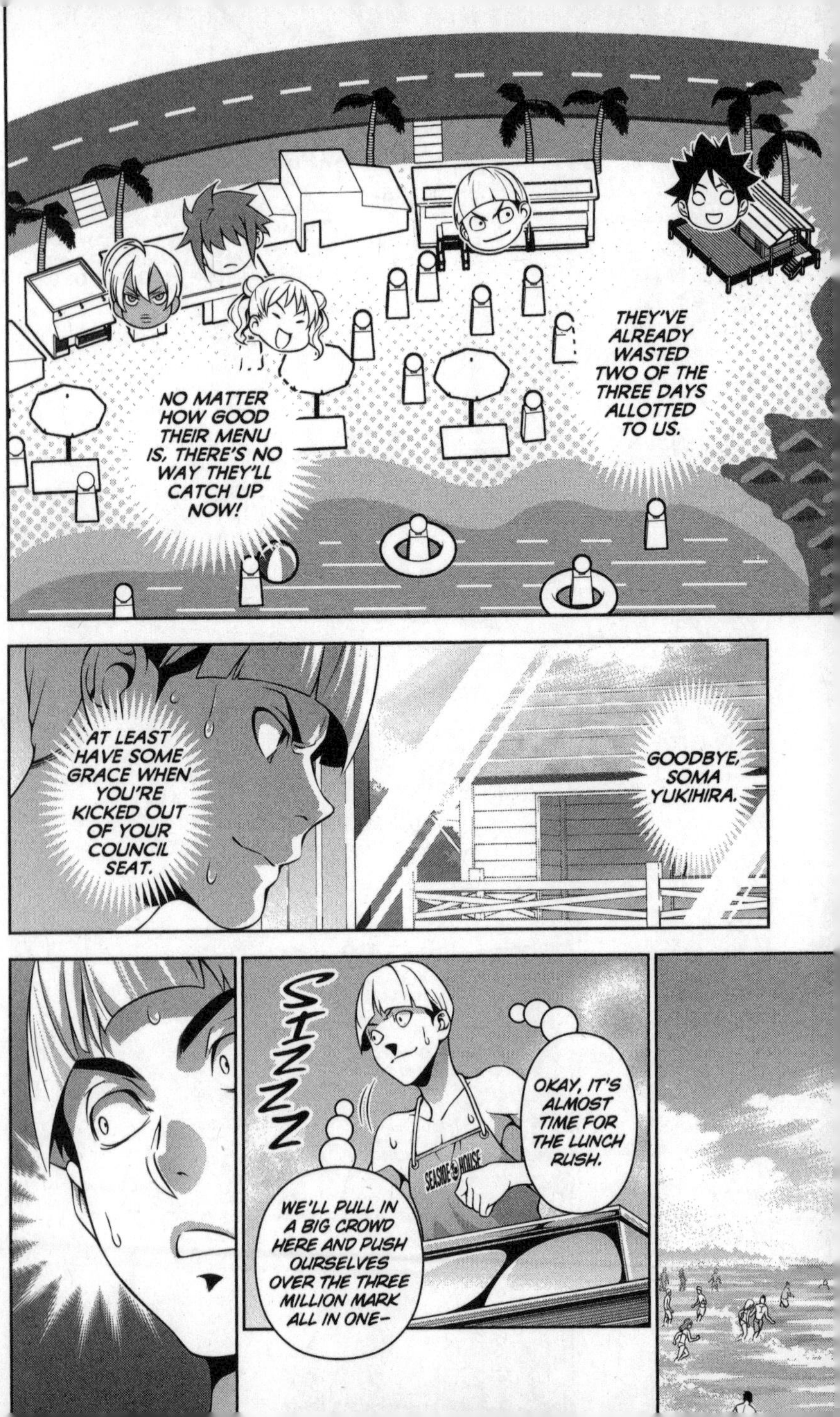
THEY'VE ALREADY WASTED TWO OF THE THREE DAYS ALLOTTED TO US.
NO MATTER HOW GOOD THEIR MENU IS, THERE'S NO WAY THEY'LL CATCH UP NOW!
GOODBYE, SOMA YUKIHIRA.
AT LEAST HAVE SOME GRACE WHEN YOU'RE KICKED OUT OF YOUR COUNCIL SEAT.
SIZZZ
OKAY, IT'S ALMOST TIME FOR THE LUNCH RUSH.
SEASIDE HOUSE
WE'LL PULL IN A BIG CROWD HERE AND PUSH OURSELVES OVER THE THREE MILLION MARK ALL IN ONE-

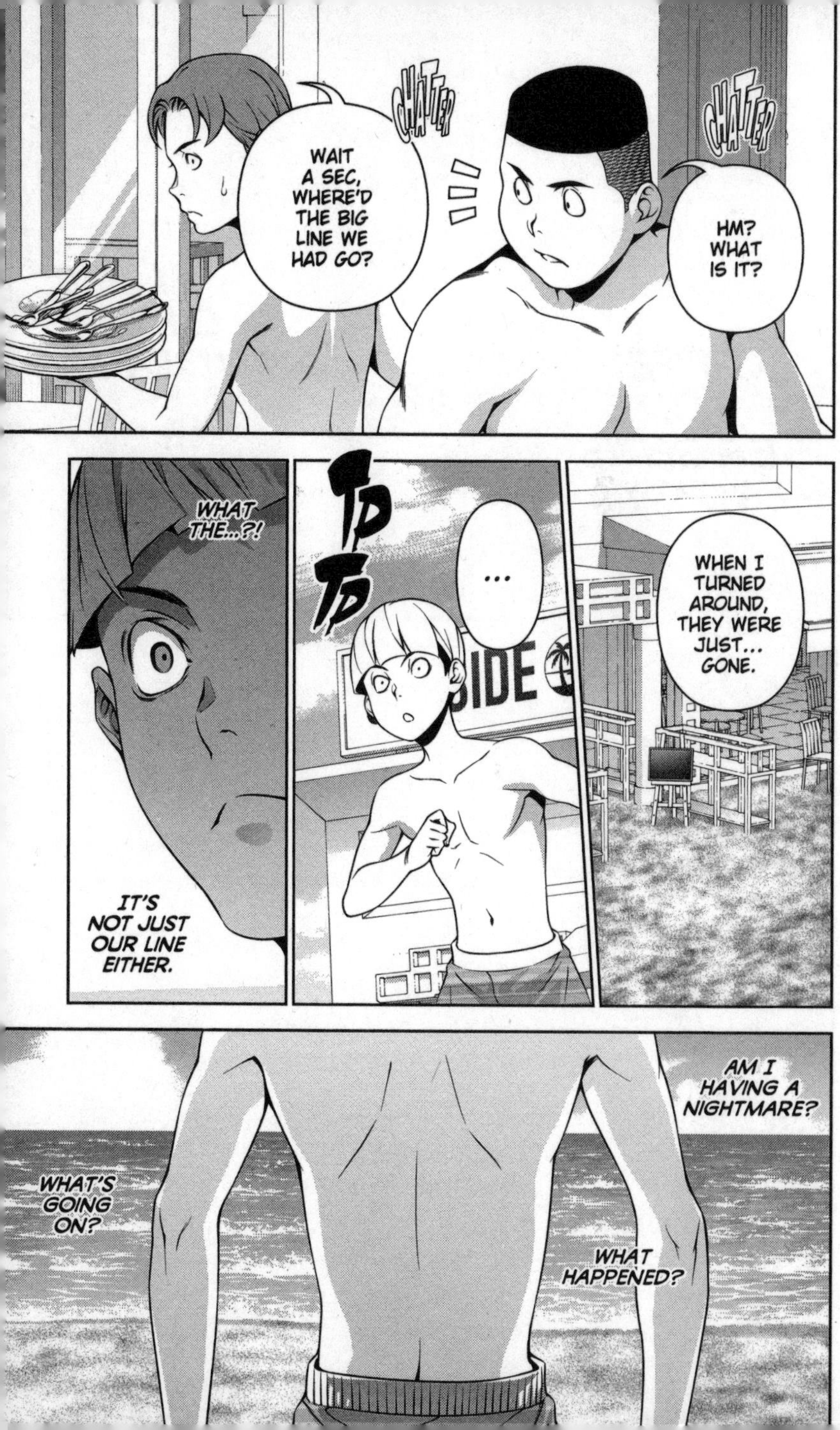
CHATTER
HM? WHAT IS IT?
CHATTER
WAIT A SEC, WHERE'D THE BIG LINE WE HAD GO?
WHEN I TURNED AROUND, THEY WERE JUST... GONE.
TP TP
...
WHAT THE...?!
IT'S NOT JUST OUR LINE EITHER.
AM I HAVING A NIGHTMARE?
WHAT'S GOING ON?
WHAT HAPPENED?

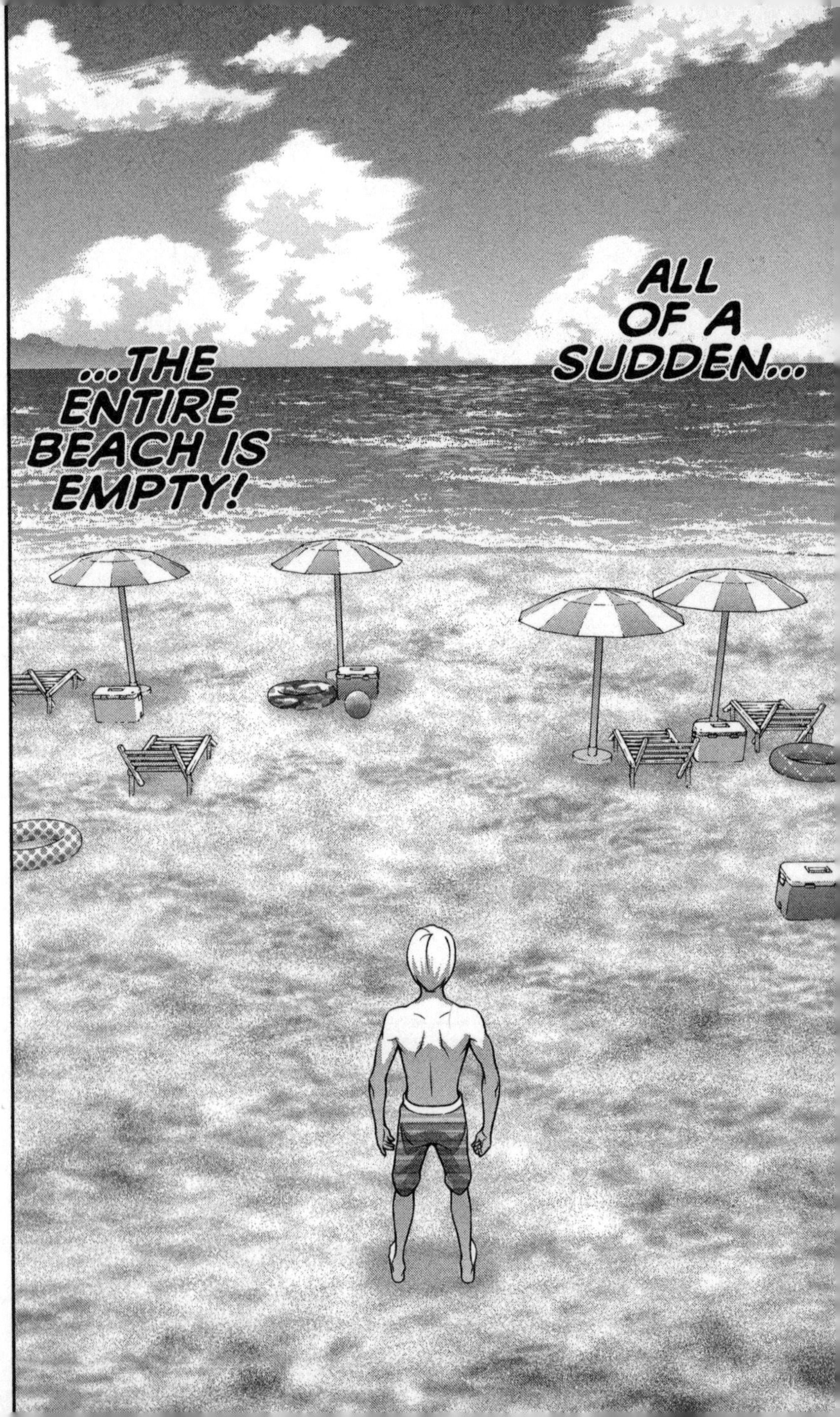
ALL OF A SUDDEN...
...THE ENTIRE BEACH IS EMPTY!

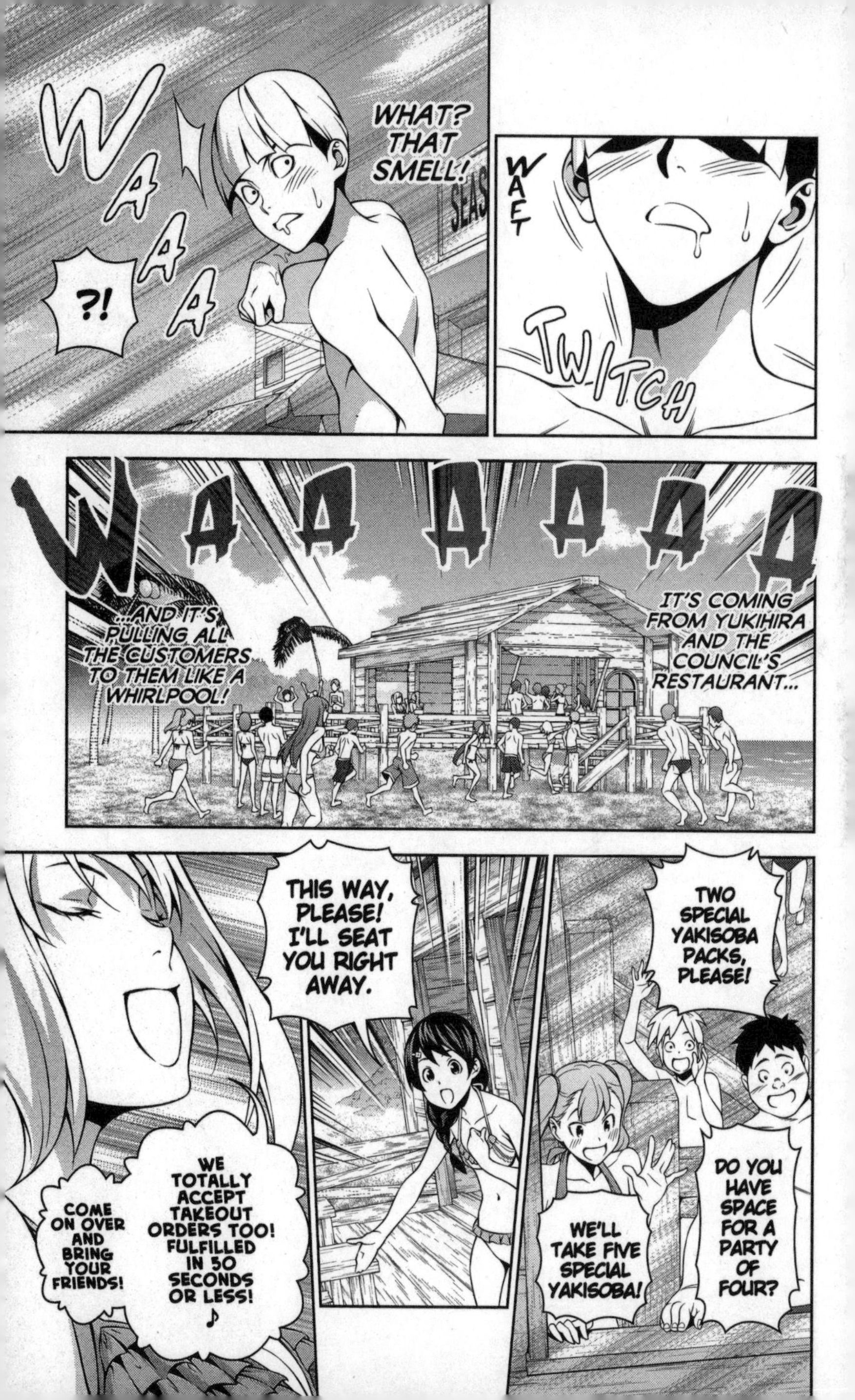
WAFT
TWITCH
WHAT? THAT SMELL!
WAAAA
?!
WAAAAAA
IT'S COMING FROM YUKIHIRA AND THE COUNCIL'S RESTAURANT...
...AND IT'S PULLING ALL THE CUSTOMERS TO THEM LIKE A WHIRLPOOL!
TWO SPECIAL YAKISOBA PACKS, PLEASE!
DO YOU HAVE SPACE FOR A PARTY OF FOUR?
WE'LL TAKE FIVE SPECIAL YAKISOBA!
THIS WAY, PLEASE! I'LL SEAT YOU RIGHT AWAY.
WE TOTALLY ACCEPT TAKEOUT ORDERS TOO! FULFILLED IN 30 SECONDS OR LESS! ♪
COME ON OVER AND BRING YOUR FRIENDS!

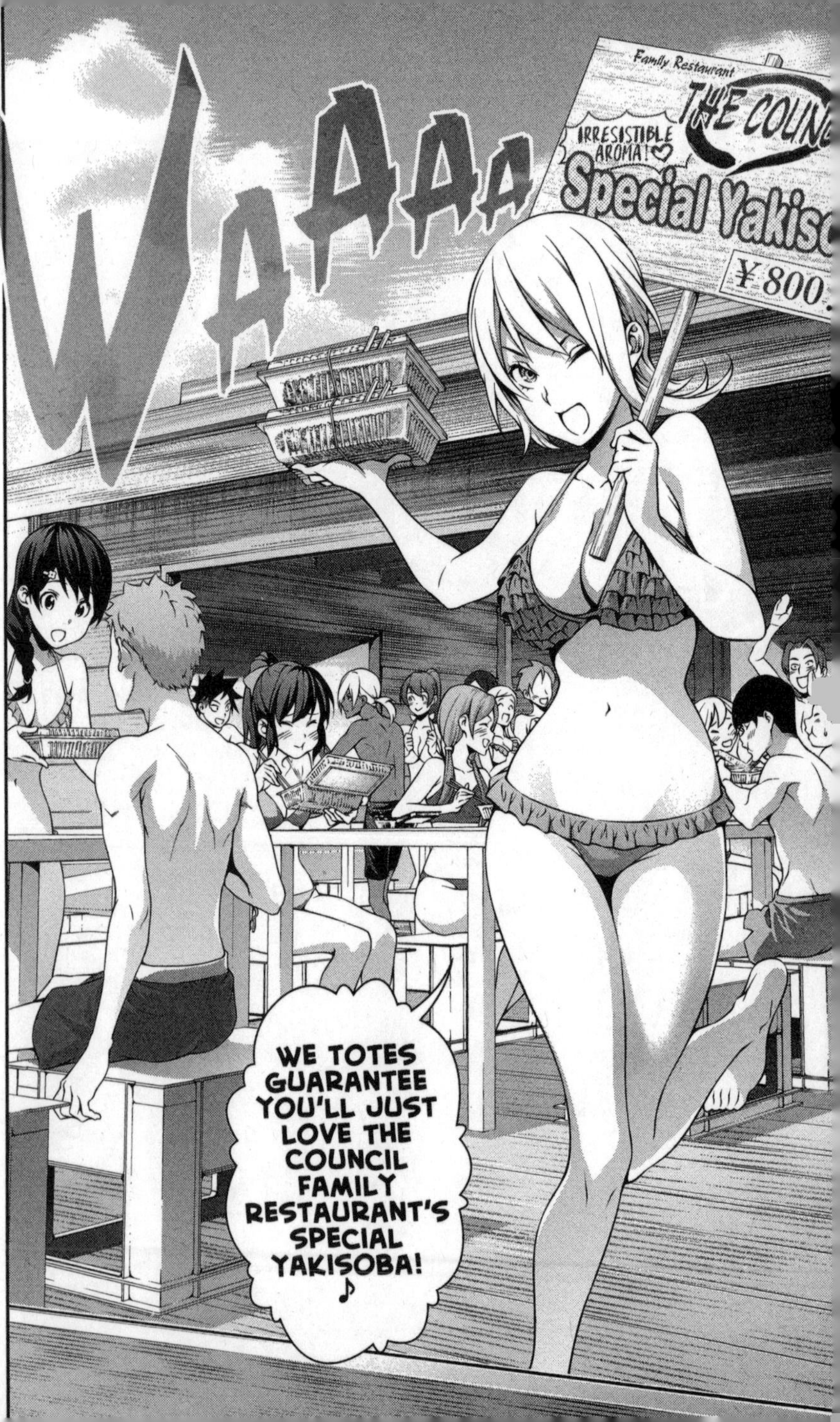
WAAAA
Family Restaurant
THE COUNC
IRRESISTIBLE AROMA!
Special Yakiso
¥800
WE TOTES GUARANTEE YOU'LL JUST LOVE THE COUNCIL FAMILY RESTAURANT'S SPECIAL YAKISOBA! ♪

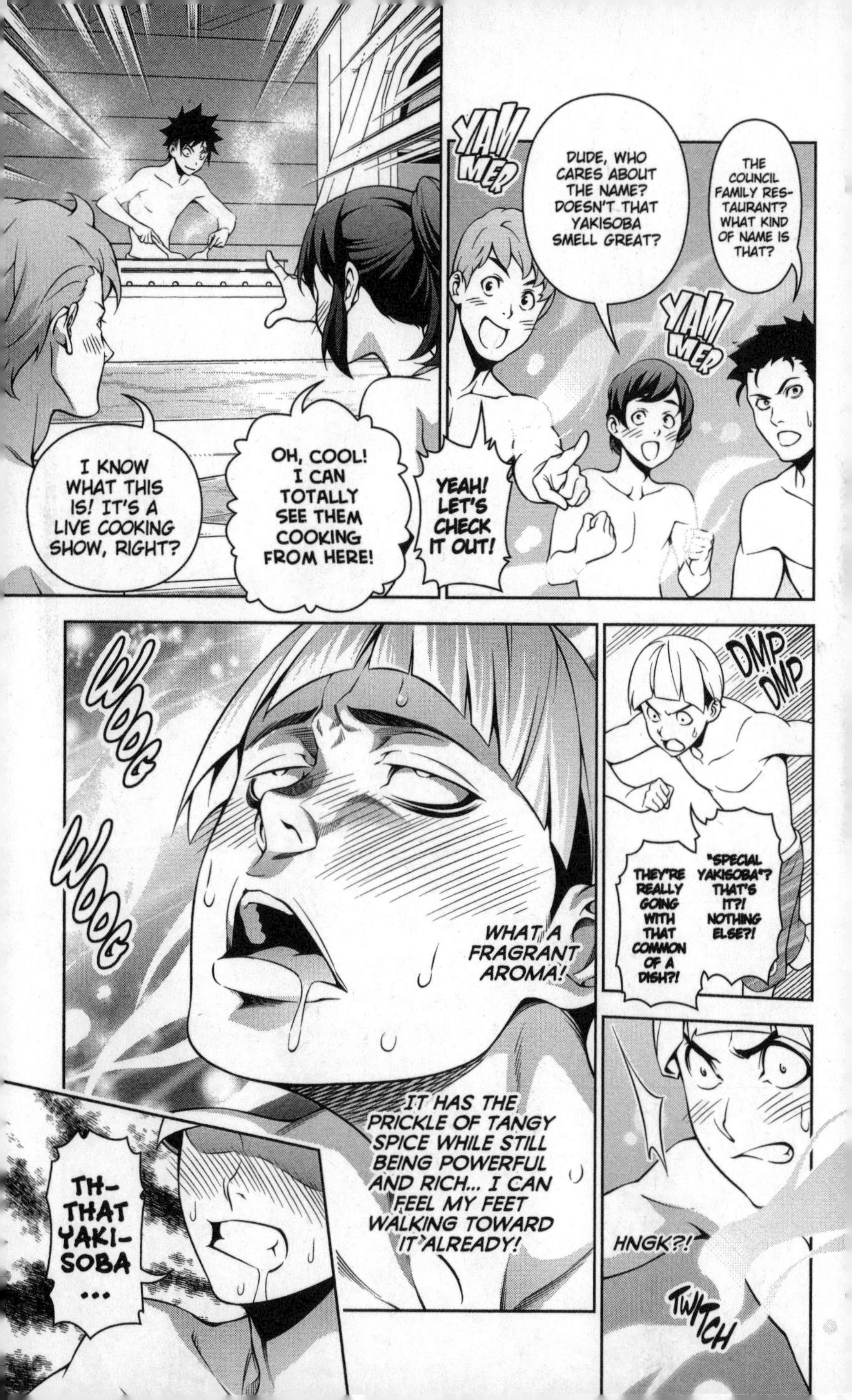
YAM MER
THE COUNCIL FAMILY RESTAURANT? WHAT KIND OF NAME IS THAT?
DUDE, WHO CARES ABOUT THE NAME? DOESN'T THAT YAKISOBA SMELL GREAT?
YAM MER
YEAH! LET'S CHECK IT OUT!
OH, COOL! I CAN TOTALLY SEE THEM COOKING FROM HERE!
I KNOW WHAT THIS IS! IT'S A LIVE COOKING SHOW, RIGHT?
DMP DMP
"SPECIAL YAKISOBA"? THAT'S IT?! NOTHING ELSE?!
THEY'RE REALLY GOING WITH THAT COMMON OF A DISH?!
HNGK?!
TWITCH
WOOG
WOOG
WHAT A FRAGRANT AROMA!
IT HAS THE PRICKLE OF TANGY SPICE WHILE STILL BEING POWERFUL AND RICH... I CAN FEEL MY FEET WALKING TOWARD IT ALREADY!
TH-THAT YAKI-SOBA...

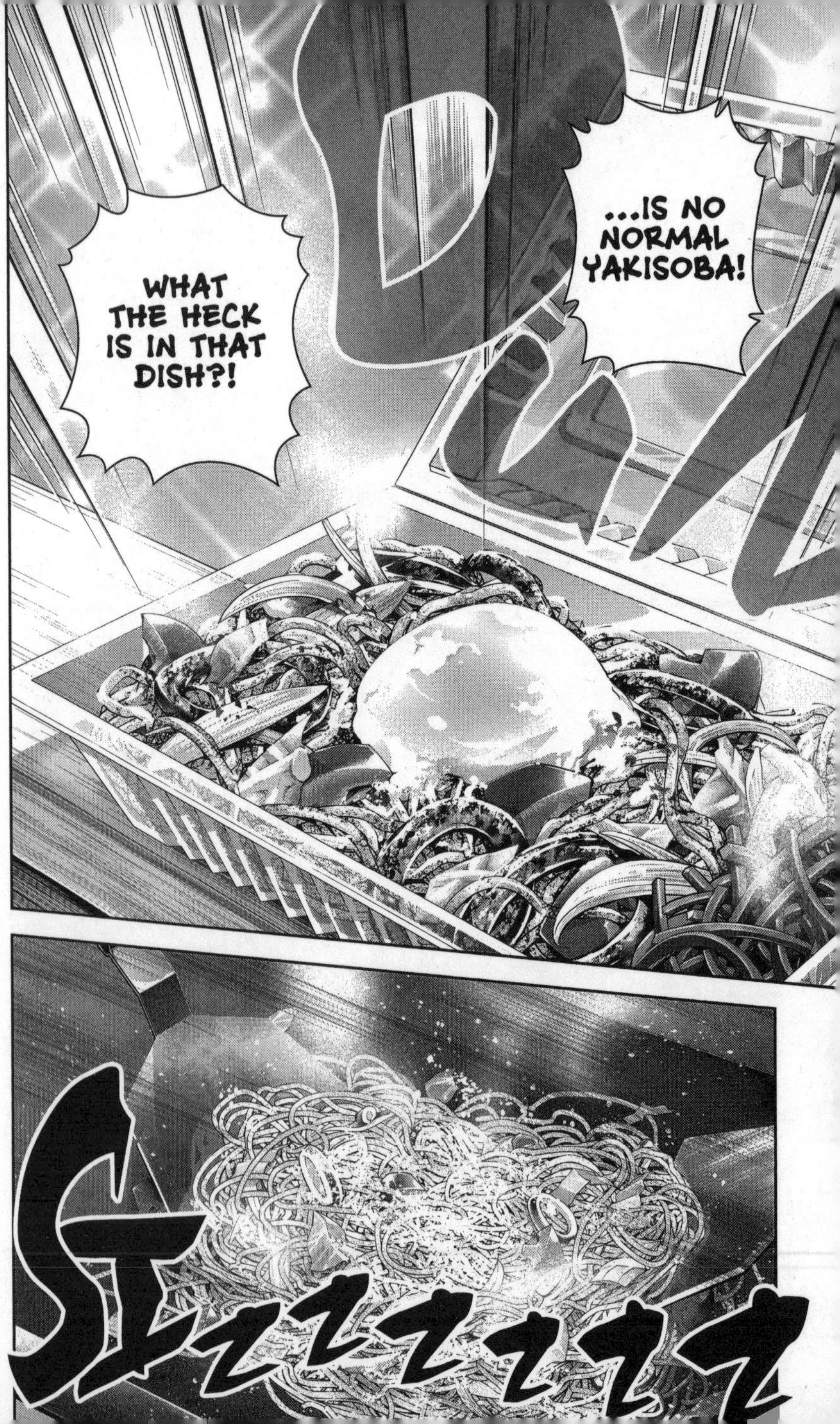
...IS NO NORMAL YAKISOBA!
WHAT THE HECK IS IN THAT DISH?!
SIZZZZZZZ

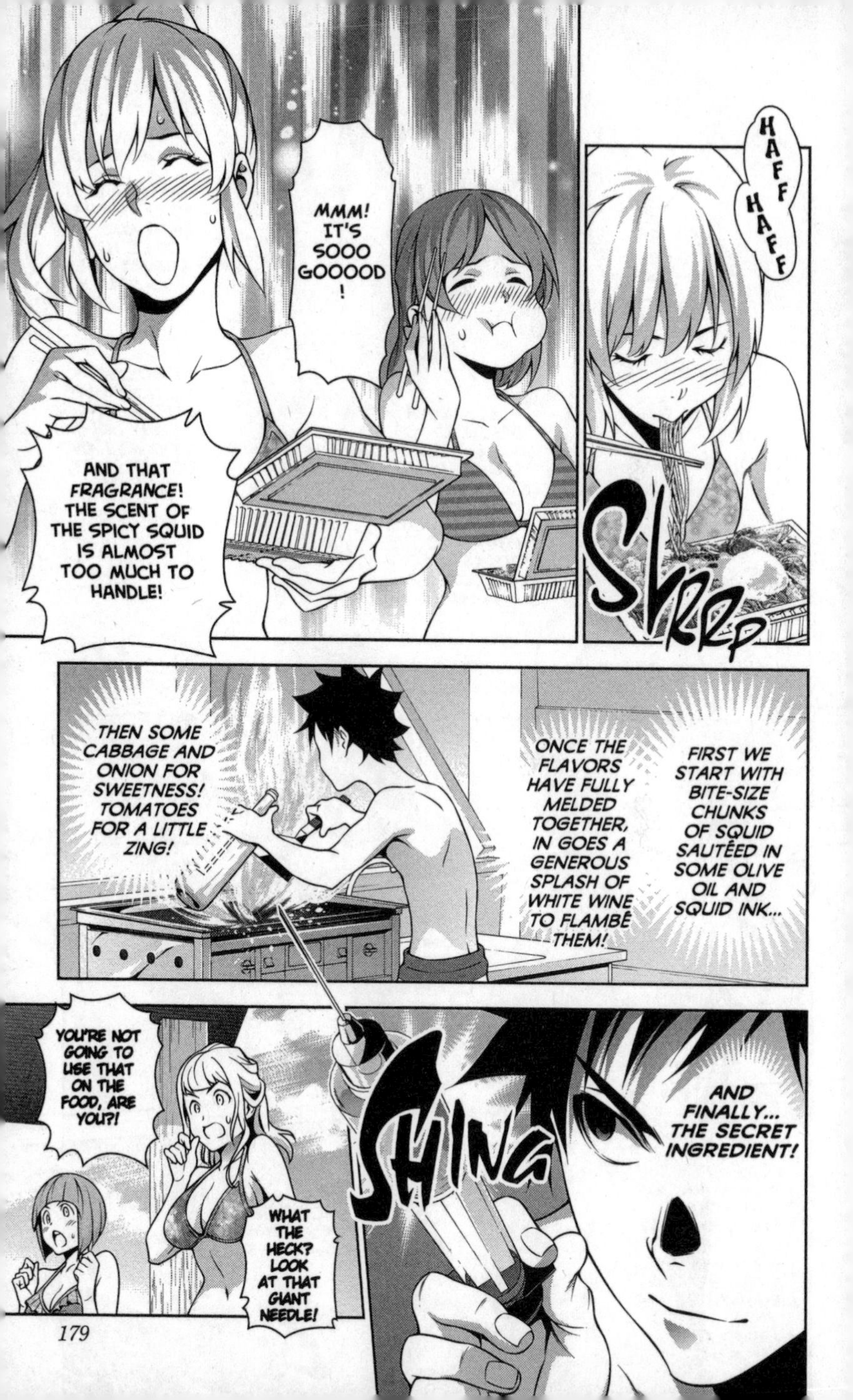
HAFF HAFF
SLRRP
MMM! IT'S SOOO GOOOOD!
AND THAT FRAGRANCE! THE SCENT OF THE SPICY SQUID IS ALMOST TOO MUCH TO HANDLE!
FIRST WE START WITH BITE-SIZE CHUNKS OF SQUID SAUTÉED IN SOME OLIVE OIL AND SQUID INK...
ONCE THE FLAVORS HAVE FULLY MELDED TOGETHER, IN GOES A GENEROUS SPLASH OF WHITE WINE TO FLAMBÉ THEM!
THEN SOME CABBAGE AND ONION FOR SWEETNESS! TOMATOES FOR A LITTLE ZING!
AND FINALLY... THE SECRET INGREDIENT!
SHING
YOU'RE NOT GOING TO USE THAT ON THE FOOD, ARE YOU?!
WHAT THE HECK? LOOK AT THAT GIANT NEEDLE!

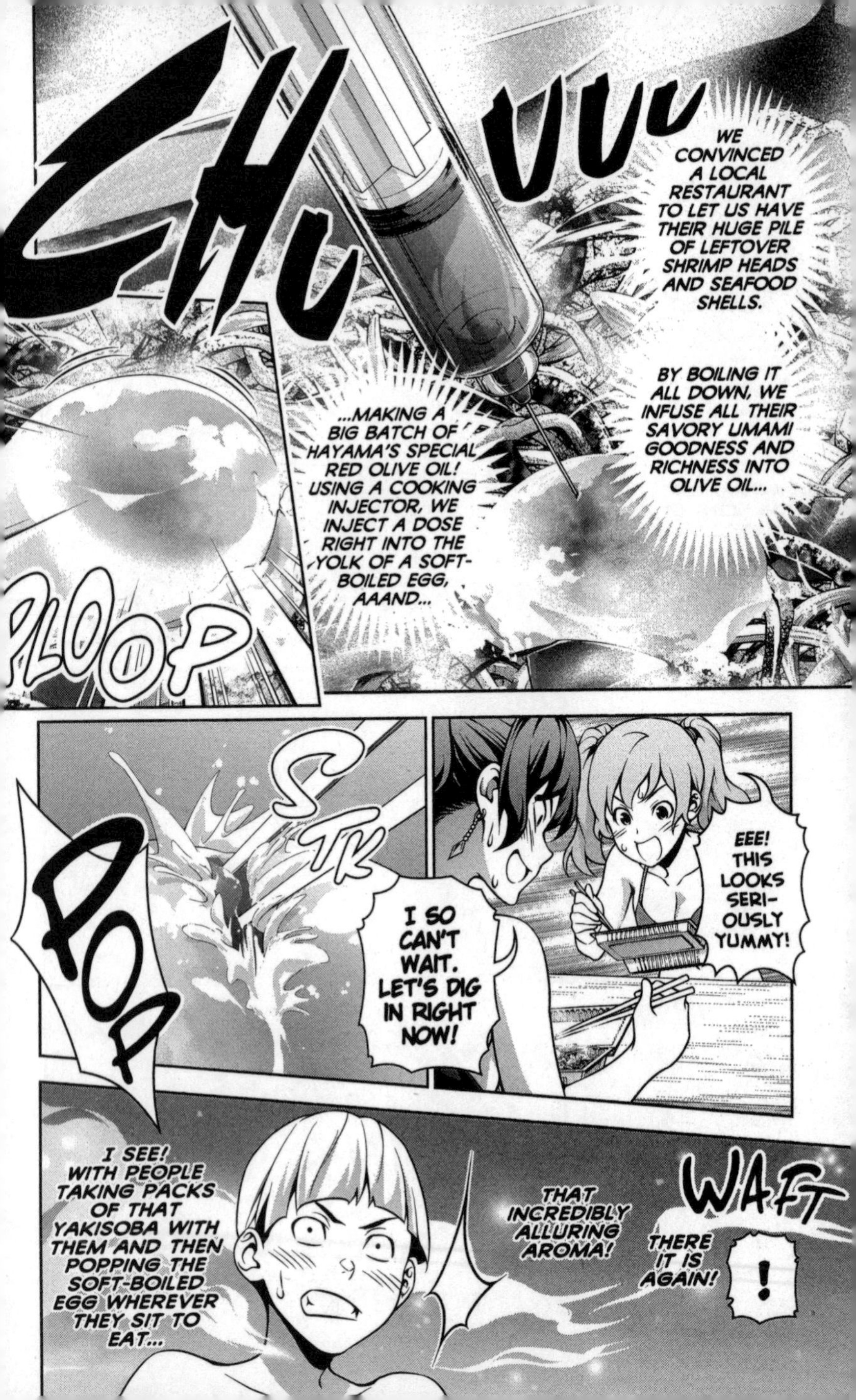
WE CONVINCED A LOCAL RESTAURANT TO LET US HAVE THEIR HUGE PILE OF LEFTOVER SHRIMP HEADS AND SEAFOOD SHELLS.
BY BOILING IT ALL DOWN, WE INFUSE ALL THEIR SAVORY UMAMI GOODNESS AND RICHNESS INTO OLIVE OIL...
...MAKING A BIG BATCH OF HAYAMA'S SPECIAL RED OLIVE OIL! USING A COOKING INJECTOR, WE INJECT A DOSE RIGHT INTO THE YOLK OF A SOFT-BOILED EGG, AAAND...
CHUUUU
PLOOP
EEE! THIS LOOKS SERI-OUSLY YUMMY!
I SO CAN'T WAIT. LET'S DIG IN RIGHT NOW!
STK
POP
WAFT
!
THERE IT IS AGAIN!
THAT INCREDIBLY ALLURING AROMA!
I SEE! WITH PEOPLE TAKING PACKS OF THAT YAKISOBA WITH THEM AND THEN POPPING THE SOFT-BOILED EGG WHEREVER THEY SIT TO EAT...

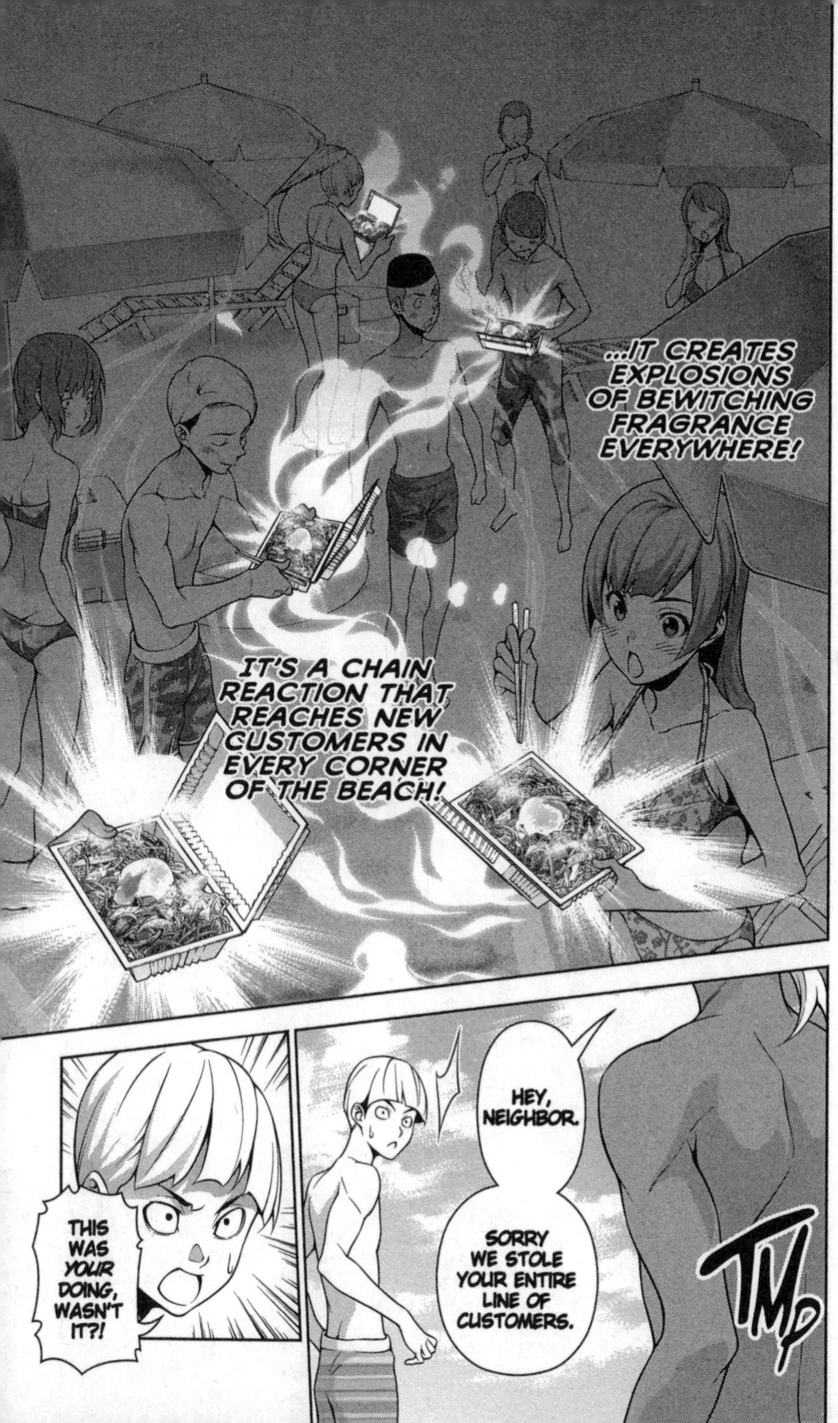
...IT CREATES EXPLOSIONS OF BEWITCHING FRAGRANCE EVERYWHERE!
IT'S A CHAIN REACTION THAT REACHES NEW CUSTOMERS IN EVERY CORNER OF THE BEACH!
HEY, NEIGHBOR.
SORRY WE STOLE YOUR ENTIRE LINE OF CUSTOMERS.
TMP
THIS WAS *YOUR* DOING, WASN'T IT?!

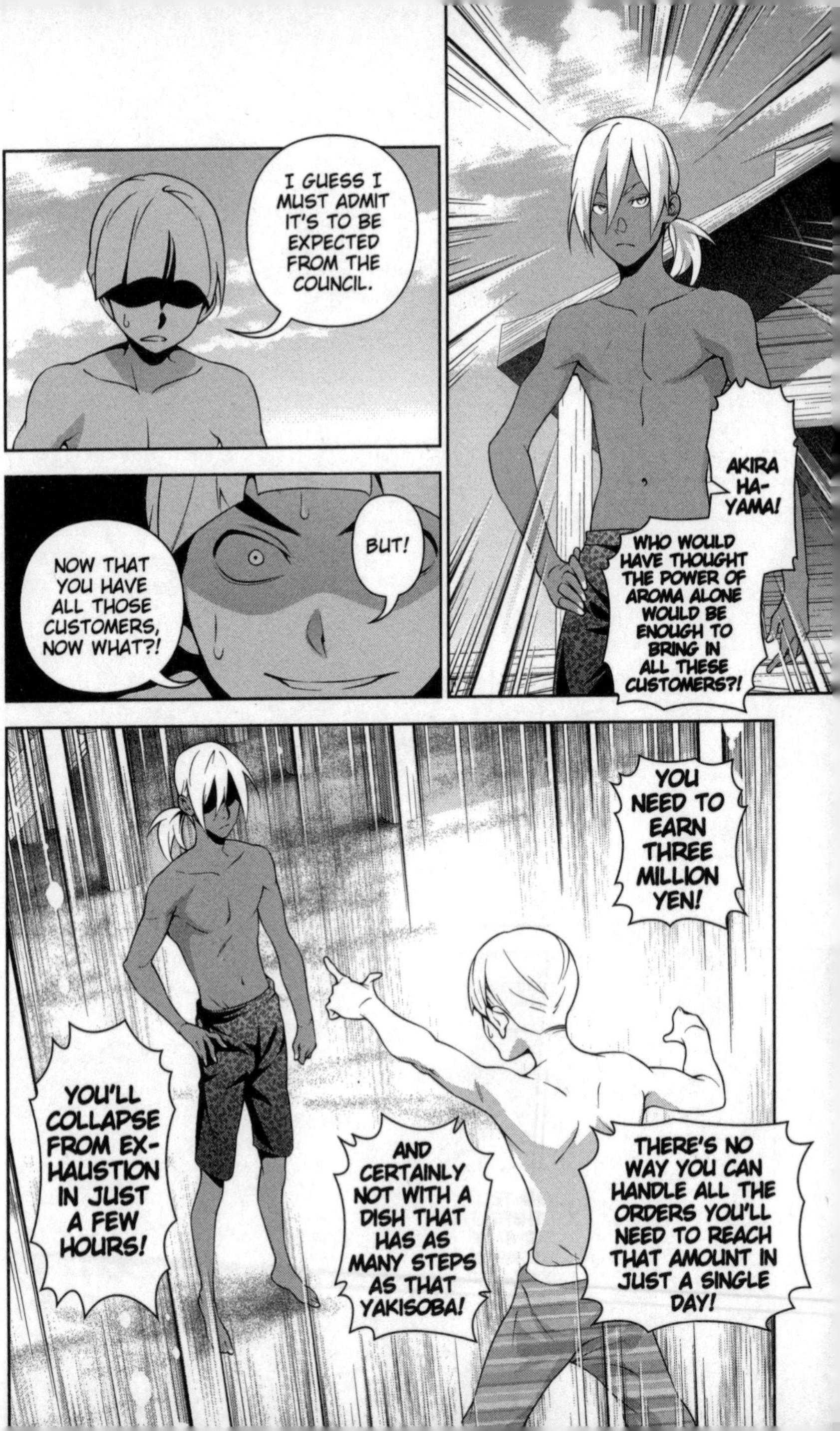
AKIRA HA-YAMA!
WHO WOULD HAVE THOUGHT THE POWER OF AROMA ALONE WOULD BE ENOUGH TO BRING IN ALL THESE CUSTOMERS?!
I GUESS I MUST ADMIT IT'S TO BE EXPECTED FROM THE COUNCIL.
BUT!
NOW THAT YOU HAVE ALL THOSE CUSTOMERS, NOW WHAT?!
YOU NEED TO EARN THREE MILLION YEN!
THERE'S NO WAY YOU CAN HANDLE ALL THE ORDERS YOU'LL NEED TO REACH THAT AMOUNT IN JUST A SINGLE DAY!
AND CERTAINLY NOT WITH A DISH THAT HAS AS MANY STEPS AS THAT YAKISOBA!
YOU'LL COLLAPSE FROM EX-HAUSTION IN JUST A FEW HOURS!

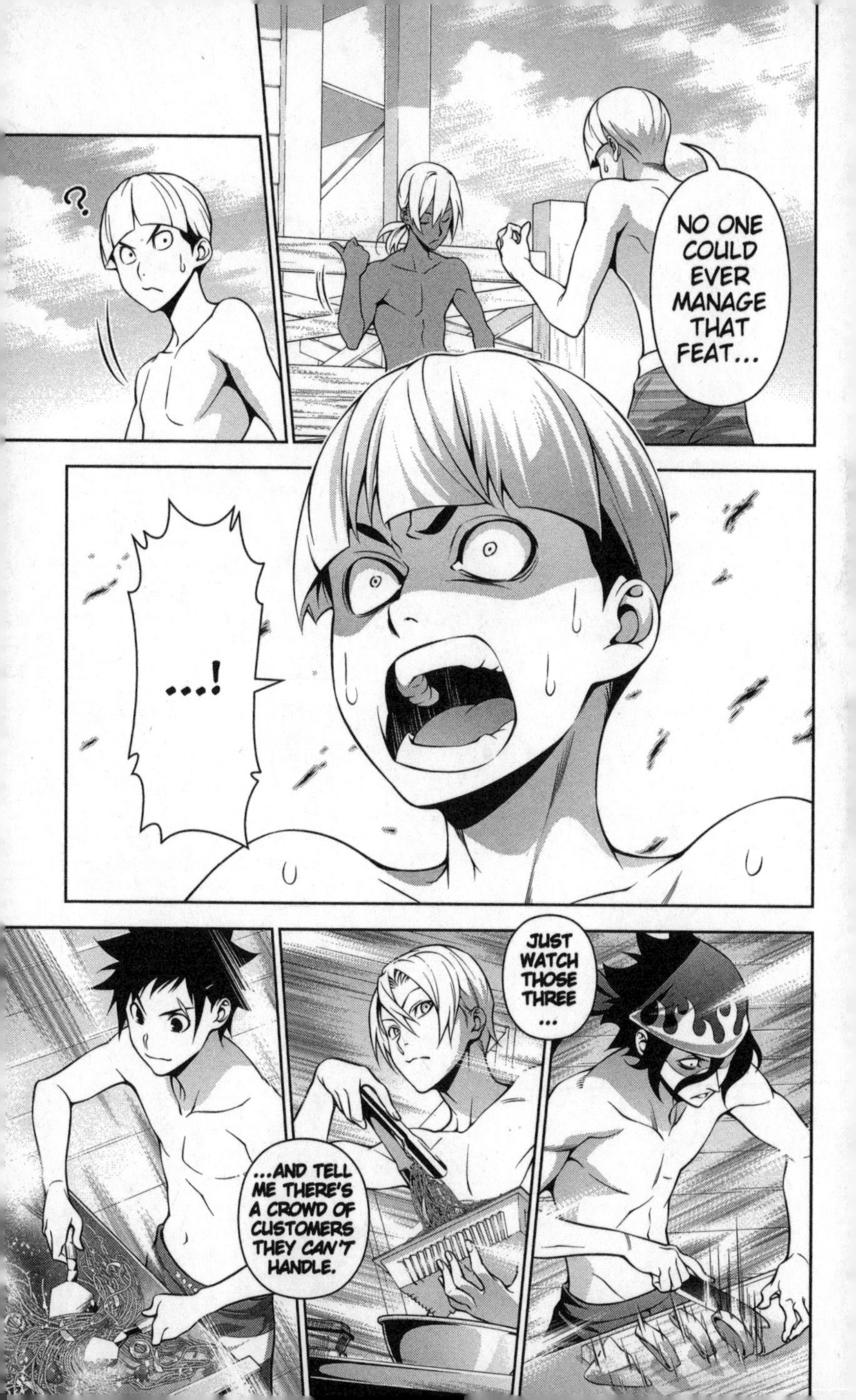
NO ONE COULD EVER MANAGE THAT FEAT...
?
...!
JUST WATCH THOSE THREE ...
...AND TELL ME THERE'S A CROWD OF CUSTOMERS THEY CAN'T HANDLE.

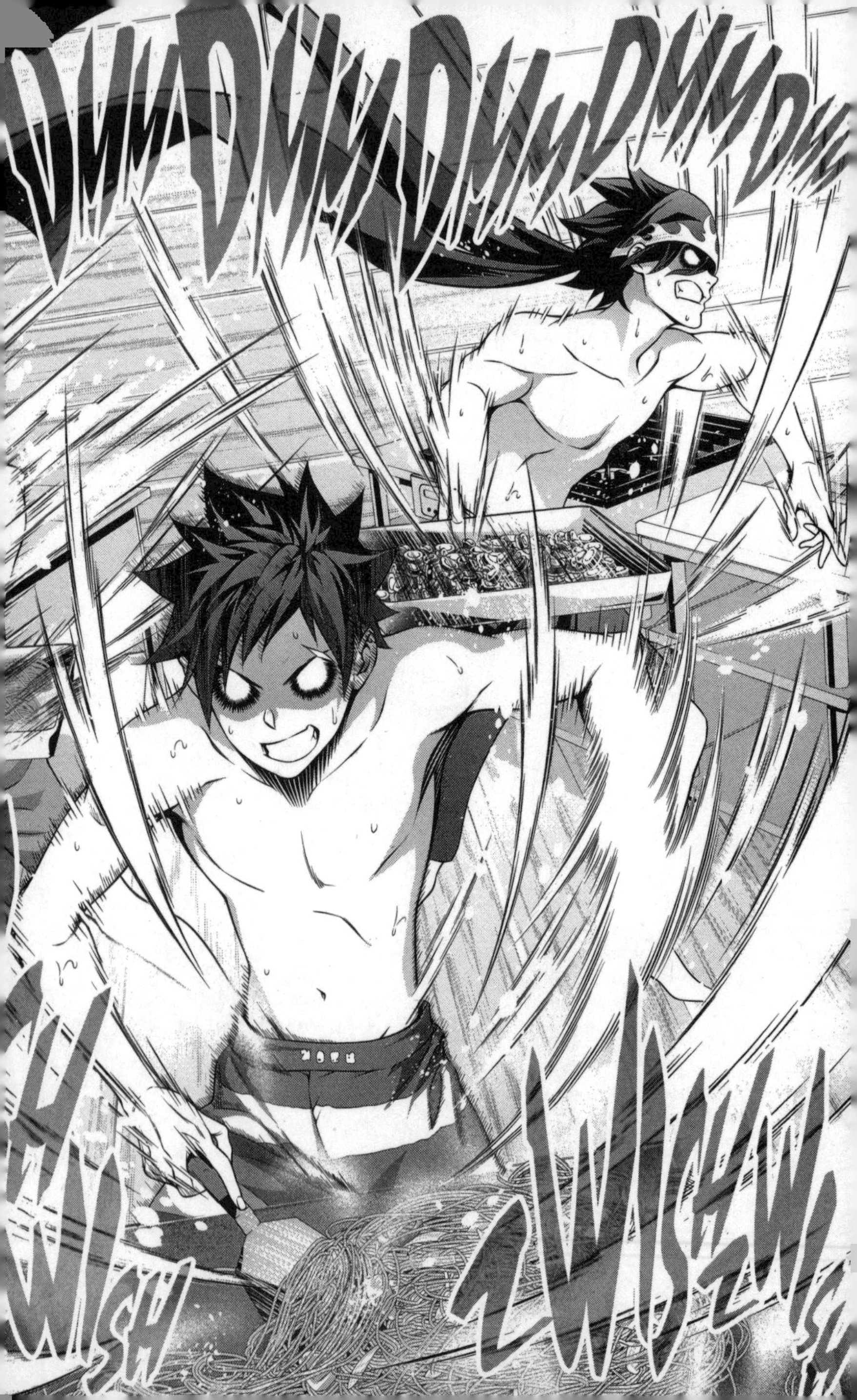

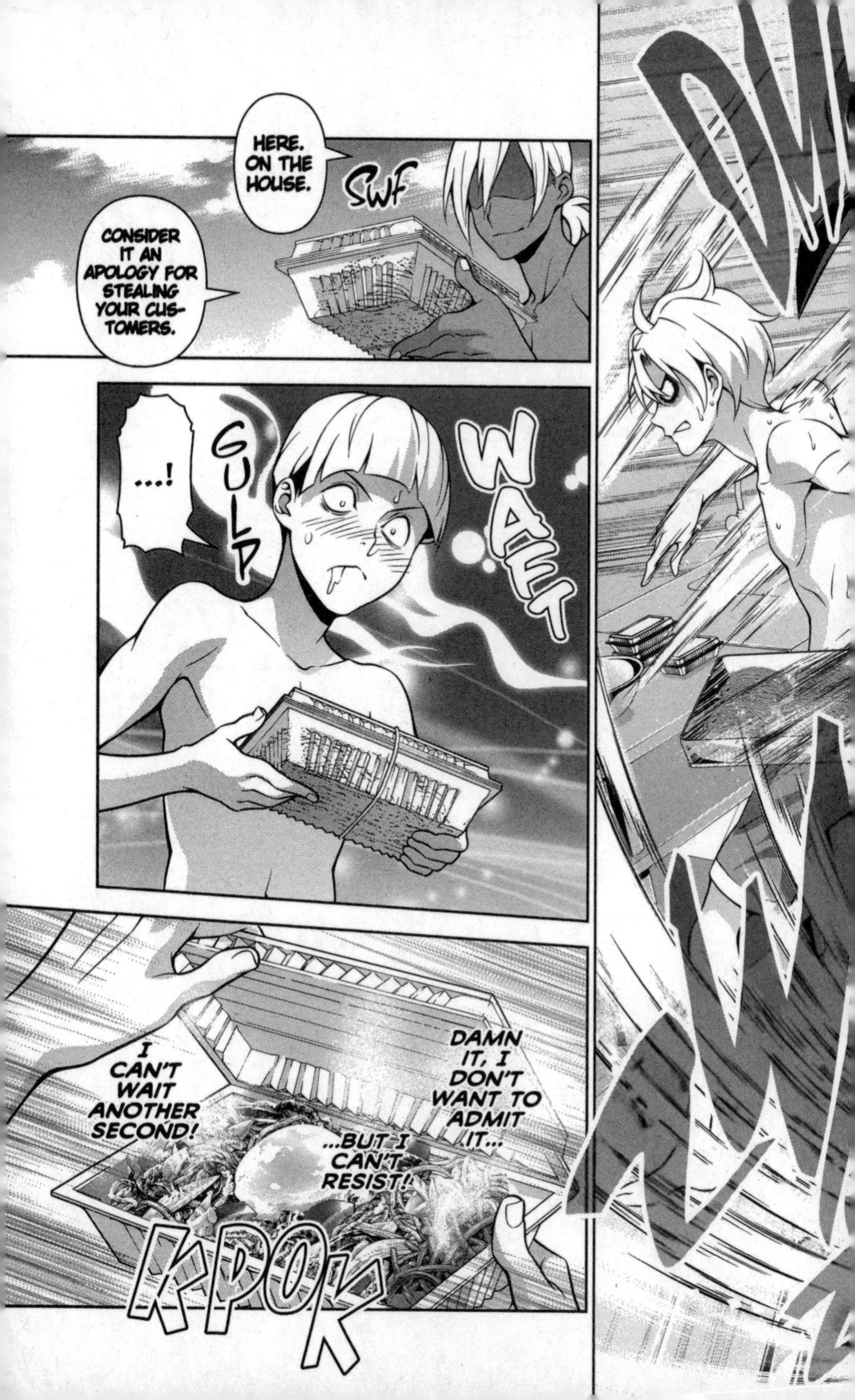
HERE. ON THE HOUSE.
SWF
CONSIDER IT AN APOLOGY FOR STEALING YOUR CUS-TOMERS.
WAFT
GULP
...!
DAMN IT, I DON'T WANT TO ADMIT IT...
...BUT I CAN'T RESIST!
I CAN'T WAIT ANOTHER SECOND!
KPOK

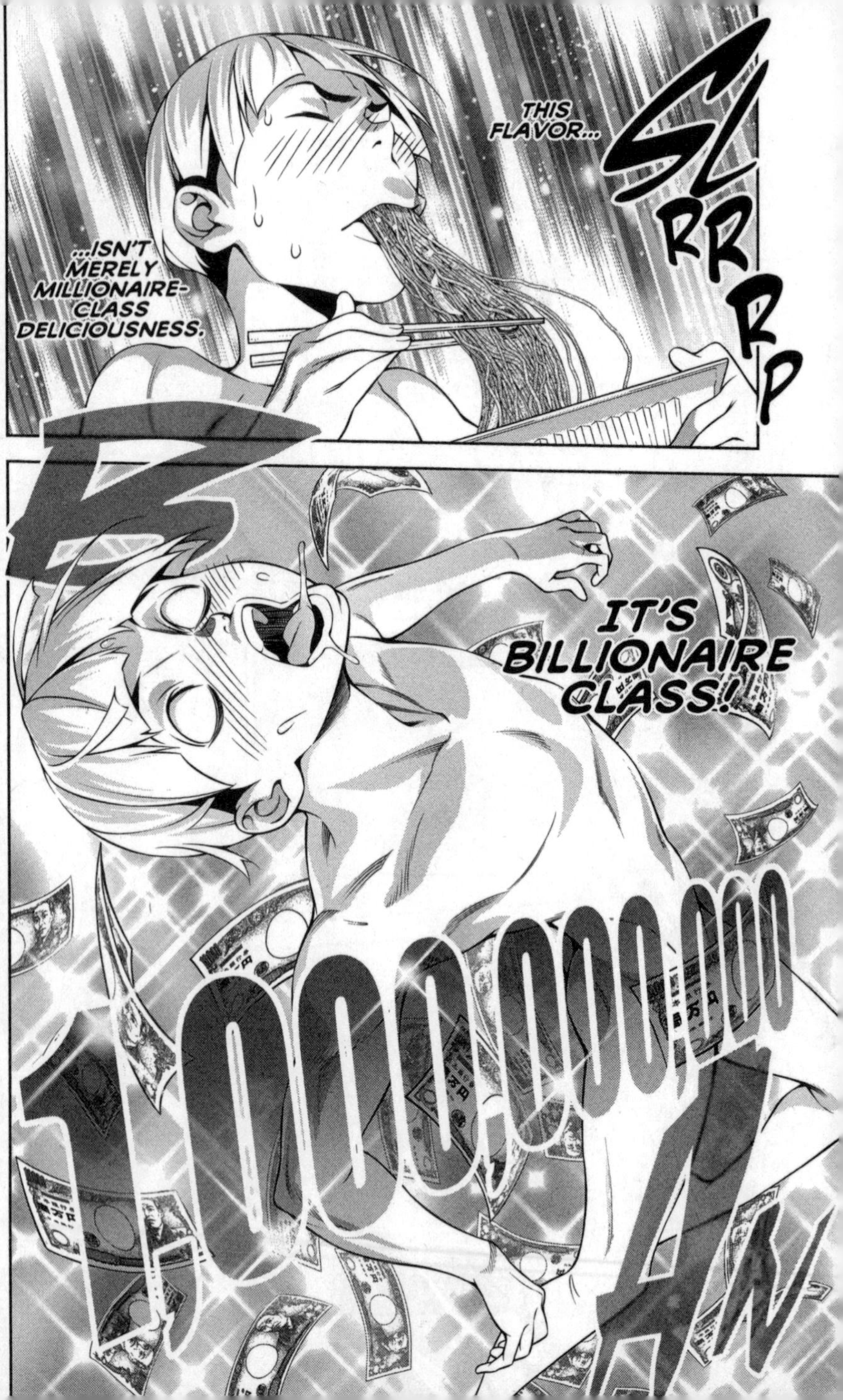
THIS FLAVOR...
SLRRRRP
...ISN'T MERELY MILLIONAIRE-CLASS DELICIOUSNESS.
IT'S BILLIONAIRE CLASS!
1,000,000,000

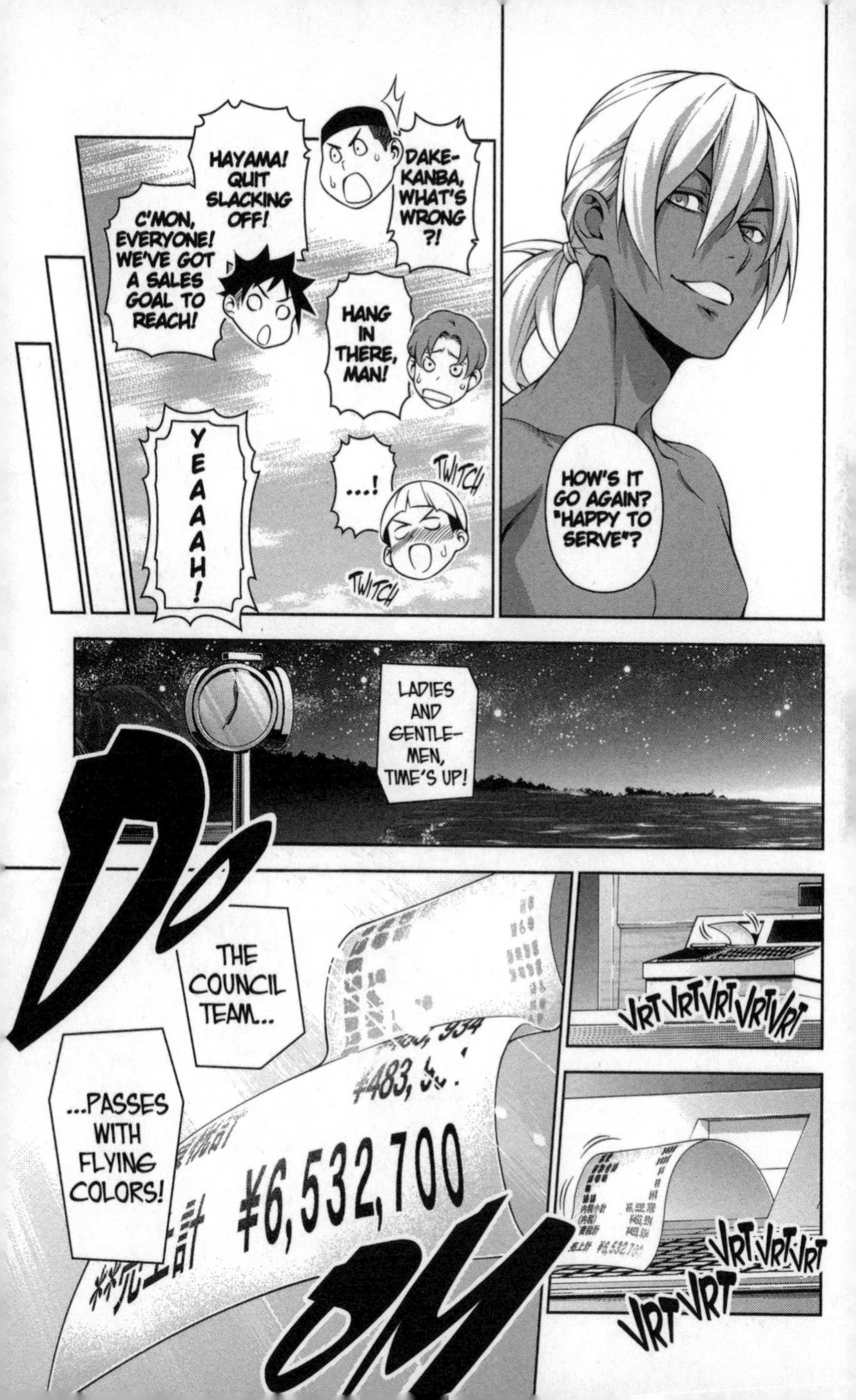
HOW'S IT GO AGAIN? "HAPPY TO SERVE"?
DAKE-KANBA, WHAT'S WRONG?!
HAYAMA! QUIT SLACKING OFF!
C'MON, EVERYONE! WE'VE GOT A SALES GOAL TO REACH!
HANG IN THERE, MAN!
...!
TWITCH
TWITCH
YEAAAAH!
LADIES AND GENTLEMEN, TIME'S UP!
VRT VRT VRT VRT VRT
VRT VRT VRT
VRT VRT
DO
THE COUNCIL TEAM...
...PASSES WITH FLYING COLORS!
¥6,532,700
OM

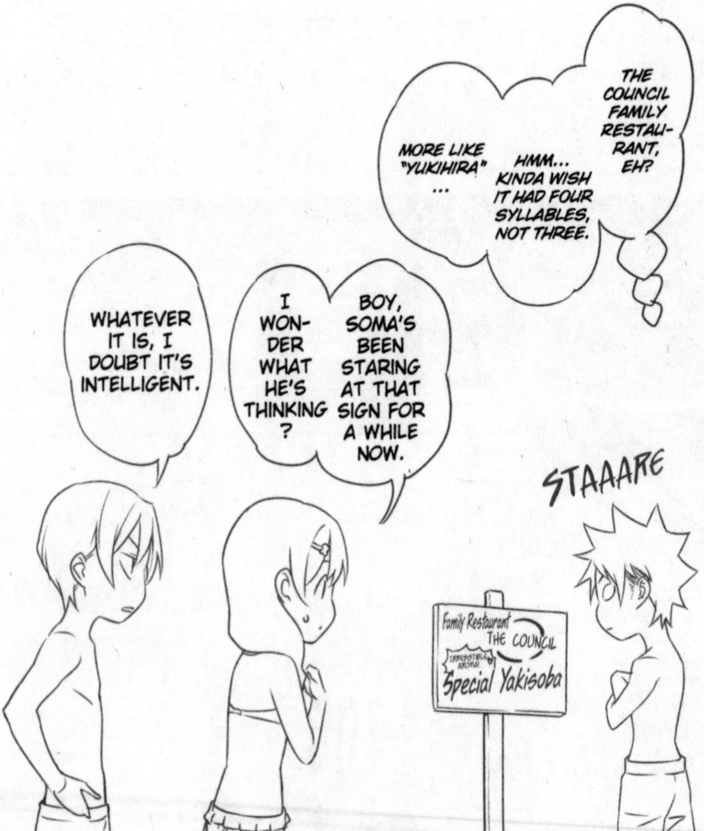
THE COUNCIL FAMILY RESTAURANT, EH?
HMM... KINDA WISH IT HAD FOUR SYLLABLES, NOT THREE.
MORE LIKE "YUKIHIRA"...
BOY, SOMA'S BEEN STARING AT THAT SIGN FOR A WHILE NOW.
I WONDER WHAT HE'S THINKING?
WHATEVER IT IS, I DOUBT IT'S INTELLIGENT.
STAAARE
Family Restaurant THE COUNCIL
IRRESISTIBLE AROMA!
Special Yakisoba

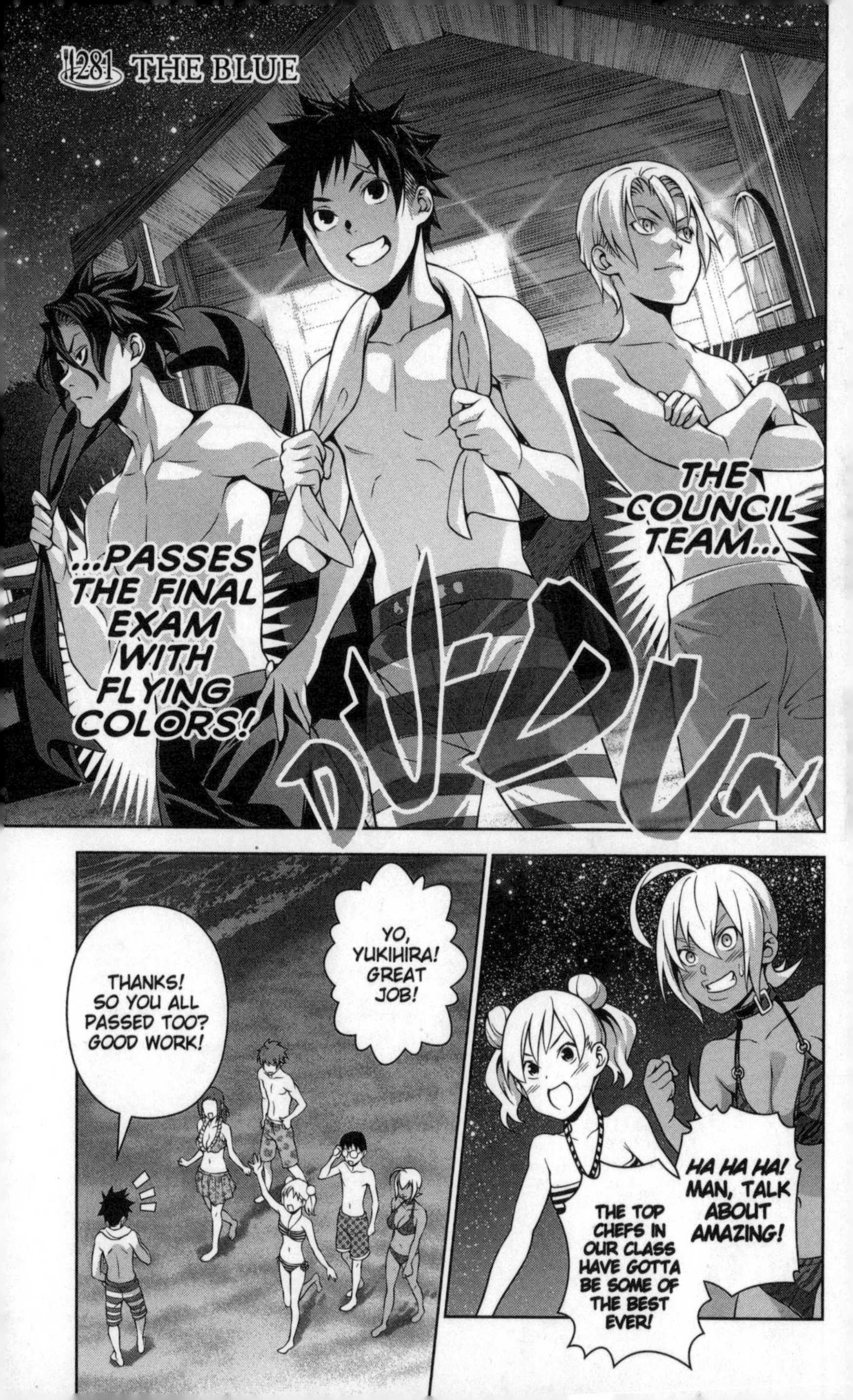
281 THE BLUE
THE COUNCIL TEAM...
...PASSES THE FINAL EXAM WITH FLYING COLORS!
DU-DUN
HA HA HA! MAN, TALK ABOUT AMAZING!
THE TOP CHEFS IN OUR CLASS HAVE GOTTA BE SOME OF THE BEST EVER!
YO, YUKIHIRA! GREAT JOB!
THANKS! SO YOU ALL PASSED TOO? GOOD WORK!

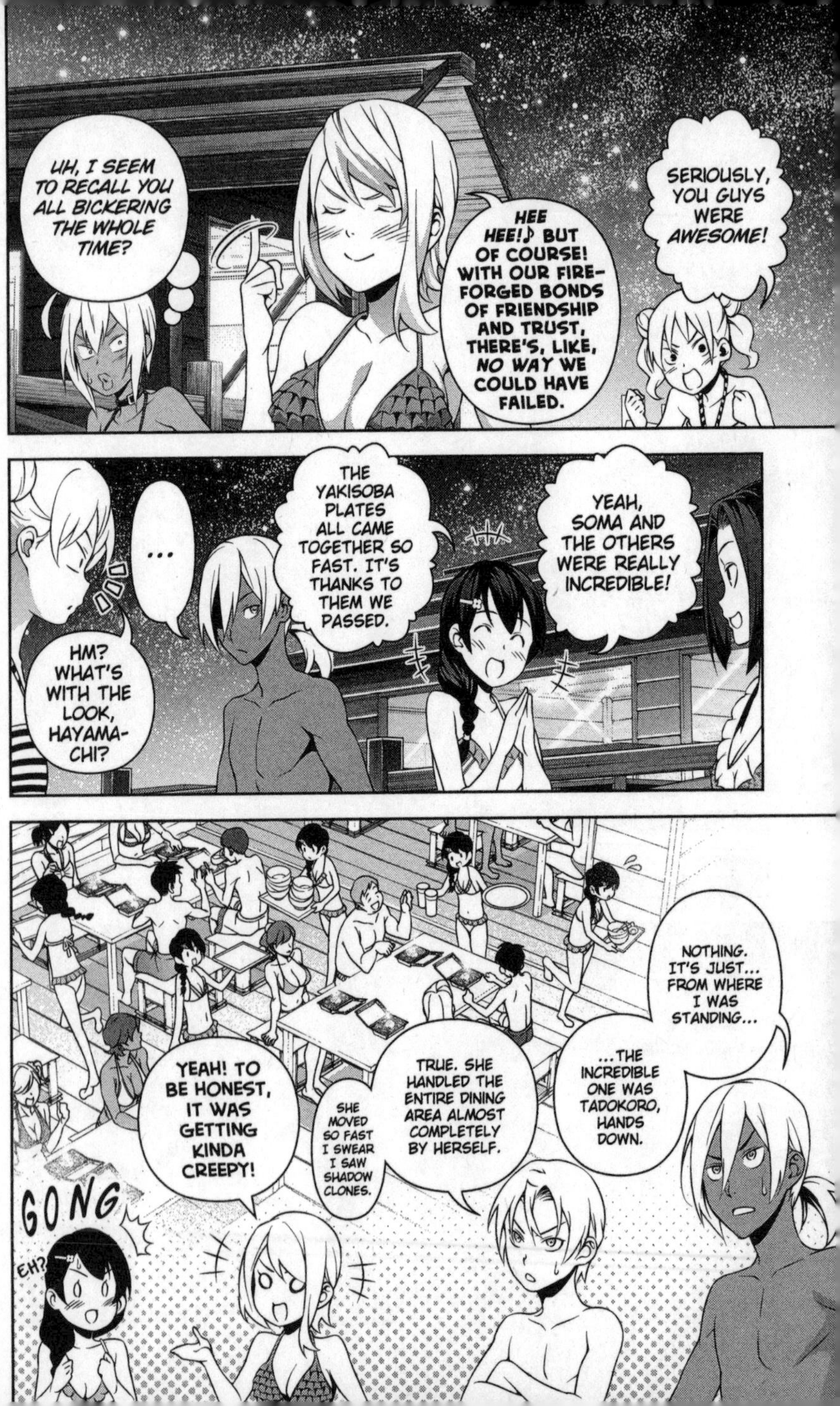
SERIOUSLY, YOU GUYS WERE AWESOME!
HEE HEE!♪ BUT OF COURSE! WITH OUR FIRE-FORGED BONDS OF FRIENDSHIP AND TRUST, THERE'S, LIKE, NO WAY WE COULD HAVE FAILED.
UH, I SEEM TO RECALL YOU ALL BICKERING THE WHOLE TIME?
YEAH, SOMA AND THE OTHERS WERE REALLY INCREDIBLE!
THE YAKISOBA PLATES ALL CAME TOGETHER SO FAST. IT'S THANKS TO THEM WE PASSED.
...
HM? WHAT'S WITH THE LOOK, HAYAMA-CHI?
NOTHING. IT'S JUST... FROM WHERE I WAS STANDING...
...THE INCREDIBLE ONE WAS TADOKORO, HANDS DOWN.
TRUE. SHE HANDLED THE ENTIRE DINING AREA ALMOST COMPLETELY BY HERSELF.
SHE MOVED SO FAST I SWEAR I SAW SHADOW CLONES.
YEAH! TO BE HONEST, IT WAS GETTING KINDA CREEPY!
GONG
EH?

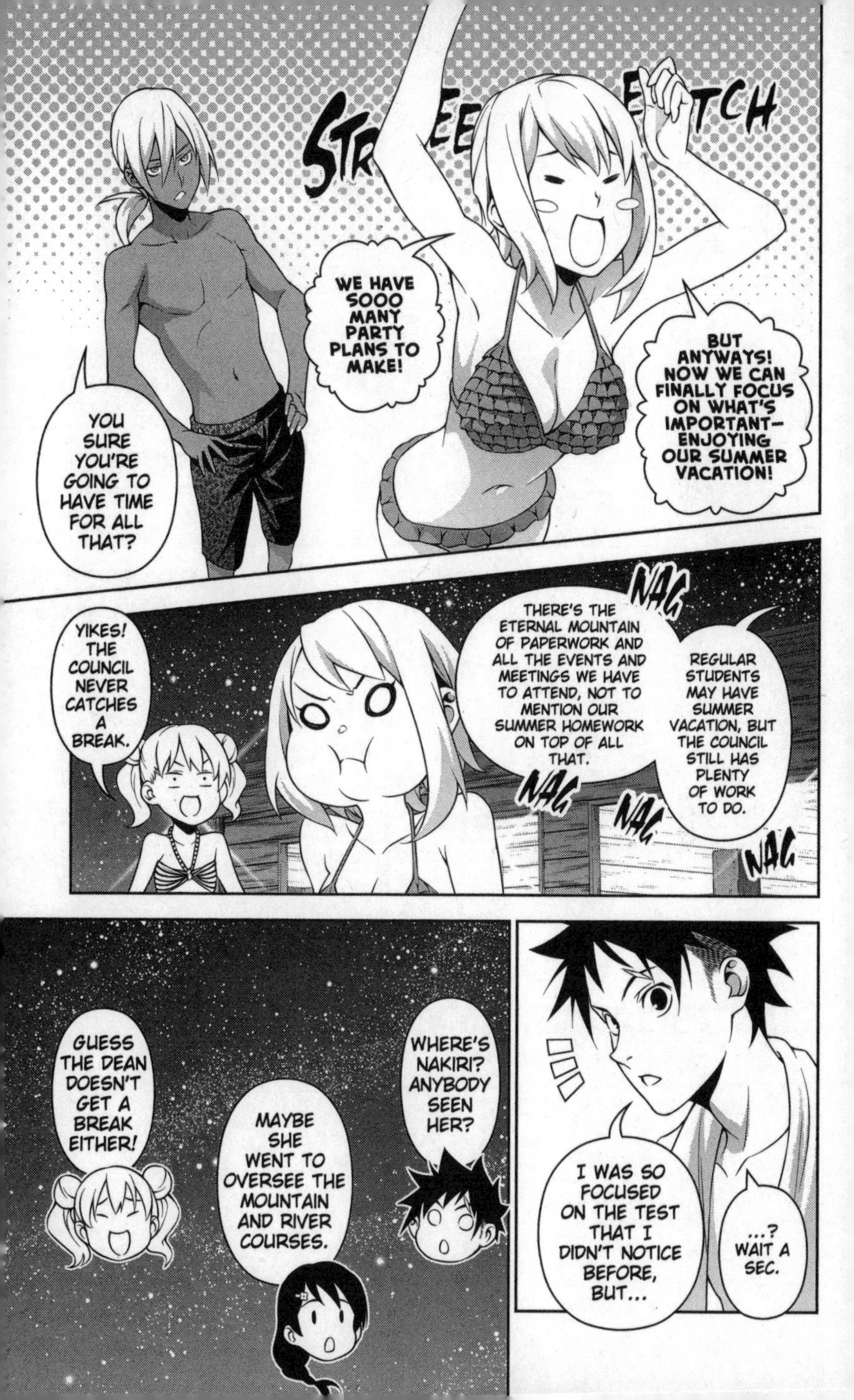
STREEETCH
BUT ANYWAYS! NOW WE CAN FINALLY FOCUS ON WHAT'S IMPORTANT—ENJOYING OUR SUMMER VACATION!
WE HAVE SOOO MANY PARTY PLANS TO MAKE!
YOU SURE YOU'RE GOING TO HAVE TIME FOR ALL THAT?
NAG
REGULAR STUDENTS MAY HAVE SUMMER VACATION, BUT THE COUNCIL STILL HAS PLENTY OF WORK TO DO.
THERE'S THE ETERNAL MOUNTAIN OF PAPERWORK AND ALL THE EVENTS AND MEETINGS WE HAVE TO ATTEND, NOT TO MENTION OUR SUMMER HOMEWORK ON TOP OF ALL THAT.
NAG
NAG
NAG
YIKES! THE COUNCIL NEVER CATCHES A BREAK.
...? WAIT A SEC.
I WAS SO FOCUSED ON THE TEST THAT I DIDN'T NOTICE BEFORE, BUT...
WHERE'S NAKIRI? ANYBODY SEEN HER?
MAYBE SHE WENT TO OVERSEE THE MOUNTAIN AND RIVER COURSES.
GUESS THE DEAN DOESN'T GET A BREAK EITHER!

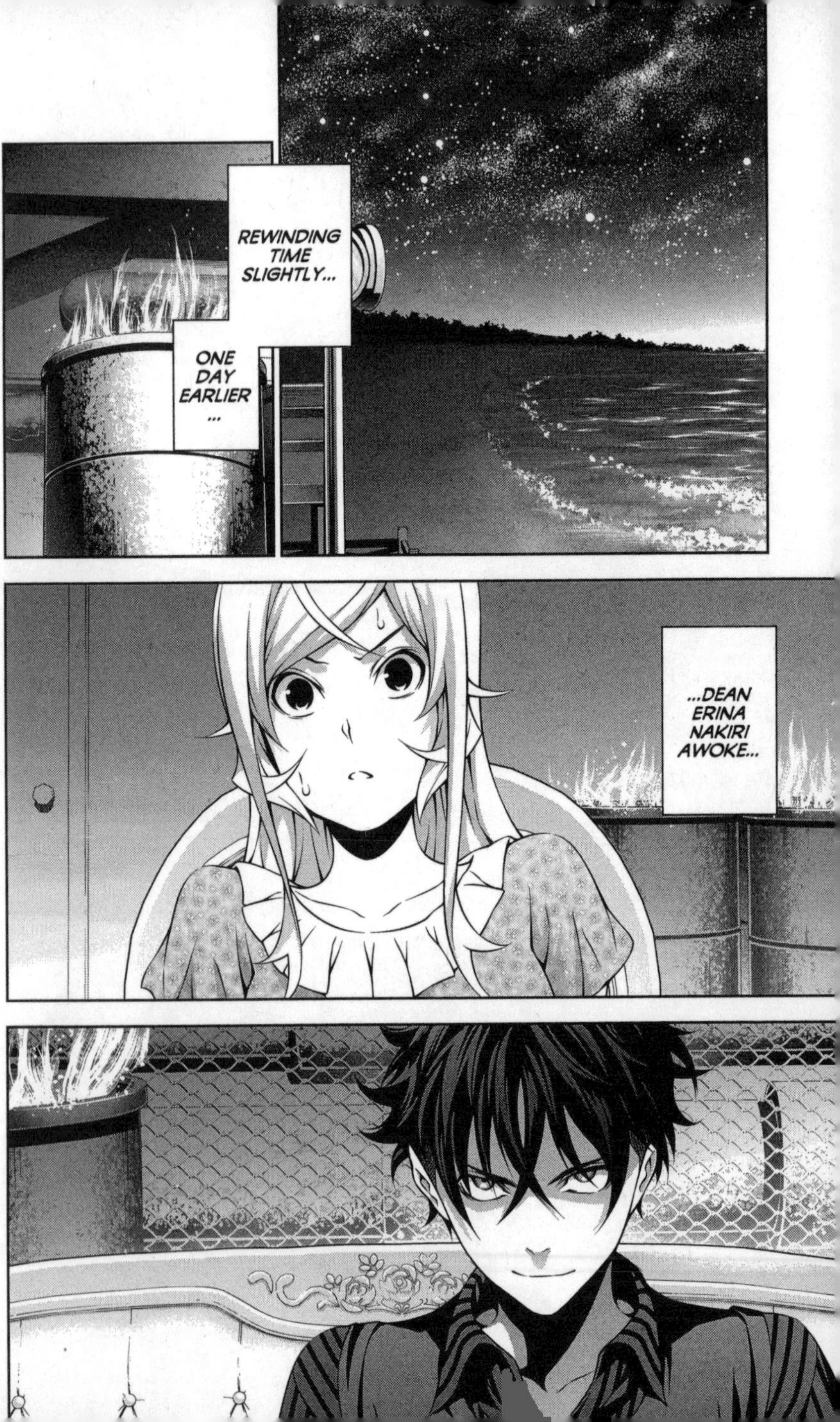
REWINDING TIME SLIGHTLY...
ONE DAY EARLIER ...
...DEAN ERINA NAKIRI AWOKE...

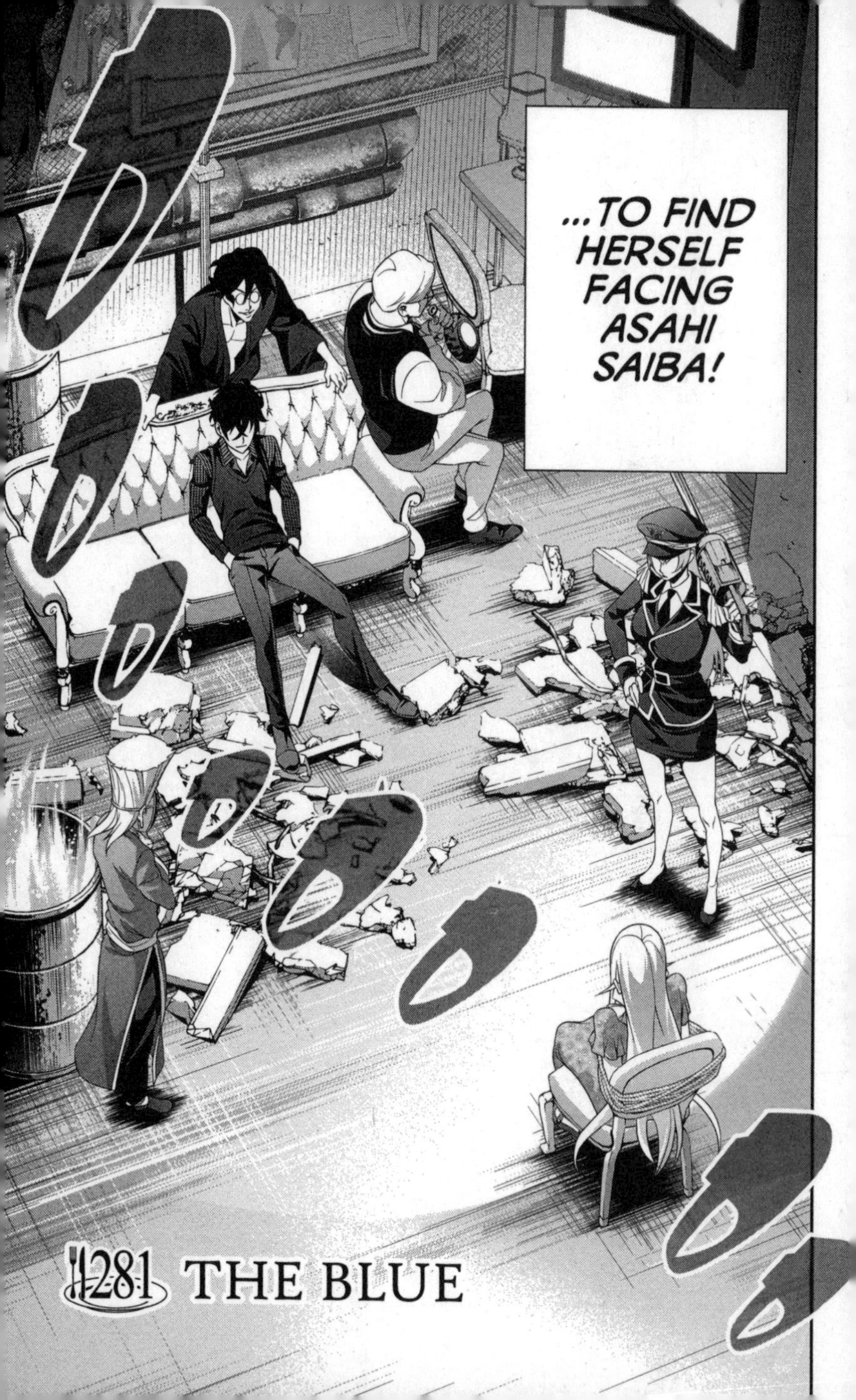
...TO FIND HERSELF FACING ASAHI SAIBA!
281 THE BLUE

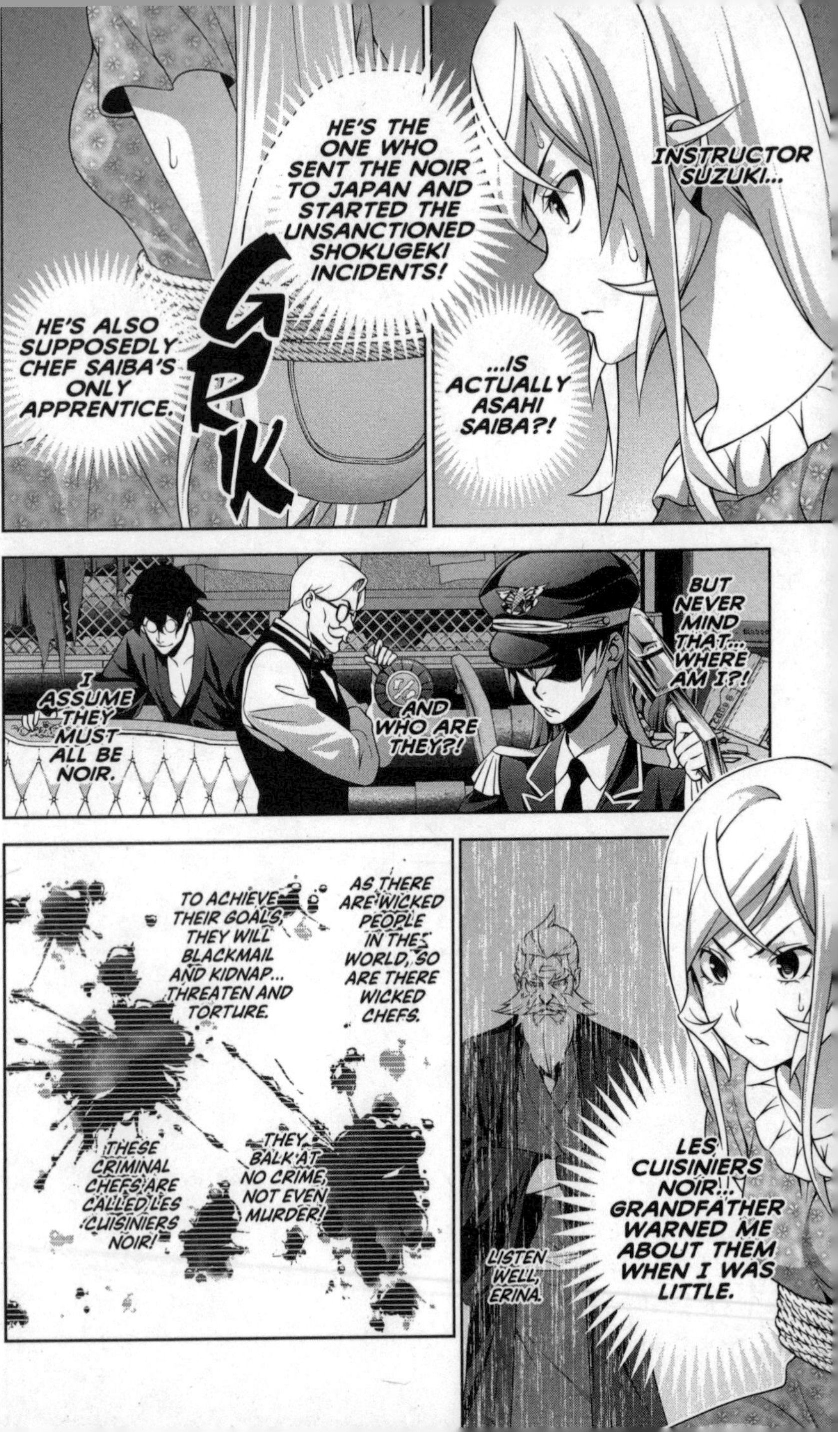
INSTRUCTOR SUZUKI...
...IS ACTUALLY ASAHI SAIBA?!
HE'S THE ONE WHO SENT THE NOIR TO JAPAN AND STARTED THE UNSANCTIONED SHOKUGEKI INCIDENTS!
GRK
HE'S ALSO SUPPOSEDLY CHEF SAIBA'S ONLY APPRENTICE.
BUT NEVER MIND THAT... WHERE AM I?!
AND WHO ARE THEY?!
I ASSUME THEY MUST ALL BE NOIR.
LES CUISINIERS NOIR... GRANDFATHER WARNED ME ABOUT THEM WHEN I WAS LITTLE.
LISTEN WELL, ERINA.
AS THERE ARE WICKED PEOPLE IN THE WORLD, SO ARE THERE WICKED CHEFS.
TO ACHIEVE THEIR GOALS, THEY WILL BLACKMAIL AND KIDNAP... THREATEN AND TORTURE.
THEY BALK AT NO CRIME, NOT EVEN MURDER!
THESE CRIMINAL CHEFS ARE CALLED LES CUISINIERS NOIR!

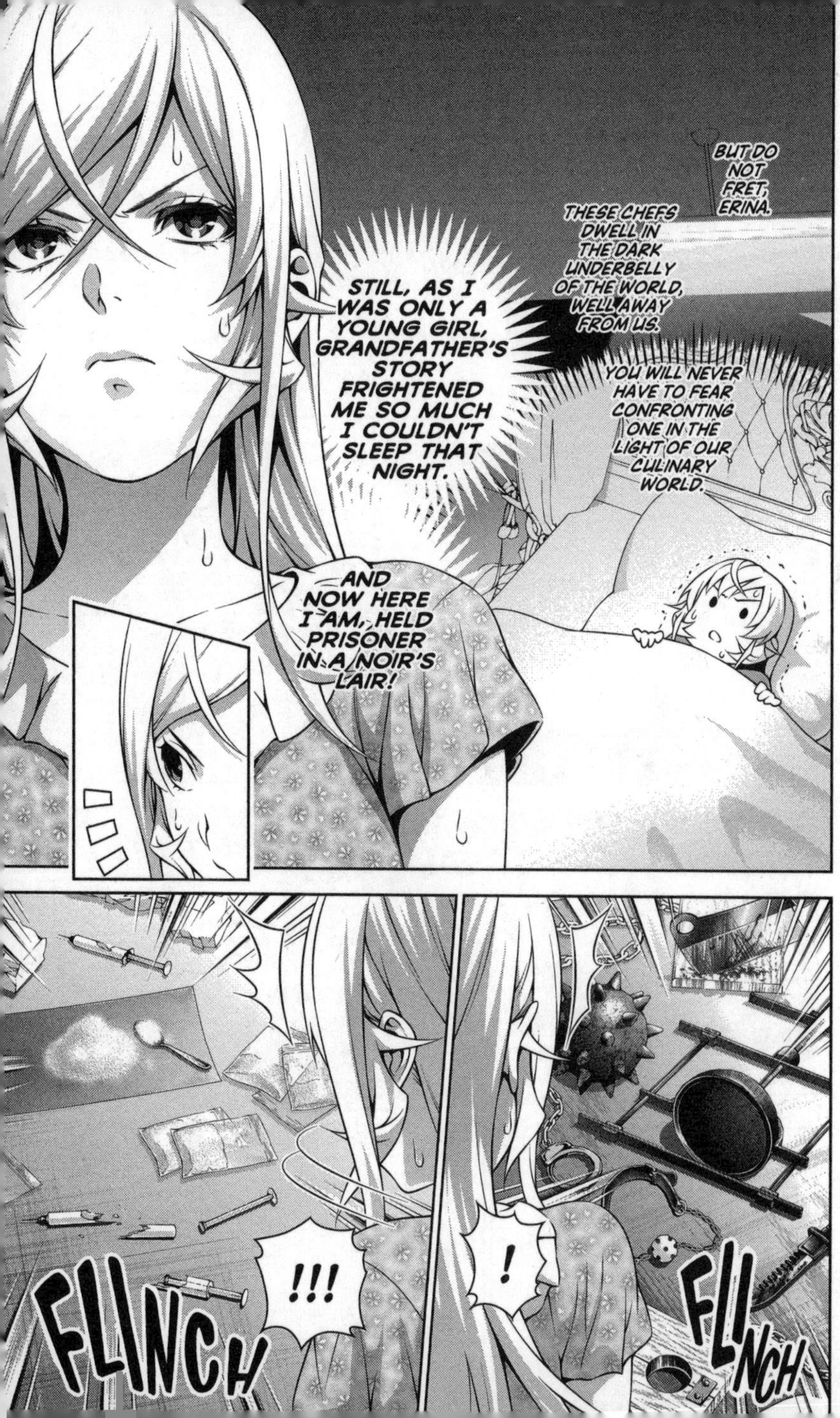
BUT DO NOT FRET, ERINA.
THESE CHEFS DWELL IN THE DARK UNDERBELLY OF THE WORLD, WELL AWAY FROM US.
YOU WILL NEVER HAVE TO FEAR CONFRONTING ONE IN THE LIGHT OF OUR CULINARY WORLD.
STILL, AS I WAS ONLY A YOUNG GIRL, GRANDFATHER'S STORY FRIGHTENED ME SO MUCH I COULDN'T SLEEP THAT NIGHT.
AND NOW HERE I AM, HELD PRISONER IN A NOIR'S LAIR!
!
FLINCH
!!!
FLINCH

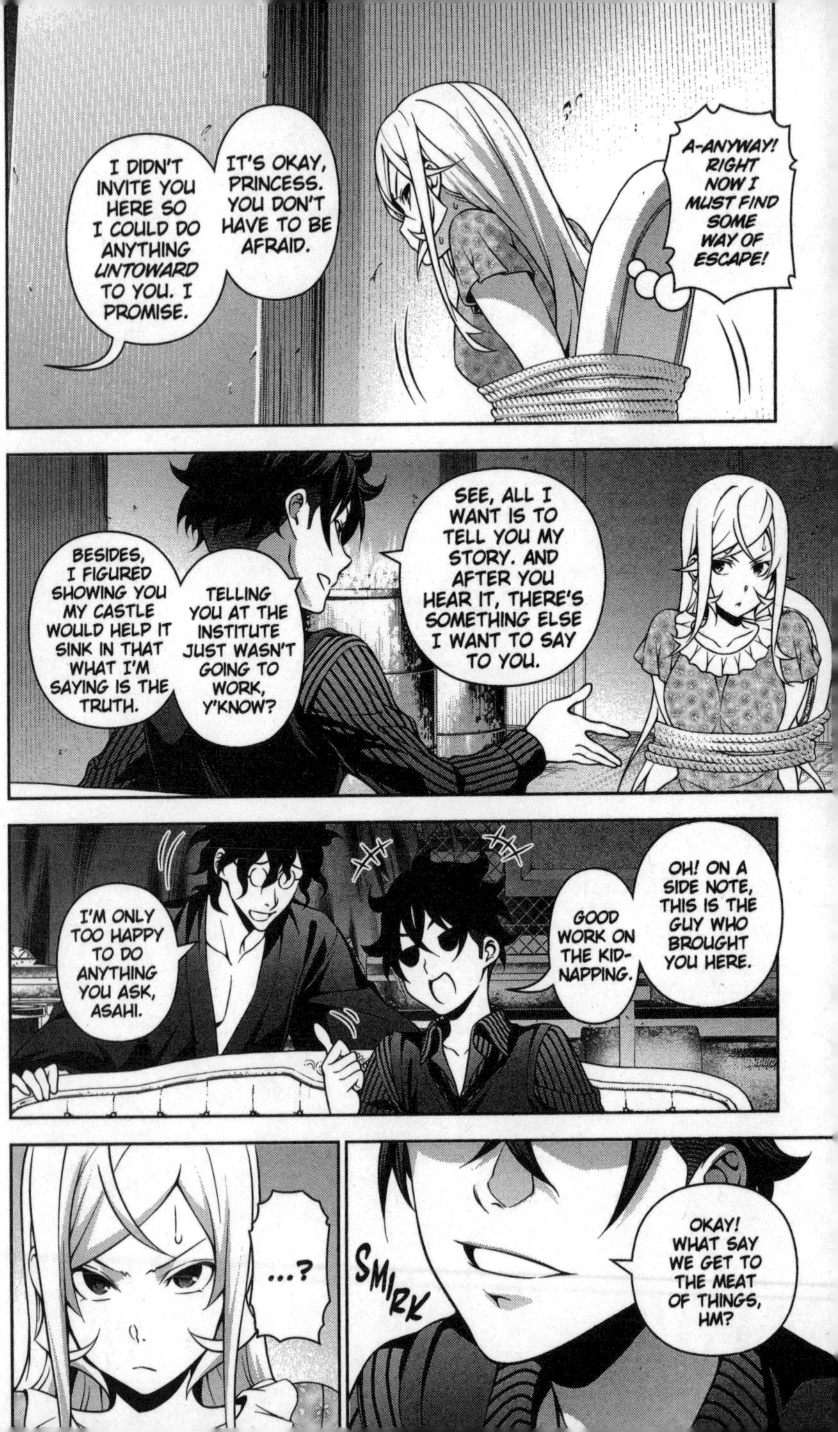
A-ANYWAY! RIGHT NOW I MUST FIND SOME WAY OF ESCAPE!
IT'S OKAY, PRINCESS. YOU DON'T HAVE TO BE AFRAID.
I DIDN'T INVITE YOU HERE SO I COULD DO ANYTHING *UNTOWARD* TO YOU. I PROMISE.
SEE, ALL I WANT IS TO TELL YOU MY STORY. AND AFTER YOU HEAR IT, THERE'S SOMETHING ELSE I WANT TO SAY TO YOU.
TELLING YOU AT THE INSTITUTE JUST WASN'T GOING TO WORK, Y'KNOW?
BESIDES, I FIGURED SHOWING YOU MY CASTLE WOULD HELP IT SINK IN THAT WHAT I'M SAYING IS THE TRUTH.
OH! ON A SIDE NOTE, THIS IS THE GUY WHO BROUGHT YOU HERE.
GOOD WORK ON THE KID-NAPPING.
I'M ONLY TOO HAPPY TO DO ANYTHING YOU ASK, ASAHI.
OKAY! WHAT SAY WE GET TO THE MEAT OF THINGS, HM?
SMIRK
...?

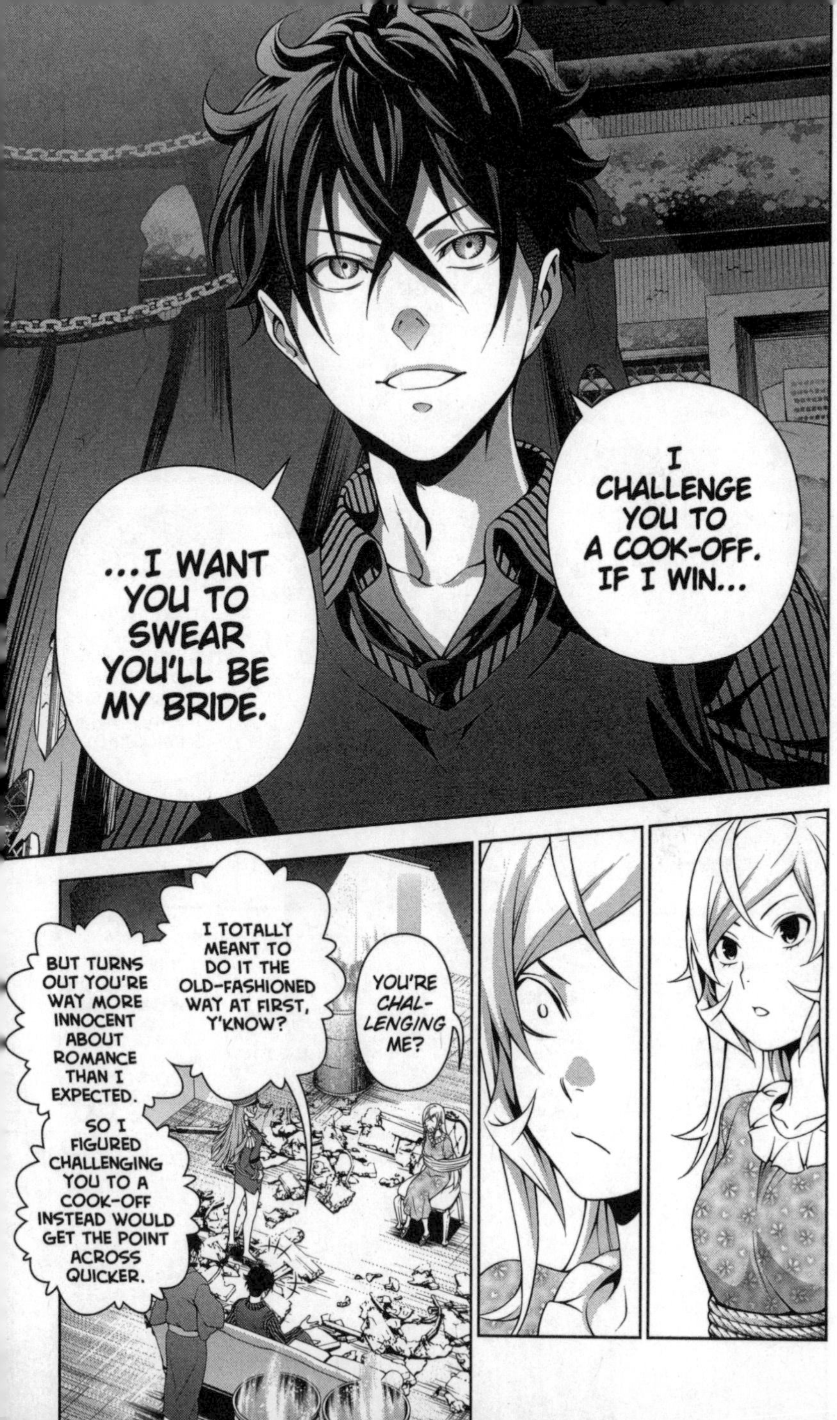
I CHALLENGE YOU TO A COOK-OFF. IF I WIN...
...I WANT YOU TO SWEAR YOU'LL BE MY BRIDE.
YOU'RE CHAL-LENGING ME?
I TOTALLY MEANT TO DO IT THE OLD-FASHIONED WAY AT FIRST, Y'KNOW?
BUT TURNS OUT YOU'RE WAY MORE INNOCENT ABOUT ROMANCE THAN I EXPECTED.
SO I FIGURED CHALLENGING YOU TO A COOK-OFF INSTEAD WOULD GET THE POINT ACROSS QUICKER.

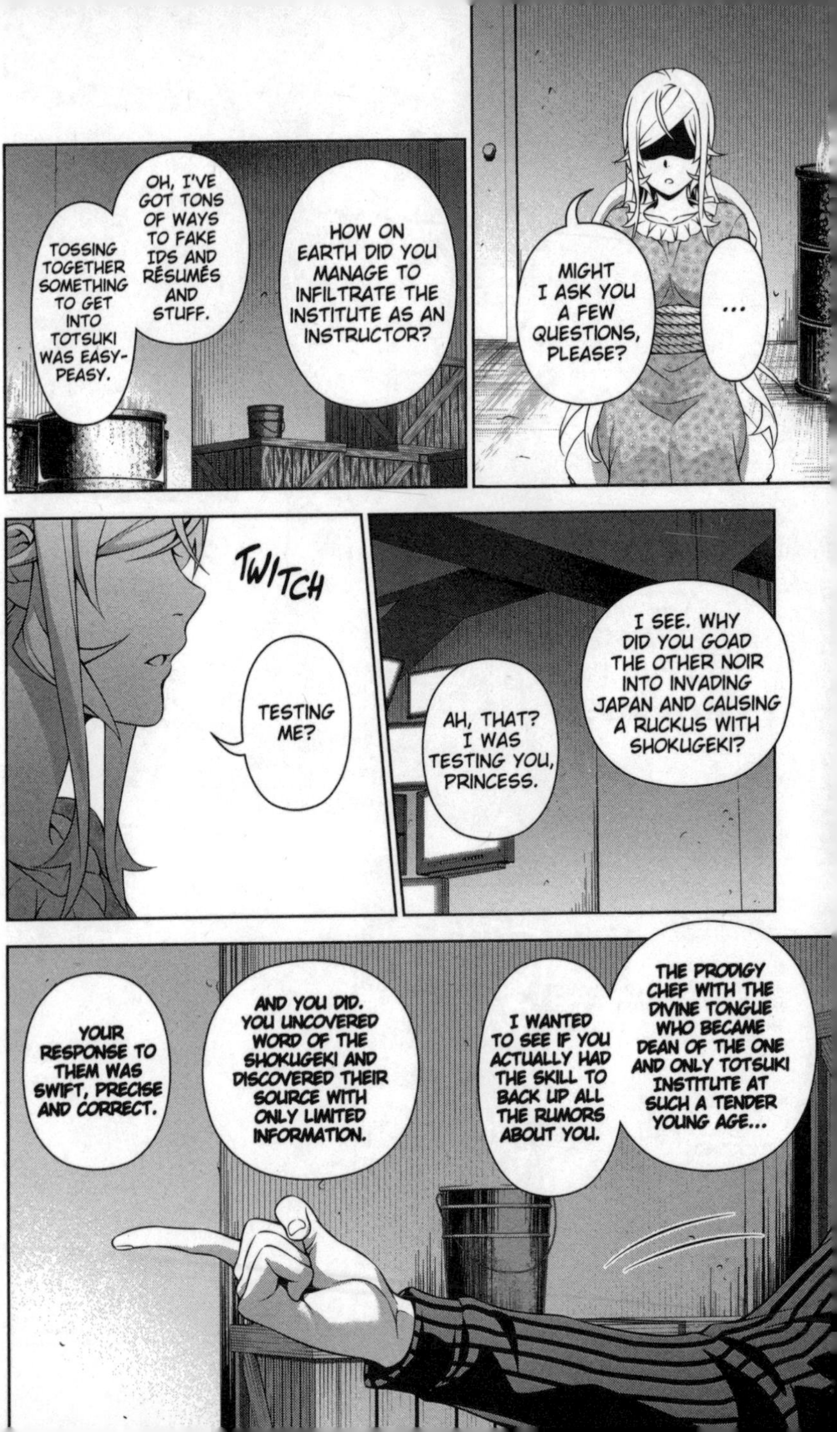
...
MIGHT I ASK YOU A FEW QUESTIONS, PLEASE?
HOW ON EARTH DID YOU MANAGE TO INFILTRATE THE INSTITUTE AS AN INSTRUCTOR?
OH, I'VE GOT TONS OF WAYS TO FAKE IDS AND RÉSUMÉS AND STUFF.
TOSSING TOGETHER SOMETHING TO GET INTO TOTSUKI WAS EASY-PEASY.
I SEE. WHY DID YOU GOAD THE OTHER NOIR INTO INVADING JAPAN AND CAUSING A RUCKUS WITH SHOKUGEKI?
AH, THAT? I WAS TESTING YOU, PRINCESS.
TWITCH
TESTING ME?
THE PRODIGY CHEF WITH THE DIVINE TONGUE WHO BECAME DEAN OF THE ONE AND ONLY TOTSUKI INSTITUTE AT SUCH A TENDER YOUNG AGE...
I WANTED TO SEE IF YOU ACTUALLY HAD THE SKILL TO BACK UP ALL THE RUMORS ABOUT YOU.
AND YOU DID. YOU UNCOVERED WORD OF THE SHOKUGEKI AND DISCOVERED THEIR SOURCE WITH ONLY LIMITED INFORMATION.
YOUR RESPONSE TO THEM WAS SWIFT, PRECISE AND CORRECT.

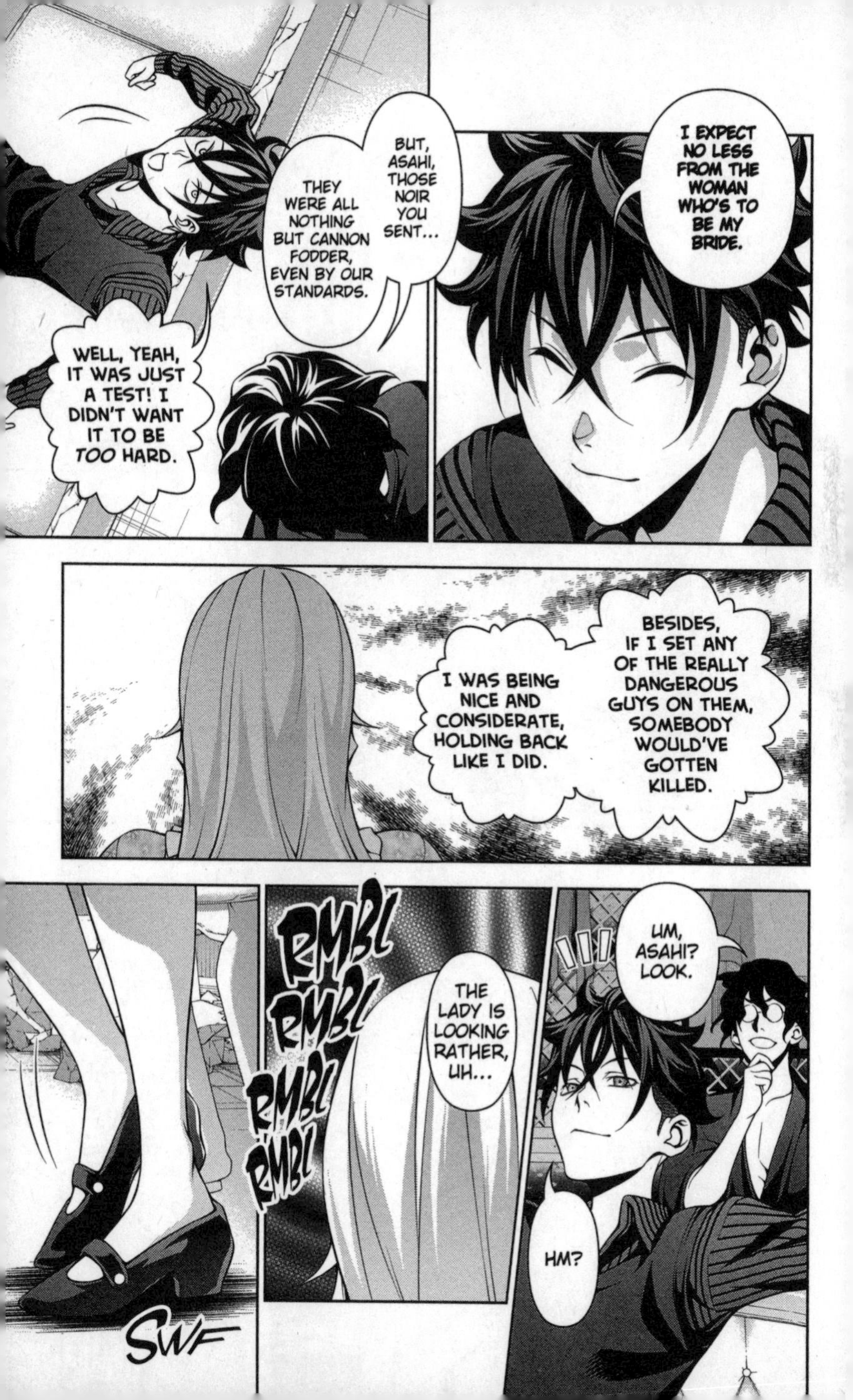
I EXPECT NO LESS FROM THE WOMAN WHO'S TO BE MY BRIDE.
BUT, ASAHI, THOSE NOIR YOU SENT...
THEY WERE ALL NOTHING BUT CANNON FODDER, EVEN BY OUR STANDARDS.
WELL, YEAH, IT WAS JUST A TEST! I DIDN'T WANT IT TO BE *TOO* HARD.
BESIDES, IF I SET ANY OF THE REALLY DANGEROUS GUYS ON THEM, SOMEBODY WOULD'VE GOTTEN KILLED.
I WAS BEING NICE AND CONSIDERATE, HOLDING BACK LIKE I DID.
UM, ASAHI? LOOK.
HM?
RMBL RMBL RMBL RMBL RMBL
THE LADY IS LOOKING RATHER, UH...
SWF

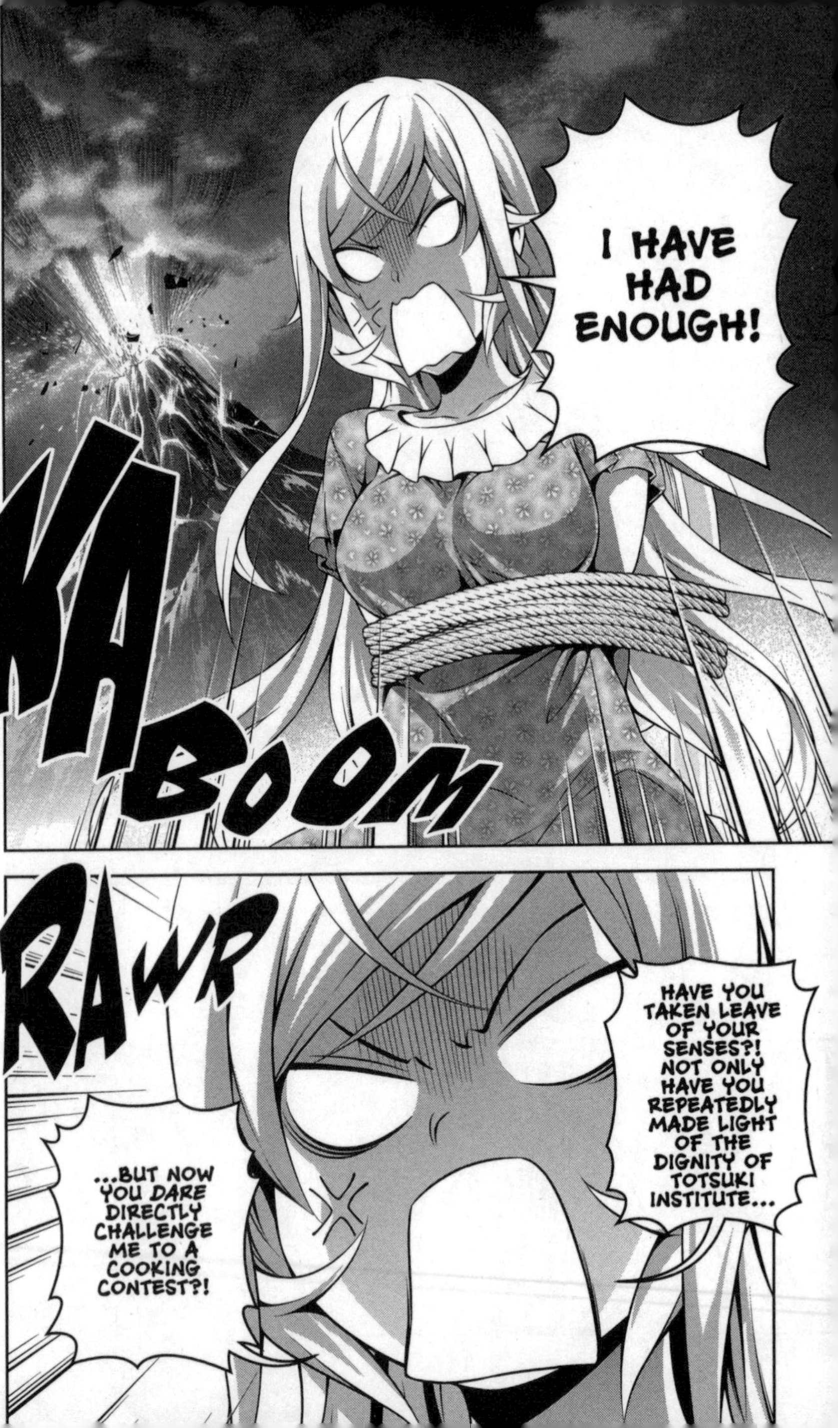
I HAVE HAD ENOUGH!
KABOOM
HAVE YOU TAKEN LEAVE OF YOUR SENSES?! NOT ONLY HAVE YOU REPEATEDLY MADE LIGHT OF THE DIGNITY OF TOTSUKI INSTITUTE...
...BUT NOW YOU *DARE* DIRECTLY CHALLENGE ME TO A COOKING CONTEST?!
RAWR

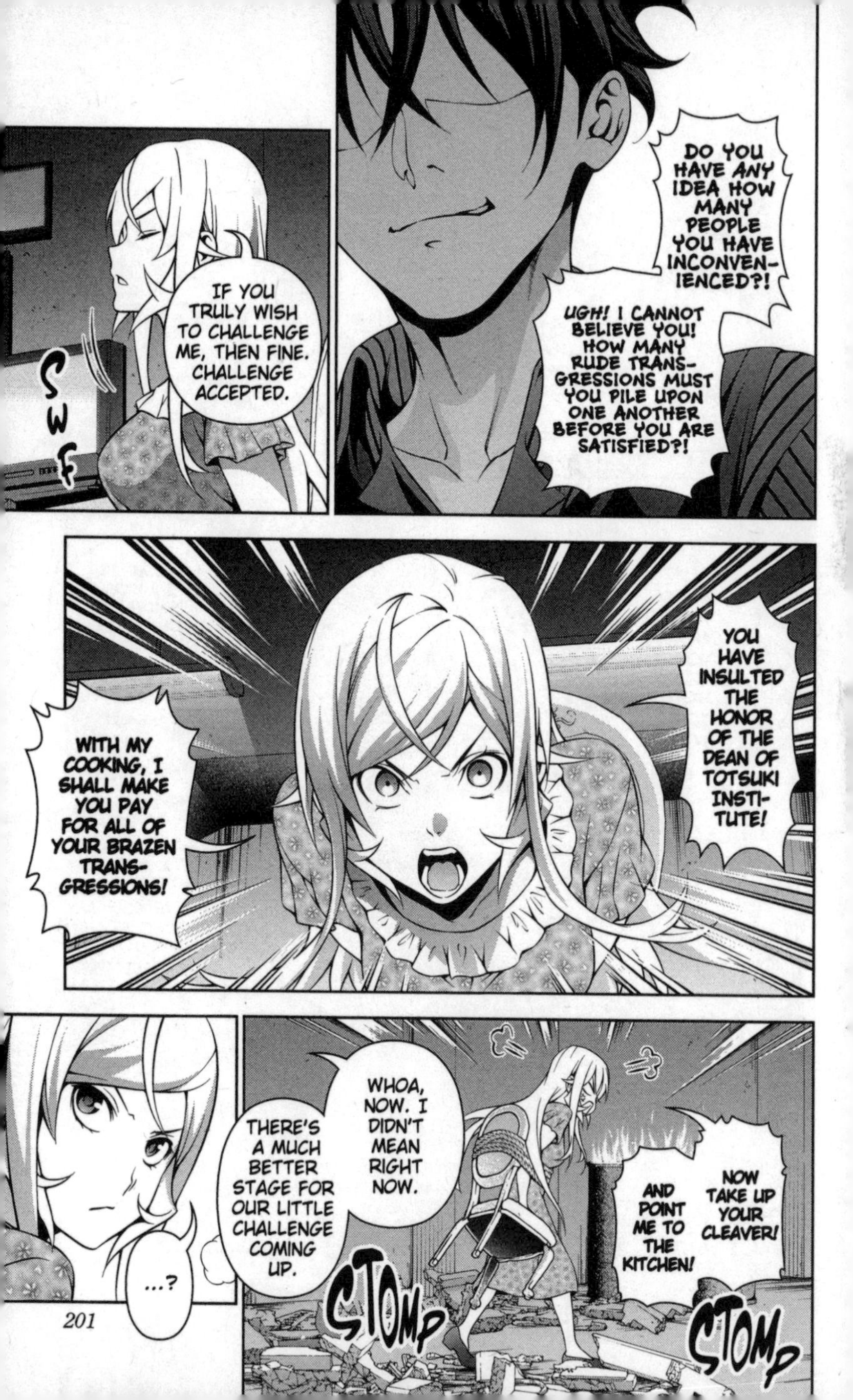
DO YOU HAVE ANY IDEA HOW MANY PEOPLE YOU HAVE INCONVEN-IENCED?!
UGH! I CANNOT BELIEVE YOU! HOW MANY RUDE TRANS-GRESSIONS MUST YOU PILE UPON ONE ANOTHER BEFORE YOU ARE SATISFIED?!
IF YOU TRULY WISH TO CHALLENGE ME, THEN FINE. CHALLENGE ACCEPTED.
SWF
YOU HAVE INSULTED THE HONOR OF THE DEAN OF TOTSUKI INSTI-TUTE!
WITH MY COOKING, I SHALL MAKE YOU PAY FOR ALL OF YOUR BRAZEN TRANS-GRESSIONS!
NOW TAKE UP YOUR CLEAVER!
AND POINT ME TO THE KITCHEN!
STOMP
STOMP
WHOA, NOW. I DIDN'T MEAN RIGHT NOW.
THERE'S A MUCH BETTER STAGE FOR OUR LITTLE CHALLENGE COMING UP.
...?

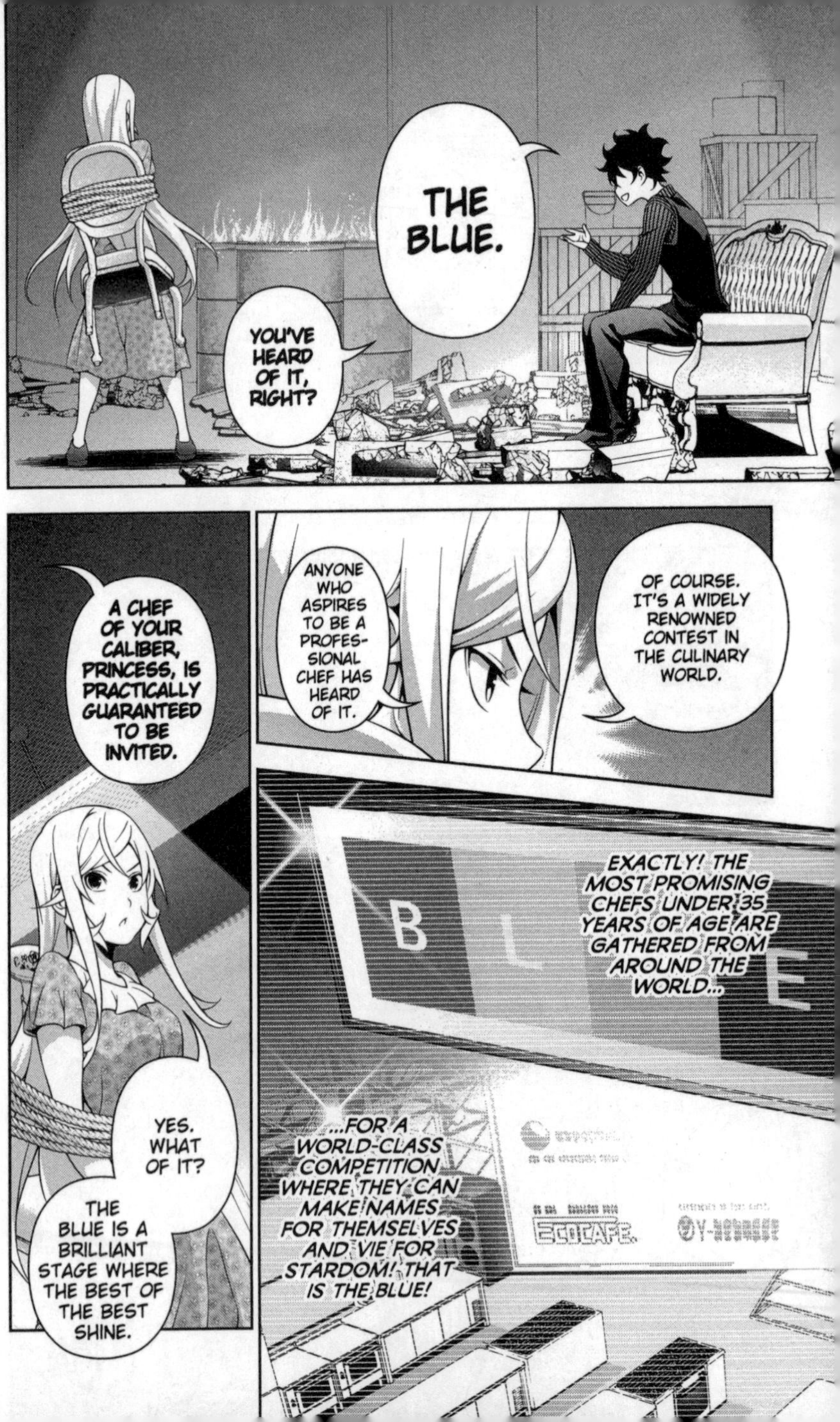
THE BLUE.
YOU'VE HEARD OF IT, RIGHT?
OF COURSE. IT'S A WIDELY RENOWNED CONTEST IN THE CULINARY WORLD.
ANYONE WHO ASPIRES TO BE A PROFES-SIONAL CHEF HAS HEARD OF IT.
EXACTLY! THE MOST PROMISING CHEFS UNDER 35 YEARS OF AGE ARE GATHERED FROM AROUND THE WORLD...
B
E
...FOR A WORLD-CLASS COMPETITION WHERE THEY CAN MAKE NAMES FOR THEMSELVES AND VIE FOR STARDOM! THAT IS THE BLUE!
ECOCAFE.
A CHEF OF YOUR CALIBER, PRINCESS, IS PRACTICALLY GUARANTEED TO BE INVITED.
YES. WHAT OF IT?
THE BLUE IS A BRILLIANT STAGE WHERE THE BEST OF THE BEST SHINE.

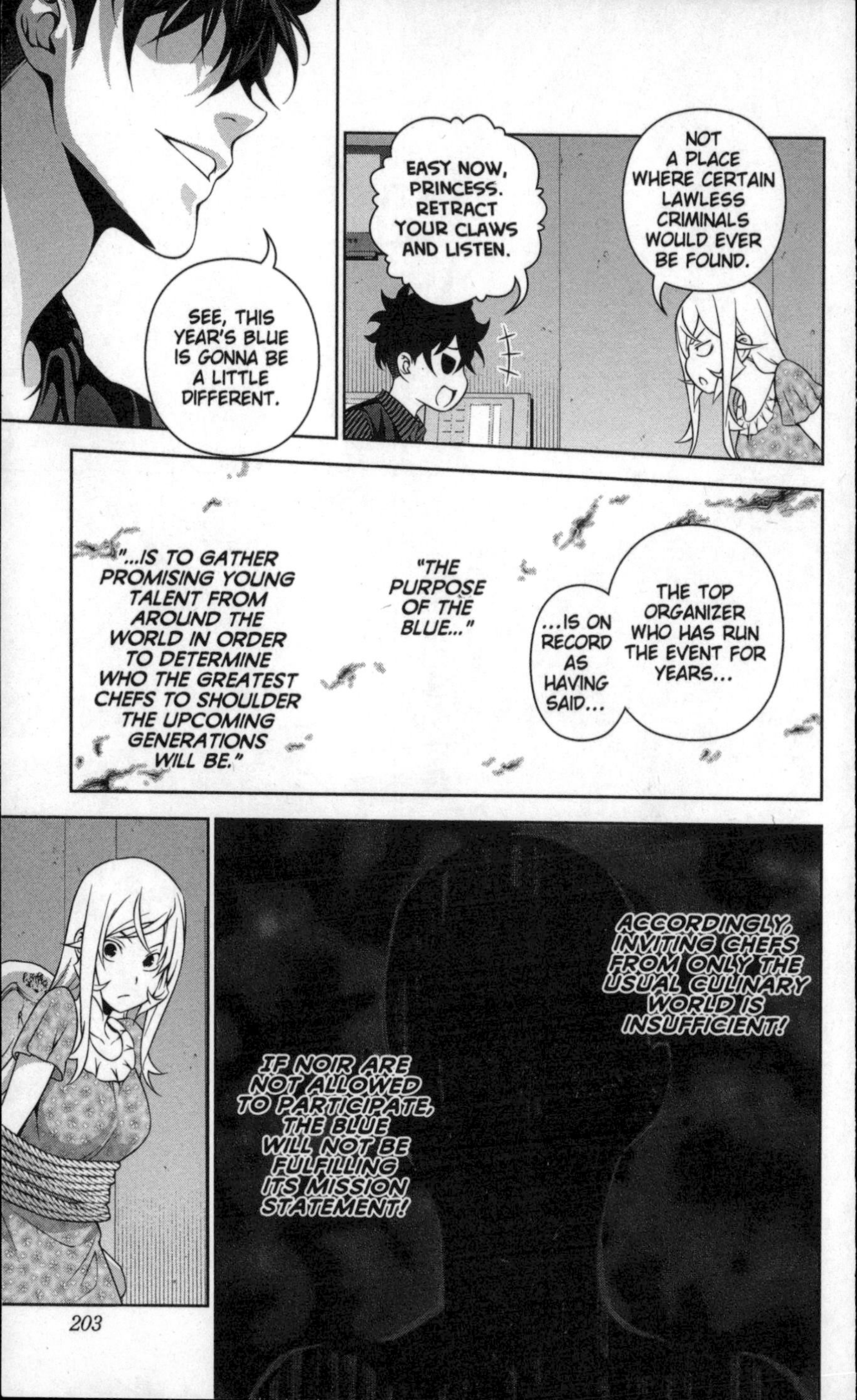
NOT A PLACE WHERE CERTAIN LAWLESS CRIMINALS WOULD EVER BE FOUND.
EASY NOW, PRINCESS. RETRACT YOUR CLAWS AND LISTEN.
SEE, THIS YEAR'S BLUE IS GONNA BE A LITTLE DIFFERENT.
THE TOP ORGANIZER WHO HAS RUN THE EVENT FOR YEARS...
...IS ON RECORD AS HAVING SAID...
"THE PURPOSE OF THE BLUE..."
"...IS TO GATHER PROMISING YOUNG TALENT FROM AROUND THE WORLD IN ORDER TO DETERMINE WHO THE GREATEST CHEFS TO SHOULDER THE UPCOMING GENERATIONS WILL BE."
ACCORDINGLY, INVITING CHEFS FROM ONLY THE USUAL CULINARY WORLD IS INSUFFICIENT!
IF NOIR ARE NOT ALLOWED TO PARTICIPATE, THE BLUE WILL NOT BE FULFILLING ITS MISSION STATEMENT!

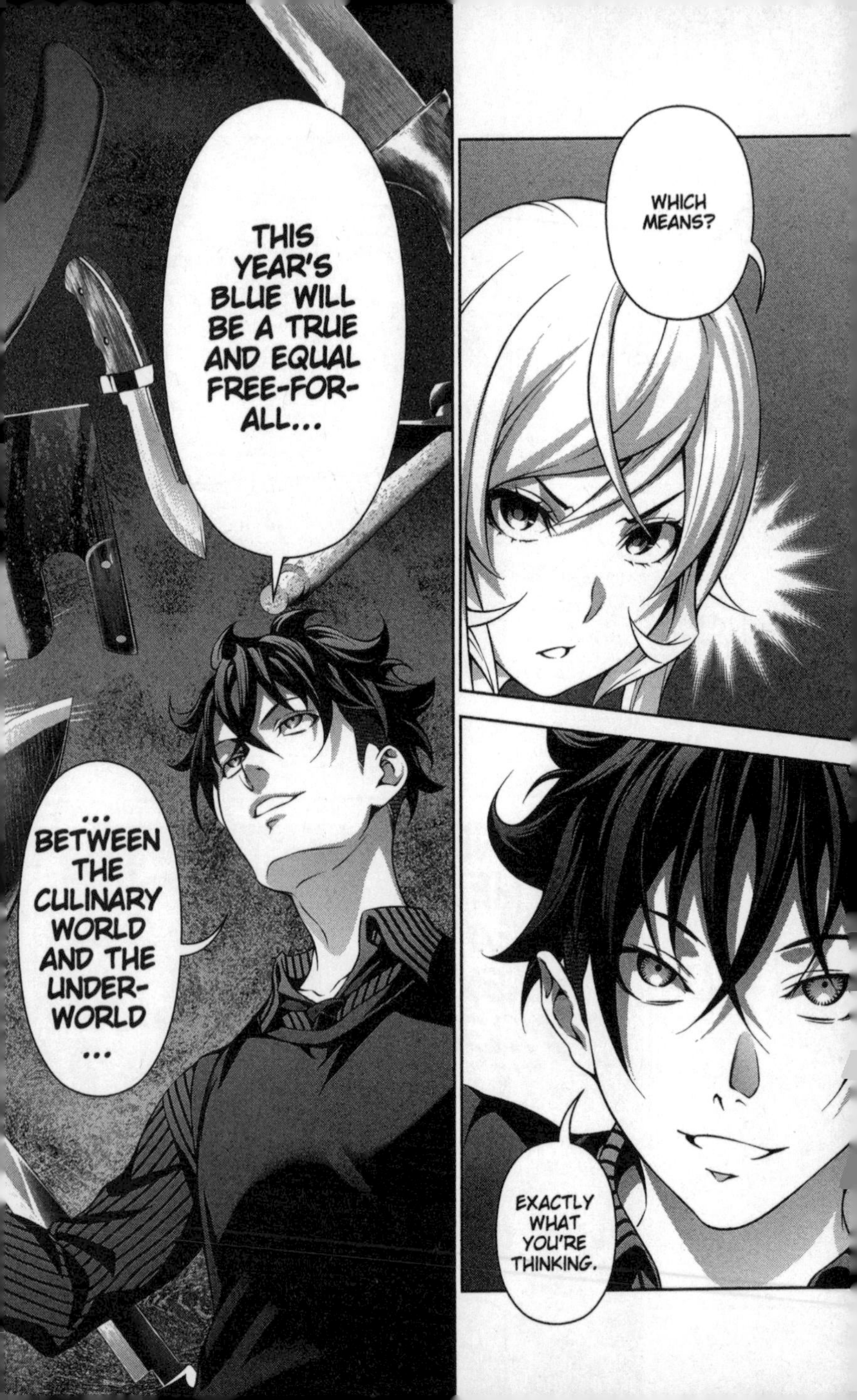
THIS YEAR'S BLUE WILL BE A TRUE AND EQUAL FREE-FOR-ALL...
... BETWEEN THE CULINARY WORLD AND THE UNDER-WORLD ...
WHICH MEANS?
EXACTLY WHAT YOU'RE THINKING.

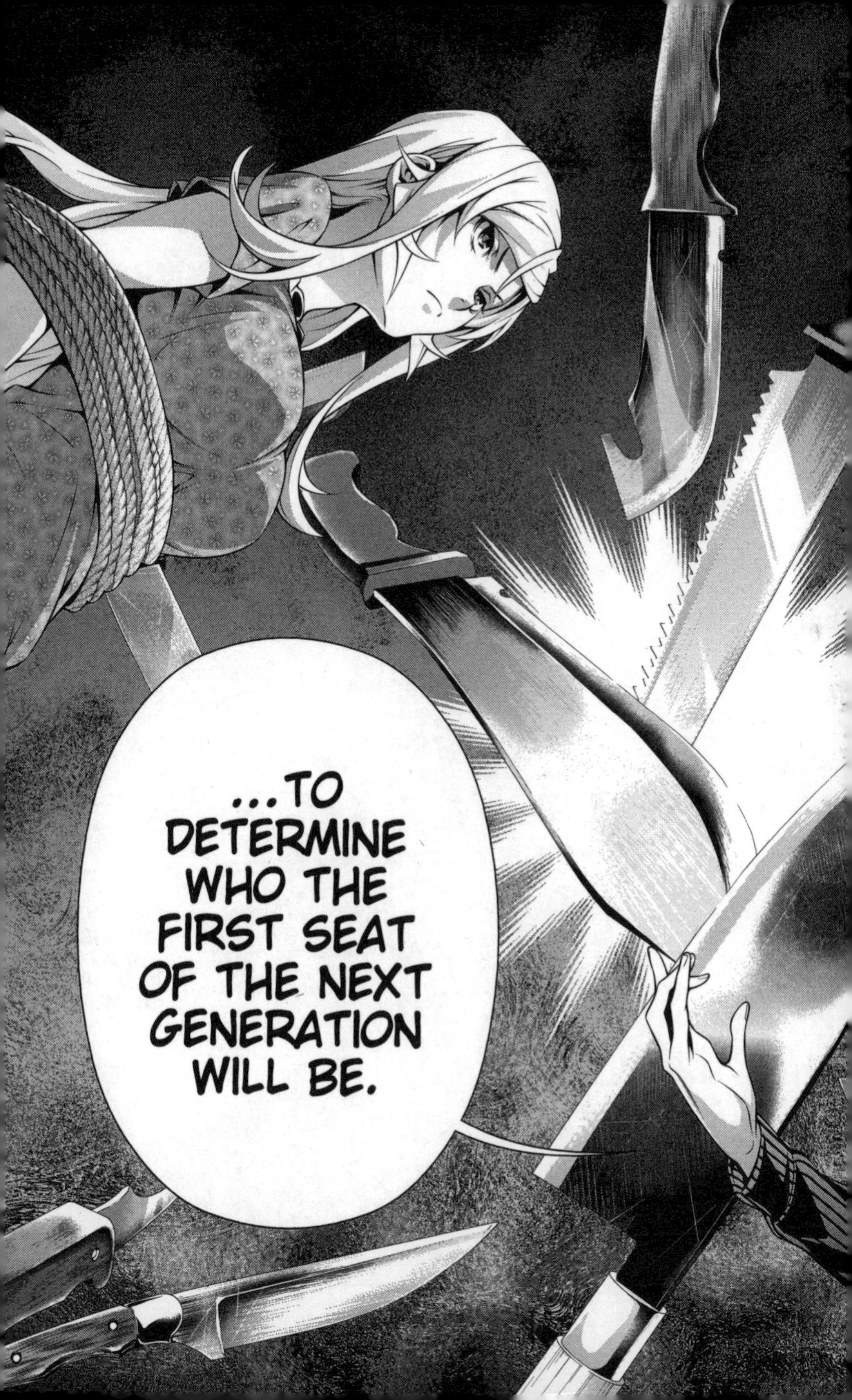
...TO DETERMINE WHO THE FIRST SEAT OF THE NEXT GENERATION WILL BE.

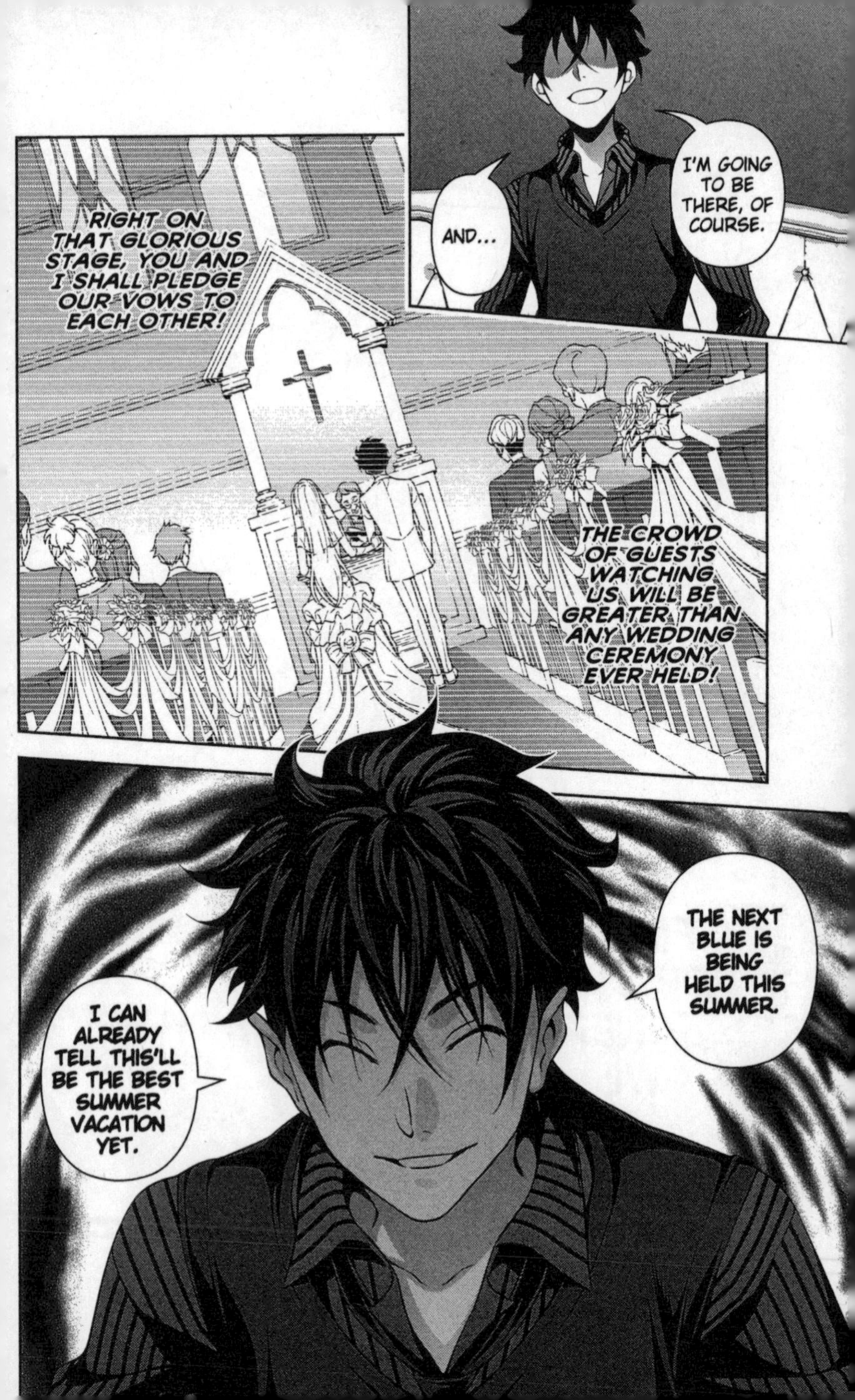
I'M GOING TO BE THERE, OF COURSE.
AND...
RIGHT ON THAT GLORIOUS STAGE, YOU AND I SHALL PLEDGE OUR VOWS TO EACH OTHER!
THE CROWD OF GUESTS WATCHING US WILL BE GREATER THAN ANY WEDDING CEREMONY EVER HELD!
THE NEXT BLUE IS BEING HELD THIS SUMMER.
I CAN ALREADY TELL THIS'LL BE THE BEST SUMMER VACATION YET.

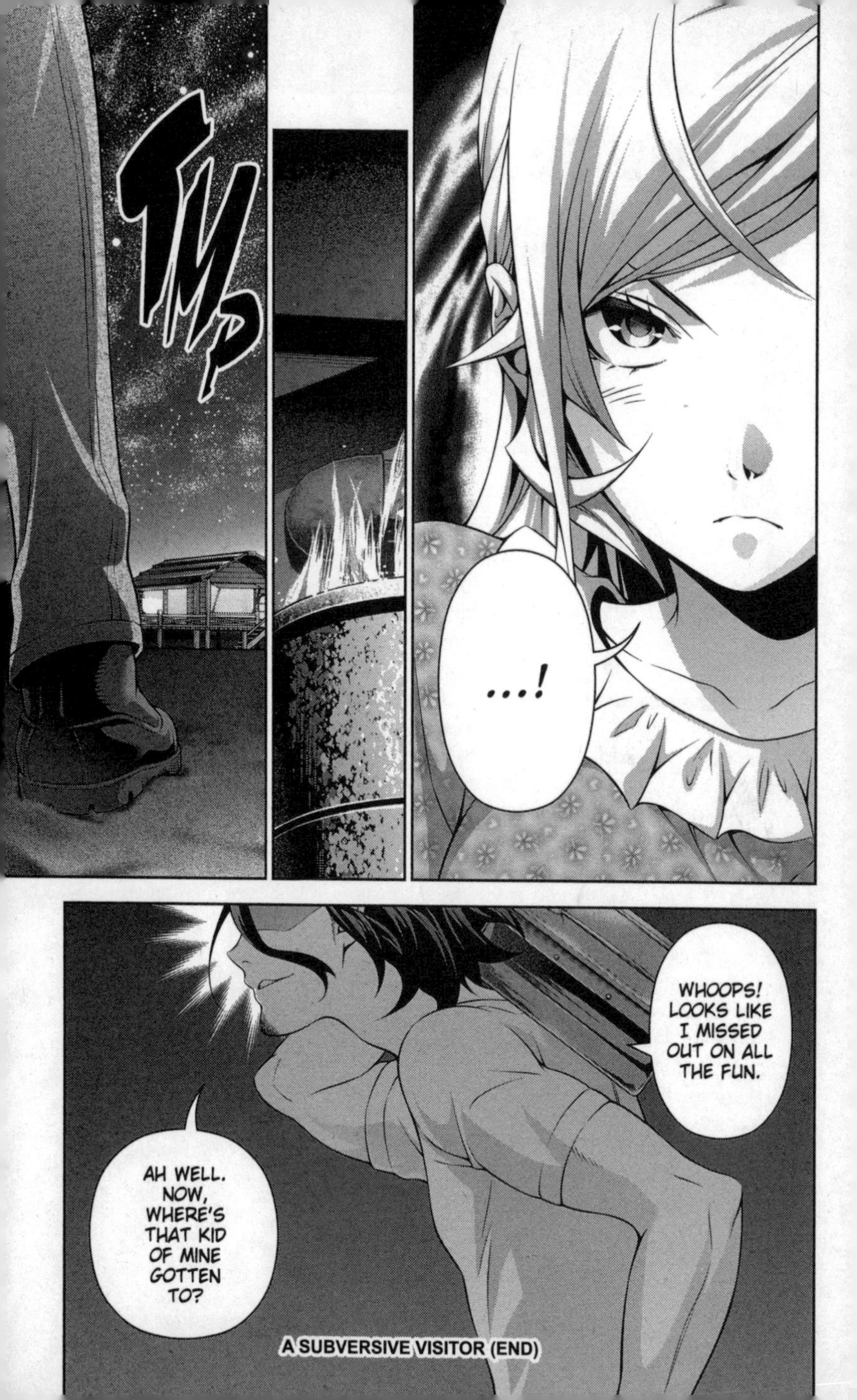
...!
TMP
WHOOPS! LOOKS LIKE I MISSED OUT ON ALL THE FUN.
AH WELL. NOW, WHERE'S THAT KID OF MINE GOTTEN TO?
A SUBVERSIVE VISITOR (END)

You're Reading in the Wrong Direction!!

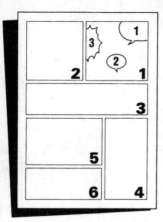

Whoops! Guess what? You're starting at the wrong end of the comic!

...It's true! In keeping with the original Japanese format, **Food Wars!** is meant to be read from right to left, starting in the upper-right corner.

Unlike English, which is read from left to right, Japanese is read from right to left, meaning that action, sound effects and word-balloon order are completely reversed... something which can make readers unfamiliar with Japanese feel pretty backwards themselves. For this reason, manga or Japanese comics published in the U.S. in English have sometimes been published "flopped"—that is, printed in exact reverse order, as though seen from the other side of a mirror.

By flopping pages, U.S. publishers can avoid confusing readers, but the compromise is not without its downside. For one thing, a character in a flopped manga series who once wore in the original Japanese version a T-shirt emblazoned with "M A Y" (as in "the merry month of") now wears one which reads "Y A M"! Additionally, many manga creators in Japan are themselves unhappy with the process, as some feel the mirror-imaging of their art skews their original intentions.

We are proud to bring you Yuto Tsukuda and Shun Saeki's **Food Wars!** in the original unflopped format.

For now, though, turn to the other side of the book and let the adventure begin...!

—Editor

◀ ● ● ● ● ● ● ● ● ● ● ● ● ● ● ●